Prince Fortun.

William Black

Alpha Editions

This edition published in 2024

ISBN 9789362091680

Design and Setting By

Alpha Editions

www.alphaedis.com

Email - info@alphaedis.com

Contents

CHAPTER I.

A REHEARSAL.

When the curtain fell on the last act of "The Squire's Daughter," the comedy-opera that had taken all musical London by storm, a tall and elegant young English matron and her still taller brother rose from their places in the private box they had been occupying, and made ready to depart; and he had just assisted her to put on her long-skirted coat of rose-red plush when an attendant made his appearance.

"Mr. Moore's compliments, your ladyship, and will you please to step this way?"

The box was close to the stage. Lady Adela Cunyngham and her brother, Lord Rockminster, followed their guide through a narrow little door, and almost at once found themselves in the wings, amid the usual motley crowd of gas-men, scene-shifters, dressers, and the like. But the company were still fronting the footlights; for there had been a general recall, and the curtain had gone up again; and probably, during this brief second of scrutiny, it may have seemed odd to these two strangers to find themselves looking, not at rows of smiling faces on the stage, but at the backs of the heads of the performers. However, the curtain once more came down; the great wedding-party in the squire's hall grew suddenly quite business-like and went their several ways as if they had no longer any concern with one another; and then it was that the squire's daughter herself—a piquant little person she was, in a magnificent costume of richly flowered white satin, and with a portentous head-gear of powdered hair and brilliants and strings of pearls—was brought forward by a handsome young gentleman who wore a tied wig, a laced coat and ruffles, satin knee-breeches, shining silken stockings, and silver-buckled shoes.

"Lady Adela," said he, "let me introduce you to Miss Burgoyne. Miss Burgoyne has been kind enough to say she will take you into her room for a little while, until I get off my war-paint. I sha'n't keep you more than a few minutes."

"It is very good of you," said the tall young matron in the crimson coat to this gorgeous little white bride, whose lips were brilliant with cherry-paste, and whose bright and frank eyes were surrounded by such a mighty mass of make-up.

"Not at all," she answered, pleasantly enough, and therewith she led the way down some steps into a long, white-tiled corridor, from which branched the various dressing-rooms. "I'm afraid I can't give you any tea now; but there's some lemonade, of my own making—it has become very popular in the theatre—you would hardly believe the number of callers I have of an evening."

By this time Lionel Moore, who was responsible for these strangers being in the theatre, had gone quickly off to his own dressing-room to change his attire, so that when the two ladies reached a certain half-open door where the prima-donna's maid was waiting for her, Lord Rockminster naturally hung back and would have remained without. Miss Burgoyne instantly turned to him.

"Oh, but you may come in too!" she said, with great complaisance.

Somewhat timorously he followed these two into a prettily furnished little sitting-room, where he was bidden to take a seat and regale himself with lemonade, if he was so minded; and then Miss Burgoyne drew aside the curtain of an inner apartment, and said to her other guest:

"*You* may come in here, if you like. Mr. Moore said you wished to know about stage make-up and that kind of thing—I will show you all the dreadful secrets—Jane!" Thereupon these three disappeared behind the curtain, and Lord Rockminster was left alone.

But Lord Rockminster liked being left alone. He was a great thinker, who rarely revealed his thoughts, but who was quite happy in possessing them. He could sit for an hour at a club-window, calmly gazing out into the street, and be perfectly content. It is true that the pale tobacco-tinge that overspread the young man's fair complexion seemed to speak of an out-of-door life; but he had long ago emancipated himself from the tyranny of field-sports. That thraldom had begun early with him, as with most of his class. He had hardly been out of his Eton jacket when gillies and water-bailiffs got hold of him, and made him thrash salmon-pools with a seventeen-foot rod until his back was breaking; and then keepers and foresters had taken possession of him, and compelled him to crawl for miles up wet gullies and across peat-hags, and then put a rifle in his hand, expecting him to hit a bewildering object on the other side of a corrie when, as a matter of fact, his heart was like to burst with excitement and fear. But the young man had some strength of character. He rebelled; he refused to be driven like a slave any longer; he struck for freedom and won it. There was still much travelling to be encountered; but when he had got that over, when he had seen everything and done everything, and there was nothing more to do or to see, then he became master of himself and conducted himself accordingly. Contemplation, accompanied by a cigarette, was now his chief good. What his meditations were no one knew, but they sufficed unto himself. He had attained Nirvana. He lived in a region of perpetual thought.

But there was one active quality that Lord Rockminster certainly did possess: he was a most devoted brother, as all the town knew. He was never tired of going about with his three beautiful sisters, or with any one of them; he would fetch and carry for them with the most amiable assiduity; "Rock" they called him, as if he were a retriever. Then the fact that they followed very different pursuits made all the greater demand on his consideration. His youngest sister, Lady Rosamund Bourne, painted indefatigably in both water and oils, and had more than once exhibited in Suffolk Street; Lady Sybil devoted herself to music, and was a well-known figure at charitable concerts; while the eldest sister, Lady Adela, considered literature and the drama as more particularly under her protection, nor had she ceased to interest herself in these graceful arts when she married Sir Hugh Cunyngham, of the Braes, that famous breeder of polled cattle. The natural consequence of all this was that Lord Rockminster found himself called to a never-ending series of concerts, theatres, private views, and the like, and always with one or other of his beautiful, tall sisters as his companion; while on a certain occasion (for it was whispered that Lady Adela Cunyngham was engaged in the composition of a novel, and her brother was the soul of good-nature) he had even gone the length of asking a publisher to dine at his club. And here he was seated in an actress's room, alone, while his sister was inspecting powder-puffs, washes, patches, and paste jewelry; and not only that, but they were about to take an actor home to supper with them. What he thought about it all he never said. He sat and stroked his small yellow moustache; his eyes was absent; and on his handsome, almost Greek, features there dwelt a perfect and continuous calm.

Presently the door was opened, and the smart-looking young baritone who had stolen away the hearts of half the women in London made his appearance. He was a young fellow of about eight-and-twenty, pleasant-featured, his complexion almost colorless, his eyes gray with dark lashes, his eyebrows also dark. In figure he was slight and wiry rather than muscular; but where he gave evidence of strength was in his magnificent throat and in the set of his head and shoulders. It may be added that he possessed, what few stage-singers appear to possess, a remarkably well-formed leg—a firm-knit calf tapering to a small ankle and a shapely foot; but, as he had now doffed his professional silken stockings and silver-buckled shoes for ordinary evening wear, his merits in this respect were mostly concealed.

No sooner had he begun to talk to Lord Rockminster than the sound of his voice summoned forth from the inner apartment Lady Adela, who, with many expressions of thanks, bade good-night to the prima-donna, and put herself under charge of the young baritone.

"My sisters are at the Mellords' to-night," said she, as she accompanied him along the corridor and up the steps and through the now almost deserted wings. "They were dining there, and we left them as we came to the theatre, and promised to pick them up on our way home. There will be a bit of a crush, I suppose; you won't mind coming in for a few minutes, will you, Mr. Moore?"

"I don't know Mrs. Mellord," said he, with becoming modesty.

"But everybody knows you—that is the great point," said this tall young Englishwoman, who looked very gracious and charming, and who, when she turned to talk to her companion, had a quick, responsive smile ever ready in her clear, intelligent, gray-blue eyes. "Oh, yes, you must come. It is one of the prettiest houses in London; and Mrs. Mellord is one of the nicest women. We will get Sybil and Rose away as soon as we can; and I shouldn't at all wonder if we found Georgie Lestrange and her brother there too. Oh, almost certain, I should say. Then we could carry them off to supper, and after that Pastora might try over her duet with Damon. But as regards the Mellords, Mr. Moore," said she, with a pleasant smile, as he handed her into her brougham, which had been brought round to the stage-door, "I shall consider you to be under my protection, and I will take care no one shall ask you to sing."

"But you know, Lady Adela, I am always delighted to sing for any friend of yours," said he, promptly enough; and then, when he and Lord Rockminster had entered the carriage, and the footman had shut the door and got on the box, away they drove through the busy midnight world of London.

It did not take them long to get from the New Theatre to the house of the famous Academician; and here, late as it was, they found plenty of people still arriving, a small crowd of onlookers scanning the various groups as they crossed the pavement. On this hot night in May, it seemed pleasantly cool to get into the great hall of white and black marble, where the miniature lake, on which floated an alabaster swan, was all banked round with flowers; and when Lady Adela had dispossessed herself of her long plush coat, it was evident she had dressed for the reception before going to the theatre, for now she appeared in a costume of silver-gray satin with a very considerable train, while there were diamond stars in her light brown hair, and at her bosom a bunch of deep crimson roses. At the head of the stairs they encountered Mrs. Mellord, who received the famous young baritone with the most marked kindness. Indeed, he seemed to be known to a considerable number of the people who were assembled in these spacious rooms of white and gold; while those who were not personally acquainted with him easily recognized him, for were not his photographs in every stationer's window in London? The Ladies Sybil and Rosamund Bourne they found in the studio, talking to the great Academician himself. These two young ladies were even taller, as they likewise were fairer in complexion, than their married sister; moreover, they were much more dignified in demeanor than she was, though that may have merely arisen from maidenly reserve. But when Mr. Mellord exhibited at the Royal Academy his much-talked-of picture of the three sisters, most people seemed to think that though the two younger ladies might have carried off the palm for their handsome, pale, regularly cut features and their calm, observant eyes, there was something in the bright, vivacious look of the eldest that outweighed these advantages; while in society, and especially as a hostess in her own house, the charm of Lady Adela's manner, and her quick, sympathetic, engaging ways made her a universal favorite. And one was tempted, in amazement, to ask how it came about that a woman so alert and intelligent, so conversant with the world, so ready to note the ridiculous side of things, could not understand what a poor and lamentable figure she made as an amateur authoress? But had the Lady Sybil any less confidence in her musical attainments, when she would undertake to play a duet with one of the most distinguished of professional musicians, she on the violin, he at the piano? And here, at this very moment, was Lady Rosamund talking to by far and away the greatest painter in England, and there was a picture before them on an easel, and she was saying to him, with perfect coolness,

"Why, I see you use cadmium yellow, Mr. Mellord! I *never* do."

Somehow an impression got abroad through these brilliant rooms that Mr. Moore was going to sing; and at length Mrs. Mellord came to the young man and frankly preferred her request.

"Oh, yes," said he, most good-naturedly.

"The serenade?" she ventured to hint.

"Oh, not the serenade!" said he, with a laugh. "Every butcher's boy in the streets whistles it."

"All England is singing it—and a good thing, too," she made answer; and then she said, with some emphasis: "I am sure no one rejoices more than myself at the great popularity of 'The Squire's Daughter.' I am very glad to see that a comedy-opera may be based on the best traditions of English music; and I hope we shall have a great deal less of the Offenbach tinkle-tankle."

"The serenade, if you like, then," said he, with, careless good-humor; what did it matter to him?

"And whom shall I get to play an accompaniment for you?"

"Oh, you needn't trouble; I can do that for myself—"

"But you must make one young lady supremely happy," said she, with insidious flattery.

He glanced round the studio.

"I see Miss Lestrange over there—she has played it for me before—without the music, I mean."

"Then I'll go and fetch her," said the indefatigable hostess; and now everybody seemed to know that Mr. Lionel Moore was about to sing "The Starry Night."

Miss Georgie Lestrange was no sooner appealed to than she came through the crowd, smiling and laughing. She was an exceedingly pretty lass, with fresh-complexioned cheeks, a pert and attractive nose, a winsome mouth, and merry blue eyes that were hardly made grave by the *pince-nez* that she habitually wore. She was very prettily dressed, too—in blue-and-silver brocade, with a high Medici collar of silver lace, puffed sleeves with twisted cords of silver, and silver fillets binding the abundant masses of her ruddy-golden hair. She sat down at the piano, and the first notes of the accompaniment deepened the silence that now prevailed, not only in this big studio, but throughout the communicating rooms.

Probably there was not a human being in the place who had not heard this serenade sung a dozen times over, for it was the most popular air of the most popular piece then being played in London; but there was some kind of novelty in listening to the same notes that had thrilled through the theatre (rather, that had sent their passionate appeal up to a certain mysterious balcony, in the dim moonlight of the stage) now pulsating through the hushed silence of these modern rooms. Lionel Moore was not a baritone of altogether rare and exceptional gifts, otherwise he might hardly have been content with even the popularity and the substantial rewards of comic opera; but he had a very excellent voice for all that, of high range, and with a resonant and finely sympathetic *timbre* that seemed easily to find its way (according to all accounts) to the feminine heart. And the music of this serenade was really admirable, of subtle and delicate quality, and yet full of the simplest melody, and perhaps none the less to be appreciated that it seemed to suggest a careful study of the best English composers. The words were conventional enough, of course; but then the whole story of "The Squire's Daughter" was as artificial as the wigs and powder and patches of the performers; and even now, when Harry Thornhill, bereft of all his gay silk and lace and ruffles, and become plain Mr. Lionel Moore, in ordinary evening dress, sang to Miss Georgie Lestrange's accompaniment, the crowd did not think of the words—they were entranced by the music. "The starry night"—this is how Harry Thornhill, in the opera, addresses Grace Mainwaring, he standing in the moonlit garden and looking up to her window—

"The starry night brings me no rest;

My ardent love now stands confessed;

Appear, my sweet, and shame the skies,

That have no splendor,

That have no splendor like thine eyes!"

The serenade was followed by a general murmur of approbation, rather than by any loud applause; but the pretty Mrs. Mellord came up to the singer and was most profuse of thanks. Prudently, however, he moved away from the piano, being accompanied by Miss Georgie Lestrange, who seemed rather pleased with the prominence this position gave her; and very soon a surreptitious message reached them both that they were wanted below. When they went down into the hall they found that Lady Adela had got her party collected, including Miss Lestrange's brother Percy; thereupon the four ladies got into the brougham and drove off, while the three gentlemen proposed to follow on foot, and have a cigarette the while. It was a pleasantly warm night, and they had no farther to go than Sir Hugh Cunyngham's house, which is one of the large garden-surrounded mansions on the summit of Campden Hill.

When at length they arrived there and had entered by the wooden gate, the semicircular carriage-drive, lit by two solitary lamps, and the front of the house itself, half-hidden among the black trees, seemed somewhat sombre and repellent at this silent hour of the morning; but they found a more cheerful radiance streaming out from the hall-door, which had been left open for them; and when they went into the large dining-room, where the ladies had already assembled, there was no lack of either light or color there, for all the candles were ablaze, and the long table was brilliant with silver and Venetian glass and flowers. And, indeed, this proved to be a very merry and talkative supper-party; for, as soon as supper was served, the servants were sent off to bed; Lord Rockminster constituted himself butler, and Percy Lestrange handed round the pheasants' eggs and asparagus and such things; so that there was no alien ear in the room. Lionel Moore, being less familiar with the house, was exempted from these duties; in truth, it was rather the women-folk who waited upon him—and petted him as he was used to be petted, wherever that fortunate young man happened to go.

However, it was not supper that was chiefly occupying the attention of this band of eager chatterers (from whom the silent Lord Rockminster, walking gravely round the table with a large jug of champagne-cup in his hand, must honorably be distinguished), it was the contemplated production of a little musical entertainment called "The Chaplet," by Dr. Boyce, which they were about to attempt, out-of-doors, on some afternoon still to be fixed, and before a select concourse of friends. And the most vivacious of the talkers was the red-headed and merry-eyed young maiden in blue silver and brocade, who seemed incapable of keeping her rosebud of a mouth closed for more than a minute at a time.

"I do think it's awfully hard on me," she was protesting. "Look how I'm handicapped! Everybody knows that Pastora was played by Kitty Olive; and everybody will say, 'That Lestrange girl has cheek, hasn't she? thinks she can play Kitty Olive's parts!' And you know Pastora is always calling attention to her fascinating appearance."

"Georgie, you're fishing for compliments!" the young matron said, severely.

"No, I'm not, Adela," said Miss Lestrange, who, indeed, looked as charming as any Kitty Olive could ever have done. "Then there's another thing: fancy my having to sing a duet with Mr. Moore! It's all very well for you to sing a song off your own bat—"

"That *would* be difficult, Georgie," Lady Adela observed.

"Oh, you know what I mean. But when you come to sing in conjunction with an artist like Mr. Moore, what then? They will say it is mere presumption, when my little squeak of a voice gets drowned altogether."

"If you give any weight to a professional opinion, Miss Lestrange," the young baritone said, "I can assure you you sing your part in that duet—or in anything else I've heard you sing—very well indeed. Very well indeed."

"Ah, now Georgie's happy," said Lady Adela, with a laugh, as the blushing damsel cast down her eyes. "Well, I propose that we all go into the drawing-room, and we'll hear for ourselves how Pastora and Damon sing together. You may make as much noise as ever you like; the children are in Hampshire; Hugh is in Scotland; the servants are out of hearing; and our neighbors are a long way off."

This suggestion, coming from the lady of the house, was of the nature of a command, and so they leisurely trooped into the great drawing-room, where the candles were still burning. But there was something else than these artificial lights that attracted the sharp eyes of Miss Georgie Lestrange the moment she entered this new apartment. There was a curious, wan kind of color about the curtains and the French windows that did not seem natural to the room. She walked quickly forward, drew the lace hangings aside, and then, suddenly, she exclaimed,

"Why, it's almost daylight! Look here, Adela, why shouldn't we have a rehearsal of the whole piece, from end to end—a real rehearsal, this time, on the lawn? and Rose can tell us all how we are to stand, and Mr. Moore will show us what we should do besides merely speaking the lines."

This bold proposal was greeted with general acclaim, and instantly there was a bustle of preparation. Lady Sybil began to tune her violin by the side of the open piano; Lady Rosamund, who was at once scene-painter and stage-manager, as it were, got out some sheets of drawing-paper, on which she had sketched the various groups; and Lady Adela brought forth the MS. books of the play, which had been prepared under the careful (and necessary) supervision of Lionel Moore.

"Rockminster will have to figure as the audience," his eldest sister said, as she was looping up her long train of silver-gray satin preparatory to going out.

"That is a part *I* could play to perfection," put in Miss Lestrange's brother.

"Oh, no," Lady Adela remonstrated. "You may be wanted for Palæmon. You see, this is how it stands. The young shepherd was originally played at Drury Lane by a boy—and in Dublin by an actress; it is a boy's part, indeed. Well, you know, we thought Cis Yorke would snap at it; and she was eager enough at first; but"—and here Lady Adela smiled demurely—"I think her courage gave way. The boy's dress looked charming as Rose sketched it for her—and the long cloak made it quite proper, you know—and very picturesque, too—but—but I think she's frightened. We can't count on her. So we may have to call on you for Palæmon, Mr. Lestrange."

"And I have taken the liberty of cutting out the song, for it's rather stupid," said Lionel Moore, "so you've only got a few lines to repeat."

"The fewer the better," replied Mr. Percy Lestrange, who was possibly right in considering that, with his far-from-regular features and his red hair and moustache, his appearance as a handsome young swain should not have too much prominence given it.

Notwithstanding that it had been Miss Lestrange's audacious proposal that they should go masquerading in the open air, she was a wise young virgin, and she took care before going out to thrust a soft silk handkerchief into the square opening of her dress; the Ladies Sybil and Rosamund followed her example by drawing lace scarfs round their necks and shoulders; it was the young matron who was reprehensibly careless, and who, when the French windows were thrown open, went forth boldly, and without any wrap at all, into the cool air of the dawn. But for a second, as they stood on the little stone balcony above the steps leading down to the garden, this group of revellers were struck silent. The world looked so strange around them. In the mysterious gray light, that had no sort of kindly warmth in it, the grass of the lawn and the surrounding trees seemed coldly and intensely green; and cold and intense, with no richness of hue at all, were the colors of the flowers in the various plots and beds. Not a bird chirped as yet. Not a leaf stirred. But in this ghostly twilight the solitary gas lamps were beginning to show pale; and in the southern heavens the silver sickle of the moon, stealing over to the west, seemed to be taking the night with it, and leaving these faintly lilac skies to welcome the uprising of the new day.

At first, indeed, there was something curiously uncanny—something unearthly and phantasmal almost—in the spectacle of these figures, the women in white, the men in black, moving through this wan light; and their voices sounded strangely in the dead silence; but ere long a soft saffron tinge began to show itself in the east; one or two scraps of cloud in the violet skies caught a faint touch of the coming dawn; there was a more generous tone on the masses of foliage, on the flower-beds, and on the grass; and now the cheerful chirping of the birds had begun among the leaves. And what more beautiful surroundings could have been imagined for the production of any pastoral entertainment? The wide lawn was bounded on one side by a dense thicket of elms and limes and chestnuts, and on the other by a tall, dark hedge of holly; while here and there was a weeping-willow, round the stem of which a circular seat had been constructed, the pendulous branches enclosing a sort of rustic bower. As this fantastic performance went forward, the skies overhead slowly became more luminous; there was a sense of warmth and clear daylight beginning to tell; the birds were singing and chattering and calling everywhere; and the sweet, pure air of the morning, as it stirred, and no more than stirred, the trembling leaves, brought with it a scent of mignonette that seemed to speak of the coming of June.

Laura, in the person of Lady Adela Cunyngham, had reproached the faithless Damon (who was no other than Mr. Lionel Moore)—

"Ungrateful Damon, is it come to this?

Are these the happy scenes of promis'd bliss?

Ne'er hope, vain Laura, future peace to prove;

Content ne'er harbors with neglected love."

—and Damon had replied (not mumbling his lines, as a privileged actor sometimes does at rehearsal, but addressing them properly to the hapless Laura)—

"Consider, fair, the ever-restless pow'r,

Shifts with the breeze, and changes with the hour:

Above restraint, he scorns a fixt abode,

And on his silken plumes flies forth the rambling god."

Then Lady Sybil took out her violin from its case and drew the bow across the strings.

"We'll let you off the song, if you like, Mr. Moore," Lady Adela said to the young baritone, but in a very half-hearted kind of way.

"Oh, no," said he, pleasantly, "perhaps this may be my only rehearsal."

"The audience," observed Lord Rockminster, who, at a little distance, was lying back in a garden-chair, smoking a cigarette—"the audience would distinctly prefer to have the song sung."

Lady Sybil again gave him the key-note from the violin; and, without further accompaniment, he thus addressed his forsaken sweetheart:

"You say at your feet that I wept in despair,

And vow'd that no angel was ever so fair;

How could you believe all the nonsense I spoke?

What know we of angels? I meant it in joke,

   I meant it in joke;

What know we of angels? I meant it in joke."

When, in his rich, vibrating notes, he had sung the two verses, all the ladies rewarded him by clapping their hands, which was an exceedingly wrong thing to do, considering that they formed no part of the audience. Then *Damon* says,

"To-day Demætus gives a rural treat,

And I once more my chosen friends must meet:

Farewell, sweet damsel, and remember this,

Dull repetition deadens all our bliss."

And Laura sadly answers,

"Where baleful cypress forms a gloomy shade,

And yelling spectres haunt the dreary glade,

Unknown to all, my lonesome steps I'll bend,

There weep my suff'rings, and my fate attend."

Here Laura ought to sing the song "Vain is every fond endeavor;" but Lady Adela said to the violinist,

"No, never mind, Syb; no one wants to hear *me* sing, until the necessity of the case arises. Let's get on to the feast; I think that will be very popular; for we must have lots of shepherds and shepherdesses; and the people will be delighted to recognize their friends. Where's your sketch, Rose? I would have groups round each of the willows, and occasional figures coming backwards and forwards through those rhododendrons."

"You must leave the principal performers plenty of stage," Lionel Moore interposed, laughing. "You mustn't hem us in with supers, however picturesque their dress may be."

And so they went on discussing their arrangements, while the refulgent day was everywhere declaring itself, though as yet no sound of the far-off world could reach this isolated garden. Nor was there any direct sunshine falling into it; but a beautiful warmth of color now shone on the young green of the elms and chestnuts and hawthorns, and on one or two tall-branching, trembling poplars just coming into leaf; while the tulip-beds—the stars, the crescents, the ovals, and squares—were each a mass of brilliant vermilion, of rose, of pale lemon, of crimson and orange, or clearest gold. This new-found dawn seemed wholly to belong to the birds. Perhaps it was their universal chirping and carolling that concealed the distant echo of the highways; for surely the heavily-laden wains were now making in for Covent Garden? At all events there was nothing here but this continuous bird-clamor and the voices of these modern nymphs and swains as they went this way and that over the velvet-smooth lawn.

And now the bewitching Pastora appears upon the scene (but would Mrs. Clive have worn a gold *pince-nez* at rehearsal?) and she has just quarrelled with her lover Palæmon—

"Insulting boy! I'll tear him from my mind;

Ah! would my fortune could a husband find!

And just in time, young Damon comes this way,

A handsome youth he is, and rich, they say."

The butterfly-hearted Damon responds at once:

"Vouchsafe, sweet maid, to hear a wretched swain,

Who, lost in wonder, hugs the pleasing chain:

For you in sighs I hail the rising day,

To you at eve I sing the lovesick lay;

Then take my love, my homage as your due—

[*Aside.*

The Devil's in her, if all this won't do."

It must be confessed that the pretty and smiling and blushing Miss Georgie Lestrange looked just a little self-conscious as she had to listen to this extremely frank declaration; but she had the part of the coquettish Pastora to play; and Pastora, as soon as she discovers that Damon has no thought of marriage, naturally declines to have anything to do with him. And here came in the duet which had first suggested this escapade:

"You say at your feet that I wept in despair,

And vow'd that no angel was ever so fair;

How could you believe all the nonsense I spoke?

What know we of angels? I meant it in joke,

I meant it in joke;

What know we of angels? I meant it in joke."

"DAMON.

From flow'r to flow'r, his joy to change,

    Flits yonder wanton bee;

From fair to fair thus will I range,

    And I'll be ever free.

From fair to fair thus will I range,

    And I'll be ever free.

"PASTORA.

You little birds attentive view,

    That hop from tree to tree;

I'll copy them, I'll copy you,

    For I'll be ever free.

"DUETTO.

Then let's divide to east and west

    Since we shall ne'er agree;

And try who keeps their promise best

    And who's the longest free.

Let's try who keeps their promise best

    And who's the longest free."

And again the audience made bold to clap their hands; for Miss Georgie Lestrange, despite her self-depreciation, sang very well indeed; and of course Lionel Moore knew how to moderate his voice, so that the combination was entirely pleasing. The further progress of the little comedy needs not to be described here; it has only to be said that the injured Laura is in the end restored to her repentant lover; and that a final duet between her and Damon closes the piece with the most praiseworthy sentiments:

"For their honor and faith be our virgins renown'd,

Nor false to his vows one young shepherd he found;

Be their moments all guided by virtue and truth,

To preserve in their age what they gain'd in their youth,

To preserve in their age what they gain'd in their youth."

Lord Rockminster rose from his chair, stretched his long legs, and threw away his cigarette.

"Very well done," said he, slowly. "Congratulate all of you."

"This is the first time I ever saw Rockminster sit out a morning performance," observed Percy Lestrange, with a playful grin.

"As for you young things," the mistress of the house said to her girl-guests, as they were all trooping in by the French windows again, "you must hurry home and get in-doors before the servants are up. I don't want this frolic to be talked about all over the town."

"A frolic, indeed!" Miss Georgie protested, as her brother was putting her cloak round her shoulders. "I don't call it a frolic at all. I call it very serious business; and I'm looking forward to winning the deepest gratitude of the English public—or at least as much of the English public as you can cram into your garden, my dear."

Then, as soon as the light wraps and dust-coats had been distributed and donned, the members of the gay little party said good-bye to Lady Adela in the front hall, and went down the carriage sweep to the gate. Here there was a division; for the Lestranges were going north by Holland Lane to Notting Hill; while Lord Rockminster and his two sisters, making for Palace Gardens Terrace, walked with Lionel Moore only as far as Campden Hill Road; thereafter he pursued his journey to Piccadilly alone.

And even now London was not fully awake, though the sun was touching the topmost branches of the trees, and here and there a high window, struck by the level rays, flashed back a gleam of gold. In this neighborhood the thoroughfares were quite deserted; silence reigned over those sleeping houses; the air was sweet and cool; now and again a stirring of wind brought a scent of summer—blossom from within the garden-enclosures. It is true that when he got down into Kensington Road he found a long procession of wagons slowly making their way into the great city; but this dull, drowsy noise was not ungrateful; in much content and idly he walked away eastward, looking in from time to time at the beautiful greensward of Kensington Gardens and Hyde Park. He was in no hurry. He liked the stillness, the gracious coolness and quietude of the morning, after the hot and feverish nights at the theatre. When at length he reached his lodging in Piccadilly, let himself in with his latch-key, and went up-stairs to his rooms, he did not go to bed at once. He drew an easy-chair to the front window, threw himself into it, lit a cigarette, and stared absently across to the branching elms and grassy undulations of the Green Park. Perhaps he was thinking of the pretty, fantastic little comedy that had just been performed up in that garden at Campden Hill—like some dream-picture out of Boccaccio. And if he chanced to recall the fact that the actor who originally played the part of Damon, at Drury Lane, some hundred and forty years ago, married in real life an earl's daughter, that was but a passing fancy. Of Lord Fareborough's three daughters, it was neither Lady Sybil nor Lady Rosamund, it was the married sister, Lady Adela Cunyngham, who had constituted herself his particular friend.

CHAPTER II.

THE GREAT GOD PAN.

Late as he went to bed, sleep did not long detain him, for, in his own happy-go-lucky, troubadour sort of life, he was one of the most occupied of men even in this great, hurrying, bustling capital of the world. As soon as he had donned his dressing-gown and come into the sitting-room, he swallowed a cup of coffee that was waiting for him, and then, to make sure that unholy hours and cigarettes had not hurt his voice, he dabbed a note on the piano, and began to practise, in the open-throated Italian fashion, those *vocalises* which sound so strangely to the uninstructed ear. He rang for breakfast. He glanced in a despairing way at the pile of letters and parcels awaiting him, the former, no doubt, mostly invitations, the latter, as he could guess, proofs of his latest sittings to the photographers, albums and birth-day books sent for his autograph, music beseeching commendation, even manuscript plays accompanied by pathetic appeals from unknown authors. Then there was a long row of potted scarlet geraniums and large white daisies which the house-porter had ranged by the window; and when he opened the note that had been forwarded with these he found that the wife of a famous statesman had observed as she drove along Piccadilly that the flowers in his balcony wanted renewal and begged his acceptance of this graceful little tribute. He took up a pair of dumb-bells, and had some exercise with them, to keep his arms and chest in good condition. He looked at himself in the mirror: no, he did not seem to have smoked inordinately; nevertheless, he made sundry solemn vows about those insidious cigarettes. Then he began to open the envelopes. Here was an imposing card, "To have the honor of meeting their royal highnesses the king and queen of ——;" here was a more modest bit of pasteboard with "*R.S.V.P.* to mess president" at the lower corner; here were invitations to breakfasts, to luncheons, to afternoon squawks, to Sunday dinners, to dances and crushes, in short, to every possible kind of diversion and frivolity that the gay world of London could devise. He went steadily on with his letters. More photographers wanted him to sit to them. Would he accept the dedication of "The Squire's Daughter Fantasia"? The composer of "The Starry Night Valses" would like a lithographic portrait of Mr. Lionel Moore to appear on the cover. A humble admirer of Mr. Lionel Moore's great impersonation of Harry Thornhill begged to forward the enclosed acrostic, and might he be allowed to print it in the *Mudborough Young Men's Mutual Improvement Magazine*? Messrs. Smith & Smith would be extremely obliged if Mr. Lionel Moore would honor them with his opinion of the accompanying pair of their patent silver-mounted automatic self-adjusting braces.

"If I don't get a secretary," he muttered to himself, "I shall soon be in a mad-house."

Nor did he pay much attention to his breakfast when it was put on the table, for there were newspapers to be opened and glanced through—country journals, most of them, with marked paragraphs conveying the most unexpected, and even startling, intelligence regarding himself, his occupations, and forthcoming engagements. Then there were the book packets and the rolls of music to be examined; but by this time he had lit an after-breakfast cigarette, and was proceeding with something of indifference. Occasionally he strolled about the room, or went to the window and looked down into the roaring highway of Piccadilly, or across to the sunny foliage and pale-blue mists of the Green Park. And then, in the midst of his vague meditations, the following note was brought to him; it had been delivered by hand:

"MY DEAR MR. MOORE,—I do so *awfully* want to see you, about a matter of *urgent importance*. Do be good-natured and come and lunch with us—any time before half-past two, if possible. It will be *so* kind of you. I hope the *morning performance* has done you no harm.

ADELA CUNYNGHAM."

Yours, sincerely,

Well, luncheon was not much in his way, for he usually dined at five; nevertheless, Lady Adela was an especial friend of his and had been very kind to him, and here was some serious business. So he hurried through what correspondence was absolutely necessary; he sent word to Green's stables that he should not ride that morning; he walked round to a certain gymnasium and had three quarters of an hour with the fencing-master (this was an appointment which he invariably held sacred); on his way back to his rooms he called in at Solomon's for a buttonhole; and then, having got home and made certain alterations in his toilet, he went out again, jumped into a hansom, and was driven up to the top of Campden Hill, arriving there shortly after one o'clock.

He found Lady Adela and Miss Georgie Lestrange in the drawing-room, or rather just outside, on the little balcony overlooking the garden, and neither of them seemed any the worse for that masquerading in the early dawn; indeed, Miss Georgie's naturally fresh and bright complexion flushed a little more than usual when she saw who this new-comer was, for perhaps she was thinking of the very frank manner in which Damon had expressed his admiration for Pastora but a few short hours ago.

"I have been telling Georgie all about the dresses at the drawing-room," said the tall young matron, as she gave him her hand and regarded him with a friendly look; "but that won't interest you, Mr. Moore. We shall have to talk about the new beauties, rather, to interest *you*."

He was a little puzzled.

"I thought, Lady Adela, you said there was something—something of importance—"

"That depends," said she, with a pleasant smile in her clear, gray-blue eyes. "I think it of importance; but it remains to be seen whether the world is of the same opinion. Well, I won't keep you in suspense."

She went to the piano, and brought back three volumes plainly bound in green cloth.

"Behold!"

He took them from her, and glanced at the title-page: "Kathleen's Sweethearts, a Novel, by Lady Arthur Castletown," was what he found there.

"So it is out at last," said he, for he had more than once heard of this great work while it was still in progress.

"Yes," said she, eagerly, "though it isn't issued to the public yet. The fact is, Mr. Moore, I want you to help me. You know all about professional people, and the newspapers, and so on—who better?—and, of course, I'm very anxious about my first book—my first big book, that is—and I don't want it to get just thrown aside without ever being glanced at. Now, what am I to do? You may speak quite freely before Georgie—she's just as anxious as I am, every bit, I believe—only what to do we can't tell."

"All that I can think of," said the ruddy-haired young damsel, with a laugh, "is to have little advertisements printed, and I will leave them behind me wherever I go—in the stalls of a theatre, or at a concert, or anywhere. You know, Adela, you can *not* expect me to turn myself into a sandwich-man, and go about the streets between boards."

"Georgie, you're frivolous," said Lady Adela, and she again turned to Lionel Moore, who was still holding the three green volumes in his hands in a helpless sort of fashion. "You know, Mr. Moore, there are such a lot of books published nowadays—crowds!—shoals!—and, unless there is a little attention drawn beforehand, what chance have you? I want a friend in court—I want several friends in court—and that's the truth; now, how am I to get them?"

This was plain speaking; but he was none the less bewildered.

"You see, Lady Adela, the theatre is so different from the world of letters. I've met one or two newspaper men now and again, but they were dramatic critics—I never heard that they reviewed books."

"But they were connected with newspapers?—then they must know the men who do," said this alert and intelligent lady. "Oh, I don't ask for anything unfair! I only ask for a chance. I don't want to be thrown into a corner unread or sold to the second-hand bookseller uncut. Now, Mr. Moore, think. You must know *lots* of newspaper men if you would only *think*: why, they're always coming about theatres. And they would do anything for you, for you are such a popular favorite; and a word from you would be of such value to a beginner like me. Now, Mr. Moore, be good-natured, and consider. But first of all come away and have some lunch, and then we'll talk it over."

When they had gone into the dining-room and sat down at table, he said,

"Well, if it comes to that, I certainly know one newspaper man; in fact, I have known him all my life; he is my oldest friend. But then he is merely the head of the Parliamentary reporting staff of the *Morning Mirror*—he's in the gallery of the House of Commons, you know, every night—and I'm afraid he couldn't do much about a book."

"Couldn't he do a little, Mr. Moore?" said Lady Adela, insidiously. "Couldn't he get it hinted in the papers that 'Lady Arthur Castletown' is only a *nom de plume?*"

"Then you don't object to your own name being mentioned?" asked this simple young man.

"No, no, not at all," said she, frankly. "People are sure to get to know. There are some sketches of character in the book that I think will make a little stir—I mean people will be asking questions; and then you know how a pseudonym whets curiosity—they will certainly find out—and they will talk all the more then. That ought to do the book some good. And then you understand, Mr. Moore," continued this remarkably naive person, "if your friend happened to know any of the reviewers, and could suggest how some little polite attention might be paid them, there would be nothing wrong in that, would there? I am told that they are quite gentlemen nowadays—they go everywhere—and—and indeed I should like to make their acquaintance, since I've come into the writing fraternity myself."

Lionel Moore was silent; he was considering how he should approach the fastidious, whimsical, sardonic Maurice Mangan on this extremely difficult subject.

"Let me see," he said, presently. "This is Wednesday; my friend Mangan won't be at the House; I will send a message to his rooms, and ask him to come down to the theatre: then we can have a consultation about it. May I take this copy of the book with me, Lady Adela?"

"Certainly, certainly!" said she, with promptitude. "And if you know of any one to whom I should send a copy, with the author's name in it—my own name, I mean—it would be extremely kind of you to let me know. It's so awfully hard for us poor outsiders to get a hearing. You professional folk are in a very different position—the public just worship you—you have it all your own way—you don't need to care what the critics say—but look at *me*! I may knock and knock at the door of the Temple of Fame until my knuckles are sore, and who will take any notice—unless, perhaps, some friendly ear begins to listen? Do you think Mr. Mangan—did you say Mangan?—do you think he would come and dine with us some evening?"

The artless ingenuousness of her speech was almost embarrassing.

"He is a very busy man," he said, doubtfully, "very busy. He has his gallery work to do, of course; and then I believe he is engaged on some important philosophical treatise—he has been at it for years, indeed—"

"Oh, he writes books too?" Lady Adela cried. "Then certainly you must bring him to dinner. Shall I write a note now, Mr. Moore—a Sunday evening, of course, so that we may secure you as well—"

"I think I would wait a little, Lady Adela," he said, "until I see how the land lies. He's a most curious fellow, Mangan: difficult to please and capricious. I fancy he is rather disappointed with himself; he ought to have done something great, for he knows everything—at least he knows what is fine in everything, in painting, in poetry, in music; and yet, with all his sympathy, he seems to be forever grumbling—and mostly at himself. He is a difficult fellow to deal with—"

"I suppose he eats his dinner like anybody else," said Lady Adela, somewhat sharply: she was not used to having her invitations scorned.

"Yes, but I think he would prefer to eat it in a village ale-house," Lionel said, with a smile, "where he could make 'the violet of a legend blow, among the chops and steaks.' However, I will take him your book, Lady Adela; and I have no doubt he will be able to give you some good advice."

It was late that evening when, in obedience to the summons of a sixpenny telegram, Maurice Mangan called at the stage-door of the New Theatre and was passed in. Lionel Moore was on the stage, as any one could tell, for the resonant baritone voice was ringing clear above the multitudinous music of the orchestra; but Mangan, not wishing to be in the way, did not linger in the wings—he made straight for his friend's room, which he knew. And in the dusk of the long corridor he was fortunate enough to behold a beautiful apparition, in the person of a young French officer in the gayest of uniforms, who, apparently to maintain the character he bore in the piece (it was that of a young prisoner of war liberated on parole, who played sad havoc with the hearts of the village maidens by reason of his fascinating ways and pretty broken English), had just facetiously chucked two of the women dressers under the chin; and these damsels were simpering at this mark of condescension, and evidently much impressed by the swagger and braggadocio of the miniature warrior. However, Mlle. Girond (the boy-officer in question) no sooner caught sight of the new-comer than she instantly and demurely altered her demeanor; and as she passed him in the corridor she favored him with a grave and courteous little bow, for she had met him more than once in Miss Burgoyne's sitting-room. Mangan returned the salutation most respectfully; and then he went on and entered the apartment in which Lionel Moore dressed.

It was empty; so this tall, thin man with the slightly stooping shoulders threw himself into a wicker-work easy-chair, and let his eyes—which were much keener than was properly compatible with the half-affected expression of indolence that had become habitual to him—roam over the heterogeneous collection of articles around. These were abundantly familiar to him—the long dressing-table, with all its appliances for making-up, the mirrors, the wigs on blocks, the gay-colored garments, the fencing-foils and swords, the framed series of portraits from "Vanity Fair," the innumerable photographs stuck everywhere about. Indeed, it was something not immediately connected with these paraphernalia of an actor's existence that seemed to be occupying his mind, even as he idly regarded the various pastes and colors, the powder-puffs and pencils, the pots of vaseline. His eyes grew absent as he sat there. Was he thinking of the Linn Moore of years and years ago who used to reveal to the companion of his boyhood all his high aims and strenuous ambitions—how he was resolved to become a Mendelssohn, a Mozart, a Beethoven? Whither had fled all those wistful dreams and ardent aspirations? What was Linn Moore now?—why, a singer in comic opera, his face beplastered almost out of recognition; a pet of the frivolous-fashionable side of London society; the chief adornment of photographers' windows.

"'Half a beast is the great god Pan,'" this tall, languid-looking man murmured to himself, as he was vacuously staring at those paints and brushes and cosmetics; and then he got up and began to walk indeterminately about the room, his hands behind his back.

Presently the door was opened, and in came Lionel Moore, followed by his dresser.

"Hallo, Maurice!—you're late," said Harry Thornhill, as he surrendered himself to his factotum, who forthwith began to strip him of his travelling costume of cocked hat, frogged coat, white leather breeches, and shining black boots in order to make way for the more brilliant attire of the last act.

"Now that I am here, what are your highness's commands?" Mangan asked.

"There's a book there—written by a friend of mine," Lionel said, as he was helping his dresser to get off the glittering top-boots. "She wants me to do what I can for her with the press. What do I know about that? Still, she is a very particular friend—and you must advise me."

Mangan rose and went to the mantelpiece and took down Volume I.

"Lady Arthur Castletown—" said he.

"But that is not her real name," the other interposed. "Her real name is Lady Adela Cunyngham—of course you know who she is."

"I have been permitted to hear the echo of her name from those rare altitudes in which you dwell now," the other said, lazily. "So she is one of your fashionable acquaintances; and she wants to secure the puff preliminary, and a number of favorable reviews, I suppose; and then you send for me. But what can I do for you except ask one or two of the gallery men to mention the book in their London Correspondent's letter?"

"But that's the very thing, my dear fellow!" Lionel Moore cried, as he was getting on his white silk stockings. "The very thing! She wants attention drawn to the book. She doesn't want to be passed over. She wants to have the name of the book and the name of the author brought before the public—"

"Her real name?"

"Yes, certainly, if that is advisable."

"Oh, well, there's not much trouble about that. You can always minister to a mind diseased by a morbid craving for notoriety if a paragraph in a country newspaper will suffice. So this is part of what your fashionable friends expect from you, Linn, in return for their patronage?"

"It's nothing of the kind; she would do as much for me, if she knew how, or if there were any occasion."

"Oh, well, it is no great thing," said Mangan, who was really a very good-natured sort of person, despite his supercilious talk. "In fact, you might do her ladyship a more substantial service than that."

"How?"

"I thought you knew Quirk—Octavius Quirk?"

"But you have always spoken so disparagingly of him!" the other exclaimed.

"What has that to do with it?" Mangan asked; and then he continued, in his indolent fashion: "Why, I thought you knew all about Quirk. Quirk belongs to a band of literary weaklings, not any one of whom can do anything worth speaking of; but they try their best to write up one another; and sometimes they take it into their heads to help an acquaintance—and then their cry is like that of a pack of beagles? you would think the press of London, or a considerable section of it, had but one voice. Why don't you take Lady Arthur's—Lady Constance's—what's her name?—why don't you take her book to the noble association of log-rollers? I presume the novel is trash; they'll welcome it all the more. She is a woman—she is not to be feared; she hasn't as yet committed the crime of being successful—she isn't to be envied and anonymously attacked. That's the ticket for you, Linn. They mayn't convince the public that Lady What's-her-name is a wonderful person; but they will convince her that she is; and what more does she want?"

"I don't understand you, Maurice!" the young baritone cried, almost angrily. "Again and again you've spoken of Octavius Quirk as if he were beneath contempt."

"What has that to do with it?" the other repeated, placidly. "As an independent writer, Quirk is quite beneath contempt—quite. There is no backbone in his writing at all, and he knows his own weakness; and he thinks he can conceal it by the use of furious adjectives. He is always in a frantic rush and flurry, that produces no impression on anybody. A whirlwind of feathers, that's about it. He goes out into the highway and brandishes a double-handed sword—in order to sweep off the head of a buttercup. And I suppose he expects the public to believe that his wild language, all about nothing, means strength; just as he hopes that they will take his noisy horse-laugh for humor. That's Octavius Quirk as a writer—a nobody, a nothing, a wisp of straw in convulsions; but as a puffer—ah, there you have him!—as a puffer, magnificent, glorious, a Greek hero, invincible, invulnerable. My good man, it's Octavius Quirk you should go to! Get him to call on his pack of beagles to give tongue; and then, my goodness, you'll hear a cry—for a while at least. Is there anything at all in the book?"

"I don't know," said Harry Thornhill, who had changed quickly, and was now regaling himself with a little of Miss Burgoyne's lemonade, with which the prima-donna was so kind as to keep him supplied. "Well, now, I shall be on the stage some time; what do you say to looking over Lady Adela's novel?"

"All right."

There was a tapping at the door; it was the call-boy.

But Lionel Moore did not immediately answer the summons.

"Look here, Maurice; if you should find anything in the book—anything you could say a word in favor of—I wish you'd come round to the Garden Club with me, after the performance, and have a bit of supper. Octavius Quirk is almost sure to be there."

"What, Quirk? I thought the Garden was given over to dukes and comic actors?"

"There's a sprinkling of everybody in it," the young baritone said; "and Quirk likes it because it is an all-night club—he never seems to go to bed at all. Will you do that?"

"Oh, yes," Maurice Mangan said; and forthwith, as his friend left the dressing-room, he plunged into Lady Adela's novel.

The last act of "The Squire's Daughter" is longer than its predecessors; so that Mangan had plenty of time to acquire some general knowledge of the character and contents of these three volumes. Indeed, he had more than time for all the brief scrutiny he deemed necessary; when Lionel Moore reappeared, to get finally quit of his theatrical trappings for the night, his friend was standing at the fireplace, looking at a sketch in brown chalk of Miss Burgoyne, which that amiable young lady had herself presented to Harry Thornhill.

"Well, what's the verdict?"

Mangan turned round, rather bewildered; and then he recollected that he had been glancing at the novel.

"Oh, *that*!" he said, regarding the three volumes with no very favorable air, "Mighty poor stuff, I should say; just about as weak as they make it. But harmless. Some of the conversation—between the women—is natural; trivial, but natural. The plain truth is, my dear Linn, it is a very foolish, stupid book, which should never have been printed at all; but I suppose your fashionable friend could afford to pay for having it printed."

"But, look here, Maurice," Lionel said, in considerable surprise, "I don't see how it can be so very stupid, when Lady Adela herself is one of the brightest, cleverest, shrewdest, most intelligent women you could meet with anywhere—quite unusually so."

"That may be; but she is not the first clever woman who has made the mistake of imagining that because she is socially popular she must therefore be able to write a book."

"And what am I to say to Octavius Quirk?"

"What are you to say to the log-rollers? Don't say anything. Get Lady Adela to ask one or two of them to dinner. You'll fetch Quirk that way easily; they say Gargantua was a fool compared to him."

"I've seen him do pretty well at the Garden, especially about two in the morning," was the young baritone's comment; and then, as he began to get into his ordinary attire, he said, "To tell you the truth, Maurice, Lady Adela rather hinted that she would be pleased to make the acquaintance of any— of any literary man—"

"Who could do her book a good turn?"

"No, you needn't put it as rudely as that. She rather feels that, in becoming an authoress, she has allied herself with literary people—and would naturally like to make acquaintances; so, if it came to that, I should consider myself empowered to ask Quirk whether he would accept an invitation to dinner—I mean, at Cunyngham Lodge. It's no use asking you, Maurice?" he added, with a little hesitation.

Maurice Mangan laughed.

"No, no, Linn, my boy; thank you all the same, I say," he continued, as he took up his hat and stick, seeing that Lionel was about ready to go, "do you ever hear from Miss Francie Wright, or have you forgotten her among all your fine friends?"

"Oh, I hear from Francie sometimes," he answered, carelessly, "or about her, anyway, whenever I get a letter from home. She's very well. Boarding out pauper sick children is her new fad; and I believe she's very busy and very happy over it. Come along, Maurice; we'll walk up to the Garden, and get something of an appetite for supper."

When they arrived at the Garden Club (so named from its proximity to Covent Garden) they went forthwith into the spacious apartment on the ground floor which served at once as dining-room, newspaper-room, and smoking-room. There was hardly anybody in it. Four young men in evening dress were playing cards at a side-table; at another table a solitary member was writing; but at the long supper-table—which was prettily lit up with crimson-shaded lamps, and the appointments of which seemed very trim and clean and neat—all the chairs were empty, and the only other occupants of the place were the servants, who wore a simple livery of white linen.

"What for supper, Maurice?" the younger of the two friends asked.

"Anything—with salad," Mangan answered; he was examining a series of old engravings that hung around the walls.

"On a warm night like this what do you say to cold lamb, salad, and some hock and iced soda-water?"

"All right."

Supper was speedily forthcoming, and, as they took their places, Mangan said,

"You don't often go down to see the old people, Linn?"

"I'm so frightfully busy!"

"Has Miss Francie ever been up to the theatre—to see 'The Squire's Daughter,' I mean?"—this question he seemed to put rather diffidently.

"No. I've asked her often enough; but she always laughs and puts it off. She seems to be as busy down there as I am up here."

"What does she think of the great name and fame you have made for yourself?"

"How should I know?"

Then there was silence for a second or two.

"I wish you'd run down to see them some Sunday, Linn; I'd go down with you."

"Why not go down by yourself?—they'd be tremendously glad to see you."

"I should be more welcome if I took you with me. You know your cousin likes you to pay a little attention to the old people. Come! Say Sunday week."

"My dear fellow, Sunday is my busiest day. Sunday night is the only night I have out of the seven. And I fancy that it is for that very Sunday evening that Lord Rockminster has engaged the Lansdowne Gallery; he gives a little dinner-party, and his sisters have a big concert afterwards—we've all got to sing the chorus of the new marching-song Lady Sybil has composed for the army."

"Who is Lady Sybil?"

"The sister of the authoress whose novel you were reading."

"My gracious! is there another genius in the family?"

"There's a third," said Lionel, with a bit of a smile. "What would you say if Lady Rosamund Bourne were to paint a portrait of me as Harry Thornhill for the Royal Academy?"

"I should say the betting was fifty to one against its getting in."

"Ah, you're unjust, Maurice; you don't know them. I dare say you judged that novel by some high literary standard that it doesn't pretend to reach. I am sure of this, that if it's half as clever as Lady Adela Cunyngham herself, it will do very well."

"It will do very well for the kind of people who will read it," said the other, indifferently.

This was a free-and-easy place; when they had finished supper, Lionel Moore lit a cigarette, and his friend a briar-root pipe, without moving from the table; and Mangan's prayer was still that his companion should fix Sunday week for a visit to the little Surrey village where they had been boys together, and where Lionel's father and mother (to say nothing of a certain Miss Francie Wright, whose name cropped up more than once in Mangan's talk) were still living. But during this entreaty Lionel's attention happened to be attracted to the glass door communicating with the hall; and instantly he said, in an undertone:

"Here's a stroke of luck, Maurice; Quirk has just come in. How am I to sound him? What should I do?"

"Haven't I told you?" said Mangan, curtly. "Get your swell friends to feed him."

Nevertheless, this short, fat man, who now strode into the room and nodded briefly to these two acquaintances, speedily showed that on occasion he knew how to feed himself. He called a waiter, and ordered an underdone beefsteak with Spanish onions, toasted cheese to follow, and a large bottle of stout to begin with; then he took the chair at the head of the table, thus placing himself next to Lionel Moore.

"A very empty den to-night," observed this new-comer, whose heavy face, watery blue eyes, lank hair plentifully streaked with gray, and unwholesome complexion would not have produced a too-favorable impression on any one unacquainted with his literary gifts and graces.

Lionel agreed; and then followed a desultory conversation about nothing in particular, though Mr. Octavius Quirk was doing his best to say clever things and show off his boisterous humor. Indeed, it was not until that gentleman's very substantial supper was being brought in that Lionel got an opportunity of artfully asking him whether he had heard anything of Lady Adela Cunyngham's forthcoming novel. He was about to proceed to explain that "Lady Arthur Castletown" was only a pseudonym, when he was interrupted by Octavius Quirk bursting into a roar—a somewhat affected roar—of scornful laughter.

"Well, of all the phenomena of the day, that is the most ludicrous," he cried, "—the so-called aristocracy thinking that they can produce anything in the shape of art or literature. The aristocracy—the most exhausted of all our exhausted social strata—what can be expected from it? Why, we haven't anywhere nowadays either art or literature or drama that is worthy of the name—not anywhere—it is all a ghastly, spurious make-believe—a mechanical manufactory of paintings and books and plays without a spark of life in them—"

"When they had finished supper, Lionel Moore lit a cigarette, and his friend a brier-root pipe."

Lionel Moore resentfully thought to himself that if Mr. Quirk had been able to do anything in any one of these directions he might have held less despairing views; but, of course, he did not interrupt this feebly tempestuous monologue.

"—We are all played out, that is the fact—the soil is exhausted—we want a great national upheaval—a new condition of things—a social revolution, in short. And we're going to get it" he continued, in a sort of triumphant way; "there's no mistake about that; the social revolution is in the air, it is under our feet, it is pressing in upon us from every side; and yet at the very moment that the aristocracy have got notice to quit their deer-forests and their salmon-rivers and grouse-moors, they so far mistake the signs of the times that they think they should be devoting themselves to art and going on the stage! Was there ever such incomprehensible madness?"

"I hope they won't sweep away deer-forests and grouse-moors just all at once," the young baritone said, modestly, "for I am asked to go to the Highlands at the beginning of next August."

"Make haste, then, and see the last of these doomed institutions" observed Mr. Quirk, with dark significance, as he looked up from his steak and onions. "I tell you deer-forests are doomed; grouse-moors are doomed; salmon-rivers are doomed. They are a survival of feudal rights and privileges which the new democracy—the new ruling power—will make short work of. The time has gone by for all these absurd restrictions and reservations! There is no defence for them; there never was; they were conceived in an iniquity of logic which modern common-sense will no longer suffer. *Bona vacantia* can't belong to anybody—therefore they belong to the king; that's a pretty piece of reasoning, isn't it? And if the crofter or the laborer says, '*Bona vacantia* can't belong to anybody—therefore they belong to me'—isn't the reasoning as good? But it is not merely game-laws that must be abolished, it is game itself."

"If you abolish the one, you'll soon get rid of the other," Maurice Mangan said, with a kind of half-contemptuous indifference; he was examining this person in a curious way, as he might have looked through the wires of a cage in the Zoological Gardens.

"Both must be abolished," Mr. Octavius Quirk continued, with windy vehemence. "The very distinction that takes any animal *feræ naturæ* and constitutes it game is a relic of class privilege and must go—"

"Then Irish landlords will no longer be considered *feræ naturæ*?" Mangan asked, incidentally.

"We must be free from these feudal tyrannies, these mediæval chains and manacles that the Norman kings imposed on a conquered people. We must be as free as the United States of America—"

"America!" Mangan said; and he was rude enough to laugh. "The State of New York has more stringent game-laws than any European country that I know of; and why not? They wanted to preserve certain wild animals, for the general good; and they took the only possible way."

Quirk was disconcerted only for a moment; presently he had resumed, in his reckless, *mouton-enragé* fashion,

"That may be; but the Democracy of Great Britain has pronounced against game; and game must go; there is no disputing the fact. Hunting in any civilized community is a relic of barbarism; it is worse in this country—it is an infringement of the natural rights of the tiller of the soil. What is the use of talking about it?—the whole thing is doomed; if you're going to Scotland this autumn, Mr. Moore, if you are to be shown all those exclusive pastimes of the rich and privileged classes, well, I'd advise you to keep your eyes open, and write as clear an account of what you see as you can; and, by Jove, twenty years hence your book will be read with amazement by the new generation!"

Here the pot of foaming stout claimed his attention; he buried his head in it; and thereafter, sitting back in his chair, sighed forth his satisfaction. The time was come for a large cigar.

And how, in the face of this fierce denunciation of the wealthy classes and all their ways, could Lionel Moore put in a word for Lady Adela's poor little literary infant? It would be shrivelled into nothing by a blast of this simulated simoom. It would be trodden under foot by the log-roller's elephantine jocosity. In a sort of despair he turned to Maurice Mangan, and would have entered into conversation with him but that Mangan now rose and said he must be going, nor could he be prevailed on to stay. Lionel accompanied him into the hall.

"That Jabberwock makes me sick; he's such an ugly devil," Mangan said, as he put on his hat; and surely that was strange language coming from a grave philosopher who was about to publish a volume on the "Fundamental Fallacies of M. Comte."

"But what am I to do, Maurice?" Lionel said, as his friend was leaving. "It's no use asking for his intervention at present; he's simply running amuck."

"If your friend—Lady What's-her-name—is as clever as you say, she'll just twist that fellow round her finger," the other observed, briefly. "Good-night, Linn."

And indeed it was not of Octavius Little, nor yet of Lady Adela's novel, that Maurice Mangan was thinking as he carelessly walked away through the dark London thoroughfares, towards his rooms in Victoria Street. He was thinking of that quiet little Surrey village; and of two boys there who had a great belief in each other—and in themselves, too, for the matter of that; and of all the beautiful and wonderful dreams they dreamed while as yet the far-reaching future was veiled from them. And then he thought of Linn Moore's dressing-room at the theatre; and of the paints and powder and vulgar tinsel that had to fit him out for exhibition before the footlights; and of the feverish whirl of life and the bedazzlement of popularity and fashionable petting; and somehow or other the closing lines of Mrs. Browning's poem would come ever and anon into his head as a sort of unceasing refrain:

"The true gods sigh for the cost and pain,—

For the reed that grows nevermore again

As a reed with the reeds in the river."

CHAPTER III.

NINA.

One morning Lionel was just about to go out (he had already been round to the gymnasium and got his fencing over) when the house-porter came up and said that a young lady wished to see him.

"What does she want?" he said, impatiently—for something had gone wrong with the clasp of his cigarette-case, and he could not get it right. "What's her name? Who is she?"

"She gave me her name, sir; but I did not quite catch it," said the factotum of the house.

"Oh, well, send her up," said he; no doubt this was some trembling *débutante*, accompanied by an ancient duenna and a roll of music. And then he went to the window, to try to get the impenitent clasp to shut.

But perhaps he would not have been so wholly engrossed with that trifling difficulty had he known who this was who had come softly up the stair and was now standing, irresolute, smiling, wondering, at the open door. She was a remarkably pretty, even handsome young lady, whose pale, clear, olive complexion and coal-black hair bespoke her Southern birth; while there was an eager and yet timid look in her lustrous, soft black eyes, and something about the mobile, half-parted mouth that seemed to say she hardly knew whether to cry or laugh over this meeting with an old friend. A very charming picture she presented there; for, besides her attractive personal appearance, she was very neatly, not to say coquettishly, dressed, her costume, which had a distinctly foreign air, being all of black, save for the smart little French-looking hat of deep crimson straw and velvet.

At last she said,

"Leo!"

He turned instantly, and had nearly dropped the cigarette-case in his amazement. And for a second he seemed paralyzed of speech—he was wholly bewildered—perhaps overcome by some swift sense of responsibility at finding Antonia Rossi in London, and alone.

"Che, Nina mia," he cried; "tu stai cca a Londra!—chesta mo, chi su credeva!—e senza manca scriverme nu viers' e lettere—Nina!—mi pare nu suonno!—"

She interrupted him; she came forward, smiling—and the parting of the pretty lips showed a sunny gleam of teeth; she held up her two hands, palm outwards, as if she would shut away from herself that old, familiar Neapolitanese.

"No, no, no, Leo," she said, rapidly, "I speak English now—I study, study, study, morning, day, night; and always I say, 'When I see Leo, he have much surprise that I speak English'—always I say, 'Some day I go to England, and when I see Leo'—"

The happy, eager smile suddenly died away from her face. She looked at him. A strange kind of trouble—of doubt and wonderment and pain—came into those soft, dark, expressive eyes.

"You—you not wish to see me, Leo?" she said, rather breathlessly—and as if she could hardly believe this thing. "I come to London—and you not glad to see me—"

Quick tears of wounded pride sprang to the long black lashes; but, with a dignified, even haughty inclination of the head, she turned from him and put her hand on the handle of the door. At the same instant he caught her arm.

"Why, Nina, you're just the spoiled child you always were! Ah, your English doesn't go so far as that; you don't know what a spoiled child is?—*è la cianciosella*, you Neapolitan girl! Why, of course I'm glad to see you—I am delighted to see you—but you frightened me, Nina—your coming like this, alone—"

"I frighten you, Leo?" she said, and a quick laugh shone brightly through her tears. "Ah, I see—it is that I have no chaperon? But I had no time—I wished to see you, Leo—I said, 'Leo will understand, and afterwards I get a chaperon all correctly.' Oh, yes, yes, I know—but where is the time?—yesterday I go through the streets—it is Leo, Leo everywhere in the windows—I see you in this costume, in the other costume—and your name so large, so very large, in the—in the—"

"The theatre-bills? Well, sit down, Nina, and tell me how you come to be in London."

She had by this time quite forgiven or forgotten his first dismay on finding her there; and now she took a chair with much quiet complaisance, and sat down, and put her black silk sunshade across her knees.

"It is simple," she said, and from time to time she regarded him in a very frank and pleased and even affectionate way, as if the old comradeship of the time when they were both studying in Naples was not to be interfered with by the natural timidity of a young and extremely pretty woman coming as a stranger into a strange town. "You remember Carmela, Leo? Carmela and her—her spouse—they have great good-fortune—they get a grand prize in the lottery—then he says, 'Carmeluccia, we will go to Paris—we will go to Paris, Carmeluccia—and why not Nina also?' Very kind, was it not?—but Andrea is always kind, so also Carmela, to me. Then I am in Paris. I say, 'It is not far to London; I go to London; I go to London and see Leo.' Perhaps I get an engagement—oh, no, no, no, you shall not laugh!" she broke in—though it was she herself who was laughing, and not he at all. "I am improved—oh, yes, a little—a little improved—you remember old Pandiani he always say my voice not bad, but that *agilità* was for me very difficult."

He remembered very well; but he also remembered that when he left Naples, Signorina Rossi was laboring away with the most pertinacious assiduity at cavatinas full of runs and scales and *fiorituri* generally; and he was quite willing to believe that such diligence had met with its due reward. But when the young lady modestly hinted that she had left her music in the hall below, and would like Leo to hear whether she had not acquired a good deal more of flexibility than her voice used to possess, and when he had fetched the music and taken it to the piano for her, he was not a little surprised to see her select Ambroise Thomas's "Io son Titania." And he was still more astonished when he found her singing this difficult piece of music with a brilliancy, an ease, a *verve* of execution that he had never dreamed of her being able to reach.

"Brava! Brava! Bravissima!—Well, you *have* improved, Nina!" he exclaimed. "And it isn't only in freedom of production, it is in quality, too, in *timbre*— my goodness, your voice has ever so much more volume and power! Come, now, try some big, dramatic thing—"

She shook her head.

"No, no, Leo, I know what I do," she said. "I shall never have the grand style—never—but you think I am improved? Yes. Well, now, I sing something else."

He forgot all about her lack of a chaperon; they were fellow-students again, as in the old days at Naples, when they worked hard (and also played a little), when they comforted each other, and strove to bear with equanimity the grumbling and querulousness of that always-dissatisfied old Pandiani. Signorina Rossi now sang the Shadow Song from "Dinorah;" then she sang the Jewel Song from "Faust;" she sang "Caro nome" from "Rigoletto," or anything else that he could suggest; and her runs and shakes and scale passages were delivered with a freedom and precision that again and again called forth his applause.

"And you have never sung in public, Nina?" he asked.

"At one concert, yes, in Naples," the young lady made answer. "And at two or three *matinées*." And then she turned to him, with a bright look. "You know this, Leo?—I am offered—no—I was offered—an engagement to sing in opera; oh, yes; it was the *impresario* from Malta—he comes to Naples—Pandiani makes us all sing to him—then will I go to Malta, to the opera there? No!"

"Why not, Nina? Surely that was a good opening," he said.

She turned away from him again, and her fingers wandered lightly over the keys of the piano.

"I always say to me, 'Some day I am in England; the English give much money at concerts; perhaps that is better.'"

"So you've come over to England to get a series of concert-room engagements; is that it, Nina?"

She shrugged her shoulders ever so slightly.

"Perhaps. One must wait and see. It is not my ambition. No. The light opera, that is—popular?—is it right?"

"Yes, yes."

"It is very popular in England," said the young Italian lady, with her eyes coming back from the music-sheets to seek those of her friend." Well, Leo, if I take a small part to begin, have I voice sufficient? What do you think? No; be frank; say to yourself, 'I am Pandiani; here is Antonia Rossi troubling me once more; it is useless; go away, Antonia Rossi, and not trouble me!' Well, Maestro Pandiani, what you say?"

"So you want to go on the stage, Nina?" said he; and again the dread of finding himself responsible for this solitary young stranger sent a qualm to his heart. It was an embarrassing position altogether; but at the same time the thought of shaking her off—of getting free from this responsibility by telling a white lie or two and persuading her to go back to Naples—that thought never even occurred to him. To shake off his old comrade Nina? He certainly would have preferred, for many reasons, that she should have taken to concert-room business; but if she were relying on him for an introduction to the lyric stage, why, he was bound to help her in every possible way. "You know you've got an excellent voice," he continued. "And a very little stage training would fit you for a small part in comedy-opera, if that is what you're thinking of, as a beginning. But I don't know that you would like it, Nina. You see, you would have to become under-study for the lady who has the part at present; and they'd probably want you to sing in the chorus; and you'd get a very small salary—at first, you know, until you were qualified to take one of the more important parts—and then you might get into a travelling company—"

"A small part?" said she, with much cheerfulness. "Oh, yes; why not? I must learn."

"But I don't know that you would like it," he said, still ruefully. "You see, Nina, you might have to dress in the same room with two or three of the chorus-girls—"

"And then?" she said, with a little dramatic gesture, and an elevation of her beautifully formed black eyebrows. "Leo, you never saw my lodgings with the family Debernardi—you have only mount the stairs—"

"My goodness, Nina, I could guess what the inside of the rooms was like, if they were anything like those interminable and horrid stairs!" he exclaimed, with a laugh. "And you who were always so fond of pretty things, and flowers, and always so particular when we went to a restaurant—to live with the Debernardis!"

"Ah, Leo, you imagine not why?" she said, also laughing, and when she laughed her milk-white teeth shone merrily. "Old Pietro Debernardi he lives in England some years; he speaks English, perhaps not very well, but he speaks; then he teach me as he knows; and when it is possible I go on the *Risposta* and sail over to Capri, and all the way, and all the return, I listen, and listen, and listen to the English people; and I remember, and I practise alone in my own room, and I say, 'Leo, he must not ridicule me, when I go to England.'"

"Ridicule you!" said he, indignantly. "I wish I could speak Italian as freely as you speak English, Nina!"

"Oh, you speak Italian very well," said she. "But why you speak still the Neapolitan dialetto—dialect, is it right?—that you hear in the shops and the streets? Ah, I remember you are so proud of it, and when I try to teach you proper Italian, you laugh—you wish to speak like Sabetta Debernardi, and Giacomo, and the others. That is the fault to learn by ear, instead of the books correctly. And you have not forgotten yet!"

"Well, Nina," he resumed, "I don't seem to have frightened you with the possibility of your having to dress in the same room with two or three chorus-girls whom you don't know; and in fact, if I happened to be acquainted with the theatre, I dare say I could get the manager to make sure you were to dress along with some nice girl, who would show you how to make-up, and all that. But you would get a very small salary to begin with, Nina; perhaps only thirty shillings a week—and an extra pound a week when you had to take up your under-study duties—however, that need not trouble you, because we are old comrades, Nina, and while you are in England my purse is yours—"

She looked at him doubtfully.

"Ah, you don't understand," he said, gently. "It's only this, Nina: I have plenty of money; if you are a good comrade and a good friend, you will take from me what you want—always—at any moment—"

The pretty, pale-olive face flushed quickly, and for a brief second she glanced at him with grateful eyes; but it was perhaps to cover her embarrassment that she now rose from the piano, and pretended to be tired of the music and of these professional schemes.

"It is enough of booziness," she said, lightly; "come, Leo, will you go for a small walk?—have you time?"

"Oh, yes, I have time," said he, "but you must not say *booziness*, Nina? it is *bizness*."

"*Beezness!—beezness!*" she said, smiling. "It is enough of *beezness*. You go for a walk with me—yes? How beautiful the weather!" she continued, in a suddenly altered tone, as she looked out at the sunlit foliage of the Green Park; and then she murmured, almost to herself, in those soft Italian vowel sounds:

"Ah, Leo mio, che sarei felice d'essere in campagna!"

It was a kind of sigh; perhaps that was the reason she had inadvertently relapsed into her own tongue. And as they went down the stairs, and he opened the door for her, the few words he addressed to her were also in Italian.

"The country!" he said. "We will just step across the street, Nina, and you will find yourself in what is quite as pretty as the country at this time of year. You may fancy yourself sitting in the Villa Reale, if you could only have a flash of blue sea underneath the branches of the trees."

But when they had crossed over and got into the comparative quiet of the Park, she resolutely returned to her English again; and now she was telling him about the people in Naples whom he used to know, and of their various fortunes and circumstances. Sometimes neither of them spoke; for all this around them was very still and pleasant—the fresh foliage of the trees and the long lush grass of the enclosures as yet undimmed by the summer dust; the cool shadows thrown by the elms and limes just moving as the wind stirred the wide branches; altogether a world of soft, clear, sunny green, unbroken except by here and there a small copper beech with its bronze leaves become translucent in the hot light. It is true that the browsing sheep were abnormally black; and the yellow-billed starlings had perhaps less sheen on their feathers than they would have had in the country; nevertheless, for a park in the midst of a great city this place was very quiet and beautiful and sylvan; and indeed, when these two sat down on a couple of chairs under a fragrant hawthorn, Nina's lustrous dark eyes became wistful and absent, and she said,

"Yes, Leo, it is as you say in the house—it all appears a dream."

"What appears like a dream to you?" her companion asked.

"To be in London, sitting with you, Leo, and hearing you speak," she answered, in a low voice. "Often I think of it—often I think of London— wondering what it is like—and I ask myself, 'Will Leo be the same after his great renown? Are we friends as before?' and now I am here, and London is not dark and terrible with smoke, but we sit in gardens—oh, very beautiful!—and Leo is talking just as in the old way—perhaps it is a dream?" she continued, looking up with a smile. "Perhaps I wake soon?"

"Oh, no, it isn't a dream, Nina," said he, "only it might pass for one, for you haven't told me how you managed to get here. It is all a mystery to me. Where are you staying, for example?"

"My lodging?" she said. "I have an apartment in the Restaurant Gianuzzi."

"Where is that?"

"Rupert Street," she answered, with a valiant effort at the proper pronunciation.

"My goodness! what are you doing, Nina?" he said, almost angrily. "Living by yourself in a foreign restaurant, in the neighborhood of Leicester Square! You'll have to come out of that at once!"

"You must not scold me, Leo," she said, in rather a hurt way. "How am I to know?"

"I am not scolding you," he said (indeed, he knew better than to do that; if once the notion had got into her little head that he was really upbraiding her, she would have been up and off in a moment, proud-lipped, indignant-eyed, with a fierce wrong rankling in her heart; and weeks it might take him to pet her into gentleness again, even if she did not forthwith set out for the South, resolved to return to this harsh, cold England no more). "I am not scolding you, Nina," he said, quite gently. "Of course you didn't know. And of course you were attracted by the Italian name—you thought you would feel at home—"

"They are very nice people, yes, yes!" she said—and still she was inclined to hold her head erect, and her mouth was a little proud and offended.

"Very likely indeed," he said, with great consideration, "but, you see, Nina, a single young lady can't stay at a restaurant by herself, without knowing some one, some one to go about with her—"

"Why," she said, vehemently, almost scornfully, "you think I not know that! An Italian girl—and not know that! Last night, hour after hour, I sit and think, 'Oh, there is Leo singing now—if I may go to the theatre!—to sit and hear him—and think of the old days—and perhaps to write home to the *maestro*, and tell him of the grand fame of his scholar.' But no. I cannot go out. There is no time yet to see about chaperon. When it comes eleven hour, I say, 'The theatre is ceased;' and I go to bed. Then this morning I know no person; I say, 'Very well, I go and see Leo; he will understand;' it is how I meet him in the Chiaja, and he says, 'Good-morning, Nina; shall we go for a little walk out to Pozzuoli'—it is just the same."

"Yes, I understand well enough, Nina," said he, good-naturedly, "and I wasn't scolding you when I said you must get some better place to stay at while you are in London. Well, now, I am going to tell you something. I don't know much about what actors and actresses are in Italy, but here in England they are exceedingly generous to any of their number who have fallen into misfortune; and a case of the kind happened a little while ago. An actor, who used to be well known, died quite suddenly and left his widow entirely unprovided for; whereupon there was a subscription got up for her, and a morning performance, too, in which nearly all the leading actors and actresses managed to do something or other; and the result is that they have been able to take the lease of a house in Sloane Street, and furnish the rooms for her, and she is to earn her living by keeping lodgers. Now, if you really want to remain in London, Nina, don't you think that might be a comfortable home for you? She is a very nice, ladylike little woman; and she's a great friend of mine, too; she would do everything she could for you. There's a chaperon for you ready-made!—for I'm afraid she has only one lodger to look after as yet, though she has all the necessary servants, and the establishment is quite complete. What do you say to that, Nina?"

Her face had brightened up wonderfully at this proposal.

"Yes, yes, yes, Leo!" she said, instantly. "Tell me how I go, and I go at once, to ask her if she can give me apartments."

He glanced at his watch.

"The fact is," said he, slowly, "I was to have lunched with a very small party to-day—at a duchess's house—at a duchess's house, think of that, Nina!"

She jumped to her feet at once, and frankly held out her hand.

"Forgive me, Leo!—I retard you—I did not know."

"Don't be in such a hurry, Nina," he said, as he also rose. "I'm going to break the appointment, that's all about it; Signorina Antonia Rossi doesn't arrive in England every day. I'll tell you what we have got to do: we will get into a hansom and drive to a telegraph-office, and I'll get rid of that engagement; then we'll go on to the Restaurant Gianuzzi, and you and I will have a little luncheon by ourselves, just to prepare us for the fatigues of the day; then you will get your things ready, and I will take you down to Mrs. Grey's in Sloane Street, and introduce you to that most estimable little lady; and then, if Mrs. Grey happens to be disengaged for the evening, she might be induced to come with you to the New Theatre, and she could take you safe home after the performance. How will that do, Nina?"

"You always were kind to me, Leo," she said—though the gratitude plainly shining in the gentle, dark eyes rendered the words quite unnecessary.

And indeed she was delighted, with a sort of childish delight, to sit in this swift hansom, bowling along the smooth thoroughfare; and she chatted and chattered in her gay, rapid, disconnected fashion; and she had nothing but contempt for the shabby Neapolitan fiacre and the jolting streets that Leo of course remembered; and when at last she found herself and her companion of old days seated at a small, clean, bright window-table in the Restaurant Gianuzzi—they being the only occupants of the long saloon— she fairly clapped her little hands together in her gladness. And then how pretty she looked! She had removed her bonnet; and the light from the window, falling on the magnificent masses of her jet-black hair gave it almost a blue sheen in places; while here and there—about the wax-like ear, for example, a tiny ringlet had got astray, and its soft darkness against the olive complexion seemed to heighten the clear, pure pallor of the oval cheek. And now all doubts as to how Leo might receive her had fled from her mind; they were on the old, familiar terms again; and she followed with an eager and joyous interest all that he had to say to her. Then how easily could she accentuate her sympathetic listening with this expressive face! The mobile, somewhat large, beautifully formed mouth, the piquant little nose with its sensitive nostrils, the eloquent dark eyes could just say anything she pleased; though, to be sure, however varying her mood might be, in accordance with what she heard and what was demanded of her, her normal expression was one of an almost childish and happy content. She poured her glass of Chianti into a tumbler, and filled that up with water, and sipped it as a canary sips. She made little pellets of bread with her dainty white fingers—but that was in forgetfulness—that was in her eagerness of listening. And at last she said,

"What is it, Leo?—you wish to frighten me with your trials?—no! for now you laugh at all these—these mortifications. Then a man is proud—he is sensitive—he is not patient as a woman—oh, you think you frighten me?—no, no!"

The fact is, he began to see more and more clearly that she was resolved upon trying her fortune on the lyric stage; and he thought it his duty to let her know very distinctly what she would have to encounter. He did not exactly try to dissuade her; but he gave her a general idea of what she might expect, and that in not too roseate colors. His chief difficulty, however, was this: he was possessed by a vague feeling that there might be some awkwardness in having Antonia Rossi engaged at the same theatre with himself; and yet, looking round all the light operas then being performed, he had honestly to confess that the only part Nina could aspire to take, with her present imperfect pronunciation of English, was that of the young French officer played at the New Theatre by Mlle. Girond. Nor did it lessen his embarrassment to find, as soon as he mentioned this possibility, that to join the New Theatre was precisely what Signorina Rossi desired.

"I don't think there would be much difficulty about it, Nina," he was forced to admit—carefully concealing his reluctance the while. "Lehmann, that is our manager, is talking about getting up a second travelling company, for the opera is so popular everywhere; and there is to be a series of rehearsals of under-studies beginning next Monday, and you could see all the coaching going on. Then you could sit in front at night, and watch Mlle. Girond's 'business:' how would you like that, Nina?—whether what she does is clever or stupid, you would have to copy it? the public would expect that—"

"Why not?" Nina said, with a pleasant smile. "Why not? I learn. She knows more; why I not learn?"

"It's a shame to throw away a fine voice like yours on a small part in comic opera," he said—still with vague dreams before him of a concert-room career for her.

"But I must begin," said she, with much practical common-sense, "and while I am in the small part, I learn to act, I learn the stage-affair, I learn better English, to the end of having a place more important. Why, Leo, you are too careful of me! At Naples I work hard, I am a slave to old Pandiani—I suffer everything—can I not work hard here in London? You think I am an infant? Certainly I am not—no, no—I am old—old—"

"But light-hearted still, Nina," he said, for she was clearly bent on laughing away his fears. Then he looked at her, with a little hesitation. "There's another thing, Nina? about the costume."

"Yes?" she asked, innocently.

"I don't know—whether you would quite like—but I'll show you Mlle. Girond's dress anyway—then you can judge for yourself," said he. He called the waiter. He scribbled on a piece of paper, "Photograph of Mlle. Girond as Capitaine Crépin in 'The Squire's Daughter.'" "Send round to some stationer's shop, will you, and get me that?"

When the messenger returned with the photograph, Lionel, rather timidly, put it before her; but, indeed, there was nothing in the costume of Mlle. Girond to startle any one—the uniform of the boy-officer was so obviously a compromise. Nina glanced at it thoughtfully.

"Well, Leo," she said, looking up, "you see no harm?"

"Harm?" said he, boldly taking up his cue, "of course not! It isn't like any uniform that ever was known; I suppose it's Mlle. Girond's own invention; but, at all events, there's nothing to prevent any modest girl wearing it. Why, I know more than one fashionable lady who would think nothing of appearing as Rosalind—and Rosalind's is a real boy's dress, or ought to be—and then they haven't the excuse that an actor or actress has, that it is a necessity of one's profession. However, there's nothing to be said about that costume, anyway; I really had forgotten that Mlle. Girond had got her pretty little blue coat made with so long a skirt. Besides, Nina, with a voice like yours, you will soon be beyond having to take parts like that."

Indeed, she was so evidently anxious to obtain an engagement in the same theatre that he himself was engaged in that his vague reluctance ultimately vanished; and he began considering when he could bring her before Mr. Lehmann, the manager, and Mr. Carey, the musical conductor, so that they should hear her sing. As to their verdict, as to what the manager would do, he had no doubt whatever. She had a valuable voice, and her ignorance of stage requirements would speedily disappear. At the very time that Lehmann was trying to get new under-studies with a view to the formation of a second travelling company, why, here was a perfect treasure discovered for him. And Lionel made certain that, as soon as Antonia Rossi had had time to study Mlle. Girond's "business," and perhaps one or two chances of actually playing the part, she would be drafted into one or other of the travelling companies, and sent away through the provinces; so that any awkwardness arising from her being in the same theatre with himself, and he her only friend in England, to whom she would naturally appeal in any emergency, would thus be obviated.

"Nina," said he, as they were driving in a hansom to Sloane Street (all her belongings being on the top of the cab), "Lehmann, our manager, is to be at the theatre this afternoon, about some scenery, I fancy, and there's a chance of our catching him if we went down some little time before the performance. Would you come along and sing one or two things? you might have the arrangement made at once."

"Will you go with me, Leo?"

"Oh, yes," he said, "I mean Mrs. Grey will take you, you know; for I will try to get places for her and you in front afterwards; but I will go with you as well. You won't be afraid?"

She laughed.

"Afraid?—no, no—what I can do I can do—there is no Pandiani to scold me if they not satisfied—that is my own *beezness*—is it right?—oh, I say to you, Leo, if you hear Pandiani when I refuse to go to Malta—you think you know the Neapolitan deealect—dialect?—no, it is not good for you to know all the wicked words of Naples—and he is old and evil-tempered—it is no matter. But in this theatre there is no Pandiani and his curses—"

"No, no, not curses, Nina," he said. "I see old Debernardi has taught you some strange English. Of course the *maestro* did not use curses to his favorite pupil—oh, yes, you were, Nina, a great favorite, though he was always grumbling and growling. However, remember this, Nina, you must sing your best this evening, and impress them; and I shouldn't wonder if Lehmann gave you exceptional terms."

"More *beezness*?" she said, with a smile that showed a gleam of her pretty teeth; the sound of the word had tickled her ear, somehow; more than once, as the cab rolled away down Kensingtonwards, he could hear her repeat to herself—"*beezness! beezness!*"

This young Italian lady seemed to produce a most favorable impression on the little, pale-faced widow, who appeared to be very grateful to Lionel Moore for having thought of her. The ground-floor sitting-room and bedroom, she explained, were occupied by her sole lodger; the young lady could have the choice of any of the apartments above. The young lady, as it turned out, was startled beyond measure at the price she was asked to pay (which, in truth, was quite moderate, for the rooms were good rooms, in a good situation, and neatly furnished), and it was only on Lionel's insisting on it that she consented to take the apartments on the second floor.

"I beg you not miscomprehend," Nina said, somewhat earnestly, to the little landlady (for was she not a friend of Leo's?). "The price is, perhaps, not too large—it is to me that it is large—"

"Oh, that's all right, Nina," Lionel broke in; "that's all settled. You see, Mrs. Grey, Miss Rossi has come over here to get an engagement in comedy opera, or perhaps to sing at concerts; and if a manager calls to see her on business, why, of course, she must be in decent rooms. You can't go and live in a slum. Mrs. Grey knows what managers are, Nina; you must take up a good position and hold your own; and—and, in fact, Nina, when you are in London you can't afford to go and climb those frightful Neapolitan stairs and hide yourself in a garret. So it's settled; and I'm going out directly to hire a piano for you."

"For how much expense, Leo?" she said, anxiously.

"Oh, we'll see about that by and by," said he.

He then explained to Mrs. Grey that Miss Nina was that very evening going along to the New Theatre to be heard by the manager and the conductor; that thereafter she wished to see the performance of "The Squire's Daughter," in which she hoped ere long to take a part herself; and that, if Mrs. Grey could find it convenient to accompany the young lady, it would be a very great obligation to him, Mr. Moore. Mrs. Grey replied to this that her solitary lodger had gone down to Richmond for two or three days; she herself had no engagement of any kind for that evening; and when, she asked, did any one ever hear of an old actress refusing an invitation to go to the theatre?

"So that's all settled, too," said this young man, who seemed to be carrying everything his own way.

Then he went out and hired a piano—necessarily a small upright—which was to be taken down to Sloane Street that same evening; next he sought out a telegraph-office, and sent a message to Mr. Lehmann and to Mr. Carey; finally he called at a florist's, and bought a whole heap of flowers for the better decoration of Signorina Rossi's new apartments. In this last affair he was really outrageously extravagant, even for one who was habitually careless about his expenditure; but he said to himself,

"Well, I throw away lots of money in compliments to people who are quite indifferent to me; and why shouldn't I allow myself a little latitude when it is my old comrade Nina who has come over to England?"

When at length he got back to the house he found it would soon be time for them to be thinking of getting down to the theatre; so he said,

"Now, look here, Mrs. Grey, when Miss Nina has done with her singing and her talk with the manager, you must take her to some restaurant and get some dinner for both of you, for you can't go on without anything until eleven. You will just have time before the performance begins. I'm sorry I can't take you; but, you see, as soon as I hear what the manager says, I must be off to dress for my part. Then, at the end of the performance, I can't ask you to wait for me; you will have to bring her home, either in a cab or by the Underground, for Nina is very economical. I hope you won't think I am treating you ill in leaving you to yourselves—"

"Why, Leo, you have given up the whole day to me!" Nina exclaimed.

"You gave up many an afternoon to me, Nina," he rejoined, "when I sprained my ankle down at that confounded Castello Dell' Ovo."

The ordeal that the *débutante* had now to undergo was, of course, made remarkably easy for her through the intervention of this good friend of hers. When they got down to the theatre they went at once on to the stage, where Nina found herself in the midst of an old-fashioned English village, with a gayly bedecked Maypole just behind her, while in front of her was the great, gaunt, empty, musty-smelling building, filled with a dim twilight, though, also, there were here and there one or two orange-points of gas. Lionel sent a messenger to the manager's office, and also told him to ask if Mr. Carey had come; then he opened Nina's roll of music for her, and began to discuss with her which piece she should choose. Fortunately Mr. Lehmann had not yet left—here he was—a stout, clean-shaven, sharp-eyed sort of person, in a frock-coat and a remarkably shiny hat; he glanced at the young lady in what she considered a very rude and unwarrantable manner, but the fact was he was merely, from a business point of view, trying to guess what her figure was like. Lionel explained all the circumstances of the case to him, and gave it as his own confident opinion that, as soon as they had heard Mlle. Rossi sing, there would be little doubt of her being engaged. At the same moment Mr. Carey appeared—a tall, blond, extremely handsome person of the fashion-plate sort; and, at a word from the manager, two or three scene-shifters went and wheeled on to the stage a small upright piano.

Nina did not seem at all disconcerted by their business-like air and want of little formal politenesses. Quite calmly she took out "Caro nome " from her music and handed it to the conductor, who was at the piano. He glanced at the sheet, appeared a little surprised, but struck the opening chords for her. Then Nina sang; and though for a second or two the sound of her own voice in this huge, empty building seemed strange—seemed wrong almost and unnatural—she had speedily recovered confidence, and was determined she would bring no discredit upon her friend Leo. Very well indeed she sang, and Lionel was delighted; while, of course, Mr. Carey was professionally interested in hearing for the first time a voice so fresh and pure and so perfectly trained; but when she had finished the manager merely said,

"Thank you, that will do; I needn't trouble you further." Then, after a word or two, partly aside, with Mr. Carey, he turned to Lionel and abruptly asked what salary she wanted—just as if Lionel had brought him some automaton and made it work.

"I think you ought to give her a very good salary," the young man said, in an undertone; "she has studied under Pandiani at Naples. And if I were you I wouldn't ask her to sing in the chorus at all; I would rather keep a voice like that fresh and unworked until she is fit to take a part."

"Singing in the chorus won't hurt her," said he, briefly, "for a while, at least, and she'll become familiar with the stage."

But here Lionel drew the manager still further aside; and then ensued a conversation which neither Nina nor Mr. Carey could in the least overhear. At the end of it Mr. Lehmann nodded acquiescence, and said, "Very well, then;" and straightway he departed, for he was a busy man, and had little time to waste on the smaller courtesies of life—especially in the case of *débutantes.*

Lionel returned to the young lady whose fate had just been decided.

"That's all right, Nina," he said. "You are engaged as under-study to Mlle. Girond, and you'll have three pounds a week as soon as you have studied her business and are ready to take the part when you're wanted. I will find you a full score, and you may get up some of the other music, when you've nothing better to do. The rehearsals of the under-studies begin on Monday—but I'll see you before then and let you know all about it. You won't mind my running away?—I'm on in the first scene. There is Mrs. Grey waiting for you—you must go and get something to eat—and when you come back, call at the stage-door, and you'll find an envelope waiting for you, with two places in it—the dress circle, if it can be managed, for I want you to be some distance away from the orchestra. Good-bye, Nina!"

She held his hand for a moment.

"Leo, I thank you," she said, regarding him with her dark eyes; and then he smiled and waved another farewell to her as he disappeared; and she was left to make her way with her patient chaperon out of this great, hollow, portentous building, that was now resounding with mysterious clankings and calls.

And it was from a couple of seats in the back of the dress-circle that Mrs. Grey and her young charge heard the comedy-opera of "The Squire's Daughter;" and Lionel knew they were there; and no doubt he sang his best—for, if Nina had been showing off what she could do in the morning, why should he not show off now, amid all these added glories of picturesque costumes and surroundings? Nina was in an extraordinary state of excitement, which she was unable altogether to conceal. Mrs. Grey could hear the little, muttered exclamations in Italian; she could see how intently that expressive face followed the progress of the piece, reflecting its every movement, as it were; she caught a glimpse of tears on the long, dark lashes when Lionel was singing, with impassioned fervor, his love-lorn serenade; and then the next moment she was astonished by the vehemence of the girl's delight when the vast house thundered forth its applause—indeed, Nina herself was clapping her hands furiously, to join in the universal roar of a recall—she was laughing with joy—she appeared to have gone mad. Then, at the end of the second act, she said, quickly,

"Mrs. Grey, can I send to him a note?—is there letter-paper?"

"Well, my dear, if we go into the refreshment-room and have a cup of tea, perhaps one of the young ladies could give us a sheet of writing-paper."

And thus it was that Lionel, when he was leaving the theatre that night, found a neatly folded little note awaiting him. He was in a considerable hurry; for he had to go home and dress and get off to a crush in Grosvenor Square, where he hoped to find Lady Adela Cunyngham, her sisters, and Miss Georgie Lestrange (there was some talk of an immediate presentation of the little pastoral comedy), so that he had only time to glance over Nina's nervously pencilled scrawl. Thus it ran:

"Leo, it is magnificent, it is splendid, you are a true artist; to-morrow I write to Pandiani, he will be overjoyed as I am. But Miss Burgoyne—*no, no, no*— she is not artist at all—she is negligent of her part, of the others in the scene—she puts up her fan and talks to you from behind it—why you allow that?—it is insult to the public! She *believes* not her part and makes all the rest false. What a shame to you, Leo; but your splendid voice, your fine timbre, carries everything! Bravo, my Leo! It is a great trionf, brilliant, beautiful, and Nina is proud of her friend. Good-night from

"NINA."

As Lionel was spinning along Piccadilly in his swift hansom, it occurred to him that if Nina were going to join the "Squire's Daughter" company, it might be just as well for her not to have any preconceived antipathy against Miss Burgoyne. For Miss Burgoyne was an important person at the New Theatre.

CHAPTER IV.

COUNTRY AND TOWN.

On this Sunday morning, when all the good people had gone to church, there was no sign of life on these far-stretching Winstead Downs. The yellow roads intersecting the undulations of black-and-golden gorse were undisturbed by even a solitary tramp; so that Lionel Moore and his friend Mangan, as they idly walked along, seemed to be the sole possessors of the spacious landscape. It was a beautiful morning, warm and clear and sunny; a southerly breeze stirred the adjacent elms into a noise as of the sea, caused the chestnuts to wave their great branches bearing thousands of milky minarets, and sent waves of shadows across the silken gray-green of a field of rye. There was a windmill on a distant height, its long arms motionless. A strip of Scotch firs stood black and near at one portion of the horizon; but elsewhere the successive lines of wood and hill faded away into the south, becoming of a paler and paler hue until they disappeared in a silvery mist. The air was sweet with the resinous scent of the furze. In short, it was a perfect day in early June, on a wide, untenanted, high-lying Surrey common.

And Maurice Mangan, in his aimless, desultory fashion, was inveighing against the vanity of the life led by certain classes in the great Babylon out of which he had just haled his rather unwilling friend; and describing their mad and frantic efforts to wrest themselves free of the demon *ennui*; and their ceaseless, eager clamor for hurry and excitement, lest, in some unguarded moment of silence, their souls should speak.

"It is quite a fallacy," he was saying, as he walked carelessly onwards, his head thrown forward a little, his hands clasped behind his back, his stick trailing after him, "it is altogether a fallacy to talk of the 'complaining millions of men' who 'darken in labor and pain.' It is the hard-working millions of mankind who are the happiest; their constant labor brings content; the riddle of the painful earth doesn't vex them—they have no leisure; they don't fear the hour of sleep—they welcome it. It is the rich, who find time drag remorselessly on their hands, who have desperately to invent occupations and a whirl of amusements, who keep pursuing shadows they can never lay hold of, who are really in a piteous case; and I suppose you take credit to yourself, Linn, my boy, that you are one of the distractions that help them to lighten the unbearable weariness of their life. Well," he continued, in his rambling way, "it isn't quite what I had looked forward to; I had looked forward to something different for you. I can remember, when we used to have our long Sunday walks in those days, what splendid ambitions you had for yourself, and how you were all burning to begin—the organist of Winstead Church was to produce his Hallelujah Chorus, and the nations were to listen; and the other night, when I was in your room at the theatre, when I saw you smearing your face and decking yourself out for exhibition before a lot of fashionable idlers, I could not help saying to myself, 'And this is what Linn Moore has come to!'"

"Yes, that is what Linn Moore has come to," the other said, with entire good-nature. "And what has Maurice Mangan come to? I can remember when Maurice Mangan was to be a great poet, a great metaphysician, a great—I don't know what. Winstead was far too small a place for him; he was to go up and conquer London, and do great and wonderful things. And what is he now?—a reporter of the gabble of the House of Commons."

"I suppose I am a failure," said this tall, thin, contemplative-looking man, who spoke quite dispassionately of himself, just as he spoke with a transparent honesty and simplicity of his friend. "But at least I have kept myself to myself. I haven't sold myself over to the Moloch of fashion—"

"Oh, your dislike of fashionable people is a mere bundle of prejudice!" Lionel cried. "The truth is, Maurice, you don't know those fashionable people you seem to despise so heartily. If you did, you would discover that they had the ordinary human qualities of other people—only that they are better educated and more courteous and pleasant in manner. Then their benevolence—if you knew how much they give away in charity—"

"Benevolence!" Mangan broke in, impatiently. "What is benevolence? It is generally nothing more or less than an expression of your own satisfaction with yourself. You are stuffed with food and wine; your purse is gorged; 'here's a handful of sovereigns for you, you poor devil crouching at the corner!' What merit is in that? Do you call that a virtue? But where charity really becomes a heroism, Linn, is when a poor, suffering, neuralgic woman, without any impulse from abundance of health or abundance of comfort, sets laboriously to work to do what she can for her fellow-creatures. Then that is something to regard—that is something to admire—"

Lionel burst out laughing.

"A very pretty description of Francie Wright!" he cried. "Francie a poor, suffering, wretched woman—because she happened to have a touch of neuralgia the last Sunday you were down here! There's very little of the poor and suffering about Francie; she's as contented and merry a lass as you'd find anywhere."

Mangan was silent for a second or two; and then he said, with a little hesitation,

"Didn't you tell me Miss Wright had not been up yet to see 'The Squire's Daughter?'"

"No, she has not," Lionel answered, lightly. "I don't know whether you have been influencing her, Maurice, or whether you have picked up some of her highly superior prejudices; anyhow, I rather fancy she doesn't quite approve of the theatre—I mean, I don't think she approves of the New Theatre, for she'd go to any other one fast enough, I suppose, if you could only get her away from her sick children. But not the New Theatre, apparently. Perhaps she doesn't care to see me making myself a motley to the view."

"She has a great regard for you, Linn. I wouldn't call her opinions prejudices," Mangan said—but with the curious diffidence he displayed whenever he spoke of Lionel's cousin.

"Oh, Francie should have lived in the fifteenth century—she would have been a follower of Savonarola," Lionel said, with a laugh. "She's far too exalted for these present days."

"Well, Linn," said his friend, "I'm glad you know at least one person who has some notion of duty and self-sacrifice, who has some fineness of perception and some standard of conduct and aim to go by. Why, those people you associate so much with now seem to have but one pursuit—the pursuit of pleasure, the gratification of every selfish whim; they seem to have no consciousness of the mystery surrounding life—of the fact that they themselves are inexplicable phantoms whose very existence might make them pause and wonder and question. No, it is the amassing of wealth, and the expending of it, that is all sufficient. I used to wonder why God should have chosen the Jews, of all the nations of the earth, for the revelation that there was something nobler than the acquisition of riches; but I suppose it was because no race ever needed it so much. And what new revelation—what new message is coming to the multitudes here in England who are living in a paradise of sensual gratification, blinded, besotted, their world a sort of gorgeous pig-stye—"

"Oh, that's all right," Lionel said, cheerfully. "Octavius Quirk has settled all that. The cure for everything is to be a blowing of the whole social fabric to bits. Then we're going to begin again all over; and the New Jerusalem will be reached when each man has to dig for his own potatoes."

"Quirk!" said Maurice Mangan, contemptuously; and then he took out his watch. "We'd better be getting back, Linn. We'll just be in time to meet your people coming out of church."

So they turned and walked leisurely across the gorse-covered downs until they reached the broad and dusty highway leading towards Winstead village. And then again they struck into a by-lane with tall hedges, the banks underneath which were bright with stitchwort and speedwell and white dead-nettle. Now and again, through a gap or a gate, they caught a glimpse of the lush meadows golden with buttercups; in one of them there was a small black pony standing in the shadow of a wide-spreading elm. They passed some cottages with pretty gardens in front; they stopped for a second to look at the old-fashioned columbine and monkshood, the none-so-pretty, the yellow and crimson wall-flower, the peony roses. Then always around them was this gracious silence, which seemed so strange after the roar of London; and if the day promised to become still hotter, at least they had this welcome breeze, that rustled the quick-glancing poplars, and stirred the white-laden hawthorns, and kept the long branches of the wych-elms and chestnuts swaying hither and thither. They were not talking much now; one of them was thinking of a pair of gray eyes.

At last they came to a turnstile, and, passing through that, found themselves in one of those wide meadows; at the farther side of it the red-tiled roof, the gray belfry, and slated spire of Winstead Church just showed above the masses of green foliage. They crossed the meadow and entered the churchyard. A perfect silence reigned over the place; they could not hear what was going on within the small building; out here there was no sound save the chirping of the birds and the continuous murmur of the trees. They walked about, looking thoughtfully at the gravestones—many of them bearing names familiar enough to them in bygone years. And perhaps one or other of them may have been fancying that when the great, busy world had done with him—and used him up and thrown him aside—here at least there would be peace preserved for him—an ample sufficiency of rest under this greensward, with perhaps a few flowers put there by some kindly hand. The dead did not seem to need much pity on this tranquil day.

Then into this universal silence came suddenly a low, booming sound that caused Lionel Moore's heart to stand still: it was the church organ—that awakened a multitude of associations and recollections, that seemed to summon up the vanished years and the dreams of his youth, when it was he himself who used to sit at the instrument and call forth those massive chords and solemn tones. Something of his boyhood came back to him; he seemed again to be looking forward to an unknown future; wondering and eager, he painted visions; and always in them, to share his greatness and his fame, there was some radiant creature, smiling-eyed, who would be at his side in sorrow and in joy, through the pain of striving and in the rapture of triumph. And now—now that the years had developed themselves—what had become of these wistful hopes and forecasts? Boyish nonsense, he would have said (except just at such a moment as this, when the sudden sound of the organ seemed to call back so much). He had encountered the realities of life since then; he had chosen his profession; he had studied hard; he had achieved a measure of fame. And the beautiful and wonderful being who was to share his triumphs with him? Well, he had never actually beheld her. A glimmer here and there, in a face or a form, had taken his fancy captive more than once; but he remained heart-whole; he was too much occupied, he laughingly assured Maurice Mangan again and again, to have the chance of falling in love.

"Getting married?" he would say. "My dear fellow, I haven't time; I'm far too busy to think of getting married."

So the radiant bride had never been found, even as the new Hallelujah Chorus that was to thrill the hearts of millions had never been written; and Linn Moore had to be content with the very pronounced success he had attained in playing in comic opera, and with a popularity in the fashionable world of London, especially among the women-folk therein, that would have turned many a young fellow's head.

When they thought the service was about over they went round to the porch and awaited the coming out of the congregation. And among the first to make their appearance—issuing from the dusky little building into this bewilderment of white light and green leaves—were old Dr. Moore and his wife, and Miss Francie Wright, who passed for Lionel's cousin, though the relationship was somewhat more remote than that. Maurice Mangan received a very hearty welcome from these good people; and then, as they set out for home, Lionel walked on with his father and mother, while Lionel's friend naturally followed with the young lady. She was not a distinctly beautiful person, perhaps, this slim-figured young woman, with the somewhat pale face, the high-arched eyebrows, and light-brown hair; but at least she had extremely pretty gray eyes, that had a touch of shrewdness and humor in them, as well as plenty of gentleness and womanliness; and she had a soft and attractive voice, which goes for much.

"It is so kind of you, Mr. Mangan," said she, in that soft and winning voice, "to bring Linn down. You know he won't come down by himself; and who can wonder at it? It is so dull and monotonous for him here, after the gay life he leads in London."

"Dull and monotonous!" he exclaimed. "Why, I have been preaching to him all the morning that he should be delighted to come down into the quietude of the country, as a sort of moral bath after the insensate racket of that London whirl. But no one ever knows how well off he is," he continued, as they walked along between the fragrant hawthorn hedges;

"it's the lookers-on who know. Good gracious, what wouldn't I give to be in Linn's place!"

"Do you mean in London, Mr. Mangan?" she asked, and for an instant the pretty gray eyes looked up.

"Certainly not!" he said, with unnecessary warmth. "I mean here. If I could run down of a Sunday to a beautiful, quiet, old-fashioned place like this, and find myself in my own home, among my own people, I wonder how many Sundays would find me in London? You can't imagine, you have no idea, what it is to live quite alone in London, with no one to turn to but club acquaintances; and I think Sunday is the worst day of all, especially if it is fine weather, and all the people have gone to the country or the seaside to spend the day with their friends."

"But, Mr. Mangan," said Miss Francie Wright, gently, "I am sure, whenever you have a Sunday free like that, we should be only too glad if you would consider us your friends—unless you think the place too dreadfully tedious, as I'm afraid my cousin finds it."

"It is very kind of you—very," said he. "And I know the old doctor and Mrs. Moore like to see me well enough, for I bring down their boy to them; but if I came by myself, I'm afraid they wouldn't care to have an idling, dawdling fellow like me lounging about the place of a Sunday afternoon."

"Will you come and try, Mr. Mangan?" said she, quietly. "For Linn's sake alone I know they would be delighted to have you here. And if it is rest and quiet you want, can't we give you the garden and a book?"

"You mustn't put such visions before me," he said. "It's too good to be true. I should be sighing for Paradise all through the week and forgetting my work. And shouldn't I hate to wake up on Monday morning and find myself in London!"

"You might wake up on Monday morning, and find yourself in Winstead," said she, "if you would take Linn's room for the night."

"Ah, no," he said, "it isn't for the like of me to try to take Linn's place in any way whatever. He has always had everything—everything seemed to come to him by natural right; and then he has always been such a capital fellow, so modest and unaffected and generous, that nobody could ever grudge him his good-fortune. Prince Fortunatus he always has been."

"In what way, Mr. Mangan?" his companion asked, rather wonderingly.

"In every way. People are fond of him; he wins affection without trying for it; as I say, it all comes to him as if by natural right."

"Yes, they say he is very popular in London, among those fine folk," observed Miss Francie, quite good-naturedly.

"Oh, I wasn't thinking of his fashionable friends," Mangan rejoined. "Being made much of by those people doesn't seem to me one of the great gifts of fortune. And yet I wonder it hasn't spoiled him. He doesn't seem the least bit spoiled, does he?"

"Really, I see so little of him," Miss Francie said, with a smile, "he honors us with so few visits, that I can hardly tell."

"No, he is not spoiled—you may take my word for it," her companion said, with decision. And then he added, "I suppose he gets too much of that petting; he is kept in such a turmoil of gayety that its evil effects have no time to sink into him. He is too busy—as he said this morning about marrying."

"What was that, Mr. Mangan?" she asked.

"He said he was too busy to think of getting married."

"Oh, indeed?" she said, with her eyes directed towards the ground. "We—we have always been expecting to hear of his being engaged to some young lady—seeing he is made so much of in London—" She could say no more, for now they were arrived at the doctor's house, which was separated from the highway by a little strip of front garden. They passed in through the gate and found the door left open for them.

"Well, Miss Savonarola," said Lionel, as he hung up his hat in the hall and turned to address her, "how have you been all this time?"

"I have been very well, Mr. Pagan," said she, smiling.

"And how are all those juvenile Londoners that you've planted about in the cottages?"

"They're getting on nicely, every one of them," said she, with quite an air of pride; and then she added, "When is your Munificence going to give me another subscription?"

"Just now, Francie," was the instant reply. "How much do you want?"

"As much as ever you can afford," said she.

He pulled from his pocket a handful of loose coin, and began to pick out the sovereigns. But Miss Francie, with a little touch of her fingers, put the money away.

"No, Linn, not from you. You've given me too much already. You give too freely; I like to have a little difficulty in obtaining subscriptions; it feels nicer somehow. But if my funds should run very low, then I'll come to you, Linn."

"Whenever you like, Francie," said he, carelessly; he poured the money into his pocket again and bade Maurice Mangan come up to his room, to get the dust of travel removed from his hands and face before going in to luncheon.

Then while Mangan was busy with his ablutions in this small upper chamber, Lionel drew a chair to the open window and gazed absently abroad on the wide stretch of country visible from the doctor's house. It was a familiar view; yet it was one not easy to get tired of; and of course on such a morning as this it lost none of its charm. Everywhere in the warm breeze and the sunshine there was a universal rustling and trembling and glancing of all beautiful things—of the translucent foliage of the limes, the pendulous blossoms of lilacs and laburnums, the swaying branches of the larch, and the masses of blue forget-me-nots in the garden below. Then there were all the hushed sounds of the country: the distant, quick footfall of a horse on some dusty road; the warning cluck of a thrush to her young ones down there among the bushes; the glad voices and laughter of some girls in an adjacent garden—they, too, likely to be soon away from the maternal nest; the crow of a cock pheasant from the margin of the wood; the clear, ringing melody of an undiscoverable lark. Everywhere white light, blue skies, and shadows of great clouds slow-sailing over the young green corn and over the daisied meadows in which the cows lay half-asleep. And when he looked beyond that low green hill, where there were one or two hares hopping about on their ungainly high haunches, and past that great stretch of receding country in which strips of red-and-white villages peeped here and there from the woods, behold! a horizon as of the sea, faint and blue and far, rising and ever rising in various hues and tones, until it was lost in a quivering mist of heat; and he could only guess that there, too, under the glowing sky, some other fair expanse of our beautiful English landscape lay basking in the sunlight and sweet air of the early summer.

Of course Lionel was the hero of the hour when they were all assembled in the dining-room—at a very sumptuously furnished board, by the way, for the hale old doctor was fond of good living and a firm believer in the virtues of port wine. Moreover, the young man had an attentive audience; for the worthy old lady at the head of the table never took her admiring eye's off this wonderful boy of hers; and Miss Francie Wright meekly listened too; while as for Maurice Mangan, who was he in his humble station to interrupt this marvellous tale of great doings and festivities? Not that Lionel magnified his own share in these things; nay, he modestly kept himself out altogether; it was merely to interest these simple country folk that he described the grand banquets, the illuminated gardens, the long marquees, and told them how the princess looked, and who it was who had the honor of taking her in to supper. But when he came, among other things, to speak of the rehearsal of the little pastoral comedy, in the clear light of the dawn, by Lady Adela Cunyngham and her friends, he had to admit that he himself was present on that occasion; and at once the fond mother took him to task.

"They passed in through the gate, and found the door left open for them."

"It's wicked, Lionel," she said, severely; "it's downright wicked to keep such hours. Look at the result of it all. You can't eat anything—you're not taking a mouthful!"

"But, you know, mother, I'm not used to luncheon," he said, cheerfully enough. "I have to dine at five every day—and I've no time to bother with luncheon, even if I could eat it."

"Take a glass of port, my lad," the old doctor said. "That will put some life into you."

"No, thanks," he said, indifferently, "I can't afford to play tricks. I have to study my throat."

"Why, what better astringent can you have than tannic acid?" the old gentleman called down the table. "I suppose you drink those washy abominations that the young men of the day prefer to honest wine; what's that I hear about lemonade? Lemonade!" he repeated, with disgust.

"It's home-brewed—it's wholesome enough; Miss Burgoyne makes some for me when she is making it for herself," the young man said; and then he turned to his mother: "Mother, I wish you would send her something from the garden—"

"Who, Lionel?"

"Miss Burgoyne—at the theatre, you know. She's very good to me—lends me her room if I have any swell friends who want to come behind—and makes me this lemonade, which is better than anything else on a hot night. Couldn't you send her something from the garden?—not flowers—she gets too many flowers, and doesn't care for them; but if you had some early strawberries or something of that kind, she would take them as a greater compliment, coming from you, than if some idiot of a young fool spent guineas on them at a florist's. And when are you coming up to see 'The Squire's Daughter,' Francie? The idea that you should never have been near the place, when I hear people confessing to each other that they have been to see it eight and ten, or even a dozen times!"

"But I am so busy, Lionel!" she said; and then perhaps an echo of something that had been said in the morning may have recurred to her mind; for she seemed a trifle confused, and kept her eyes downcast, while Lionel went on to tell them of what certain friends of his were going to do at Henley Regatta.

After luncheon they went out into the garden, and took seats in the shade of the lilac-trees, in the sweet air. Old Mrs. Moore had for form's sake brought a book with her; but she was not likely to read much when the pride of her eyes had come down on a visit to her, and was now talking to her, in his off-hand, light-hearted way. Maurice Mangan had followed the doctor's example and pulled out his pipe—which he forgot to light, however. He seemed dissatisfied. He kept looking back to the house from time to time. Was there no one else coming out? There was the French window of the drawing-room still open; was there no glimmer of a gray dress anywhere—with its ornamentation of a bunch of scarlet geraniums? At last he made bold to say to the doctor:

"Where has Miss Francie gone to? Isn't she coming out too?"

"Oh, she's away after those London brats of hers, I have no doubt," the old gentleman said. "You won't see her till teatime, if even then." Whereupon Mangan lit his pipe, and proceeded to smoke in silence, listening at times and absently to Lionel's vivacious talking to his mother.

In fact, before Miss Francie Wright returned that afternoon, Lionel found that he had to take his departure, for there are no trains to Winstead on Sunday, and he would have to walk some three miles to the nearest station. When he declared he had to go, the old lady's protests and entreaties were almost piteous.

"You come to see us so seldom, Lionel! And of course we thought you'd dine with us, at the very least; and if you could stay the night as well, you know there's a room for Mr. Mangan too. And we were looking forward to such a pleasant evening."

"But I have a long-standing engagement, mother; a dinner engagement—I could not get out of it."

"And you are dragging Mr. Mangan away up to town again, on a beautiful afternoon like this, when we know he is so fond of the country and of a garden—"

"Not at all," Lionel said. "I need not spoil Maurice's day, if I have to spoil my own; he'll stay, of course; and I suppose Francie will be back directly."

"I'm sure, Mr. Mangan," the old lady said, turning at once to her other guest, "if Lionel must really go, we shall be delighted if you will remain and dine with us—I hope you will—and you can have Lionel's room if you will stay the night as well."

"Thank you, I couldn't do that," said he, very gratefully, "but if you will have me, I shall be very glad to stay on, and go up by a late train. In the meantime, I think I'll walk to the station with Linn."

"And come back with a good appetite for dinner," said the doctor, calling after him. "We'll have something better than lemonade, I warrant ye!"

They have slow trains on these Surrey lines on Sunday; by the time that Lionel had got up to town and driven to his rooms and dressed, it was very near the hour at which he was due at the Lansdowne Gallery, where Lord Rockminster was giving a dinner-party, as a preliminary to the concert and crush that were to follow. And no sooner had he alighted from his hansom, and entered the marble vestibule of the gallery, than whom should he descry ascending the stairs in front of him but Mr. Octavius Quirk.

"Lady Adela hasn't let the grass grow under her feet," he said to himself. "Captured her first critic already!"

Lady Adela was at the head of the stairs receiving her brother's guests; and the greeting that she accorded to Mr. Octavius Quirk was of a most special and gracious kind. She was very complaisant to Lionel also, and bade him go and see if the place they had given him at dinner was to his liking. He took this as a kind of permission to choose what he wanted (within discreet limits); and as he just then happened to meet Miss Georgie Lestrange, he proposed to that smiling and ruddy-haired damsel that they should go and examine for themselves—and perhaps alter the dispositions a little. So they passed away through those brilliantly lit galleries (which served as a picture-exhibition on week-days), and at the farther end of the largest room they found the oblong dinner-table, which was brilliant with flowers and fruit, with crystal and silver. Of course Lionel and his companion had to be content with very modest places, for this was a highly distinguished company which Lord Rockminster had invited; but at all events they made sure they were to sit together, and that arrangement seemed to be satisfactory to them both.

This was rather a magnificent little banquet; and Lionel, looking down the long, richly colored table, may once or twice have thought of the quiet, small dining-room at Winstead (perhaps with the curtains still undrawn, and the evening light shining blue in the panes), and of the solitary guest whom he had left to talk to those good people; but indeed he was not permitted much time for reverie, for the young lady with the *pince-nez* was a most lively chatterer; she knew everything that was going on in London, and seemed to take a particularly active interest therein. Among other solemn items of information which she communicated to her companion, she mentioned that the issue of Lady Adela's novel had been postponed.

"Yes, it's quite ready, you know," she continued, in her blithe, discursive, happy-go-lucky fashion; "all quite ready; but she doesn't want it to go before the public until there has been a little talk about it, don't you understand? She wants some of the society papers to mention it; but she isn't quite sure how to get that done, and nobody seems able to help her— it's really distressing. Do you see that hideous creature down there at the corner?"

"Yes."

"He's a writer," observed this artless maiden, in mysterious tones.

"You don't say so!"

"Yes, he is—writes in all kinds of places. Why, now I think of it, Lady Adela said he was a friend of yours! I'm sure she did. So you pretend not to know him—is that on account of his complexion? Have you any more such *beauties* among your acquaintances, Mr. Moore? I thought he might be taking me in to dinner; and that's why I was so glad you brought me to look at the cards. Very rude, wasn't it? but you had permission, hadn't you? And there's another one coming to-night."

"Another what?"

"A writing man. But this other one is an American. Of course Lady Adela wants to have the curiosity of the American public excited just as well as the English. Have you heard Lady Sybil's marching-song yet?"

"No."

"Well, I think it is charming—really charming. Rockminster was dining with the officers of the Coldstream Guards the other evening, and he promised to send a copy to the bandmaster as soon as it is published. But Sybil wants more than that, of course; she wants to see whether the commander-in-chief wouldn't recommend it, so that it could be taken up by all the regiments. Wouldn't that be splendid?—to think that Sybil should provide a marching-song for the whole British army!"

"Yes, indeed," said he, with great politeness. "And why shouldn't the commander-in-chief recommend it? A marching-song is as important as a new button. But I must get a look at the music, if we are all to join in the chorus."

The dinner was not long-protracted, for there was to be a concert during the evening; and, indeed, people began to arrive early—strolling through the galleries, looking at the pictures, or talking together in small groups. It was during this promiscuous assembling that Octavius Quirk got hold of Lionel, and, with savage disgust, drew his attention to a hostler-looking person who had just come into the room.

"Do you see that ill-conditioned brute; what's he doing here?"

Lionel glanced in the direction indicated.

"I don't know who he is."

"Don't you know Quincey Hooper? the correspondent of the *Philadelphia Roll-Call*—a cur who toadies every Englishman he meets, and at the same time sneers at everything English in his wretched Philadelphia rag."

Then Lionel instantly bethought him of Miss Lestrange's hint; was this the correspondent who was to arouse the interest of the great American Continent in Lady Adela's forthcoming novel, even as Octavius Quirk was expected to write about it in England? But surely, with the wide Atlantic lying between their respective spheres of operation, there was no need for rivalry? Why did Mr. Quirk still glare in the direction of the new-comer with ill-disguised, or rather with wholly undisguised, disdain?

"Why," said he, in his tempestuously frothy fashion, "I've heard that creature actually discussing with another American what sort of air a man should assume in entering a drawing-room! Can you conceive of such a thing? Where *did* all that alarmed self-consciousness of the modern American come from—that unceasing self-consciousness that makes the American young man spend five sixths of his waking time in asking himself if he is a gentleman? Not from the splendid assurance, the belief in himself, the wholesome satisfaction of old John Bull. It's no use for the modern American to say he is of English descent at all!" continued this boisterous controversialist, who was still glaring at the hapless mortal at the door, as if every windy sentence was being hurled at his head. "Not a bit! there's nothing English about him, or his ways, or his sympathies, or character. Fancy an Englishman considering what demeanor he should assume before entering a drawing-room! The modern American hasn't the least idea from whom he is descended; what right has he to claim anything of our glorious English heritage?—or to say there is English blood in him at all? Why, as far back as the Declaration of Independence, the people of English birth or parentage in the Eastern States were in a distinct minority! And as to the American of the future—look at the thousands upon thousands of Germans pouring into the country as compared with the English immigration. That is the future American—a German; and it is to be hoped he will have some back-bone in him, and not alarm himself about his entering a drawing-room! America for the Americans?—it's America for the Germans! I tell you this: in a generation or two the great national poet of America will be—Goethe!"

Happily, at this moment, Lady Adela came up, and Lionel most gladly turned aside, for she had evidently something to say to him privately.

"Mr. Moore, I want to introduce you to Mr. Hooper—to Mr. Quincey Hooper—he doesn't seem to know anybody, and I want you to look after him a little—"

"No, no, Lady Adela, you must really excuse me," said he, in an undertone, but he was laughing all the same. "I can't, really. I beg your pardon, but indeed you must excuse me. I've just had one dose of literature—a furious lecture about—about I don't know what—oh, yes, immigration into

America. And do you know this—that in a generation or two the great national poet of America will be Goethe?"

"What?" said she.

He repeated the statement; and added that there could be no doubt about it, for he had it on Mr. Octavius Quirk's authority.

"Well, it's a good thing to be told," she said, sweetly, "for then you know." And therewithal, as there was a sudden sound of music issuing from the next gallery, she bade Lionel take her to see who had begun—it was Lady Sybil, indeed, who was playing a solo on the violin to an accompaniment of stringed instruments, while all the crowd stood still and listened.

The evening passed pleasantly enough. There were one or two courageous amateurs who now and again ventured on a song; but for the most part the music was instrumental. A young lady, standing with her hands behind her back, gave a recitation, and attempted to draw pathetic tears by picturing the woes of a simple-minded chimney-sweep who accidentally killed his tame sparrow, and who never quite held up his head thereafter; he seemed to pine away somehow, until one morning they found him dead, his face downward on the tiny grave in which he had buried his little playfellow. Another young lady performed a series of brilliant roulades on a silver bugle, which seemed to afford satisfaction. A well-known entertainer sat down to the piano and proceeded to give a description of a fashionable wedding; and all the people laughed merrily at the clever and sparkling way in which he made a fool of—not themselves, of course, but their friends and acquaintances. And then Lionel Moore went to his hostess.

"Don't you want me to do anything?" he said.

"You're too kind," Lady Adela made answer, with grateful eyes. "It's hardly fair. Still, if I had the courage—"

"Yes, you have the courage," he said, smiling.

"If I had the courage to ask you to sing Sybil's song for her?"

"Of course I will sing it," he said.

"Will you? Will you really? You know, I'm afraid those two girls will never give enough force to it. And it is a man's song—if you wouldn't mind, Mr. Moore."

"Where can I get the music? I'll just look it over."

Quite a little murmur of interest went through the place when it was rumored that Lionel Moore was about to sing Lady Sybil's "Soldiers' Marching Song," and when he stepped on to the platform at the upper end of the gallery, people came swarming in from the other rooms. Lady Sybil herself was to play the accompaniment—the grand piano being fully opened so as to give free egress to the marshalled chords; and when she sat down to the keyboard, it was apparent that the tall, pale, handsome young lady was not a little tremulous and anxious. Indeed, it was a very good thing for the composer that she had got Lionel Moore to sing the song; for the quite trivial and commonplace character of the music was in a large measure concealed by the fine and resonant quality of his rich baritone notes. The chorus was not much of a success—Lady Sybil's promised accomplices seemed to have found their courage fail them at the critical moment; but as for the martial ditty itself, it appeared to take the public ear very well; and when Lionel finally folded the music together again, there was quite a little tempest of clapping of hands. Here and there a half-hearted demand for a repetition was heard; but this was understood to be merely a compliment to Lady Sybil; and indeed Lionel strolled out of the room as soon as his duties were over. Fortunately no one was so indiscreet as to ask him what he privately thought of the "Soldiers' Marching Song," or of its chances of being recommended to the British Army by his royal highness the commander-in-chief.

When at length Lionel thought it was about time for him to slip away quietly from these brilliant, busy, murmuring rooms, he went to bid his hostess privately good-night.

"It was so awfully kind of you, Mr. Moore," she said, graciously, "to give us the chance of making Mr. Quirk's acquaintance. He is so interesting, you know, so unconventional, so original in his opinions—quite a treat to listen to him, I assure you. I've sent him a copy of my poor little book; some time or other I wish you could get to know what he thinks of it?"

"Oh, yes, certainly. I will ask him," Lionel said; and again he bade her good-night, and took his leave.

But as he was going by the entrance into a smaller gallery, which had been turned into a sort of supper-room (there was a buffet at one end, and everywhere a number of small tables at which groups of friends could sit down, the gentlemen of the party bringing over what was wanted) he happened to glance in, and there, occupying a small table all by himself, was Mr. Octavius Quirk, Lionel at once made his way to him. He found him with a capacious plate of lobster-salad before him, and by the side of that was a large bottle of champagne.

"Going to sit down?" Quirk asked—but with no great cordiality; it was for one person, not for two, that he had secured that bottle.

"No; I dined here," said Lionel, with innocent sarcasm.

"My dear fellow," observed the other, earnestly, "a good dinner is the very best preparation in the world for a good supper."

"I hear Lady Adela has sent you her book; have you looked at it?" Lionel asked.

"Yes, I have," said the other, with his mouth full of lobster-salad. "Capital! I call it capital! Plenty of *verve* and go—knowledge of society—nobody can do that kind of thing like the people who are actually living in it. Her characters are the people one really meets, you know—they are in the world—they belong to life. Oh, yes, a capital novel! Light, airy, amusing, sparkling—I tell you it will be the book of the season!"

"Oh, I'm very glad to hear that," said Lionel, thoughtfully; and then he went and got his light overcoat and crush-hat, and descended the wide stone-steps, and made his way home to his rooms in Piccadilly.

CHAPTER V.

WARS AND RUMORS.

Little could Lionel Moore have anticipated what was to come of his introducing his old comrade Nina to the New Theatre. At first all went well; and even the prima-donna herself was so good as to extend her patronage to Lionel's *protégée*; insomuch that, arriving rather early at the theatre one evening, and encountering Nina in the corridor, she said to her,

"You come into my room, and I'll show you my make-up."

It was a friendly offer; and the young Italian girl, who was working hard in every way to fit herself for the stage, was glad to be initiated still further into these mysteries of the toilet. But when she had followed Miss Burgoyne into the sacred inner room, and when the dresser had been told she should not be wanted yet awhile, Nina, who was far from being a stupid person, began to perceive what had prompted this sudden invitation. For Miss Burgoyne, as she was throwing off her things, and getting ready for her stage-transformation, kept plying her guest with all sorts of cunning little questions about Mr. Moore—questions which had no apparent motive, it is true, so carelessly were they asked; but Nina, even as she answered, was shrewd enough to understand.

"So you might call yourself quite an old friend of his," the prima-donna continued, busying herself at the dressing-table. "Well, what do you think of him now?"

"How, Miss Burgoyne?" Nina said.

"Why, you see the position he has attained here in London—very different from what he had when he was studying in Naples, I suppose. Don't you hear how all those women are spoiling him? What do you think of that? If I were a friend of his—an intimate friend—I should warn him. For what will the end be—he'll marry a rich woman, a woman of fashion, and cease to be anybody. Fancy a man's ruining his career—giving up his position, his reputation—becoming nobody at all—in order to have splendid horses and give big dinner-parties! Of course she'll have her doll, to drive by her side in the Park; but she'll tire—and then? And he'll get sick-tired, too, and wish he was back in the theatre; and just as likely as not he'll take to drinking, or gambling, or something. Depend on it, my dear, a professional should marry in the profession; that's the only safe thing; then there is a community of interests, and they understand each other and are glad of each other's success. Don't you think so yourself?"

Nina was startled by the sudden appeal; but she managed to intimate that, on the whole, she agreed with Miss Burgoyne; and that young lady proceeded to expand her little lecture and to cite general instances that had come within her own knowledge of the disastrous effects of theatrical people marrying outside their own set. As to any lesson in the art of making-up, perhaps Miss Burgoyne had forgotten the pretext on which she asked Nina to come to her room. Her maid was called in to help her now. And at last it was time for Nina to go, for she also, in her humble way, had to prepare herself for the performance.

But this friendliness on the part of the prima-donna towards the young baritone's *protégée* did not last very long. For one thing, Lionel did not come to Miss Burgoyne's sitting-room as much as he used to do, to have a cup of tea and a chat with one or two acquaintants; he preferred standing in the wings with Nina, who was a most indefatigable student, and giving her whispered criticisms and comments as to what was going forward on the stage. When Miss Burgoyne came upon them so employed, she passed them in cold disdain. And by degrees she took less and less notice of Miss Ross (as Nina was now called), who, indeed, was only Miss Girond's under-study and a person of no consequence in the theatre. Finally, Miss Burgoyne ceased to recognize Miss Ross, even when they happened to be going in by the stage-door of an evening; and Nina, not knowing how she had offended, nevertheless accepted her fate meekly and without protest, nor had she any thought of asking Lionel to intervene.

But worse was to befall. One day Lionel said to her,

"Nina, I never knew any one work harder than you are doing. Of course it's very handy your having Mrs. Grey to coach you; and you can't do better than stand opposite that long mirror and watch yourself doing what she tells you to do. She's quite enthusiastic about you; perhaps it's because you are so considerate—she says you never practise until the other lodgers have gone out. By the way, that reading dialogue aloud is capital; I can hear how your English is getting freer and freer; why, in a little while you'll be able to take any part that is offered you. And in any case, you know, the English audiences rather like a touch of foreign accent; oh, you needn't be afraid about that. Well, now, all this hard work can't go on forever; you must have a little relaxation; and I'm going to take you and Mrs. Grey for a drive down to Hampton Court, and we'll dine there in the evening, in a room overlooking the river—very pretty it is, I can tell you. What do you say? Will next Friday do? Friday is the night of least consequence in a London theatre; and if you can arrange it with Mrs. Grey, I'll arrange it with Lehmann; my under-study is always glad of a chance of taking the part. You persuade Mrs. Grey, and I'll manage Lehmann. Is it a bargain?"

So it came about that on a certain bright and sunny morning in June Lionel was standing at the window of a private room in a hotel near the top of Regent Street, where he proposed (for he was an extravagant young man) to entertain his two guests at lunch before driving them down to Hampton Court. He had ordered the wine and seen that the flowers on the table were all right; and now he was looking down into the street, vaguely noticing the passers-by. But this barouche that drove up?—there was something familiar about it—wasn't it the carriage he had sent down to Sloane Street?—then the next moment he was saying to himself,

"My goodness gracious! can that be Nina?"

And Nina it assuredly was; but not the Nina of the black dress and crimson straw hat with which he had grown familiar. Oh, no; this young lady who stepped down from the carriage, who waited a second for her friend, and then crossed the pavement, was a kind of vision of light summer coolness and prettiness; even his uninstructed intelligence told him how charmingly she was dressed; though he had but a glimpse of the tight-fitting gown of cream-white, with its silver girdle, the white straw hat looped up on one side and adorned on the other with large yellow roses, the pale-yellow gloves with silver bangles at the wrists, the snow-white sunshade, with its yellow satin ribbons attached. The vision of a moment—then it was gone; but only to reappear here at the open door. And who could think of her costume at all when Nina herself came forward, with the pretty, pale, foreign face so pleasantly smiling, the liquid black eyes softly bespeaking kindness, the half-parted lips showing a glimmer of milk-white teeth.

"Good-morning, Leo!"

"Good-morning, Nina! They say that ladies are never punctual; but here you are to the moment!"

"Then you have to thank Mrs. Grey—and your own goodness in sending the carriage for us. Ah, the delightful flowers!" said she, glancing at the table, and her nostrils seemed to dilate a little, as if she would welcome all their odors at once. "But the window, Leo—you will have the window open? London, it is perfectly beautiful this morning!—the air is sweet as of the country—oh, it is the gayest city in the world!"

"I never saw London fuller, anyway," said he, as he rang the bell, and told the waiter to have luncheon produced forthwith.

Nina, seated at table in that cool summer costume, merely toyed with the things put before her (except when they came to the strawberries); she was chattering away, with her little dramatic gestures, about every conceivable subject within her recent experience, until, as she happened to say something about Naples, Lionel cruelly interrupted her by asking her if she had heard lately from her sweetheart.

"Who?" she said, with a stare; and also the little widow in black looked up from her plate and seemed to think it a strange question.

"Don't you pretend to have forgotten, Nina," Lionel said, reprovingly. "Don't you look so innocent. If you have no memory, then I have."

"But who, Leo?" she demanded, with a touch of indignation. "Who?—who?—who? What is it you mean?"

"Nina, don't you pretend you have forgotten poor Nicolo Ciana."

"Oh, Nicolo!" she exclaimed, with supreme contempt (but all the same there was a faint flush on the clear olive complexion). "You laugh at me, Leo! Nicolo! He was all, as they say here, sham—sham jewelry, sham clothes, all pretence, except the oil for his hair—that was plenty and substantial, yes. And a sham voice—he told lies to the *maestro* about his wonderful compass—"

"Now, now, Nina, don't be unjust," he said. "Mrs. Grey must hear the truth. Mrs. Grey, this was a young Italian who wanted to be better acquainted with Miss Nina here—I believe he used to write imploring letters to her, and that she cruelly wouldn't answer them; and then he wrote to Maestro Pandiani, describing the wonderful tenor voice he had, and saying he wanted to study. I suppose he fancied that if the *maestro* would only believe in the mysterious qualities of this wonderful organ of his he would try to bring them out; and in the meantime the happy Nicolo would be meeting Nina continually. A lover's stratagem—nothing worse than that! What is the harm of saying that you could take the high C if you were in ordinary health, but that your voice has been ill-used by a recent fever? It was Nina he was thinking of. Don't I remember how I used to hear him coming along the garden-paths in the Villa Reale—if there were few people about you could hear his vile falsetto a mile off—and always it was:

'Antoniella, Antonià,

Antoniella, Antonià;

Votate, Nenna bella, votate ccà,

Vedimmo a pettenessa comme te stà.'"

"Leo," she said, with proud lips, "he never called me '*Nenna mia*'—never! He dared not!"

In another instant, he could see, there would have been protesting tears in her eyes; and even Mrs. Grey, who did not know the meaning of the familiar Neapolitan phrase,[1] noticed the tremulous indignation in the girl's voice.

"Of course not, Nina," he said, at once; "I was only joking—but you know he did use to sing that confounded 'Antoniella, Antonià,' and it was always you he was thinking of."

"I did not think of *him*, then!" said she, almost instantly recovering her self-control. "Him? No! When I go out—when I was going out in the *Santa Lucia*, I looked at the English gentlemen—all so simple and honest in their dress—perhaps a steel watch-chain to a gold watch—not a sham gold chain to no watch! Then they looked so clean and wholesome—is it right, wholesome?—not their hair dripping with grease, as the peasant-girls love it. And then," she added, with a laugh, for her face had quickly resumed its usual happy brightness of expression, "then I grow sentimental. I say to myself, 'These are English people—they are going away back to England, where Leo is—can they take him a message?—can they tell him they were going over to Capri, and they met on the ship—on the steamer—an Italian girl, who liked to look at the English, and liked to hear the English speak?' And then I say 'No; what is the use; what would any message do; Leo has forgotten me.'"

"Oh, yes," said he, lightly, "you must have been quite certain that I had forgotten my old comrade Nina!"

They got a beautiful, warm, sunny afternoon for their drive down to Hampton Court; nor was it fated to be without incident either. They had passed along Oxford Street and were just turning out of the crowded thoroughfare to enter Hyde Park—and Lionel, as a man will, was watching how his coachman would take the horses through the Marble Arch—when Nina said, in a low voice,

"Leo!"

"Well?" said he, turning to her.

"Did you not see?"

"See what?"

"The carriage that went past." Nina said, looking a little concerned. "Miss Burgoyne was in it—she bowed to you—"

"Did she? I didn't see her—I'll have to apologize to her to-morrow," said he, carelessly. "Perhaps the compliment was meant for you, Nina."

"For me? Ah, no. Miss Burgoyne speaks no more to me."

"She doesn't speak to you? Why?" he asked, in some amazement.

The young Italian lady made a little gesture of indifference.

"How do I know? But I am not sorry. I do not like her—no! she is not—she is not—straightforward, is it right?—she is cunning—and she has a dreadful temper—oh! I have heard;—I have heard such stories! Again, she is not an artist—I said that to you from the beginning, Leo—no, not an artist: why does she talk to you from behind her fan, when she should regard the others on the stage? Why does she talk always and always to you, when she has nothing to say?"

"Oh, but she finds plenty to say!" he observed.

"Yes," said Nina, contemptuously, "she has always plenty to say to you on the stage, if she has not a word the moment the scene is over. Why? You don't understand! You don't reflect! I will tell you, Leo, if you are so simple. You think she does not know that the public can see she talks to you? She knows it well; and that is why she talks. It is to boast of her friendship with you, her alliance with you. She says to the ladies in the stalls, 'See here, I can talk to him when I please—you are away—you are outside.' It is her vanity. She says to them, 'You can buy his portrait out of the shop-window perhaps—you can ask him to your house perhaps—and he goes for an hour, among strangers—but see here—every night I am talking to him'—"

"Yes, and see here, Nina," he said, with a laugh, "how about my vanity?—don't you think of that? Who could have imagined I was so important a person! But the truth is, Nina, they've lengthened out that comic scene inordinately with all that gagging, and Miss Burgoyne has nothing to do in it; if she hides her talking behind her fan—"

"Hides?" said Nina, with just a trace of scorn. "No; she shows! It is display! It is vanity! And you think a true artist would so forget her part—would wish to show the people that she talks privately—"

"Miss Nina is quite right, you know, Mr. Moore," said the little widow in black, and she was entitled to speak with authority. "I didn't think it looked well myself. A ballet-girl would catch it if she went on the same way."

"What would you have her do?" he said—for he was a very tolerant and good-natured person. "Sit and look on at that idiotic comic gag?"

"Certainly," said the little dame, with decision. "She is in the scene. She is not Miss Burgoyne; she is Grace Mainwaring; and she ought to appear interested in everything around her."

"Oh, well, perhaps I have been to blame," he said, rather uneasily. "I dare say I encouraged her. But really I had no idea the audience could have noticed it."

"It was meant for them to notice it," Nina said, vindictively; and then, as she would have nothing more to say on this wretched subject, she turned to look at the gay lilacs and laburnums in the neighborhood of the Serpentine, at the shimmering blue of the wide stretch of water, and at the fleet of pleasure-boats with their wet oars gleaming in the golden sunlight.

Her equanimity was soon restored; she would have nothing further to say of Miss Burgoyne on such a gracious afternoon; and, indeed, when they had crossed the Thames at Putney, and got into the opener country down by Barnes and East Sheen and Richmond, she was chattering away in her delight over everything they encountered—the wide commons, the luxuriant gardens, the spacious mansions, the magnificent elms, the hawthorn-trees, red and white, that sweetened all the soft summer air. Of course when they arrived at the top of Richmond Hill they halted for a minute or two at the Star and Garter to water the horses, while they themselves had a stroll along the terrace, a cup of tea, and a look abroad over the wide, hazy, dream-like landscape stretching far out into the west. Then they crossed the river again at Richmond Bridge; they bowled along by Twickenham and Teddington; finally they drove through the magnificent chestnut-avenues of Bushey Park, which were just now in their finest blossom. When they stopped at the Mitre, it was not to go in; Nina was to be shown the gardens of Hampton Court Palace; there would be plenty of time for a pleasant saunter before dinner.

Miss Burgoyne, indeed! Nina had forgotten all about Miss Burgoyne as the little party of three passed through the cool gray courtyard of the palace and entered into the golden glow of the gardens—for now the westering sun was rich and warm on the tall elms and limes and threw deep shadows on the greensward under the short black yews. They walked down towards the river, and stood for a long time watching the irregular procession of boats—many of them pulled by young girls in light summer dresses that lent some variety of color to this sufficiently pretty picture. It was altogether an attractive scene—the placid waters, the soft green landscape, the swift, glancing boats, from which from time to time came a ripple of youthful laughter or song. And indeed Nina was regarding rather wistfully those maidens in palest blue or palest pink who went swinging down with the stream.

"Those young ladies," she said, in an absent kind of way, to the little widow, who was standing beside her, "it is a pleasant life they live. It is all amusement. They have no hard work; no anxieties; no troubles; everything is made gentle for them by their friends; it is one enjoyment, and again and again; they have no care."

"Don't be so sure of that, Miss Nina," Mrs. Grey said, with a quiet smile. "I dare say many a one of those girls has worked as hard at her music as ever you have done, and has very little to show for it. I dare say many a one of them would be glad to change her position for yours—I mean, for the position you will have ere long. Do you know, Mr. Moore," she said, turning to Nina's other companion, "that I am quite sure of this—if Miss Burgoyne's under-study was drafted into a travelling company, I am quite sure Miss Nina here could take her place with perfect confidence."

"I don't see why not," he said, as if it were a matter of course.

"Then you know what would happen," Mrs. Grey continued, turning again to the young lady, in whose future she seemed greatly interested. "Miss Burgoyne would want a holiday, or her doctor would order her to give her voice a fortnight's rest, or she might catch a bad cold—and then comes your chance! You know the music thoroughly? you know every bit of Miss Burgoyne's 'business;' and Mr. Moore would be on the stage, or in the wings, to guide you as to your entrances and exits. That will be a proud night for me, my dear; for I'll be there—oh, yes, I'll be there; and if I have any stage experience at all, I tell you it will be a splendid triumph—with such a voice as yours—and there won't be any more talk of keeping you as under-study to Miss Girond. No," she added, with a shrewd smile, "but there will be something else. Miss Burgoyne won't like it; she doesn't like rivals near the throne, from what I can hear. She'll try to get you drafted off into one of the country companies—mark my words."

"The country?" said Nina, rather aghast. "To go away into the country?"

"But look at the chance, my dear," said the little ex-actress, eagerly. "Look at the practice—the experience! And then, if you only take care of your voice, and don't strain it by overwork, then you'll be able to come back to London and just command any engagement you may want."

"To come back to London after a long time?" she said, thoughtfully; and she was somewhat grave and reserved as they strolled idly back through the gardens, and through the Palace buildings, to the riverside hotel.

But no far-reaching possibilities of that kind were allowed to interfere with Nina's perfect enjoyment of this little dinner-party that had been got up in her honor. They had a room all to themselves on an upper floor; the windows were thrown wide open; even as they sat at table they could look abroad on the spacious landscape whose meadows and hedges and woods stretched away into distant heights crowned by a solitary windmill. Indeed, the young lady was so rude as to leave the table more than once, and go and stand at the open window; there was a charm in the dying-out of the day—in the beautiful colors now encircling the world—in the hushed sounds coming up from the stream—that she could not withstand. The evening glow was warm on the rose-hued front of the palace and on the masses of sunny green foliage surrounding it; on the still, blue river the boats were of a lustrous bronze; while the oars seemed to be oars of shining gold as they dipped and flashed. By and by, indeed, the glory faded away; the stream became gray and ghostly; there were no more ripples of laughter or calls from this side to that; and Nina resumed her place more contentedly at the table, which was all lit up now. She made her small apologies; she said she did not know that England was such a beautiful place. Lionel, who in no way resented her thus withdrawing herself from time to time, had been leisurely talking to Mrs. Grey of theatrical things in general; and, now that coffee was coming in, he begged permission to light a cigarette. Altogether it was a simple, friendly, unpretentious evening, that did not seem to involve any serious consequences. As night fell, they set out on their homeward drive; and through the silent country they went, under the stars. Lionel left his two friends at their door in Sloane Street; and as he was driving home to his lodgings, if he thought of the matter at all, he no doubt hoped that he had given his friends a pleasant little treat.

But there was more to come of it than that. On the following evening Lionel got down to the theatre rather later than usual, and had to set to work at once to get ready, so that he had no opportunity of seeing Miss Burgoyne until he actually met her on the stage. Now, those of the public who had seen this piece before could not have perceived any difference of manner on the part of the coquettish Grace Mainwaring towards the young gentleman who had so unexpectedly fallen in her way—to wit, Harry Thornhill; but Lionel instantly became aware of it; and while he was endeavoring, after the fashion of the young stage gallant, to convey to Miss Grace Mainwaring the knowledge that she had suddenly captured his fancy and made him her slave for life, he was inwardly reflecting that he should have come down earlier to the theatre, and apologized to Miss Burgoyne for the unintentional slight of the previous day. As soon as the scene was over and they were both in the wings, he hastened to her (they had left the stage by opposite sides) and said,

"Oh, Miss Burgoyne, something very awkward happened yesterday—I am so sorry—I want to apologize—"

"I hope you will do nothing of the kind," said she, haughtily, "it is quite unnecessary."

"Oh, but look here, I'm really very sorry," he was endeavoring to say, when she again interrupted him:

"If you choose to go driving through London with chorus-girls," said she, in measured and bitter tones, "I suppose your attention must be fully occupied."

And therewith she marched proudly away from him; nor could he follow her to protest or explain, for he was wanted on the stage in about a second. He felt inclined to be angry and resentful; but he was helpless; he had to attend to this immediate scene.

Meanwhile Miss Burgoyne did not long preserve that lofty demeanor of hers; the moment she left him her rage got the better of her, for here was the Italian girl most inopportunely coming along the corridor; and just as poor Nina came up Miss Burgoyne turned to her maid, who was holding open the dressing-room door for her, and said aloud, so that every one could overhear,

"Oh, we don't want foreigners in English opera; why don't they take a barrel-organ through the streets, or a couple of canaries in a cage?"

Nor was that all; for here was Mlle. Girond; and the smart little boy-officer, as she came along the passage, was gayly singing to herself,

"Le rôti, la salade,

L'amour, la promenade

  À deux dans les

    Dans les

  Deux dans les

À deux dans les bluets!"

"Oh, there's another of the foreign chimpanzees!" exclaimed Miss Burgoyne, in her fury; and she dashed into her room, and slammed the door behind her.

Mlle. Girond stood staring at the door; then she turned to look at Nina; then she burst out laughing.

"Quel ouragan, grand Dieu!" she cried. "Ma pauvre enfant, qu'allez vous faire maintenant?" She turned to the door and laughed again. "Elle a la tête près du bonnet, n'est-ce pas?—mon Dieu, elle s'enflamme comme de la poudre!"

But Nina did not stay to make any explanation; somewhat paler than usual, and quite silent and reserved, she took up her position in the wings; nor had she a word to say to Lionel when he came off the stage and passed her—with a nod and a smile of greeting—on his way to his room.

Then things went from bad to worse, and swiftly. On the very next afternoon, which was a Sunday, Lionel was about to walk down to Sloane Street, to have a chat and a cup of tea with Mrs. Grey and Nina; but before going he thought he would just have time to scribble a piece of music in an album that Lady Rosamund Bourne had sent him and affix his name thereto. He brought his writing materials to the table and opened the big volume; and he was glancing over the pages (Lady Rosamund had laid some very distinguished people, mostly artists, under contribution, and there were some interesting sketches) when the house-porter came up and presented a card. Lionel glanced at the name—Mr. Percival Miles—and wondered who the stranger might be; then he recollected that surely this was the name of a young gentleman who was a devoted admirer of Miss Burgoyne. Miss Burgoyne had, indeed, on one occasion introduced the young man to him; but he had paid little heed; most likely he regarded him with the sort of half-humorous contempt with which the professional actor is apt to look upon the moon-struck youths who bring bouquets into the stalls and languish about stage-doors. However, he told the house-porter to ask the gentleman to step up-stairs.

But he was hardly prepared for what followed. The young gentleman who now came into the room—he was a pretty boy, of the fair-haired English type, with a little yellow moustache and clear, gray eyes—seemed almost incapable of speech, and his lips were quite pale.

"In—in what I have to say to you, Mr. Moore," he said, in a breathless kind of way, "I hope there will be no need to mention any lady's name. But you know whom I mean. That—that lady has placed her interests in my hands—she has appealed to me—I am here to demand reparation—in the usual way—"

"Reparation—for what?" Lionel asked, staring at the young man as if he were an escaped lunatic.

"Your attentions," said the hapless boy, striving hard to preserve a calm demeanor, "your attentions are odious and objectionable—she will not submit to them any longer—"

"My attentions?" Lionel said. "If you mean Miss Burgoyne, I never paid her any—you must be out of your senses!"

"Shuffling will do you no good," said this fierce warrior, who seemed to be always trying to swallow something—perhaps his wrath. "The lady has placed her interests in my hands; I demand the only reparation that is possible between gentlemen."

"Look here, my young friend," Lionel said, in a very cool sort of fashion, "do you want to go on the stage? Is that a specimen of what you can do? For it isn't bad, you know—for burlesque."

"You won't fight?" said the young man, getting paler and more breathless than ever.

"No, I will not fight—about nothing," Lionel said, with perfect good-humor. "I am not such an ass. If Miss Burgoyne is annoyed because I passed her on Friday without recognizing her, that was simply a mistake for which I have already apologized to her. As for any cock-and-bull story about my having persecuted her with odious attentions, that's all moonshine; she never put that into your head; that's your own imagination—"

"By heavens, you shall fight!" broke in this infuriate young fool, and the next moment he had snatched up the ink-bottle from the table before him and tossed it into his enemy's face. That is to say, it did not quite reach its aim; for Lionel had instinctively raised his hand, and the missile fell harmlessly on to the table again—not altogether harmlessly, either, for in falling the lid had opened and the ink was now flowing over Lady Rosamund's open album. At sight of this mishap, Lionel sprang to his feet, his eyes afire.

"I've a mind to take you and knock your idiotic brains against that wall," he said to the panting, white-faced youth. "But I won't. I will teach you a lesson instead. Yes, I will fight. Make what arrangements you please; I'll be there. Now get out."

He held the door open; the young man said, as he passed,

"You shall hear from me."

And then Lionel went back to Lady Rosamund's ill-fated album, and began to sponge it with blotting-paper, while with many a qualm he considered how he was to apologize to her and make some kind of plausible explanation. Fortunately the damage turned out to be less serious than at first sight appeared. The open page, which contained a very charming little sketch in water-color by Mr. Mellord, was of course hopelessly ruined; but elsewhere the ink had not penetrated very far; a number of new mounts would soon put that right. Then he thought he would go to Mr. Mellord and lay the whole affair before him, and humbly beg for another sketch (artists always being provided with such things); so that, as regarded the album, no great harm had been done.

But as he was sitting in Mrs. Grey's little parlor, at tea, Nina fancied he looked a little preoccupied and was not talking as blithely as usual, and she made bold to ask him if anything were the matter.

"Yes," said he, "something is the matter. I'm afraid I've made a fool of myself." And then he added, with a smile, "Nina, I'm going to fight a duel."

"A duel, Leo?" she said, faintly.

"Yes; and what I fear about it is the ridicule that may follow. But don't be alarmed, Nina," he said, cheerfully, "I don't think I'm going to fall on the deadly field of battle; I can take care of myself. The trouble is that the whole thing is so preposterous—so absolutely ridiculous! The fact is, what the young gentleman really wants is a thorough good caning, and there's nobody to give it him. Very well, he must have something else; and I propose to teach him a wholesome lesson. I'm not going to take the trouble of crossing over to France or Belgium—I dare say that will be the programme—for nothing. Then there's another thing, Nina: I am the challenged party; I ought to have the choice of weapons. Well, now, I am not a very good shot; but I'm considered a very fair fencer; and I suppose you would say that I should be magnanimous and choose pistols? Oh, no; I'm not going to do anything of the kind. There might be a very awkward accident with pistols—that is to say, if our bloodthirsty seconds put in more than half a charge of powder. But with swords I fancy I shall be rather master of the situation; and perhaps a little prod or a scratch, just to show him the color of his own blood, will do him a world of good. It may turn out the other way, no doubt; I've heard of bad fencers breaking through one's guard just by pure ignorance and accident; but the betting is against that kind of thing."

"But what is it all about, Leo?" Nina exclaimed; she was far more concerned about this mad project than he appeared to be.

"Oh, I can't tell you that," said he, lightly, "without telling you the name of the lady—for of course there is a lady in it—and that is never allowed."

Nina sprang to her feet and stretched out her hands towards him.

"I know—I know!" she said, in a breathless sort of way. "Leo, you will not deny it to me—it is Miss Burgoyne! Ah, do I not know!—she is a serpent!—a cat!—a devil!—"

"Nina," he said, almost angrily, "what are you talking about? Do you suppose Miss Burgoyne would want a duel fought just because I happened to pass her, by accident, without raising my hat?—it's absurd."

"Ah, there is more than that, Leo!" Nina cried, eagerly; and then she paused, in some hesitation and embarrassment. "Yes, there is more than that," she repeated, as if with an effort, and there was a slight flush in the pretty, pale face. "Why should I not say it to you? You are too simple, Leo. You do not understand. She wishes to have the reputation to be allied with you—in the theatre—out of the theatre. Then she sees that you drive with me in an open carriage; she hates me—what more natural? And she is angry with you—"

"Now, Nina," said he, "do you think any woman could be so mad as to want to have a duel fought simply because she saw me driving past in a carriage with Mrs. Grey and you—is it reasonable?"

"Leo, you did not see her last night," Nina said, but still with a little embarrassment, "when she meets me in the corridor—oh, such a furious woman!—her face white, her eyes burning. As for her insulting me, what may I care? I am a foreigner, yes; if one says so, I am not wounded. Perhaps the foreigners have better manners a little?—but that is not of importance; no, what I say is, she will be overjoyed to have you fight a duel about her—why, it is glory for her!—every one will talk—your names will be joined in newspapers—when the people see you on the stage they will say, 'Ah, ah, he is back from fighting the duel; he must be mad in love with Miss Burgoyne.' A duel—yes, so unusual in England—every one will talk— ah, that will be the sweetest music for Miss Burgoyne's ears in the whole world—prouder than a queen she will be when the public have your name and her name rumored together. And you do not understand it, Leo!"

He had been listening in silence, with something of vexation deepening upon his features.

"What you say only makes matters worse and worse!" he exclaimed, presently. "If that were true, Nina—just supposing that were the true state of the case—why, I should be fighting a duel over a woman I don't care twopence about, and with a young jackass whom I could kick across the street! That is what I ought to have done!—why didn't I throw him downstairs? But the mischief of it is that the thing is now inevitable; I can't back out? I declare I never was in such a quandary in my life before!"

"And you will go and put yourself in danger, Leo," Nina said, indignantly, "that a deceitful woman has the pride to hear the public talk! Have you the right to do it? You say there are sometimes accidents—both with swords as pistols—yes, every one knows it. And you put your life in danger—for what? You care nothing for your friends, then?—you think they will not heed much if—if an accident happens? You think it is a light matter— nothing—a trifle done to please a boy and a wicked-minded woman? Leo, I say you have no right to do it! You should have the spirit, the courage, to say 'no!' You should go to that woman and say, 'You think I will make sport for you?—no, I will not!' And as for the foolish boy, if he comes near to you, then you take your riding-whip, Leo, and thrash him!—thrash him—thrash him!" Nina exclaimed, with her teeth set hard; indeed, her bosom was heaving so with indignation that Mrs. Grey put her hand gently on the girl's shoulder, and reminded her that Lionel was in sufficient perplexity, and wanted wise counsel rather than whirling words.

As for Lionel himself, he had to leave those good friends very shortly; for he was going out to dinner, and he had to get home to dress. And as he was walking along Piccadilly, ruminating over this matter, the more he thought of it the less he liked the look of it: not that he had been much influenced by Nina's apprehensions of personal harm, but that he most distinctly feared the absurdity of the whole affair. Indeed, the longer he pondered over it, the more morose and resentful he became that he should ever have been placed in such an awkward position; and when he was going up-stairs to his room, he was saying to himself, with gloomy significance:

"Well, if that young fool persists, I'd advise him to look out; I'm not going over the water for nothing."

[1]

Nenna mia or *Nenna bella* is the pet phrase used by the Neapolitan young man in addressing his sweetheart. *Nenna* has nothing to do with *Nina*, which is a contraction of Antonia.

CHAPTER VI.

A DEPARTURE.

There was but little sleep for Nina that night. She was sick at heart to think that in return for the unceasing kindness Lionel had shown her since her arrival in England, she should be the means of drawing him into this foolish embroilment. She saw the situation of affairs clearly enough. Miss Burgoyne was an exacting, irritable, jealous woman, who had resented Nina's presence in the theatre almost from the beginning, and who had been driven into a sudden fury by the sight of Lionel (he taking no notice of her either) driving past with this interloping foreigner. Moreover, Miss Burgoyne was inordinately vain: to have the popular young baritone fight a duel on her account—to have their names coupled together in common talk—what greater triumph could she desire than that? But while Miss Burgoyne might be the ostensible cause of the quarrel, Nina knew who was the real cause of it; and again and again she asked herself why she had ever come to England, thus to bring trouble upon her old ally and companion Leo.

And then in that world of visions that lies just outside the realm of sleep— in which great things become small, and small things acquire a fantastic and monstrous importance—she worried and fretted because Lionel had laughingly complained on the previous evening that henceforth there would be no more home-made lemonade for him. Well, now, if she—that is to say, if Nina—were in her humble way to try what she could do in that direction? It might not be so good as the lemonade that Miss Burgoyne prepared; but perhaps Lionel would be a little generous and make allowance? She would not challenge any comparison. She and Mrs. Grey between them would do their best, and the result would be sent anonymously to his rooms in Piccadilly; if he chose to accept it—well, it was a timid little something by way of compensation. Nina forgot for the moment that within the next few days an unlucky sword-thrust might suddenly determine Lionel's interest in lemonade, as in all other earthly things; these trivial matters grew large in this distorted land of waking dreams; nay, she began to think that if she were to leave England altogether, and go away back to Naples, and perhaps accept an engagement in opera at Malta, then matters would be as before at the New Theatre; and when Lionel and Miss Burgoyne met in the corridor, it would be, "Good-evening, Miss Burgoyne!" and "Good-evening, Mr. Moore!" just as it used to be. There would be no Italian girl interfering, and bringing dissension and trouble.

But the next morning, when the actual facts of the case were before her clearer vision, she had better reason for becoming anxious and restless and miserable. As the day wore on, Mrs. Grey could hardly persuade her to run down to the Crystal Palace for the opening of the Handel Festival, though, as the little widow pointed out, Mr. Moore had procured the tickets for them, and they were bound to go. Of course, when once they were in the great transept of the Palace, in the presence of this vast assemblage, and listening to the splendid orchestra and a chorus of between three and four thousand voices dealing with the massive and majestic strains of the "Messiah," the spell of the music fell upon Nina and held absolute sway over her. She got into a curious state of exaltation; she seemed breathless; sometimes, Mrs. Grey thought, she shivered a little with the strain of emotion. And all the time that Mr. Santley was singing "Why do the nations," she held her hand tightly over her heart; and when he had finished—when the thrilled multitude broke forth into an extraordinary thunder of enthusiasm—Nina murmured to herself,

"It is—it is like to take my life-blood away."

But when they were in the train again, and on their way up to town, it was evident to her companion that the girl had returned to her anxious fears.

"Mrs. Grey," she said, suddenly, "I speak to Miss Burgoyne to-night."

"Oh, no, don't do that, Miss Nina!" said Mrs. Grey, with much concern, for she knew something of the circumstances of the case. "I hope you won't do that! You might simply make matters worse. Mr. Moore would not have spoken to you if he thought you would interfere, depend upon that. And if Miss Burgoyne is vexed or angry, what good would you do? I hear she has a sharp tongue; don't *you* try her temper, my dear," the little woman pleaded.

But Nina did not answer these representations; and she was mostly silent and thoughtful all the way to town. When they reached London, they had some tea at the railway-station, and she went on at once to the theatre. She was there early; Miss Burgoyne had not arrived; so Nina lingered about the corridor, listening to Mlle. Girond's pretty chatter, but not hearing very much.

At length the prima-donna appeared; and she would have passed Nina without recognition, had not the latter went forward a step, and said, somewhat timidly,

"Miss Burgoyne!"

"What?" said Miss Burgoyne, stopping short, and regarding the Italian girl with a by-no-means-friendly stare.

"May I have a word with you?" Nina said, with a little hesitation.

"Yes; what is it?" the other demanded, abruptly.

"But—but in private?" Nina said again. "In your room?"

"Oh, very well, come in!" Miss Burgoyne said, with but scant courtesy; and she led the way into her sitting-room, and also intimated to her maid that she might retire into the inner apartment. Then she turned to Nina.

"What is it you want?"

But the crisis found Nina quite unprepared. She had constructed no set speech; she had formulated no demand. For a second or so she stood tongue-tied—tongue-tied and helpless—unable to put her passionate appeal into words; then, all of a sudden, she said,

"Miss Burgoyne, you will not allow it—this folly! It is madness that they fight about—about nothing! You will not allow it!—what is it to you?—you have enough fame, enough reputation as a prima-donna, as a favorite with the public—what more? Why should you wish more—and at such a dreadful risk?—"

"Oh, I don't know what you're talking about!" said Miss Burgoyne. "What are you talking about?"

"The duel—" said Nina, breathlessly.

"What duel?"

Nina stared at her.

"Ah, you do not know, then?" she exclaimed.

"What don't I know?" Miss Burgoyne said, impatiently. "What are you talking about! What duel? Is it something in the evening papers? Or have you taken leave of your senses?"

Nina paid no heed to these taunts.

"You do not know, then," she asked, "that—that Mr. Moore is going to fight a duel—with a young gentleman who is your friend? No?—you do not know it?"

It was Miss Burgoyne's turn to stare in amazement.

"Mr. Moore?" she repeated, with her eyes (which were pretty and coquettish enough, though they were not on the same plane) grown wide and wondering. "A friend of mine? And you come to me—as if I had anything to do with it? Oh, my goodness!" she suddenly exclaimed, and a curious smile of intelligence began to dawn upon her face. "Has that young donkey carried the matter so far as that?"

But she was not displeased; nay, she was rather inclined to laugh.

"Well, that would make a stir, wouldn't it? And how did you find it out?—who told *you*? A duel? I thought he was talking rather mysteriously yesterday morning—Conrad the Corsair kind of thing—glooms and daggers—so it was a duel he was thinking of? But they are not really going to fight, Miss Ross," continued Miss Burgoyne, who had grown quite friendly. "You know people can't give up an engagement at a theatre to go and fight a duel: it's only French gentlemen who have no occupation who do that sort of thing. A duel?—a real, actual duel—do you seriously mean it?"

The prospect seemed to afford her great satisfaction, if not even a cause for merriment.

"Miss Burgoyne, you will not permit it!" Nina exclaimed.

"I?" said the other. "What have I to do with it? If two men want to fight, why shouldn't they?" said she, with apparent carelessness.

"Ah, but you know well what you have to do with it," Nina said, with some touch of scorn. "Yes, you pretend; but you know it well. The young man he goes from you yesterday to provoke the duel—you have been talking to him—and yet you pretend. You say, why should they not fight? Then it is nothing to you that one friend or the other friend may be killed?—that is nothing to you?—and you know you can prevent it if you choose. You do not wish to interfere—it will be amusing to read in the papers! Oh, very amusing! And if the one is killed?"

"But you know, Miss Ross, they don't go such lengths nowadays," said Miss Burgoyne, with great good-humor. "No, no; it's only honor and glory they go out for; it's only the name of the thing; they don't want to kill each other. Besides, if two men mean to fight, how can a woman interfere? What is she supposed to know of the cause of quarrel? These things are not supposed to be known."

"Then," said Nina, whose lips had grown still more indignant and scornful, "this is what I say: if anything happens, it is your conscience that will speak to you in after time. You wish them to fight, yes, for your vanity to be pleased!—you wish it said that they fight about you! And that is a trionf for you—something in the papers—and you do not care what harm is done if you are talked about! That is your friendship!—what do you care?—any one may be sacrificed to your vanity—"

"I suppose if they were fighting about you, you wouldn't say a word against it!" observed Miss Burgoyne, coolly. In fact the vehement reproaches that Nina had addressed to her did not seem to have offended her in the least;

for she went on to say, in the best of tempers: "Well, Miss Ross, I have to thank you for bringing me the news. But don't be alarmed; these dreadful duels, even when they get into the newspapers, seldom show much harm done. And in the meantime will you excuse me?—Jane is grumbling in there, I know. Tell me anything you may hear about it by and by—and meanwhile I am very much obliged to you." So Nina found herself dismissed, neither her piteous appeal nor her indignant protest having had apparently any effect whatever.

But Miss Burgoyne, while transforming herself into Grace Mainwaring, had plenty of time to think over this startling position of affairs, and to consider how she could best use it to her own advantage. She had a nimble brain; and it may have occurred to her that here was a notable chance for her to display the splendid magnanimity of her disposition—to overwhelm Mr. Lionel Moore with her forgiveness and her generous intervention on his behalf. At all events, in the first scene in which these two met on the stage, Harry Thornhill became instantly aware that the merry and mischievous Grace Mainwaring appeared bent on being very friendly towards him— even while she looked curiously at him, as if there were something in her mind. Moreover, she seemed in excellent spirits; there was no perfunctory "drag" in her give-and-take speeches with the adventurous young gentleman whom fate had thrown in her way. He was very well pleased to find the scene going so well; he sang his share in the parting duet with unusual *verve*; she responded with equal animation; the crowded house gave them an enthusiastic recall. But the public could not tell that, even in the midst of this artistic triumph, the audacious young lover had his own thoughts in his head; and that he was really saying to himself, "What the mischief is she at now?"

He was to learn later on in the evening. Just as he got dressed for the ball-room scene, a message was brought him that Miss Burgoyne would like to see him for a minute or two as soon as he was ready. Forthwith he went to her room, tapped at her door, entered, and found himself the sole occupant; but the next moment the curtain concealing the dressing-room was opened about five feet from the ground; and there (the rest of her person being concealed) he beheld the smiling face of Grace Mainwaring, with its sparkling eyes and rouge and patches, to say nothing of the magnificent white wig with its nodding sprays of brilliants.

"Just a moment, Mr. Moore," said she, "and I shall be with you directly"— and therewith the vision was gone, and the crimson curtains came together again.

Very shortly thereafter the Squire's Daughter came forth in all the splendor of her white satin and pearls; and she lost no time in letting him know why he had been summoned.

"You are a very bloodthirsty man," said she, in accents of grave reproach (though her eyes were not so serious), "and I am ashamed of you that you should think of harming that poor boy; but I am not going to allow it—"

"Why, who told you anything about it?" he said; for he could not pretend not to know what she meant.

"A little bird," she made answer, with much complacence. "And the idea that you should really want to do such a thing!—how many voices like yours are there wandering about in comedy-opera that you should consider you have any right to run such a risk? I don't mean being killed—I mean catching a cold! I suppose you have got to take your coat and waistcoat off—on Calais sands—with a wind blowing in from the sea; that is a nice thing for your chest and throat, isn't it? Well, I'm going to step in and prevent it. I consider you have treated me very badly—pretending you didn't see me, when you were so very particularly engaged; but never mind; I never bear malice; and, as I say, I'm going to step in and prevent this piece of folly."

"Very much obliged, I am sure," he said, politely. "When men propose to fight, it is so extremely pleasant to find a woman appear to throw a protecting arm over them!"

"Oh, I am not going to be repelled by any of your ferocious sentiments," said she, good-naturedly. "I am a friend of both of you—I hope; and I won't have anything of the kind—I tell you I won't allow it—"

"I'm afraid your intervention has come too late," said he, quietly.

"Why?" she demanded.

"Oh, it isn't worth speaking about," said he. "The young gentleman went a little too far—he has got to be taught a lesson, that is all—"

"Oh, listen to him!—listen to his bloodthirstiness!" she exclaimed, in affected horror; and then she suddenly altered her tone. "Come, now, Mr. Moore, you're not seriously going to try to harm that poor boy! He is a very nice boy, as honest and simple-minded as you could wish. And such a pretty boy, too—no, no, it is quite absurd—"

"You are right there," said he. "It is quite absurd. The whole thing is absurd. But it has gone too far."

Here Miss Burgoyne was called.

"Will you leave it in my hands?" she said, leisurely rising from her chair, and tucking up her long train so that she might safely pass into the wings.

"Certainly not," said he. "You have no right to know anything about it. The quarrel was forced upon me; I had no wish to harm your pretty boy, nor have I much now—except in trying to keep myself from being harmed. But that is all over now; and this thing has to be seen through to the end now."

He held open the door for her; and then he accompanied her along the passage and up the steps, until they were both ready for their entrance on the stage.

"Men are so obstinate," said she, with an air of vexation; "so obstinate and foolish. But I don't care; I'll see if I can't get something done; I won't allow two dear friends of mine to do anything so stupid if I can help it. Why, the idea!—getting into a quarrel with a harmless young fellow like that! You ought to have been kind to him for my sake—for he really is such a dear boy—so simple and good-natured—"

"*But where is Grace?*" said a voice out there in the wide ball-room; and as this was Miss Burgoyne's cue, she tripped lightly on to the stage with her smiling answer: "*One kiss, papa, before the guests arrive.*" And, as it turned out, there was no further opportunity of talk that night between Miss Burgoyne and Mr. Lionel Moore.

But two days thereafter, and just as Lionel was about to go out for his morning ride, the house-porter brought him a card. It was Mr. Percival Miles who was below.

"Ask the gentleman to come up."

Here were the preliminaries of battle, then. Lionel had a vague kind of notion that the fire-eating youth ought not to have appeared in person—that he ought to have been represented by a friend; however, it was not of much consequence. He only hoped that there would be no further altercation or throwing of ink-bottles; otherwise he considered it probable that this interview would terminate in a more English manner than the last.

The young gentleman came in, hat in hand. He was apparently very calm and dignified.

"Mr. Moore," said he, slowly, as if he were repeating words already carefully chosen, "I am about to take an unusual course. I have been asked to do so—I have been constrained to do so—by the one person whose wish in such a matter must be respected. I have come to apologize to you for my conduct of the other day."

"Oh, very well," said Lionel, but somewhat coldly; he did not seem well satisfied that this young man should get off so easily, after his unheard-of insolence. Indeed, Lionel was very much in the position of the irate old Scotchwoman whose toes were trodden upon by a man in a crowd. "I beg your pardon," said the culprit. "Begging my paurdon 'll no dae," was the retort, "I'm gaun to gie ye a skelp o' the lug!"

"I hope you will accept my apology," the pale-faced young gentleman continued in the same stiff and embarrassed manner. "I don't know whether it is worth while my offering any excuse for what I did—except that it was done under a misapprehension. The—the lady in question seemed annoyed—perhaps I mistook the meaning of certain phrases she used—and certainly I must have been entirely in error in guessing as to what she wished me to do. I take the whole blame on myself. I acted hastily—on the spur of the moment; and now I am exceedingly sorry; and I ask your pardon."

"Oh, very well," Lionel said, though somewhat ungraciously. "But you see you are getting rather the best of this performance. You come here with a ridiculous cock-and-bull story, you threaten and vapor and kick up mock-heroics, you throw a bottle of ink over a book belonging to a friend of mine—and then you are to get off by saying two or three words of apology!"

"What can I do more?" said the humble penitent. "I have tried to explain. I—I was as ready to fight as you could be; but—but now I obey the person who has the best right to say what shall be done in such an affair. I have made every apology and explanation I could; and I ask your pardon."

"Oh, very well," Lionel said again.

"Will you give me your hand, then?" Mr. Percival Miles asked; and he somewhat timidly advanced a step, with outstretched palm.

"That isn't necessary," said Lionel, making no other response.

The fair-haired young warrior seemed greatly embarrassed.

"I—I was told—" he stammered; but Lionel, who was now inclined to laugh, broke in on his confusion.

"Did Miss Burgoyne say you weren't to come away without shaking hands with me—is that it?" he asked, with a smile.

"Y—yes," answered the young gentleman, blushing furiously.

"Oh, very well, there's no trouble about that," Lionel said, and he gave him his hand for a second; after which the love-lorn youth somewhat hastily withdrew, and no doubt was glad to lose himself in the busy crowd of Piccadilly.

That same afternoon Lionel drove down to Sloane Street. He was always glad to go along and have a friendly little chat about musical affairs with the eagerly enthusiastic Nina; and, as this particular evening was exceedingly fine and pleasant, he thought he might induce her to walk in to the theatre by way of Belgrave Square and the Green Park. But hardly had they left the house when Nina discovered that it was not about professional matters that Lionel wanted to talk to her on this occasion.

"Nina," said he, with befitting solemnity, "I have great news for you. I am saved. Yes, my life has been saved. And by whom, think you? Why, by Miss Burgoyne! Miss Burgoyne is the protecting goddess who has snatched me away in a cloud just as my enemy was about to pin me to the earth with his javelin."

"There is to be no duel, Leo?" she said, quickly.

"There is not," he continued. "Miss Burgoyne has forbidden it. She has come between me and my deadly foe and held up a protecting hand. I don't know that it is quite a dignified position for me to find myself in, but one must recognize her friendly intentions, anyway. And not only that, Nina, but she sent me a bottle of lemonade yesterday! Just think of it! to save your life is something, but to send you lemonade as well—that is almost too much goodness."

Poor Nina! If this careless young man had only looked at the address on the wrapper of the bottle he could easily have guessed whose was the handwriting—especially recognizable in the foreign-looking L and M. That timidly proffered little gift was Nina's humble effort at compensation; and now he was bringing it forward as a proof of Miss Burgoyne's great good-nature! And it was Miss Burgoyne who had intervened to prevent this absurd duel—Miss Burgoyne, who knew nothing at all about it until Nina told her! Nina, as they now walked along towards Constitution Hill, was too proud to make any explanation; only she thought he might have looked at the address on the wrapper.

"Seriously," he said to his companion, "seriously, Nina, she has put me under a very great obligation and shown herself very magnanimous as well. There is no doubt she was offended with me about something or other; and she had the generosity to put all that aside the moment she found I was embroiled in this stupid affair. And, mind you, I'm very glad to be out of it. It would have looked ridiculous in the papers; and everything gets into the papers nowadays. Of course that young idiot had no right to go and tell her about the duel; but I suppose he wanted to figure as a hero in her eyes—

poor devil! he seems pretty bad about her. Well, now that her intervention has got me out of this awkward scrape, how am I to show my gratitude to her? what do you say, Nina?"

But Nina had nothing to say.

"There's one thing I can do for her," he continued. "You know how fond actors and actresses are of titled folks. Well, Miss Burgoyne is going down to Henley Regatta with a lot of other professionals, and I am going too, with another party—Lady Adela Cunyngham has got a house-boat there. Very well, if I can find out where Miss Burgoyne is—and I dare say she will be conspicuous enough, though she's not very tall—I will take Lord Rockminster to pay his respects to her and leave him with her; won't that do! They have already been introduced at the theatre; and if Rockminster doesn't say much, I have no doubt she will chatter enough for both. And Miss Burgoyne will be quite pleased to have a lord all to herself."

"Leo," said Nina, gently, "do you not think you yourself have too much liking for—for that fine company?"

"Perhaps I have," said he, with perfect good-humor. "What then? Are you going to lecture me, too? Is Saul among the prophets? Has Maurice Mangan been coaching you as well?"

"Ah, Leo," said she, "I should wish to see you give it all up—yes—all the popularity—and your fine company—and that you go away back to Pandiani—"

"Pandiani!" he exclaimed. "Here's romance, indeed! You want us both to become students again, and to have the old days at Naples back again—"

"No, no, no!" she said, shaking her head. "It is the future I think of. I wish to hear you in grand opera or in oratorio—I wish to see you a great artist— that is something noble, something ambitious, something to work for day and night. Ah, Leo, when I hear Mr. Santley sing 'Why do the nations'— when I see the thousands and thousands of people sitting entranced, then I say to myself, 'There is something grand and noble to speak to all these people—to lift them above themselves, to give them this pure emotion, surely that is a great thing—it is high, like religion—it is a purification—it is—'" But here she stopped, with a little gesture of despair. "No, no, Leo, I cannot tell you—I have not enough English."

"It's all very well," said he, "for you to talk about Santley; but where will you get another voice like his?"

"Leo, you can sing finer music than 'The Starry Night,'" she said. "You have the capacity. Ah, but you enjoy too much; you are petted and spoiled, yes? you have not a great ambition—"

"I'll tell you what I seem to have, though, Nina," said he. "I seem to have a faculty of impressing my friends with the notion that I could do something tremendous if only I tried; whereas I know that this belief of theirs is only a delusion."

"But you do not try, Leo," said this persistent counsellor. "No? life is too pleasant for you; you have not enthusiasm; why, your talk is always *persiflage*—it is the talk of the fashionable world. And you an artist!"

However, at this moment Lionel suddenly discovered that this leisurely stroll was likely to make them late in getting to the theatre; so that perforce they had to leave these peaceful glades of the Green Park and get into Piccadilly, where they jumped into a hansom-cab and were rapidly whirled away eastward.

But if Lionel was to be reproached for his lack of ambition, that was a charge which could not be brought against certain of those fashionable friends of his at whom Nina (in unconscious collusion with Maurice Mangan) seemed inclined to look askance. At the very height of the London season Lady Adela Cunyngham and her sisters, Lady Sybil and Lady Rosamund Bourne, had taken the town by storm; and it seemed probable that, before they departed for Scotland, they would leave quite a trail of glory behind them in the social firmament. The afternoon production of "The Chaplet," in the gardens of Sir Hugh's house on Campden Hill, had been a most notable festivity, doubtless; but then it was a combination affair; for Miss Georgie Lestrange had shared in the honors of the occasion; moreover, they had professional assistance given them by Mr. Lionel Moore. It was when the three sisters attacked their own particular pursuits that their individual genius shone, and marked success had attended their separate efforts. His royal highness, the commander-in-chief, it is true, had not as yet invited the colonels of the British army to recommend Lady Sybil's "Soldiers' Marching Song" to the band-masters of the various regiments, but, in default of that, this composition was performed nightly, as the concluding ceremony, at the international exhibition then open in London; and as the piece was played by the combined bands of the Royal Marines, with the drums of the 1st Battalion Grenadier Guards, the Highland Pipers of the 2d Battalion Scots Guards, and the drums of the 2d Battalion Grenadier Guards, the resultant noise was surely sufficient to satisfy the hungriest vanity of any composer, professional or amateur, who ever lived. Then not only had Lady Rosamund exhibited a large picture at the Lansdowne Gallery (a decorative work this was, representing the manumission of a slave, with the legend underneath, "*Hunc hominem liberum esse volo*"), but also the proprietors of an illustrated weekly newspaper had published in their summer number, as a colored supplement, what she had ventured to call "An All-the-year-round

Valentine." She had taken the following rhyme (or perhaps some one had found it for her)—

"In these fair violets of the veins,

The verdure of the spring remains;

Ripe cherries on thy lips display

The lustre of the summer day;

If I for autumn were to seek,

I'd view the apples on thy cheek;

There's nought could give me pain in thee,

But winter in thy heart to see."

—and she had drawn four pretty little landscapes, which, when reproduced on one sheet by chromo-lithography, looked very neat and elegant, while the fair artist was much gratified to observe her name figuring on the placards at railway-stations or on the boards in front of stationers' shops, as she drove along Kensington High Street.

But, of course, the crowning achievement of the gifted family was Lady Adela Cunyngham's novel. If it was not quite the success of the season, as far as the outer world was concerned, it certainly was the most-talked-of book among Lady Adela's own set. Every character in it was identified as somebody or another; and although Lady Adela, as a true artist, maintained that she did not draw individuals, but types, she could not stem the tide of this harmless curiosity, and had to submit to the half-humorous inquiries and flattering insinuations of her friends. As for the outer world, if it remained indifferent, that only showed its lack of gratitude; for here, there, and everywhere, among the evening and weekly papers (the morning papers were, perhaps, too busy with politics at the time), attention was drawn to Lady Arthur Castletown's charming and witty romance of modern life. Alp called to Alp, and deep to deep, throughout Satan's invisible world; "Kathleen's Sweethearts" was dragged in (apparently with ten men pushing behind) for casual allusion in "Our Weekly Note-book;" Lady Arthur's smart sayings were quoted in the gossip attached to this or that monthly magazine; the correspondent of a country journal would hasten to say that it was not necessary to inform *his* readers that Lady Arthur Castletown was, in reality, Lady Adela Cunyngham, the wife of the well-known breeder of polled cattle, Sir Hugh Cunyngham of the Braes. In the midst of all this Lionel went to his friend Maurice Mangan.

"Look here, Maurice," said he, "that book can't be as bad as you tried to make out."

"It is the most insensate trash that was ever put between boards," was the prompt reply.

"But how can that be? Look at what the papers say!"

"The papers—what papers? That isn't what the papers say—that is what the small band of log-rollers say, calling industriously to one another, like frogs in a pond. Didn't I tell you what would happen if you got hold of Octavius Quirk, or any one of them? How many dinners did your swell friends expend on Quirk?"

"Oh, I don't know. He is pretty often at the house."

"He is pretty often at the house, is he?" Mangan repeated.

"I hope they won't ask him to Scotland," Lionel said, ruefully. "I can't bear the fellow; it's just as you say, he's always in a whirlwind of insistence— about nothing; and he doesn't grin through a horse-collar, he roars and guffaws through it. But then, you see, he has been very kind about this book; and, of course, a new author, like Lady Adela, is grateful. I admit what you say is right enough—perhaps the family are a little anxious for notoriety; but so are a good many other people; and there's no great harm in writing or painting or composing music as well as you can. Mind, I think there's a little professional jealousy about you, Maurice," continued this sage Mentor. "You don't like a woman of fashion to come into your literary circles. But why shouldn't she? I'm sure I don't object when any one of them tries to produce a little dramatic or musical piece; on the contrary, I would rather help. And look at Mellord—the busiest painter of the day— look at the trouble he takes in advising Lady Rosamund; she has the free *entrée* into his studio, no matter who is sitting to him. I think, for amateurs, the work of all the three sisters is very creditable to them; and I don't see why they shouldn't like to have the appreciation of the public, just as other people like it."

"My dear fellow," Mangan said, but with obvious indifference, "do you think I resent the fact of your friend Lady Arthur or Lady Adela writing a foolish novel? Far from it. You asked my opinion of it, and I told you; if you don't see for yourself that the book is absolute trash—but harmless trash, as I think—then you are in a happy condition of mind, for you must be easily pleased. Come, let's talk of something worth talking about. Have you been down to Winstead lately?"

"No—never since that Sunday."

"Do you know, your people were awfully good to me," this long, lank, lazy-looking man went on—but now he seemed more interested than when talking about Lady Adela's novel. "I never spent a more delightful evening—never. I wonder they did not turn me out, though; for I stayed and stayed, and never noticed how late it was getting. Missed the last train, of course, and walked all the way up to London; not a bit sorry, either, for the night was cool, and there was plenty of starlight; I'd walk twice as far to spend another such evening. I—I'm thinking of going down there next Sunday," he added, with a little hesitation.

"Why not?" Lionel said, cordially enough.

"You see," Mangan continued, still rather hesitatingly, "the fact is—I'm rather in the way of getting illustrated papers—and—and summer numbers—and children's books—I mean, when I want them, I can get them—for lots of these things come to the newspaper offices, and they're not much use to anybody; so I thought I would just make up a parcel and send it down to Miss Frances, don't you understand, for her sick children—"

"I dare say you went and spent a lot of money." Lionel said, with a laugh.

"And she was good enough to write back that it was just what she wanted; for several of the children—most of them, I should say—couldn't read, but they liked looking at pictures. And then she was kind enough to add that if I went down next Sunday, she would take me to see how the things had been distributed—the pictures hung up on walls, and so forth—and—and that's why I think I may go down."

"Oh, yes, certainly," Lionel said, though he did not understand why any such excuse was necessary.

"Couldn't you come down, too, Linn?" Mangan suggested.

"Oh, no, I couldn't, I'm so busy," was the immediate reply. "I'm going to Scotland the first or second week in August. The doctor advises me to give my voice a long rest; and the Cunynghams have asked me to their place in Ross-shire. Besides, I don't care about singing in London when there's nobody but country cousins, and none too many of them. Of course I'll have to go down and bid the old folks good-bye before starting for Scotland, and Francie, too. Mind you tell that wicked Francie that I am very angry with her for not having come up to see 'The Squire's Daughter.'"

"Linn," said his friend, after a second, "why don't you take the old people over to Aix or some such place for a month? They're so awfully proud of you; and you might take Miss Frances as well; she seems to work so hard—she deserves a rest. Wouldn't that be as sensible as going to Scotland?"

"My good chap, I would do that in a moment—I should be delighted," said he—for he was really a most generously disposed young man, especially as regarded money; time was of greater consideration with him. "But it's no use thinking of such a thing. The old folks are much too content with home; they won't travel. And Francie—she wouldn't come away from those precious babes. Well, I'm off. Mind you scold Francie for me!"

"Perhaps," said Mangan, as he accompanied his friend to the door.

So it was that on a certain evening in August, Lionel Moore drove up to Euston Station and secured a sleeping-berth in the train going north; and no doubt the consciousness that after a long spell of hard work he was entering upon a well-earned holiday was a very welcome and comfortable thing. If only he had been a little more reflective, he might have set to work (here in the railway-carriage, as he lit his cigar, and proceeded to fix up his reading-lamp) and gone on to consider how entirely satisfactory all his circumstances were at this moment. Prince Fortunatus, indeed! Was ever any one more happily situated? Here he was, young, full of health and high spirits, excellent-tempered, and sufficiently good-looking; he had acquired a liberal measure of fame and popularity; he had many friends; he had ample means, for he did not know the difference between a backer and a layer, nor yet the difference between a broker and a jobber—in fact, gambling, either in stocks or on the turf, had never even occurred to him as a thing worth thinking about. But there was something further than all this for which he ought to have been profoundly grateful. As the long train thundered away into the night, there was no dull misery of farewell weighing heavily upon him; there were no longing fancies wandering wistfully back to a certain house, a certain figure, a pair of too-eloquent eyes. He dragged no lengthening chain with him on this journey north. For, notwithstanding his pleasant companionship with Nina, and her constant sympathy with him and her interest in his professional career; notwithstanding the affectionate regard of his cousin Francie, which was none the less sincere that it remained unspoken and only to be guessed at; notwithstanding the somewhat jealous favor which the prima-donna of the New Theatre seemed inclined to bestow on him; notwithstanding the pert coquetries and fascinations of Miss Georgie Lestrange, to say nothing of the blandishments and pettings showered upon him by crowds of ladies of exalted rank, this fortunate young man (so far at least as he was himself aware) was going away to Scotland quite heart-whole.

CHAPTER VII.

IN STRATHAIVRON.

It was still early in the afternoon when Lionel found himself driving along a loftily-winding road overlooking the wide and fertile valley of the Aivron. Right down below him, and visible through the birch-trees, was the river itself, of a brilliant, clear-shining blue, save where in some more distant sweeps it shone a silver-white; on the other side of the broad strath rose a range of hill fringed along its base with wood, but terminating in the west in far altitudes of bare rock and heather; while now and again he could catch a glimpse of some still more distant peak or shoulder, no doubt belonging to the remote and mountainous region of Assynt. And there, in the middle of the plain, stood the shooting-lodge for which he was bound—a long, rambling building or series of buildings, with all sorts of kennels and out-houses and deer-houses attached; and as he was regarding this goal and aim of his journey, and wondering how he was going to get across the swift-flowing stream, behold! a white fluttering of handkerchiefs just outside the porch. It was a signal to him, he knew; and he returned it more than once—until, indeed, he discovered that his driver was leaving the road and about to take the horses down a rudely cut track on the hillside.

"I say, isn't there a bridge anywhere?" he asked; for he was not used to such exploits.

"Aw, no, there's no bridge," the old Highland driver said, coolly, as he jammed down the brake. "But we'll do ferry well at the ford; the water is not so high the now."

"And when the water is high, what do they do then?" Lionel asked, as he regarded with some concern the almost vertical pole and the straining harness.

"Aw, well, there uss a boat; and if there's a spate on the ruvver they can come and go; but not with the heavy things. Ay, I hef seen tons of coal waiting for them at Invershin for near a fortnight when there wass a heavy spate on the ruvver. The leddies are so particular nowadays; peat will not do for them for the cooking; naw, they must hef coal."

But now the horses were entering the stream, and the old man's loquacity ceased. The animals, however, seemed quite accustomed to this performance; without any hesitation they adventured into the rapid current, and splashed their way forward, getting such footing as was possible among the big, loose stones and shingle. Indeed, the passage was effected with very little trouble, if with a good deal of jolting and bumping; and thereafter there was a pleasant trot along some sufficiently smooth greensward up to the door of the lodge.

Yes, here were the three tall and handsome sisters, looking very picturesque in their simple Northern attire? and here was Miss Georgie Lestrange conspicuous in a Tam o' Shanter of bright blue; and no sooner had the young man descended from the wagonette than they surrounded him, laughing and questioning, and giving him the heartiest of welcomes. How could he answer them all at once? When the poor man was taken into the dining-room, and set down to his solitary luncheon, they were all for waiting on him and talking to him at the same time.

"It is so awfully kind of you to come," Lady Adela said, with one of her most gracious smiles. "Now we shall hear about something else than dogs and guns and grouse."

"Oh, Mr. Moore," cried Lady Rosamund (who was the youngest, and had a bit of a temper, and was allowed to interfere when she liked), "do you know a masque called 'Alfred'? You do? how delightful! Well, then, you remember the visions of the future kings and queens that pass before Alfred when he is in the Isle of Athelney? how can I get that done in the open air? What kind of gauze do you use in the theatre? Could you get me a bit? And would painted shades do instead of living persons?—you see we have so few people to come and go on up here."

"And, Mr. Moore," cried Lady Sybil, "how are we to manage about an accompaniment? A single violin is no use out in the open. Would it be too dreadful if we had a harmonium concealed somewhere? We could get one from Inverness; and you know a harmonium would do very well for the music that introduces the visions."

"Mr. Moore," put in Miss Georgie Lestrange, with a complaining air, "fancy their having given me another of Kitty Clive's characters; isn't it too bad? Why, I'll go on and on until I identify myself with her altogether; and then, you know, Kitty Clive wasn't—I'm afraid she wasn't quite—"

"Oh, Mrs. Clive was all right; she was a great friend of Dr. Johnson," Lionel made answer, to reassure the young lady.

"But I wish you girls would leave off chattering, and let Mr. Moore get something to eat," the young matron said, impatiently; and she herself was so kind as to go and fetch the claret jug from the glide-table and fill his glass.

However, there was peace in store for him. When he had finished with this late lunch, Lady Adela begged him to excuse them if they left him to shift for himself; they were busy dressmaking, she said. Would she send for one of the keepers, who would show him one or two of the nearest pools, so that he might try for a salmon? The gentlemen had all gone down the strath, to test some new rifle, she thought; this was out of consideration for her, for she could not bear shooting close to the house; would he walk in that direction, and see what they were doing?

"Don't you trouble," he said, instantly. "You leave me to myself. I like to wander about and find out my surroundings. I shall go down to the river, to begin with; I saw some picturesque bits higher up when we were coming along."

"You'll almost certainly find Honnor Cunyngham there," said Miss Lestrange. "I suppose she has gone storking, as usual."

"Stalking?" said he, in some amazement.

"No, no—storking, as I call it. She haunts the side of the river like a crane or a heron," said the red-haired damsel. "I think she would rather land a salmon than go to heaven."

"Georgie," said the young matron, severely, "you are not likely ever to do either; so you needn't be spiteful. Come away and get to work. Mr. Moore, we dine at eight; and, if you are anywhere up or down the strath, you'll hear the bell over the stables rung at seven, and then at half-past."

So they went off and left him; and he was not displeased; he passed out by the front door, lit a cigar, and strolled down towards the banks of the Aivron. It was a bright and sweet-aired afternoon; he was glad to be at the end of his journey; and this was a very charming, if somewhat lonely, stretch of country in which he now found himself. The wide river, the steep hillside beyond hanging in foliage, the valley narrowing in among rocks and then leading away up to those far solitudes of moorland and heather, broken only here and there by a single pine—all these features of the landscape seemed so clear and fine in color; there was no intervening haze; everything was vivid and singularly distinct, and yet aërial and harmonious and retiring of hue. But of course it was the stream—with its glancing lights, its living change and motion, its murmuring, varying voice—that was the chief attraction; and he wandered on by the side of it, noting here and there the long, rippling shallows where the sun struck golden on the sand beneath, watching the oily swirls of the deep black-brown pools as if at any moment he expected to see a salmon leap into the air, and not even uninterested in the calm eddies on the other side, where the smooth water mirrored the yellow-green bank and the bushes and the overhanging birch-trees. He sat down for a while, listening absently to this continuous, soothing murmur, perhaps thinking of the roar of the great city he had left.

He was quite content to be alone; he did not even want Maurice Mangan to be discoursing to him—in those seasons of calm in which questions, long unanswered, perhaps never to be answered, will arise.

Then he rose and went on again, for, from the high-road along which he had driven, he had caught a glimpse of a wilder part of the glen, where the river seemed to come tumbling down a rocky chasm, with some huge boulders in mid-channel; and even now he could hear the distant, muffled roar of the waters. But all of a sudden he stopped. Away along there, and keeping guard (like a stork, as Miss Georgie Lestrange had suggested) above the pool that lay on this side of the double waterfall, was a young lady, her back turned towards him. So far as he could make out, she wasn't doing anything; a long fishing-rod, with the butt on the ground, she held idly in her right hand; while with her left hand she occasionally shaded her face across towards the west—probably, as he imagined, she was waiting for some of those smooth-sailing clouds to come and obscure the too-fierce light of the sun. He knew who she was; this must be Honnor Cunyngham, Lady Adela's sister-in-law; and of course he did not wish to intrude on the young lady's privacy; he would try to pass by behind her unobserved, though here the strath narrowed until it was almost a defile.

He was soon relieved from all anxiety. Sharper eyes than his own had perceived him. The young lady wheeled round; glanced at him for a second; turned again; and then a thin, tall, old man, who had hitherto been invisible to him, rose from his concealment among the rocks close to her and came along the river bank. He was a very handsome old man, this superannuated keeper, with his keen, aquiline nose, his clear, gray eyes, and frosted hair.

"Miss Honnor says will you hef a cast, sir? There's some clouds will be over soon."

"Oh, no, thank you, I could not dream of interrupting her," Lionel said; and then it occurred to him that he ought to go and thank the young lady herself for this frank invitation. "I—I'll go along and tell her so."

As he walked towards her he kept his eye, somewhat furtively, on her, though now she had turned her back again; and all he could make out was that she had a very elegant figure; that she was tall—though not so tall as her three sisters-in-law; and that her abundant brown hair was short and curly and kept close to her head, almost like a boy's. Were not her shoulders a trifle square-set for a woman?—but perhaps that appearance was owing to her costume, for she wore a Norfolk jacket of gray homespun that looked as if it could afford a good defence against the weather. She was entirely in gray, in fact; for her short-skirted dress was of the same material; and so also was the Tam o' Shanter, adorned with salmon flies, that she wore on her shapely head of golden-brown curls. Oh, yes, she looked sufficiently picturesque, standing there against the glow of the western skies, with the long salmon-rod in her right hand; but he was hardly prepared for what followed. The moment that she heard him draw near, she wheeled round and regarded him for a second—regarded him with a glance that rather bewildered him by reason of its transparent honesty and directness. The clear hazel eyes seemed to read him through and through, and yet not to be aware of their own boldness; and he did not know why he was so glad to hear that she had a soft and girlish voice, as she said,

"You are Mr. Moore. I am Lady Adela's sister—of course you know. Won't you take my rod? There will be some shadow very soon, I think."

"Oh, certainly not—certainly not," said he. "But I should be delighted if you would let me stay and look on; it would interest me quite as much—every bit as much."

"Oh, stay by all means," said she, turning to look at the western sky. "But I wish you would take my rod. What are they all about to let you come wandering out alone, on the first day of your arrival?"

"Oh, that's quite right," said he, cheerfully. "Lady Adela and the young ladies are all busy dressmaking."

"Ye may be getting ready, Miss Honnor," old Robert interposed. "There'll be a cloud over the sun directly."

Thus admonished, the tall young fisher-maiden stepped down by the side of a rock overhanging this wide, black-swirling pool, and proceeded to get her tackle in order.

"You know I'll give you my rod whenever you like to take a turn," said she, addressing Lionel even as she was getting the fly on to the water. "But we can't afford to waste a moment of shadow. I have done nothing all day on account of the sunlight."

And now the welcome shade was over, and, after a preliminary cast or two to get the line out, she was sending her fly well across, and letting it drift quietly down the stream, to be recovered by a series of small and gentle jerks. Lionel was supposed to be looking on at the fishing; but, when he dared, he was stealing covert glances at her; for this was one of the most striking faces he had seen for many a day. There was a curiously pronounced personality about her features, refined as they were; her lips were proud—and perhaps a little firmer than usual just now, when she was wielding a seventeen-foot rod; her clear hazel eyes were absolutely fearless; and her broadly marked and somewhat square eyebrows appeared to lend strength rather than gentleness to the intellectual forehead. Then the stateliness of her neck and the set of her head; she seemed to recall to him some proud warrior-maiden out of Scandinavian mythology—though she was dressed in simple homespun and had for her only henchman this quiet old Robert, who, crouching down under a birch-tree, was watching every cast made by his mistress with the intensest interest. And at last Lionel was startled to hear the old man call out, but in an undertone—"Ho!"

Honnor Cunyngham began coolly to pull in her line through the rings.

"What is it?" Lionel asked, in wonder.

"I rose a fish then, but he came short," she said, quietly. "We'll give him a rest. A pretty good one, wasn't he, Robert?"

"Ay, he wass that, Miss Honnor, a good fish. And ye did not touch him?"

"Not at all; he'll come again sure enough."

And then she turned to Lionel? and he was pleased to observe, as she went on to speak to him about her sisters-in-law and their various pursuits, that, proud as those lips were, a sort of grave good-humor seemed to be their habitual expression, and also that those transparently honest, hazel eyes had a very attractive sunniness in them when she was amused.

"The dressmaking," she said. "Of course you know what that is about. They are preparing another of those out-of-door performances. Oh, yes, they are very much in earnest," she went on, with a smile that lightened and sweetened the pronounced character of her face.

"And you are to be entertained this time. They are not going to ask you to do anything. Last time, at Campden Hill, you took a principal part, didn't you?—but this time you are merely to be a guest—a spectator."

"And which are you to be, Miss Cunyngham?" he made bold to ask.

"I? Oh, they never ask me to join in those things," she said, pleasantly enough. "The sacred fire has not descended on me. They say that I regard their performances as mere childish amusement; but I don't really; it isn't for a Philistine like myself to express disdain about anything. But then, you see, if I were to try to join in with my clever sisters, and perhaps when they were most in earnest, I might laugh; and enthusiasts couldn't be expected to like that, could they?"

She spoke very honestly and fairly, he thought, and without showing anything like scorn of what she did not sympathize with; and yet somehow he felt glad that he was not expected to take a part in this new masque.

"From what I remember of it," said he, "I suppose it will be mostly a pageant—there is plenty of patriotic sentiment in it, but hardly any action, as far as I recollect. Of course, I know it chiefly because the poet Thomson wrote it, or partly wrote it, and because he put 'Rule Britannia' into it. Isn't it odd," he added, with a touch of adroit flattery (as he considered), "that the two chief national songs of England, 'Ye Mariners of England' and 'Rule Britannia' should both have been written by Scotchmen?"

She paid no heed to this compliment; indeed he might have known that the old Scotch families (many of them of Norman origin, by the way) have so intermarried with English families that they have very little distinct nationality, though they may be proud enough of their name. This young lady was no more Scotch than himself.

"I will try him again now," said she, with a glance at the water, and forthwith she set to work with rod and line, beginning a few yards farther up the stream, and gradually working down to where she had risen the fish. As she came near the spot, Lionel could see that she was covering every inch of water with the greatest care, and also that at the end of each cast she let the fly hang for a time in the current. He became quite anxious himself. Was she not quite close to the fish now? Or had he caught too clear a glimpse of the fly on the previous occasion, and gone away? Yes, she must be almost over him now; and yet there was no sign. Or past him? Or he might have turned and gone a yard or two farther down? Then, as this eagerly interested spectator was intently watching the swirls of the deep pool, there was a sudden wave on the surface, she struck up her rod slightly, and the next moment away went her line tearing through the water, while the reel screamed out its joyous note of recognition. Old Robert jumped to his feet. At the same instant the fish made another appalling rush, far away on the opposite side of the river, and at the end of it flashed into the air—a swift gleam of purple-blue and silver that revealed his splendid size. Lionel was quite breathless with excitement. He dared not speak to her, for fear of distracting her attention. But she was apparently quite calm; and old Robert looked on without any great solicitude, as if he knew that his young mistress needed neither advice nor assistance. Meanwhile the salmon had come back into the middle of the stream, where it lay deep, only giving evidence of its existence by a series of vicious tugs.

"I don't like that tugging, Robert," she said. "He knows too much. He has pulled himself free from a fly before."

"Ay, ay, I'm afraid of that too," old Robert said, with his keen eyes fixed on every movement of the straining line.

Then the fish lay still and sulked; and she took the opportunity of moving a little bit up-stream and reeling in a yard or two.

"Would you like to take the rod now, Mr. Moore?" she said, generously.

"Oh, certainly not," he exclaimed. "I would not for worlds you should lose the salmon—and do you think I could take the responsibility?"

He ceased speaking, for he saw that her attention had once more been drawn to the salmon, which was now calmly and steadily making up-stream. He watched the slow progress of the line; and then, to his horror, he perceived that the fish was heading for the other side of a large gray rock that stood in mid-channel. If he should persist in boring his way up that farther current, would not he inevitably cut the line on the rock? What could she do? Still nearer and nearer to the big boulder went that white line, steadily cutting through the brown water; and still she said not a word, though Lionel fancied she was now putting on a heavier strain. At last the line was almost touching the stone; and there the salmon lay motionless. He was within half a yard of certain freedom, if only he had known; for the water was far too deep to allow of old Robert wading in and getting the line over the rock. But just as Lionel, far more excited than the fisher-maiden herself, was wondering what was going to happen next, the whole situation of affairs was reversed in a twinkling; the salmon suddenly turned and dashed away down-stream until it was right at the end of the pool, and there, in deep water on the other side, it resumed its determined tugging, so that the pliant top of the rod was shaken as if by a human hand.

"That is what frightens me," she said to Lionel. "I don't like that at all."

But what could he do to help her? Eager wishes were of no avail; and yet he felt as if the crowning joy of his life would be to see that splendid big fish safely out there on the bank. All his faculties seemed to be absorbed in the contemplation of that momentous struggle. The past and the future were alike cut off from him—he had forgotten all about the theatre and its trumpery applause—he had no thought but for the unseen creature underneath the water, that was dashing its head from side to side, and then boring down, and then sailing away over to the opposite shallows, exhausting every manœuvre to regain its liberty. He could not speak to her; what was anything he could say as compared with the tremendous importance of the next movement on the part of the fish? But she was calm enough.

"He doesn't tire himself much, Robert," she said. "He keeps all his strength for that tugging."

But just as she spoke the salmon began to come into mid-stream again, and she stepped a yard or two back, reeling in the line swiftly. Once or twice she looked at the top of the rod: there was a faint strain on, nothing more. Then her enemy seemed inclined to yield a little; she reeled in still more quickly; knot after knot of the casting-line gradually rose from the surface; at last they caught sight of a dull, bronze gleam—the sunlight striking through the brown water on the side of the fish. But he had no intention of giving in yet; he had only come up to look about him. Presently he headed up-stream again—quietly and steadily; then there was another savage shaking of his head and tugging; then a sharp run and plunge; and again he lay deep, jerking to get this unholy thing out of his jaw. Lionel began to wonder that any one should voluntarily and for the sake of amusement undergo this frightful anxiety. He knew that if he had possession of the rod, his hands would be trembling; his breath would be coming short and quick; that a lifetime of hope and fear would be crowded into every minute. And yet here was this girl watching coolly and critically the motion of the line, and showing not the slightest trace of excitement on her finely cut, impressive features. But he noticed that her lips were firm; perhaps she was nerving herself not to betray any concern.

"I think I am getting the better of him, Robert," said she, presently, as the fish began to steer a little in her direction.

"I would step back a bit, Miss Honnor," the keen-visaged old gillie said; but he did not step back; on the contrary, he crouched down by the side of a big boulder, close to the water, and again he tried his gaff, to make sure that the steel clip was firmly fixed in the handle.

"And yet here was this girl watching coolly and critically the motion of the line."

Yes, there was no doubt that the salmon was beaten. He kept coming nearer and nearer to the land, led by the gentle, continuous strain of the pliant top, though ever and anon he would vainly try to head away again into deep water. It was a beautiful thing to look at: this huge, gleaming creature taken captive by an almost invisible line, and gradually yielding to inevitable fate. Joy was in Lionel's heart. If he had wondered that any one, for the sake of amusement, should choose to undergo such agonies of anxiety, he wondered no more. Here was the fierce delight of triumph. The struggle of force against skill was about over; there was no more tugging now; there were no more frantic rushes or bewildering leaps in the air. Slowly, slowly the great fish was being led in to shore. Twice had old Robert warily stretched out his gaff, only to find that the prize was not yet within his reach. And then, just as the young lady with the firm-set lips said, 'Now, Robert!' and just as the gaff was cautiously extended for the third time, the salmon gave a final lurch forward, and the next instant—before Lionel could tell what had happened—the fly was dangling helplessly in the air, and the fish was gone.

"*Au Yeea!*" said Robert, in an undertone, to himself; while Lionel, as soon as he perceived the extent of the catastrophe, felt as though some black horror had fallen over the world. He could not say a word; he seemed yearning to have the fish for one second again where he had lately seen it— and then wouldn't he have gladly jumped into the stream, gaff in hand, to secure the splendid trophy! But now—now there was nothing but emptiness and a lifeless waste of hurrying water.

And as regards the young lady? Well, she smiled—in a disconcerted way, to be sure; and then she said, with apparent resignation,

"I almost expected it. I never do hope to get a tugging salmon; all the way through I was saying to myself we shouldn't land him. However, there's no use fretting over lost fish. We did our best, Robert, didn't we?"

"Indeed you could not hef done better, Miss Honnor," said the old gillie. "There wass no mistake that you made at ahl."

"Very well," said she, cheerfully; and she looked in a kindly way towards the old man. "I did everything right? and as for you, no one will tell me that the best gillie in Ross-shire did anything wrong; so we have nothing to reproach ourselves with, Robert, have we?"

"But it is such a dreadful misfortune!" exclaimed Lionel, who could hardly understand this equanimity. "Another couple of seconds, and you must have had him."

"Well, now, Robert," said she, briskly, "shall we go up and try the tail of the Long Pool? Or go down to the Stones?"

"We'll chist go up to the tail of the Long Pool, Miss Honnor," said he; and he took the rod from her, picked up her waterproof, and set out; while Lionel, without waiting for any further invitation, accompanied her.

And as they walked along, picking their way among boulders and bracken and heather, he was asking her whether the heart-breaking accidents and bitter disappointments of salmon-fishing were not greater than its rewards; as to which she lightly made answer:

"You must come and try. None of the gentlemen here are very eager anglers; I suppose they get enough of salmon-fishing in the spring. Now if you care about it at all, one rod is always enough for two people, and we could arrange it this way—that you should take the pools where wading is necessary. They'll get a pair of waders for you at the lodge. At present old Robert does all the wading that is wanted; but of course I don't care much about playing a fish that has been hooked by somebody else. Now, you would take the wading pools."

"Oh, thank you," said he, "but I'm afraid I should show myself such a duffer. I used to be a pretty fair trout-fisher when I was a lad," he went on to say; and then it suddenly occurred to him that the offer of her companionship ought not to be received in this hesitating fashion. "But I shall be delighted to try my hand, if you will let me; and of course you must see that I don't disturb the best pools."

So they passed up through the narrow gorge, where the heavy volume of water was dashing down in tawny masses between the rocks, and got into the open country again, where the strath broadened out in a wide expanse of moorland. Here the river ran smooth between low banks, bordered now and again by a fringe of birch, and there was a greater quiet prevailing, the farther and farther they got away from the tumbling torrents below. But when they reached the Long Pool no fishing was possible; the afternoon sun struck full on the calm surface of the water; there was not a breath of wind to stir the smooth-mirrored blue and white; they could do nothing but choose out a heathery knoll on the bank, and sit down and wait patiently for a passing cloud.

"I suppose," said she, clasping her fingers together in her lap—"I suppose you are all eagerness about to-morrow morning?"

"Oh, I am not going shooting to-morrow," said he.

"What!" she exclaimed. "To be on a grouse-moor on the Twelfth, and not go out?"

"It is because it is the Twelfth; I don't want to spoil sport," said he, modestly. "And I don't want to make a fool of myself either. If I could shoot well enough, and if there were a place for me, I should be glad to go out with them; but my shooting is, like my fishing, a relic of boyhood's days; and I should not like to make an exhibition of myself before a lot of crack shots."

"That is only false pride", said she, in her curiously direct, straightforward way. "Why should you be ashamed to admit that there are certain things you can't do as well as you can do certain other things? There is no particular virtue in having been brought up to the use of a gun or rod. Take your own case. You are at home on the stage. There you know everything—you are the master, the proficient. But take the crack shots and put them on the stage, and ask them to do the simplest thing—then it is their turn to be helpless, not to say ridiculous."

"Perhaps," said he, rather tentatively, "you mean that we should all of us keep to our own walks in life?"

"I'm sure I don't mean anything of the kind," said she, with much frankness. "I only mean that if you are not a first-rate shot, you need not be ashamed of it; you should remember there are other things you can do well. And really you must go out to-morrow morning. My brother was talking about it at breakfast; and I believe the proposal is that you go with him and Captain Waveney. If any little mistake is made, Captain Waveney is the man to retrieve it—at least so I've heard them say."

"At all events," said he, "if I go with them at all, it will not be under false pretences. I shall warn them, to begin with, that I am a bad shot; then I can't be found out. And they must put me in a position where I can't do much harm."

"I dare say you shoot very well," she said, with a smile. "Gentlemen always talk like that on the evening before the Twelfth, if they have come to a strange moor."

But now she had risen again, for a breath of wind was stirring along the strath, while some higher air-currents were slowly bringing certain fleecy clouds across from the west. As soon as the welcome shade had stolen over the river, she began to cast; and on this smooth water he could see more clearly what an excellent line this was that she sent out. Not a long line—perhaps twenty-three or twenty-four yards—but thrown most admirably, the fly lighting on the surface like a snowflake. Moreover, he was now a little bit behind her, so that he could with impunity regard the appearance of this newly-found companion—her lithe and agile form, the proud set of her neck and head, the beautiful close masses of her curly, golden-brown hair, and the fine contour of her sun-tanned cheek. Then the vigorous exercise in which she was engaged revealed all the suppleness and harmonious proportions of her figure; for here was no pretty wrist-work of trout-fishing, but the wielding of a double-handed salmon-rod; and she had taught herself the gillies' method of casting—that is to say, she made the backward cast by throwing both arms right up in the air, so that, as she paused to let the line straighten out behind, her one hand was on a level with her forehead, and the other more than a foot above that. Lionel thought that before he tried casting in the presence of Miss Honnor Cunyngham, he should like to get a few quiet lessons from old Robert.

However, all this expenditure of skill proved to be of no avail. She could not move a fin; nor had Robert any better luck, when, they having come to a shallow reach, she allowed the old man, who was encased in waders, to get into the water and fish along the opposite bank. When he came ashore again, his young mistress said,

"Dame Fortune hasn't forgiven us for letting that first one go." And old Robert, who had probably never heard of Dame Fortune (or may have considered the phrase a polite and young-lady-like form of swearing), merely made answer,

"Ay, Miss Honnor, we'll go and try the Small Pool, now."

The Small Pool lies between the Long Pool and the Rock Pool; it is a circular, deep, black hole, in which the waters collect before dashing and roaring down between the great gray boulders; and to fish it you must get out on certain knife-like ledges that seem to offer anything but a secure foothold. However, Miss Honnor did not think twice about it; and, indeed, as she made her way out on those narrow slips of rock, Lionel perceived that her boots, which were laced in front like men's boots, if they were small enough as regarded that portion covering the foot, were provided with most sensibly wide soles, which, again were studded with nails. And there, balancing herself as best she might, she got out a short line, and began industriously to cover every inch of the surging and whirling water. A most likely-looking place, Lionel thought to himself, as he sat and looked on. But here also they were doomed to disappointment. It is true she hooked a small sea-trout—and was heartily glad when it shook itself free, thereby saving her time and trouble. All the rest of her labor was expended for nothing; so finally she had to reel up and make her way ashore, where she surrendered her rod to the old gillie.

Then they passed down through the narrow defile again and came in view of the wide path—now all saffron-tinted in the evening sunlight—with the lodge and its straggling dependencies in the midst of the plain. Perhaps it was this sight of the house that recalled to her what they had been talking of some time before; for, as they walked along the river-bank, she was again urging him to go out on the following morning; and not only that, but she declared he must have one or two days' deer-stalking while he was in the North. If he missed, then he missed; why should he care what foresters and gillies thought of him? Of course he was very grateful to her for all her kind patronage; but he could not help thinking it rather odd to find a woman lending courage to a man—counselling him to be independent and to have no fear of ridicule.

"I recollect," he said to her, "once hearing Lord Rockminster say that until a man has gone deer-stalking he can have no idea what extremes of misery a human being is capable of enduring."

"Lord Rockminster is incurably lazy," she said. "I think if you found yourself riding along this strath some night about eight or nine o'clock, knowing that away up among the hills you had left a stag of ten or twelve points to be sent for and brought down the next morning—then I think you wouldn't be reflecting on the discomforts you had gone through, or, if you did, it would be with pride. Why," said she, "you surely didn't come to the Highlands to play at private theatricals?"

"I get enough of the theatre in the South," he said, "as you may well imagine."

But here was a bend of the river sheltered from the weltering sun by a steep and wooded hill; and Miss Cunyngham, at old Robert's suggestion, began work again. It was really most interesting to watch this graceful casting; Lionel, sitting down on the heather and smoking a cigarette, seemed to want no other occupation; he forgot what the object of throwing a fly was, the throwing of the fly seemed to be enough in itself. He had grown to think that all these oily sweeps of brown water, touched here and there by dark, olive-green reflections, were useful only as showing where the fly dropped; there was no fish watching the slow jerking of the "Bishop" across the current; the one salmon that haunted the Rock Pool had put in an appearance and gone away long ago. But suddenly there was a short, sharp scream of the reel; then silence.

"What is it, Robert?" she said—apparently holding on to something. "Another sea-trout?"

"Oh, no, Miss Honnor, I am not thinking that—"

The words were hardly out of his mouth when it became abundantly clear that the unknown creature in the deeps had not the least intention of concealing his identity. A sudden rush down-stream, followed by a wild splashing and thrashing on the surface, was only the first of a series of performances that left Miss Honnor not one single moment of breathing-space. Either she was following him rapidly down the river, or following him up again, or reeling in swiftly as he came sailing towards her, or again she could only stand in breathless suspense as he flung himself into the air and then beat and churned the water, shaking the line this way and that.

"Oh, you wicked little wretch!" she cried, at a particularly vicious flourish out of the water; but this was the kind of fish she liked; this was a fish that fought fair—a gentlemanly fish, without the thought of a sulk in him—a very Prince Rupert even among grilse; this was no malevolent, underhand, deep-boring tugger. Indeed, these brilliant dashes and runs and summersaults soon began to tell The gallant little grilse was plainly getting the worst of it. He allowed himself to be led; but, whenever she stepped back on the bank and tried to induce him to come in, at the first appearance of shallow water he would instantly sheer off again with all the strength that was left in him. Fortunately he seemed inclined to head up-stream; and she humored him in that, for there the water was deeper under the bank. Even then he fought splendidly to the last. As soon as he got to recognize that an enemy was waiting for him—an enemy armed with some white, shining thing that he more than once warily slipped out of—he would make struggle after struggle to keep away—until at last there was a sudden, swift, decisive stroke of the steel clip, and Robert had his glittering prize safely ashore.

"What o'clock is it, Mr. Moore?" said Miss Honnor—but she seemed pleased with the result of this brisk encounter.

He looked at his watch.

"Half-past seven," he said.

"Yes; I thought I heard the first bell; we must make haste home. Not but that my sisters are very good to me," she continued, as she took the fly that Robert handed her and stuck it in her Tam o' Shanter; "if I happen to have got hold of a fish, I am allowed to come in to dinner anyhow. And then, you know, there is no great ceremony at this bungalow of a place; it's different at the Braes, if Lady Adela happens to have a large house-party—then I have to behave like other folk. What do you say, Robert—seven pounds? Well, he made a good fight of it. And I'm glad not to be going home empty-handed."

So Lionel picked up her waterproof and put it over his arm; she shouldered her fishing-rod, after having reeled in the line; the handsome old gillie brought up the rear with the gaff and the slung grilse; and thus equipped the three of them set out for the lodge—across the wide valley that was now all russet and golden under the warm light still lingering in the evening skies.

CHAPTER VIII.

THE TWELFTH.

When Lionel went down early next morning, he found Lady Adela's father in sole possession; and was not long in discovering that the old earl was in a towering rage.

"Good-morning!" said this tall, pale, stooping-shouldered old gentleman, whose quite hairless face was surmounted by a brown wig. "Well, what do you think of last night's performance? What do you think of it? Did you ever know of any such gross outrage on common decency? Why, God bless my soul and body, I never heard of such a thing!"

Lionel knew quite well what he meant. The fact was that a Free Church minister whom Sir Hugh Cunyngham had met somewhere had called at Aivron Lodge; as the custom of that part of the country is, he was invited to stay to dinner; he sat late, told many stories, and drank a good deal of whiskey, until it was not judged prudent to let him try to get his pony across the ford, even if hospitality had not demanded that he should be offered a room for the night; and then, when every one was thinking of getting away to bed, the worthy man must needs insist on having family worship, to which the servants had also to be summoned. It was the inordinate length of this service at such a time of night that had driven old Lord Fareborough to the verge of madness.

"Look at me!" he said to Lionel, in tones of deep and bitter indignation. "Look at me—a skeleton—a wreck of a human being, who can only get along by the most careful nursing of his nervous system. My heart is affected; I have serious doubts about the state of my lungs? it is only through the most assiduous nursing of my nerves that I exist at all. And what is more maddening than enforced restraint—imprisonment—no chance of leaving the room, with all those strange servants at the door; why, God bless my soul, I call it an outrage! I yield to no one in respect for the cloth, whether it is worn by a Presbyterian, or a Catholic, or one of my own church; but I say that no one has a right to thrust religious services down my throat! What the devil did Cunyngham mean by asking him to stay to dinner at all?"

"As I understand it," said Lionel, with a becoming diffidence, "it was some suggestion of Captain Waveney's. He said the Free Church ministers were particular friends of the crofters—and of course the good-will of the crofters is of importance to a shooting-tenant—"

"The good-will of the crofters!" the bewigged old nobleman broke in, impatiently. "Are you aware, sir, that the Strathaivron Branch of the Land League met last week and passed a resolution declaring salmon to be ground-game? What are you to do with people like that? How are you to reason with them? What is the use of pacifying them? They are in the hands of violent and malevolent revolutionaries—it is war they want—it is 1789 they want—it is plunder and robbery and confiscation they want—and the right of every man to live idle at the cost of the state! Why, God bless my soul! the idea that you are to try to pacify these ignorant savages—"

But here Lionel, who began to fancy that he had discovered another Octavius Quirk, was afforded relief; for the minister himself appeared; and at the very sight of him Lord Fareborough indignantly quitted the room. The minister, who was a rather irascible-looking little man with a weather-reddened face and rusty whiskers, inquired of Lionel whether it was possible to procure a glass of milk; but when Lionel rang the bell and had some brought for him, the minister observed that milk by itself was a dangerous thing in the morning; whereupon the butler had to be sent for, who produced the spirit-decanter; and then, and finally, the minister, boldly discarding the milk altogether, poured out for himself a good solid dram, and drank it off with much evident satisfaction.

Now the ladies began to make their appearance, some of them going along to the gun-room to hear what the head keeper had to say, others of them trooping out by the front door to guess at the weather. Among the latter was Miss Honnor Cunyngham; and Lionel, who had followed her, went up to her.

"A beautiful morning, isn't it?" he said.

"I'm afraid it's too beautiful," said she, in reply. "Look up there."

And she was right. This was far too picturesque and vivid a morning to portend well for a shooting-day. Down at the farther end of the strath, the skies were banked up with dark and heavy clouds; the lake-like sweep of the river was of a sombre and livid blue; and between the indigo stream and the purple skies, a long neck of land, catching the sunlight, burned the most brilliant gold. And even as they stood and looked, a faint gray veil gradually interposed between them and the distant landscape; a rainbow slowly formed, spanning the broad valley; and then behind the fairy curtain of the shower they could see the yellow river-banks, and the birchwoods, and the farther-stretching hills all vaguely and spectrally shining in the sun.

"But this is a very peculiar glen," said she. "It often threatens like that when it means nothing. You may get a perfectly dry, still day after all. And, Mr.

Moore, may I ask you if what you said about your shooting yesterday afternoon was entirely true or only a bit of modesty?"

"If it comes to that," he said, "I never shot a grouse in my life—no, nor ever shot *at* one."

"Because," she continued, with a certain hesitation which was indeed far removed from her usual manner, "because you—you seem rather sensitive to criticism—to other people's opinion—and if you wouldn't think it impertinent of me to offer you some hints—well, for what they are worth—"

"But I should be immensely grateful!" he answered at once.

"Well," she said, in an undertone, so that no one should overhear, "you know, on the Twelfth, with such still weather as we have had for the last week or two, the birds are never wild; you needn't be in the least anxious; you won't be called upon for snap-shots at all; you can afford to take plenty of time and get well on to the birds before you fire. You see, you will be in the middle; you will take any bird that gets up in front of you; my brother and Captain Waveney will take the outside ones and the awkward cross-shots. And if a covey gets up all at once, they won't expect you to pick out the old cock first; they'll do all that; in fact, you must put yourself at your ease, and not be anxious, and everything will be right."

"Honnor!" called Lady Adela, "Come away at once—breakfast is in." So that Lionel had no proper opportunity of thanking the young lady for her friendly counsel and the interest she took in his small affairs.

Breakfast was a merry meal; for, as soon as the things had been brought in, the servants were allowed to leave; and while Lady Adela poured out the tea and coffee, the gentlemen carved for themselves at the sideboard or handed round the dishes at table. The Rev. Mr. MacNachten, the little Free Church minister, was especially vivacious and humorous, abounding with facetious anecdotes and jests and personal reminiscences; until, observing that breakfast was over, he composed his countenance and proceeded to return thanks. The grace (in spite of Lord Fareborough's nervous qualms) was comparatively a short one; and at the end of it they all rose and were for going their several ways.

But this was not to the minister's mind.

"Your leddyship," said he, addressing his hostess in impressive tones, "it would be ill done of us to be assembled on such an occasion without endeavoring to make profitable use of it. I propose to say a few words in season, if ye will have the kindness to call in the servants."

Lady Adela glanced towards her husband with some apprehension on her face (for she knew the importance attached to the morning of the Twelfth); but whatever Sir Hugh may have thought, he made no sign. Accordingly there was nothing for it but that she should ring the bell and summon the whole household; and in a few minutes the door of the room was surrounded by a group of Highland women-servants and gillies, the English servants rather hanging back in the hall. The breakfast-party had resumed their seats; but the minister remained standing; and presently, when perfect silence had been secured, he lifted up his voice in prayer.

Well, it was a sufficiently earnest prayer, and it was listened to with profound attention by the smart-looking lasses and tall and swarthy gillies clustering about the door; but to the English part of his audience its chief features were its curiously exhortatory and argumentative character and also its interminable length. As the minister went on and on, the frown of impatience on Lord Fareborough's face deepened and deepened; he fretted and fumed and fidgeted; but, of course, he could not bring disgrace on his son-in-law's house by rising and leaving the room. Nor did it convey much consolation to the sportsmen to hear the heavy tramp of the head keeper just outside the windows; for they knew that Roderick must be making use of the most frightful language over this unheard-of delay.

But at last this tremendous oration—for it was far more of an oration than a prayer—came to an end; and the congregation drew a long breath and were about to seize their newly found liberty when the minister quietly remarked:

"We will now sing the Hundred and Twenty-First Psalm."

"God bless my soul!" exclaimed Lord Fareborough, aloud; and Lady Adela flushed quickly; for it was not seemly of her father to give way to such anger before those keen-eyed and keen-eared Highland servants.

However, the Rev. Mr. MacNachten took no heed. He began to sing, in a slow and raucous fashion, and to the melancholy tune of "Ballerma,"

"'I to the hills will lift mine eyes,

From whence doth come mine aid;'"

and presently there came from the door a curious nasal wail, men and women singing in unison, and seemingly afraid to trust their voices. As for the people in the room no one tried to join in this part of the service—no one except Honnor Cunyngham, who appeared to know the words of the Psalm and the music equally well, for she accompanied the minister throughout, singing boldly and simply and without shyness, her clear voice making marked contrast with his raven notes. Nor was this all; for, when the Psalm was finished, the minister said,

"My friends, when it hath pleased the Lord that we should meet together, we should commune one with another, to the perfecting of ourselves for that greater assemblage to which I hope we are all bound." And then, without further preface, he proceeded to exhort them to well-doing in all the duties of life—as masters and mistresses, as servants, as parents, as children, as brothers, as fellow-Christians; while at the end of each rambling and emphatic passage there came in a verse from Ecclesiastes: "Let us hear the conclusion of the whole matter: Fear God, and keep his commandments: for this is the whole duty of man."

Alas! there was no conclusion to this matter. The little, violent-faced minister warmed to his work, insomuch that several times he used a Gaelic phrase the better to impress those patient listeners at the door, while he paid less and less attention to the congregation in the room. Indeed, the hopeless resignation that had at first settled down on some of their faces had given place to a most obvious resentment; but what did that matter to Mr. MacNachten, who was not looking their way? Again and again Sir Hugh Cunyngham forlornly pulled out his watch, but the hint was not taken. Lord Fareborough was beside himself with unrest; he drummed his fingers on the table-cloth; he crossed one leg, and then the other; while more than once he made a noise between his tongue and his teeth, which fortunately could not be heard far amid the rolling periods of the sermon. Captain Waveney, who was master of the ceremonies in all that concerned the shooting—even as he was Sir Hugh's right-hand man in the matter of cattle-breeding at the Braes—on several occasions, when a momentary pause occurred, jumped to his feet as if on the assumption that the discourse was finished; but this ruse was quite ineffectual, for the preacher took no notice of him. And meanwhile the huge figure of Roderick Munro could be seen marching up and down outside the windows, while a pair of wrathful eyes glared in from time to time; and Lady Adela, noticing these baleful glances, began to hope that the irate head keeper would not secretly instruct a gillie to go and throw the minister into the river as he was crossing the ford on his way home.

"May God forgive the scoundrel!" cried Lord Fareborough, when, the long sermon at length being over and the small crowd allowed to disperse, he was free to hasten along to the gun-room to get his boots. "And I am expected to shoot after having my nerves tortured like this! Who are going with me? Rockminster and Lestrange? Well, they must understand that I will not be hurried and flurried—I say I will not be hurried and flurried. I don't want to fall down dead—my heart won't recover this morning's work for months to come? God bless my soul, who asked that insolent scoundrel to stay the night? And what's that, Waveney—the ladies coming out to lunch? The ladies coming out to lunch on the Twelfth—and the day half over; they must be out of their senses!"

"That is the arrangement," Captain Waveney said, with rather a rueful laugh, as he, too, was lacing up his boots. "Lady Rosamund is going to take a sketch of the luncheon-party."

"Let her take a sketch of the devil!" said this very angry and inconsiderate papa. "Why can't she do it some other day?—why the Twelfth? Good heavens! is everything conspiring to vex and annoy me so that I sha'n't be able to hit a haystack?"

"Sir Hugh never says 'no' to anything that Lady Rosamund asks," observed Captain Waveney, with much good-humor.

"Sir Hugh be—" And here Lord Fareborough expressed a wish about his son-in-law and host that was probably only a figure of speech.

"Well, I don't know about that," the other replied, complacently, as he went to the couch and removed the cloth laid over the guns to protect them from the fine peat-dust (for a huge peat-fire burned continuously in this great gun-room, for the drying of garments brought home wet from the shooting or fishing). "I don't know about that; but at present the arrangement is that we lunch at the top of the Bad Step; and I believe that Miss Cunyngham is coming back from the Junction Pool, so that Lady Rosamund may have her sketch complete."

Indeed, this untoward incident of the minister's misplaced zeal seemed to throw a certain gloom over the small party to which Lionel soon found himself attached, as it moved away from the house. The tall, brown-bearded head keeper was in a sullen rage, though he could only reveal his wrath in sharp little sentences of discontent. Sir Hugh had also been put out at losing the best part of the morning; and Captain Waveney, who was a dapper little man, full of brisk spirits, did not care to talk to silent persons. As for Lionel, he was certainly very nervous and anxious; but none the less resolved to remember and act upon Honnor Cunyngham's advice. The tail of the procession was brought up by a gillie leading, or rather holding in, two brace of remarkably handsome Gordon setters, and another gillie in charge of a patient-eyed pony with a couple of panniers slung over its back.

However, the busy work of the day soon banished these idle regrets. When they had climbed a bit of the hillside, and passed through a gate in a rude stone wall, they stopped for a second to put cartridges in their guns; the keeper had two of the dogs uncoupled; while the gillie, putting a strap on the coupling of the other two, led them away to a convenient knoll, where he lay down, the gillie with the pony following his example. And scarcely had the two dogs begun to work this open bit of moorland when one of them suddenly ceased its wide ranging—suddenly as if it had been turned to stone; and then slowly, slowly it began to draw forward, its companion, a younger dog, backing beautifully and looking on with startled, watchful eyes. It was an anxious moment for the famous young baritone of the New Theatre; for the dog was right in front of him; and as the three guns, in line, stealthily moved forward, he made sure that this bird was going to get up just before him. Despite all his resolve to be perfectly cool and calm, his heart was beating quickly; and again and again he was repeating to himself Honnor Cunyngham's counsel, and wondering whether he would disgrace himself at the very outset, when some bewildering brown thing sprang from the ground, there was a terrific whir, a crack from Captain Waveney's gun—and away along there the grouse came tumbling down into the heather. Almost at the same moment there was another appalling whir on his right—followed by a bang from Sir Hugh's gun—and another bird fell headlong. After the briefest pause for reloading, the setter, that had obediently dropped at the first shot, was encouraged to go forward, the guns warily following. But it turned out that this had been an outlying brace of birds; the dogs were soon ranging freely again; Roderick picked up the slain grouse, and the whole party went on.

"Sorry you didn't get the first shot, Mr. Moore," said Sir Hugh, who was a short, thick-set man, with a fresh-colored face, iron-gray hair, and keen, light-blue eyes.

"I wish the birds would all rise to you two," Lionel said. "Then I shouldn't have to pitch into myself for missing."

"Oh, you'll soon get into the way of it," Sir Hugh said, good-naturedly. "There's never much doing along this face."

"I'll bet Bruce is on to something," Captain Waveney exclaimed, suddenly. In fact, only one of the ranging setters was now in sight; and Roderick had quickly run up to the top of a heathery knoll, to have them both in view. At the same moment they saw him hold up his arm to warn the inattentive Venus.

"How, Venus! How, Venus!" he called, in a low voice; and immediately the dog, observing that its companion was drawing on to a point, became rigid.

The guns were on the scene directly; and they were just in time; for, with a simultaneous rattle of wings that seemed to fill the air, a small covey of birds sprang from the heather and appeared to vanish into space. At least Lionel saw nothing of the others; his attention was concentrated on one that seemed to be flying away in a straight line from him; and after pausing for half a second (during which he was calling on himself to be cool) he pulled the trigger. To his inexpressible satisfaction the bird stopped in mid-air and came down with a thump on the heather, where it gave but one flutter and then lay still. He turned to see what his companions had done, with their brisk fusillade. But he could not make out. They were still watching the setter, that was again being encouraged to go on, lest a stray bird or two might still be in hiding. However, the quest was fruitless. The whole of the small covey had risen simultaneously. So Roderick picked up the dead birds and put them on a conspicuous stone, at the same time signalling to the gillie with the pony, who was slowly coming up. Then the shooting-party went forward again.

"How many birds rose then?" Lionel asked of his host.

"Five."

"And you got them all?" he said, judging by what he had seen the head keeper pick up.

"Oh, yes, we got them all. They spread out like a fan. Waveney got one brace and I another. I suppose," he added, with a smile, "you were too intent on your own bird to notice?"

"Yes, I was," he said, honestly; but he was none the less elated, for he knew that a good beginning would give him confidence.

And it did. They were soon at a part of the moor where the fun grew fast and furious; and, keeping as close as he could to certainties, or what looked like certainties, he was doing fairly well. As for the other two, he could only judge of their prowess by the birds the keeper picked up; for he kept strictly to his own business and rarely adventured on a second shot. But it was clear that both Sir Hugh and Captain Waveney were highly pleased with the way things were going. There were plenty of birds; they lay well; the dogs were working beautifully; and the bag was mounting up at a rate that promised to atone for the delay of the morning. In fact, they were now disposed to regard that episode as rather a comical affair.

"I say, Waveney," Sir Hugh remarked, as they paused for a moment to have a sip of cold tea, for the day was hot, "you'd better confess it; you put up the old minister to give us that frightfully long service this morning. It was a joke on Lord Fareborough—now, wasn't it?"

"It may have been; but I had nothing to do with it, anyway," was the answer. "Not I. Too serious a joke. I thought his lordship was going to have a fit of apoplexy when he came into the gun-room."

"My good fellow, don't talk like that!" the other exclaimed. "If you mention apoplexy to him, he'll add that on to the hundred and twenty diseases and dangers that threaten his life every moment. Apoplexy! What has he got already?—gout, asthma, heart disease, his lungs giving way, his liver in a frightful condition, his nervous system gone to bits—and yet, all the same, the old hypocrite is going to try for a stag before he leaves. I suppose he'll want Roderick to carry him as soon as he quits the pony! Well, come along, Mr. Moore; we've done pretty well so far, I think."

But it was not Lionel who needed any incitement to go forward; he was far more eager than any of his companions, now that he had been acquitting himself none so ill. Moreover, he had youth on his side and a sound chest, while nature had not given him a pair of well-formed calves for nothing; so that he faced the steep hillsides or got over the rough ground with comparative ease, rejoicing the while in the unwonted freedom of knickerbockers. It was Sir Hugh, with his bulky habit of body, who got blown now and again; as for Captain Waveney, he was a pretty tough subject and wiry. So they fought bravely on, to atone for the inhuman detention of the morning; and by the time it was necessary to make for the appointed luncheon rendezvous they had the wherewithal to give a very excellent account of themselves.

Now, several times during the morning they had come in view of the Aivron, winding far below them through the wide strath, or narrowing to a thread as it rose towards the high horizon-line in the west; and always, when there was a momentary chance, Lionel's eye had sought these distant sweeps and bends for some glimpse of the lonely angler-maiden, and sought in vain. The long valley seemed empty; and some little feeling of shyness prevented his asking his companions to point out the Junction Pool, whither, as he understood, she had been bound in the morning. And as they now approached the appointed place of meeting, he was quite disturbed by the fancy that she might have strayed away into unknown regions and be absent from this general picnic; and the moment they came in sight of the group of people who were strolling about, or looking on while the servants spread out the table-cloth on the heather and brought forth the various viands, one swift glance told him she was not present. Here was a disappointment! He wanted to tell her how he had got on, under her kind instruction—this was his own explanation of the pang her absence caused him; but presently he had found another; for Lady Rosamund was grouping the people for her sketch; and what would the sketch be without Honnor Cunyngham in it? He made bold to say so.

"Oh, you can't depend on Honnor," Lady Adela said. "She may have risen a fish, or may have got hold of one. But if you want to know whether she is likely to turn up, you might go out to that point, Mr. Moore, and then you'll be able to see whether she is coming anywhere near the Bad Step."

Willingly enough he went down through the scattered birch-trees to a projecting point overlooking the river from a very considerable height; and there, right below him, he discovered what it was they called the Bad Step. The precipice on which he stood going sheer down into the Aivron, the path along the stream left the banks some distance off, came up to where he stood, and then descended again by a deep gorge probably cut by water-power through the slaty rock. And even as he was regarding this twilit chasm it suddenly appeared to him that there were two figures away down there, crossing the burn at the foot; and then one of them, in gray—unmistakably the fisher-maiden herself—began the ascent. How she managed to obtain a footing he could not make out; for the path was no path, but merely a zig-zag track on the surface of the loose shingle—shingle so loose that he could see it yield to her every step, while the débris rolled away down to the bed of the burn. But still she fought her way upward, and at last she stood face to face with him, smiling, but a little breathless.

"That's a frightful place to come up," said he.

"Oh, it's nothing, when you know it," she said, lightly. "Tell me, how did you get on this morning?"

"Thanks to you, I think I did pretty well," said he.

"I'm awfully glad of that," said she; and the soft, clear hazel eyes repeated her words in their own transparent way.

"I remembered all your instructions," he continued (and he was in no hurry that Miss Cunyngham should go on to the luncheon-party; while old Robert stood patiently by). "And I was very fortunate in getting easy shots. Then when I did miss, either Sir Hugh or Captain Waveney was sure to get the bird? I never saw such smart shooting."

"What have you done?"

"Altogether?"

"Yes."

"I don't know. The panniers are being emptied, to make a show for Lady Rosamund's sketch. I fancy there are close on sixty brace of grouse, with some blue hares and a snipe and a wild duck."

"What has Lord Fareborough's party done?"

"I don't know? they have just shown up—so you needn't hurry on unless you are hungry."

"But I am—very hungry," said she, with a laugh. "I have been hard at work all the morning."

"Oh, in that case," he said, eagerly, "by all means come along, and I'll get you something at once. You and I needn't wait for the emptying of the other panniers. Oh, yes, that will do first-rate; I'm a duffer at shooting, you know, Miss Cunyngham, but I'm a splendid forager at a picnic. Let me carry the gaff for you."

"Oh, no, thank you," she said, "I merely use it as a walking-stick coming up the Bad Step."

"And there," he exclaimed, as they went on through the birch-wood, "look at the selfishness of men! You ask all about my shooting; but I never asked what luck you had with your fishing."

"Well, I've had rather bad luck," she said, simply. "I lost a fish in the Geinig Pool, after having him on for about five minutes, and I rose another in the Horse-Shoe Pool and couldn't get him to come again all I could do. But I mean to call upon him in the afternoon."

A sudden inspiration flashed into his brain.

"I should like to come and see you try for him," he said, quickly. "I suppose they wouldn't mind my sending home my gun?"

"Mr. Moore!" she said, with her eyes downcast. "They'd think you were mad to leave a shooting-party on the Twelfth. You can see a salmon caught, or catch one yourself, any time."

He felt a little bit snubbed, he hardly knew why; but of course she knew what was right in all such things; and so he humbly acquiesced. Indeed, he could not contest the point, for now they had come upon the picnic-party, where luncheon was in full swing. Lord Fareborough had declared on his arrival that he would not wait for the completion of his daughter's sketch; his nervous system was not to be tried in any such fashion; luncheon must be proceeded with at once, and Lady Rosamund could make her drawing when the gentlemen were smoking afterwards. Lady Adela wanted to wait for Mr. Moore, but she, too, was overruled by the impatient hypochondriac. So Lionel set to work to form a seat for Miss Honnor, out of some bracken that the gillies had cut and brought along; and also he exclusively looked after her—to Miss Georgie Lestrange's chagrin; for Lord Rockminster was too lazy to attend to any one but himself, and what girl likes being waited on by her brother when other young men are about?

And now the burly and broad-shouldered host of all these people called on them to unanimously forgive the minister for the injury he had unintentionally done them in the morning.

"It wasn't the good man's fault at all; it was Waveney's," Sir Hugh continued, as he got hold of a spoon and delved it into a pigeon-pie. "I assure you it was a practical joke that Captain Waveney played upon the whole of you. He gave the minister a little hint—and the thing was done."

Lord Fareborough glared at the culprit as if he expected to see the heavens fall upon him; but Lady Adela observed, with a touch of dignity,

"I hope I know Captain Waveney well enough not to believe that he would turn any religious service into a practical joke."

"I hope so, too, Lady Adela," the dapper little captain instantly replied, though without any great embarrassment. "That's hardly my line of country. But there's another thing: Sir Hugh may ask you to believe anything, but he won't make you believe that I could trifle with such a sacred subject as the morning of the Twelfth."

"Faith, you're right there, Waveney," Sir Hugh said, with a laugh. "Well, we've done our best to make up for the loss of time. And now, Rose, if you want to have your sketch, fire away! I'm going to light a pipe; but, mind, we sha'n't stop here very long. You'd better put in us men at once; and then you can draw in the ladies and the game and the luncheon at your leisure."

"And if you want me, Rose," Honnor Cunyngham said, "please put me in at once, too; for I'm going away back to the Horseshoe Pool."

"My dear child," Lady Adela protested, "you'll break your neck some day going down that Bad Step. I really think Hugh should have a windlass at the top and let people down by a rope. Now look alive, Rose, and get your sketch begun; I can see the gentlemen are all impatient to be off. And mind you have Mr. Moore rolling up a cigarette: it won't be natural otherwise."

She was right about one thing, anyway; the sportsmen were undoubtedly impatient to be off; and it is to be feared that Lady Rosamund's sketch suffered by the restlessness of her models. Indeed, after a very little while, Lord Fareborough indignantly rose, and declared he never had known a Twelfth of August so shamelessly sacrificed. He, for one, would have no more of it. He called to the under-keeper to bring along the gillies and the dogs; whereupon Lady Rosamund, who had a temper not quite in consonance with the calm and statuesque beauty of her features, closed her sketch-book and threw it aside, saying she would make the drawing some other day when she found the gentlemen a little more considerate.

And soon Lionel and his two companions were at their brisk occupation again; though ever and anon his thoughts would go wandering away to the Horseshoe Pool, and his fancy was picturing the fisher-maiden on the summit of a great gray boulder, while a fifteen-pounder raced and chased in the black deeps below. Sometimes he tried to get a glimpse of the upper stretches of the river; but this was a dangerous trick when all his attention was demanded by the work on hand. In any case his scrutiny of those far regions was unavailing; for the Horseshoe Pool is on the Geinig, a tributary of the Aivron, and not visible from the hill-slopes along which they were now shooting.

The bag mounted up steadily; for the afternoon, despite the threats of the morning, remained fine and clear and still; the birds lay close, and the two outside guns were skilful performers. As for Lionel, he had now acquired a certain confidence; he took no shame that he reserved for himself the easy shots; the nasty ones he could safely leave to his companions. At last, as they came in sight of a lovely little tarn lying under a distant hillock, and could descry two small dots floating on the surface of the water, Sir Hugh said to his head keeper,

"See here, Roderick, are those duck or mergansers?"

The keeper took a long look before he made reply.

"I'm not sure, Sir Hugh, but I am thinking they are mergansers, for I was seeing two or three lately."

"Very well, call in the dogs. I'm going to sit down and have a pipe. I suppose you'll do the same, Mr. Moore—though I must say this for you that you can walk. You have the advantage of youth, and you haven't as much to carry as I have. Well, I propose we have a few minutes' rest? and we will occupy ourselves in watching Waveney stalk those mergansers. There's a job for you, Waveney. They are the most detestable birds alive to have near a forest or a salmon-stream."

"Why, what harm can they do to the salmon?" Lionel asked, as he saw Captain Waveney at once change the cartridges in his gun for No. 4's and set off down the hillside.

"They snap up the parr, of course," said his heavy-shouldered host, as he drew out a wooden pipe and a pouch of black Cavendish, "but that isn't the worst: they disturb the pools most abominably—swimming about under water they frighten the salmon out of their senses. But when you get them about a deer-forest they are a still more intolerable nuisance; you are never safe; just as you are getting up to the stag, creeping along the course of a burn, perhaps, bang! goes one of those brutes like a sky-rocket, and the whole herd are instantly on the alert. Oh, that's a job old Waveney likes well enough; and it will give the dogs a rest as well as ourselves."

By this time the stalker had got out of sight. He was making a considerable detour, so as to get round by the back of the hillock unobserved; and when he came into view again, he was on the other side of the valley. The mergansers, if they were mergansers, were still swimming about unsuspectingly, though sometimes at a considerable distance apart.

"Does Miss Cunyngham shoot as well as fish?" Lionel ventured to ask.

"She has tried it," her brother said, as he called up Roderick and gave him a dram out of his capacious flask. "And I think she might shoot very well, but she doesn't care about it. It is too violent, she says. The sudden bang disturbs the charm of the scenery—something of that kind—I'm not up in these things; but she's an odd kind of girl. Tremendously fond of quietude and solitude; we've found her in the most unexpected places—and there *are* some lonely places about these hills. I tell her she shouldn't go on these long excursions without taking old Robert with her; supposing she were to sprain her ankle, she might have to remain there all night and half the next day before we could find her. Sooner or later I know she'll startle some solitary shepherd out of his senses: he'll come back to his hut swearing that he has seen a Gray Lady where no mortal woman could be. Hullo, there's Waveney again—he'll soon be on them."

They could see him stealing across the top of the hillock, and then making his way down behind certain rocks that served as a screen between him and the birds. Then he disappeared again.

"Why doesn't he fire?" Lionel asked, presently. "He must be quite close to them."

"Not so close as you imagine," was the answer. "Probably he is waiting until they come nearer together."

The next moment there stepped boldly forth the slight, brown figure; the birds instantly rose from the water and, with swift, straight flight, made down the valley; but they had not got many yards when there were two white puffs of smoke, both birds almost simultaneously came tumbling to the ground, and then followed the double report of a gun.

"Waveney has got his eye in to-day for certain," Sir Hugh said. "But what's the use of his bringing the birds along?—they're no good to anybody."

"I thought perhaps they might be of some use for salmon-flies," Captain Waveney explained, as he came up. "Aren't they, Roderick?"

The keeper regarded the two birds contemptuously, and shook his head.

"Well, Waveney, we will give you five minutes' grace, if you like," Sir Hugh said. "Sit down and have a pipe."

But this slim and wiry warrior had not even taken the gun from his shoulder.

"No, no," said he, "if you are ready, I am. I can get plenty of smoking done in the South."

So they began again; but the afternoon was now on the wane, and the beats were leading them homewards. Only two small incidents that befell the novice need mentioning. The first happened in this wise: the dogs were ranging widely over what appeared to be rather a barren beat, when suddenly one of them came to a dead point a considerable distance on. Of course Captain Waveney and Sir Hugh hurried forward; but Lionel could not, for he had got into trouble with a badly jammed cartridge. Just as he heard the first shot fired, he managed to get the empty case extracted and to replace it with a full one; and then he was about to hasten forward when he saw the covey rise—a large covey it was—while Captain Waveney got a right and left, and Sir Hugh fired his remaining barrel, for he had not had time to reload. At the same instant Lionel found that one of the birds had doubled back and was coming right over his head; up went his gun; he blazed away; and down rolled the grouse some dozen yards behind him.

"Well done!" Sir Hugh called out, "A capital shot!"

"A ghastly fluke, Sir Hugh!" Lionel called out, in return. "I simply fired in the air."

"And a very good way of firing, too!" was the naïve rejoinder.

But his next achievement was hardly so creditable. They were skirting the edge of a birch-wood that clothed the side of a steep precipice overlooking the Aivron, where there were some patches of bracken among the heather, when the setter in front of him—a young dog—began to draw rather falteringly on to something.

"Ware rabbit, Hector!" the keeper said, in an undertone.

But meanwhile the older dog, that was backing in front of Captain Waveney, whether it was impatient of this uncertainty on the part of its younger companion, or whether it was jealous, managed, unobserved, to steal forward a foot or two, until suddenly it stopped rigid.

"Good dog, Iris, good dog!" Captain Waveney said (for he had overlooked that little bit of stealthy advance), and he shifted his gun from his right hand to his left, and stooped down and patted the animal's neck—though all the time he was looking well ahead.

Then all at once there was a terrific whir of wings; Waveney quickly put his gun to his shoulder—paused—took it down again; at the same moment Lionel, finding a bird within his proper field, as he considered—though it was going away at a prodigious speed—took steady aim and fired. That distant object dropped—there was not a flutter. Of course the keeper and

Sir Hugh were still watching the young dog; but when this doubtful scent came to nothing, Sir Hugh turned to Lionel.

"That was a long shot of yours, Mr. Moore," said he. "And very excusable."

"Excusable?" said Lionel, wondering what he had done this time.

"Of course you knew that was a blackcock?" the other said.

"A blackcock?" he repeated.

"Didn't you hear Roderick call out? Didn't you see Waveney put up his gun and then take it down?"

"Neither the one nor the other; I only saw a bird before me—and fired."

"Oh, well, there's no great harm done; if a man has no worse sin on his conscience than shooting a blackcock on the Twelfth, he should sleep sound o' nights. Waveney is fastidious. I dare say, if the bird had come my way, I should not have resisted the temptation."

Lionel considered that Sir Hugh was an exceedingly considerate and good-natured person; and in fact when they picked up the dead bird, and when he was regarding its handsome plumage, it cannot fairly be said that he was very sorry for his venial mistake. Only he considered he was bound in honor to make confession to Miss Cunyngham.

Alas! he was to see little of Miss Cunyngham that night. As soon as dinner was over—and Sir Hugh and his satellite had left the dining-room to enter up the game-book, write labels for special friends, and generally finish up the business of the day—Lady Adela proposed a game of Dumb Crambo; and in this she was heartily backed up by the Lestranges, for Miss Georgie seemed to think that the mantle of Kitty Clive had descended upon her shoulders, while her brother evidently regarded himself as a facetious person. Speedily it appeared, however, that there was to be a permanent and stationary audience. Lord Fareborough—especially after dinner, when his nervous system was still in dark deliberation as to what it meant to do with him—was too awful a personage to be approached; Honnor Cunyngham good-humoredly said that she was too stupid to join in; and Lord Rockminster declared that if that was her excuse, it applied much more obviously to himself. Accordingly, the remaining members of the house-party had to form the entertainers; and never had Lionel entered into any pastime with so little zest. These people could not act a bit, and yet he had to coach them; and then he and they had to go into the drawing-room and perform their antics before that calm-browed young lady (who nevertheless regarded the proceedings with the most friendly interest) and her companion, the stolid young lord. He could not help acknowledging to himself that Miss Honnor Cunyngham and Lord Rockminster formed a remarkably handsome couple as they sat together there on a couch at right angles with the fireplace; but the distinguished appearance of the audience did not console him for the consciousness that the performers were making themselves absurd. He was impatient, ashamed, of the whole affair. Dark and sullen thoughts went flashing through his brain of saving up every penny he could get hold of and going away into some savage wilderness in Ross or Sutherland, to be seen of actors and amateurs no more. His gun and his rod would be his sole companions; his library would consist of St. John, Colquhoun, "Stonehenge," and Francis (not of Assisi); by moor and stream he would earn his own subsistence; and theatres and fashionable life and the fantastic aspirations and ambitions of *les Precieuses Ridicules* would be banished from him forever. But fortunately a nine-o'clock dinner had driven this foolish entertainment late, so that it did not last long; the ladies were unanimously willing to retire; the gentlemen thereupon trooped off to the gun-room to have a smoke and a glass of whiskey and soda water; and very soon thereafter the deep-breathing calm of the whole household told that the labors of the Twelfth were over.

CHAPTER IX.

VENATOR IMMEMOR.

And why was it, when, in course of time, it became practicable to arrange a deer-stalking expedition for him, why was it that he voluntarily chose to encounter what Lord Rockminster had called the very extremes of fatigue and human misery? He knew that he was about to undergo tortures of anxiety and privation; and, what was worse, he knew he was going to miss. He had saturated his mind with gillies' stories of capital shots who had completely lost their nerve on first catching sight of a stag. The "buck-ague" was already upon him. Not for him was there waiting away in these wilds some Muckle Hart of Ben More to gain a deathless fame from his rifle-bullet. He was about to half-kill himself with the labors of a long and arduous expedition, and at the end of it he foresaw himself returning home defeated, dejected, in the deepest throes of mortification and chagrin.

And look what he was giving up. Here was a whole houseful of charming women all ready to pet him and make much of him; and in their society he would be at home, dealing with things with which he was familiar. Lady Sybil would be grateful to him if he helped her with the music she was arranging for "Alfred: a Masque;" he could be of abundant service, too, to Lady Rosamund, who was now making individual studies for her large drawing of "Luncheon on the Twelfth;" though perhaps he could not lend much aid to Lady Adela, who was understood to be getting on very well with her new novel. But, at all events, he would be in his own element; he would be among things that he understood; he would be no trembling ignoramus adventuring forth into the unknown. And yet when, early in the morning, the old and sturdy pony was brought round to the door, and when the brown-bearded Roderick had shouldered the rifle and was ready to set forth, Lionel had little thought of surrendering his chance to any one else.

"I call this very shabby treatment," his burly and good-humored host said, as he stood at the open door. "When a man goes stalking, if there's a pretty girl in the house, she ought to make her appearance and give him a little present for good luck. It's an understood thing; it's an old custom; and yet there isn't one of those lazy creatures down yet."

"This is the best I can do for you, old fellow," Percy Lestrange said, at the same moment. "I can't give you the flask, for my sister Georgie gave it to me; but I will lend it to you for the day; and it's filled with an excellent mixture of curaçoa and brandy. You'll want some comfort? and I don't expect they'll let you smoke. What do you think of my crest?"

He handed the silver flask to Lionel, who found engraved on the side of it a merry and ingenious device, consisting of two briar-root pipes, crossed, and surrounded by a heraldic garter bearing the legend "*Dulce est de-sip-ere in loco?*" Was this Miss Georgia's little joke? Anyhow, he pocketed the flask with much gratitude; he guessed he might have need of it, if all tales were true.

"I hope you'll get a presentable head," Sir Hugh said, "The stags themselves are not in very good condition yet; but the horns are all right—the velvet's off."

"It doesn't much matter," Lionel made answer, contentedly. "I know beforehand I am going to miss. Well, good-bye, for the present! Go ahead, Maggie!"

But at the same moment there was a glimmer of a gray dress in the twilight of the hall; and the next moment Honnor Cunyngham appeared on the doorstep, the morning light shining on her smiling face.

"Mr. Moore," she said, coming forward without any kind of embarrassment, "there's an old custom—didn't my brother tell you?—you must take a little gift from some one in the house, just as you are going away, for good luck. You haven't yet? Here it is, then."

"It is exceedingly kind of you," said he; "and I wish I could make the omen come true; but I have no such hope. I know I am going to miss."

"You are going to kill a stag!" said she, confidently. "That is what you are going to do. Well, good-bye, and good-luck!"

So the little party of three—Lionel, Roderick, and the attendant gillie—straightway left the lodge and began to make for the head of the strath. And it was not altogether about deer that Lionel was now thinking. The tiny, thin packet he held in his hand seemed to burn there. What was it Honnor Cunyngham had brought down-stairs for him? However trivial it might be, surely it was something he could keep. She had given it to him for good luck; but her wishes were not confined to this one day? Then, when he had got some distance from the house, so that his curiosity could not be observed, he threw the reins on Maggie's neck, and proceeded to open this small packet covered with white paper. What did he find there?—why-only a sixpence—a bright new sixpence—not to be compared in value with the dozens on dozens of presents which were lavished upon him by his fair admirers in London—courteous little attentions which, it must be confessed, he had grown to regard with a somewhat callous indifference.

Only a small, bright coin this was; and yet he carefully wrapped up the precious talisman again in its bit of tissue paper; and as carefully he put it away in a waistcoat pocket, where it would be safe, even among the rough-and-tumble experiences that lay before him. The day seemed all the happier, all the more hopeful, that he knew this little token of friendly sympathy was in his possession. Ought not a lucky sixpence to have a hole bored in it? He could wear it in secret, even if she might not care to see it hanging at his watch-chain? and who could tell what subtle influence it might not bring to bear on his fortunes, wholly apart from the stalking of stags? He grew quite cheerful; he forgot his nervousness; he was talking gayly to the somewhat taciturn Roderick, who, nevertheless, no doubt much preferred to find his pupil in this confident mood.

Their course at first lay along the nearer bank of the Aivron; but, when they had got away up the strath towards the neighborhood of the Bad Step—which was, of course, impassable for the pony—Lionel had to separate from his companions and ford the river, following up the other side. Fortunately there was not much water in the stream; old Maggie knew her way well enough; and with nothing more than an occasional stumble among the slippery boulders and loose stones they reached the opposite bank in safety. About a mile farther up the return crossing had to be made; but this second ford was shallow and easy; and thenceforward the united party went on together. At last they struck the Geinig; and here a rude track took them away from the valley of the Aivron altogether, into a solitary land of moor and rock.

It was a still and rather louring morning; but yet he did not perceive any gloom in it at all; nay, there was rather a tender and wistful beauty up in this lonely wilderness he was entering. The heavy masses of cloud hung low and brooding over the purple hills; the heavens seemed to be in close communion with the murmuring streams in these otherwise voiceless solitudes; the long undulations were not darkly stained, they only lay under a soft, transparent shadow. Even among the grays and purple-grays of the sky there was here and there a mild sheen of silver; and now and again a pale radiance would begin to tell upon an uprising slope, until something almost like sunlight shone there, glorifying the lichened rocks and the crimson heather. This was one of the days that Honnor Cunyngham loved; and he, too, had got to appreciate their sombre beauty, the brooding calm, the gracious silence, when he went with her on her fishing expeditions into the wilds. And here was her favorite Geinig—sometimes with tawny masses boiling down between the boulders, sometimes sweeping in a black-brown current round a sudden curve, and sometimes racing over silver-gray shallows; but always with this continuous murmur that seemed to offer a kind of companionship where there was no other sound or sign of life. And would she be up here later on? he asked himself, with a curious kind of interest. Would she have a thought for the small party that had passed in the early morning and disappeared into the remote and secret fastnesses among those lonely hills? Might she linger on in the evening, in the hope of finding them coming home again—perchance with joyful news? For, after all, this lucky sixpence had buoyed up his spirits; he was not so entirely certain he would miss, if anything like a fair chance presented itself; and he knew that if that chance did offer, he would bring all that was in him to bear on the controlling of his nerves—he would not breathe—his life would be concentrated on the small cleft of the rifle—if his heart cracked in twain the instant after the trigger was pulled.

But these vague and anxious speculations were soon to be discarded for the immediate interests of the moment. They were getting near to the ground—after a sufficiently rough journey of close on eight miles; and now, as they came to the bed of a little burn, Lionel was bidden to descend from his venerable steed; the saddle was taken off; and old Maggie was hobbled, and left to occupy herself with the fresh, sweet grass growing near to the stream.

"Now look here, Roderick," Lionel said, "I'm entirely in your hands, and mind you don't spare me. Since I'm in for it, I mean to see it through."

"When it is after a stag we are, there is no sparing of any one," said Roderick, significantly, as he took out his telescope. "And you will think of this, sir, that if we are crahling along, and come on the deer without expecting it, and if they see you, then you will lie still like a stone. Many's the time they will chist stand and look at you, if you do not move; and then slowly, slowly you will put your head down in the heather again, and wait till I tell you what to do. But if you go out of sight quick—ay, so will they."

At first, as it appeared to Lionel, they went forward with a dangerous fearlessness, the keeper merely using his natural eye-sight to search the slopes and corries; but presently he began to go more warily; again and again he paused, to watch the motion of the white rags of cloud clinging to the hillsides; and occasionally, as they got up into the higher country, he would lie down with his back on a convenient mound, cross one knee over the other, and, with this rest for his telescope, proceed to scrutinize, inch by inch, the vast prospect before him. There was no more talking now. There was a kind of stealthiness in their progress, even when they walked erect; but it soon appeared to Lionel that Roderick, who went first, seemed to be keeping a series of natural eminences between them and a certain distant tract of this silent and lonely land. It was only a guess; but it accounted for all kinds of circuitous little turns; anyhow, there was nothing for him but to follow blindly whither he was led. Of course he kept his eyes open; but there was no sign of life anywhere in this barren wilderness; there was nothing but the empty undulations of heath and thick grass, with sometimes a little tarn coming in sight, and always the farther hills forming a sort of solitary amphitheatre along the horizon.

Suddenly Roderick stopped short, and quietly put out his hand to arrest the progress of his companions. Involuntarily they stooped; and he not only did likewise, but presently he was on his back on the heather, with the telescope balanced as before. After a long and earnest scrutiny, he offered the glass to Lionel.

"They're there," he said, "but in an ahfu' bad place for us."

Eagerly Lionel got hold of the telescope and tried to balance it as the keeper had done; but either his hand was trembling, or the wind had a purchase on the long tube, or he was unaccustomed to its use; at all events he could make out nothing but nebulous and uncertain patches of color.

"Tell me where they are," he said, quickly, as he put aside the glass. "I have good eyes."

"Do you see the gray scar on the hillside yonder?—then right below that the rocks—and then the open place—can you see them now? Ay, and there's not a single hind with them—"

"They're all stags?" exclaimed Lionel, breathlessly.

"Every one," said Roderick. "And when there's no hinds with them, it is easier to get at them, for they're not near so wary as the hinds; but that is a bad place where they are feeding the now—a terrible bad place. I'm thinking it is no use to try to get near them there; but they will keep feeding on and on until they get over the ridge; and what we will do now is we will chist go aweh down wind, and get round to them from anither airt."

It was little that Lionel knew what was involved in this apparently simple scheme. At first everything was easy enough; for, when they had fallen back out of sight of the deer, they merely set forth upon a long walk down wind, going erect, without any trouble. It is true that Lionel in time began to think that the keeper, instead of having the deer in mind, was bent on a pilgrimage into Cromarty or Sutherland, or perhaps towards the shores of the Atlantic; but this interminable tramp was a mere trifle compared with their labors when they began to go up wind again. For now there was nothing but stooping and crawling and slouching behind hillocks, up peat-hags, and through marshy swamps; while the heat produced by all this painful toil was liable to a sudden chill whenever a halt was called to enable Roderick to writhe his prostrate figure up to the top of some slight eminence, where, raising his head inch by inch, he once more informed himself of the whereabouts of the deer. There seemed to be no end to this snake-like squirming along the ground and creeping behind rocks and hillocks; in fact, they were now in a quite different tract of country from that in which they had first caught sight of the stags—a much more wild and sombre landscape was this, with precipitous black crags overhanging a sullen and solitary loch that had not a bush or a tree along its lifeless shores. As for Lionel, he fought along without repining. His arms were soaking wet up to the elbows; his legs were in a like condition from the knee downward. Then he was damp with perspiration; while ever and anon, when he had to lie prone in the moist grass, or crouch like a frog behind a rock, the cold wind from the hills sent a shiver down his spine or seemed to strike like an icy dagger through his chest. But he took it all as part of the day's work. There was in his possession a little silver token that afforded him much content. He would acquit himself like a man—if he could; at any rate, he would not grumble.

After what seemed ages of this inconceivable torture, Lionel was immensely relieved to find the keeper, after a careful survey from the top of a mound to which he had crawled, motion with his hand to him to come up to his side. This he did with the greatest circumspection, scarcely raising his head above the grass and heather; and then, when he had joined Roderick, he began to peer through the waving stalks and twigs just before his eyes. Suddenly his gaze was arrested by certain brown tips—tips that were moving; were these the stags' horns, he asked himself, in a kind of bewilderment of fear? There could be no doubt of it. The beasts were now lying down—he could not see their bodies—but clearly enough he could make out their branching antlers, as they lazily moved their heads, or perhaps turned to flick a fly away.

"They're too far off, aren't they?" Lionel whispered—and, despite all his sworn resolves to keep calm, he felt his heart going as if it would choke him.

"They're lying down now," Roderick said, with professional coolness, "and they're right out in the open; it is no use at all trying to get near them until they get up in the afternoon and begin to feed again, and then maybe they will feed over the shoulder yonder. No use at all," said he; but just at this moment his quick eye caught sight of something else that had just appeared on the edge of one of the lower slopes, and the expression of his face instantly changed—into something like alarm. "Bless me, look at that now!"

Lionel slowly and cautiously turned his head; and then, quite clearly, he could see a small company of seven or eight stags that had come along from quite a different direction. They paused at the crest of the slope, looking all about them.

"Was ever anything so mischievous?" Roderick exclaimed, in smothered vexation. "If they come over this way they will get our wind; and then it is good-bye to all of them. And we cannot get away neither—well, well, was there ever the like now? There is only the one chance—mebbe they will go along to the others, and keep with them till they begin feeding in the afternoon. Indeed, now, it is a terrible peety if we are to miss such a chance—and not a hind anywhere to be on the watch!"

Happily, however, Roderick's immediate fears were soon dispelled. The new-comers slowly descended the slope; then they bore up the valley again; and after walking about awhile, they followed the example of the rest of the herd and lay down on the heather.

"Ay, ay, that is better now," Roderick said, with much satisfaction. "That is ferry well now. And since there is nothing to be done till the whole of them get up to feed in the afternoon, we will chist creep aweh into a peat-hag and wait there, and you can have your lunch, sir."

So there was another crawling performance down from this exposed height; and eventually the small party managed to hide themselves in a black and moist peat-hag, where their extremely frugal repast was produced.

"But look here, Roderick," Lionel said, "it's only twelve o'clock now; do you mean to say we have to stop in this wet hole till two or three in the afternoon?"

"Ay, chist that," the keeper said, coolly. "They will begin to feed about three; and until they go over the ridge, it is no use at all trying to get near them."

"And what are we to do all the time?"

"Chist wait," Roderick said, with much simplicity; and then he and the gillie withdrew a little way down the peat-hag, so that they might have their luncheon and a cautious whispering in Gaelic by themselves.

It was tantalizing in the last degree. The breathless consciousness that the deer were close by made him all the more impatient for the half-dreaded opportunity of having a shot at one of them. He wished it was well over. If he were going to miss, he wanted to have his agony of mortification encountered and done with, instead of enduring this maddening delay. The peat-hag became a prison; and a very uncomfortable prison, too. His sandwiches were soon disposed of; thereafter—what? He dared not smoke; he had no book with him; the keeper and the gillie, having withdrawn themselves, were exchanging confidences in their native tongue. His clothes were wet and cold and clammy; Percy Lestrange's flask appeared to afford him no comfort whatever. And of course the longer he brooded over the chances of hit or miss, the more appalling became the responsibility. How much depended on that fifteenth part of a second! He was half inclined to say, "Here, Roderick, I can bear this anxiety no longer. Let us get as near the deer as we can; sight the rifle for a long distance, you whistle the stags on to their legs—and I'll blaze into the thick of them. Anything to get the shot over and done with!"

Indeed, this intolerable waiting was about as bad a thing as could have happened to his nerves; but it did not last quite as long as the keeper had anticipated; for about two o'clock Roderick ascertained that the stags were up again and feeding. This was good news—anything was good news, in fact, that broke in upon this sickening suspense; had Lionel been informed that the deer had taken alarm and disappeared at full gallop, he would have said "Amen!" and set out for home with a light heart. But, by and by, when it was discovered that the stags had gone over the ridge—one of them remained on the crest for a long time, staring right across the valley, so that the stalkers dared not move hand or foot—when this last sentinel had also withdrawn, the slouching and skulking devices of the morning had to be resumed. Not a word was spoken; but Lionel knew that the fateful moment was approaching. Then, when they began to ascend the ridge over which the stags had disappeared, their progress culminated in a laborious crawl, Roderick going first, with the rifle in one hand, Lionel dragging himself after, the gillie coming on as best he might. It was slow work now. The keeper went forward inch by inch, as if at any moment he expected to find a stag staring down upon him. And at last he lay quite still; then, with the slightest movement of his disengaged hand, he beckoned Lionel to come up beside him.

Now was the time for all his desperate and summoned calmness. He shut his lips firm, breathing only by his nose; he gradually pushed his way through the tall, withered grass; and at last, when he was almost side by side with Roderick, he peered forward. They were startlingly near, those brown and dun beasts with the branching antlers!—he almost shrank back—and yet he gazed and gazed with a strange fascination. The stags, which were not more than fifty or sixty yards off, were quite unconscious of any danger; they were quietly feeding; sometimes one of them would cease and raise his head and look lazily around. Just at this moment, too, a pale sunlight began to shine over the plateau on which they stood; and a very pretty picture it lit up—the silver-gray rocks, the wide heath, and those slim and elegant creatures grouped here and there as chance directed. Every single feature of the scene (as he discovered long thereafter) was burned into Lionel's brain; yet he was not aware of it at the time; his whole attention, as he imagined, was directed towards keeping himself cool and restrained and ready to obey Roderick's mute directions. The rifle was stealthily given to him, and as stealthily pushed through the grass. With his fore-finger the keeper indicated the stag at which Lionel was to fire; it was rather lighter in color than the others, and was standing a little way apart. Lionel took time to consider, as he thought; in reality it was to still the quick pulsation of his heart; and as he did so the stag, unfortunately for him, moved, so that, instead of offering him an easy broadside shot, it almost faced him, with its head down. Still, at any moment it might afford a fairer mark; and so, with the utmost caution, and with his lips still shut tight, he slowly raised himself somewhat, and got the rifle into his hands. Yes, the stag had again moved; its shoulder was exposed; his eyes inquired of Roderick if now was the time; and the keeper nodded assent.

The awful crisis had arrived; and he seemed to blind himself and deaden himself to all things in this mortal world except the little notch in the rifle, the shining sight, and that fawn-colored object over there. He took a long breath; he steadied and steadied the slightly trembling barrel until it appeared perfectly motionless; and then—he fired!

Alas! at the very moment that he pulled the trigger—when it was too late for him to change his purpose—the stag threw up its head to flick at its side with its horns, and thus quite altered its position; he knew he ought not to fire—but it was too late—too late—and in the very act of pulling the trigger he felt that he had missed.

Roderick sprang to his feet; for the deer, notwithstanding that they could not have discerned where the danger lay, with one consent bounded forward and made for a rocky defile on the farther side of the plateau.

"Come on, sir! Come on, sir!" the keeper called to Lionel. "You've hit him. Come along, sir!"

"I haven't hit him—I missed—missed clean!" was the hopeless answer.

"I tell ye ye've hit him!" the keeper exclaimed. "Run, sir, run!—if he's only wounded he may need the other barrel. God bless me, did ye not hear the thud when the ball struck?"

Thus admonished Lionel unwittingly, but nevertheless as quickly as he could, followed the keeper; and he could show a nimble pair of heels when he chose, even when he was hampered with this heavy rifle. Not that he had any heart in the chase. The stag had swerved aside just as he fired; he knew he must have missed. At the same time any one who goes out with a professional stalker must be content to become as clay in the hands of the potter; so Lionel did as he was bid; and though he could not overtake Roderick, he was not far behind him when they both reached the pass down which the deer had fled.

And there the splendid animals were still in view—bounding up a stony hillside some distance off, in straggling twos and threes, and going at a prodigious speed. But where was the light-colored stag? Certainly not among those brown beasts whose scrambling up that steep face was sending a shower of stones and débris down into the silent glen below.

"I'm thinking he's no far aweh," Roderick said, eagerly scanning all the ground in front of them. "We'll chist go forrit, sir; and you'll be ready to shoot, for, if he's only wounded, he may be up and off again when he sees us."

"But do you really think I hit him?" Lionel said, anxiously enough.

"I *sah* him struck," the keeper said, emphatically. "But he never dropped—no, not once on his knees even. He was off with the best of them; and that's what meks me think he was well hit, and that he's no far aweh."

So they went forward on the track of the herd, slowly, and searching every dip and hollow. For Lionel it was a period of agonizing uncertainty. One moment he would buoy himself up with the assurance that the keeper must know; the rest he convinced himself that he had missed the stag clean. Now he would be wondering whether this wide, undulating plain really contained the slain monarch of the mists; again he pictured to himself that light-colored, fleet-footed creature far away in advance of all his companions, making for some distant sanctuary among the mountains.

"Here he is, sir!" Roderick cried, with a quick little chuckle; and the words sent a thrill through Lionel such as he had never experienced in his life before. "No—he's quite dead," the keeper continued, seeing that the younger man was making ready to raise his rifle again. "I was thinking he was well hit—and no far aweh."

At the same moment Lionel had eagerly run forward. With what joy and pride—with what a curious sense of elation—with what a disposition of good-will towards all the world—he now beheld this splendid beast lying in the deep peat-hag that had hitherto hidden it from view. The stag's last effort had been to clear this gully; but it had only managed to strike the opposite bank with its forefeet when the death-wound did its work, and then the hapless animal had rolled back with its final groan into the position in which they now found it. In a second, Roderick was down in the peat-hag beside it, holding up its head by one of the horns, and examining the bulletmark.

"Well, sir," said he, with a humorous smile that did not often lighten up his visage, "if this is what you will be calling the missing of a stag, it is a ferry good way to miss it; for I never sah a better shot in my life."

"It's a fluke, then, Roderick; I declare to you I was certain I had missed," said he—though he hardly knew what he was saying; a kind of bewilderment of joy possessed him—he could not keep his eyes off the dead stag—and now, if he had only chanced to notice it, his hand was certainly trembling. Probably Roderick did not know what a fluke was; in any case his response was:

"Well, sir, I'm chist going to drink your good health; ay, and more good luck to you, sir; and it's ferry glad I am that you hef got your first stag!" and therewith he pulled out his small zinc flask.

"Oh, but you mustn't draw on your own supplies!" Lionel exclaimed, in the fulness of his pride and gratitude. "See, here is a flask filled with famous stuff. You take it—you and Alec; I don't want any more to-day."

"Do not be so sure of that," the keeper said, shrewdly, and he modestly declined to take Percy Lestrange's decorated flask. "It's a long walk from home we are; far longer than you think; and mebbe there will be some showers before we get back home."

"I don't care if there's thunder and lightning all the way!" Lionel cried, gayly. "But I'll tell you what, Roderick, I wish you'd lend me your pipe. Have you plenty of tobacco? A cigarette is too feeble a thing to smoke by the side of a dead stag. And—and on my way south I mean to stop at Inverness, and I'll send you as much tobacco as will last you right through the winter; for you see I'm very proud of my first stag—and, of course, it was all owing to your skill in stalking."

Roderick handed the young man his pipe and pouch.

"Indeed, you could not do better, sir, than sit down and hef a smoke, while me and Alec are gralloching the beast. Then we'll drag him to a safe place, and cover him up with heather, and send for him the morn's morning."

"Couldn't you put him on the pony and take him down with us? I can walk," Lionel suggested; for had he not some dim vision in his mind of a triumphal procession down the strath, towards the dusk of the evening, with perhaps a group of fair spectators awaiting him at the door of the lodge?

"Well, sir," the keeper made answer, as he drew out his gralloching knife, "you see, there's few things more difficult than to strap a deer on the back of a powny when there's no proper deer-saddle. No, sir, we'll just leave him in a safe place for the night and send for him in the morning."

"And do you call that a good head to get stuffed Roderick?" the young man asked, still gazing on his splendid prize.

"Aw, well, I hef seen better heads, and I hef seen worse heads," the keeper said, evasively. "But the velvet is off the horns whatever."

This was tremendously strong tobacco that Roderick had handed him, and yet, as it seemed to him, he had never smelt a sweeter fragrance perfuming the soft mountain air. Nor did these appear grim and awful solitudes any longer; they were friendly solitudes, rather; as he sat and peacefully and joyously smoked, he studied every feature of them—each rock and swamp and barren slope, every hill and corrie and misty mountain-top; and he knew that while life remained to him he would never forget this memorable scene—with the slain stag in the foreground. No, nor how could he ever forget that wan glare of sunlight that had come along the plateau where the deer were quietly feeding?—he seemed to see again each individual blade of grass close to his face, as well as the noble quarry that had held him breathless. And then he took out the bright little coin; surely Honnor Cunyngham could not object to his wearing it, seeing that it had proved itself such a potent charm? He rejoiced that he had not been frightened off his expedition by tales of its monotonous sufferings and dire fatigues. This was something better than arranging an out-of-door performance for a parcel of amateurs! Stiff and sore he was, his clothes were mostly soaked and caked with mire, and he did not know what he had not done to his shins and knees and elbows; but he did not mind all that; Honnor Cunyngham was right—as he rode down Strathaivron that evening towards the lodge, it would not be of fatigues and privations he would be thinking! it would be of the lordly stag left away up there in the hills, to be sent for and brought down in triumph the next day.

By the time they had got the stag conveyed to a place of concealment, and carefully covered over with heather, the afternoon was well advanced; then they set out for the little corrie in which the pony had been left. But Lionel was now to discover that they had come much farther into these wilds than he had imagined; indeed, when they at length came upon the stolid and unconcerned Maggie, he did not in the least regret that it was a riding-saddle, not a deer-saddle, they had brought with them in the morning. He had offered to walk these remaining eight miles in order to have the proud satisfaction of taking the stag home with them; now he was just as well content that it was he, and not the slain deer, that Maggie was to carry down to Strathaivron. So he lit another cigarette, got into the saddle, and with a light heart set forth upon the long and tedious jog-jog down towards the region of comparative civilization.

Yet it was hardly so tedious, after all. He was mentally going over again and again every point and incident of the day's thrilling experiences; and now it seemed as if it were a long time since he had been squirming through the heather, with all his limbs aching, and his heart ready to burst. He recalled that beautiful picture of the stags feeding on the lonely plateau; he wondered now that he was able to steady the rifle-barrel until it ceased to be tremulous; he asked himself whether he had not in reality pulled the trigger just before the stag swerved its head aside. And what would have been his feelings now, supposing he had missed? Riding home in silence and dejection—trying to account for the incomprehensible blunder—fearing to think of what he would have to say to the people at the lodge. And he was not at all sorry to reflect that, as soon as the little party got back home, Miss Honnor Cunyngham should see for herself that he, a mere singer out of comedy-opera, was not afraid to face the hardships that had proved too much for Lord Rockminster—yes, and that he had faced them to some purpose.

Very friendly sounded the voice of the Geinig, when it first struck upon his ear; they were getting into a recognizable neighborhood now; here were familiar features—not a waste of the awful and unknown. But it was too much to expect that Miss Cunyngham should still be lingering by any of those pools; the evening was closing in; she must have set out for home long ago, fishing her way down as she went. They passed a shepherd's solitary cottage; the old man came out to hear the news—which was told him in Gaelic. They reached the banks of the Aivron, and trudged along under the tall cliffs and through the scattered birch and hazel. Then came the fording of the river—the tramp along the other side—the return ford—and the small home-going party was reunited again. They skirted the glassy sweeps of the Long Pool, the darker swirls of the Small Pool, and the saffron-tinted masses of foam hurling down between the borders of the Rock Pool; and then at last they came in view of the spacious valley, and far away in the midst of it Strathaivron Lodge.

Had they been coming back with bad news this might have been rather a melancholy sight, perhaps—the long, wide strath with the wan shades of twilight stealing over the meadows and the woods and the winding river; but now (to Lionel at least) it was nothing but beautiful. If the glen itself looked ghostly and lifeless and colorless, there were warmer hues overhead; for a pale salmon-flush still suffused the sky; and where that half-crimson glow, just over the dark, heather-stained hill, faded into an exquisite transparent lilac, there hung a full moon—a moon of the lightest and clearest gold, with its mysterious continents appearing as faint gray films. The prevailing peace seemed to grow more profound with the coming of the night. But this was not a night to be feared—this was a night to be welcomed—a night with that fair golden moon hanging high in the heavens, the mistress and guardian of the silent vale.

When Lionel rode up to the door of the lodge, he found all the gentlemen of the house congregated there and dressed for dinner. Sir Hugh held up his hand.

"No, not one word!" he cried. "Not necessary. I can always tell. It is written in every line of your face."

"It isn't a hind, is it?" inquired Lord Rockminster, doubtfully.

"A hind of ten points!" Lionel said, with a laugh, as he pushed his way through. "Well, I must see if I can have a hot bath to soften my bones."

"My good fellow, it's waiting for you," his host said. "I told Jeffreys the moment I saw you coming down the strath. We'll put back dinner a bit; but be as quick as you can."

At the same moment there appeared a white-draped figure on the landing above, leaning over the balustrade.

"What have you done, Mr. Moore?" called down the well-known voice of Honnor Cunyngham.

"I've got a stag," he said, looking up with a good deal of satisfaction—or gratitude, perhaps?—in his eyes.

"How many points?"

"Ten."

"Well done! Didn't I tell you you would get a stag?"

"It's all owing to the lucky sixpence you gave me," he said; and she laughed, as she turned away to go to her room.

After a welcome bath he dressed as quickly as he could for dinner—dressed so quickly, indeed, that he thought he was entitled to glance at the outside of the pile of letters awaiting him there on the mantelpiece. He had a large correspondence, from all kinds of people; and when he was in a hurry this brief scrutiny of the address was all he allowed himself; he usually could tell if there was anything of unusual importance. On the present occasion the only handwriting that arrested him for a second was Nina's; and some sort of half-understood compunction made him open her letter. Well, it was not a letter; it was merely a little printed form, such as is put about the stalls and boxes of a theatre when an announcement has to be made. This announcement read as follows:

"NOTICE: In consequence of the sudden indisposition of MISS BURGOYNE, the part of 'Grace Mainwaring' will be sustained this evening by MISS ANTONIA ROSS"

—while above these printed words Nina had written, in a rather trembling hand: "*Ah, Leo, if you were only here to-night!*" Apparently she had scribbled this brief message before the performance; perhaps haste or nervousness might account for the uncertain writing. So Nina was to have her great opportunity after all, he said to himself, as he went joyfully down-stairs to join the brilliant assemblage in the drawing-room. Poor Nina!—he had of late almost forgotten her existence.

CHAPTER X.

AIVRON AND GEINIG.

Honnor Cunyngham was quite as proud as Lionel himself that he had killed a stag; for in a measure he was her pupil; at all events it was at her instigation that he was devoting himself to these athletic sports and pastimes, and so far withdrawing himself from the trivialities and affectations of the serious little band of amateurs. Not that Miss Cunyngham ever exhibited any disdain for those pursuits of her gifted sisters-in-law; no; she listened to Lady Sybil's music, and regarded Lady Rosamund's canvases, and even read the last MS. chapter of Lady Adela's new novel (for that great work was now in progress) with a grave good-humor and even with a kind of benevolence; and it was only when one or the other of them, with unconscious simplicity, named herself in conjunction with some master of the art she was professing—wondering how *he* could do such and such a thing in such and such a fashion when *she* found another method infinitely preferable—it was only at such moments that occasionally Honnor Cunyngham's clear hazel eyes would meet Lionel's, and the question they obviously asked was "Is not that extraordinary?" They did not ask "Is not that absurd?" or "How can any one be so innocently and inordinately vain?" they only expressed a friendly surprise, with perhaps the smallest trace of demure amusement.

On the other hand, if Miss Cunyngham rather intimated to this young guest and stranger that, being at a shooting-lodge in the Highlands, he ought to devote himself to the healthful and vigorous recreations of the place, instead of dawdling away his time in drawing-room frivolities, it was not that she herself should take possession of him as her comrade on her salmon-fishing excursions. He soon discovered that he was not to have any great encouragement in this direction. She was always very kind to him, no doubt; and she had certainly proposed that, if he cared to go with her, he could take the wading portions of the pools; but beyond that she extended to him very little companionship, except what he made bold to claim. And the fact is, he was rather piqued by the curious isolation in which this young lady appeared to hold herself. She seemed so entirely content with herself, so wholly indifferent to the little attentions and flatteries of ordinary life, always good-natured when in the society of any one, she was just as satisfied to be left alone. Now, Lionel Moore had not been used to this kind of treatment. Women had been only too ready to smile when he approached; perhaps, indeed, familiar success had rendered him callous; at all events, he had managed to get along so far without encountering any violent experience of heart-aching desire and disappointment and despair. But this young lady, with the clear, fine, intellectual face, the proud lips, the calm, observant eyes, puzzled him—almost vexed him. Nina, for example, was a far more sympathetic companion; either she was enthusiastically happy, talkative, vivacious, gay as a lark, or she was wilfully sullen and offended, to be coaxed round again and petted, like a spoiled child, until the natural sunshine of her humor came through those wayward clouds. But Miss Cunyngham, while always friendly and pleasant, remained (as he thought) strangely remote, imperturbable, calm. She did not seem to care about his society at all. Perhaps she would rather have him go up the hill?—though the birds were getting very wild now for a novice. In any case, she could not refuse to let him accompany her on the morning after his deer-stalking expedition; for all the story had to be told her.

"I suppose you are very stiff," she said, cheerfully, as they left the lodge—he walking heavily in waders and brogues—old Robert coming up behind with rod and gaff. "But I should imagine you do not ask for much sympathy. Shall I tell you what you are thinking of at this moment? You have a vague fear that the foxes may have got at that precious animal during the night; and you are anxious to see it safely down here at the lodge; and you want to have the head sent at once to Mr. Macleay's in Inverness, so that it mayn't get mixed up with the lot of others which will be coming in when the driving in the big forests begins. Isn't that about it?"

"You are a witch," said he, "or else you have been deer-stalking yourself. But, you know, Miss Honnor, it's all very well to go on an expedition like that of yesterday once in a way—as a piece of bravado, almost; and no doubt you are very proud when you see the dead stag lying on the heather before you; but I am not sure I should ever care for it as a continuous occupation, even if I were likely to have the chance. The excitement is too furious, too violent. But look at a day by the side of a salmon river!" continued this adroit young man. "There is absolute rest and peace—except when you are engaged in fighting a salmon; and, for my own part, that is not necessary to my enjoyment at all. No; I would rather see you fish; then I know that everything is going right—that every pool is being properly cast over—that Robert is satisfied. And in the meantime I can sit and drink in all the beauty of the scenery—the quietude—the loneliness; that is a real change for me, after the busy life of London. I have got to be great friends with this river; I seem to have known it all my life; when we were coming home last evening, after being away in those awful solitudes, the sound of the Geinig was the most welcome thing I ever heard, I think."

"It is to the Geinig we are going now," said his companion, who appeared quite to ignore the insidious appeal conveyed in these touching sentiments. "I promised to leave all the Aivron pools to Mr. Lestrange. But we may take the Junction Pool, for he won't have time to come beyond the Bad Step; and, by the way, Mr. Moore, if you feel stiff after yesterday, going up and down the Bad Step won't do you any harm."

Well, the ascent of this Bad Step (whether so named from the French or the Gaelic nobody seemed to know) was not so difficult, after all, for it was gradual; and a brief breathing-space on the summit showed them the far-stretching landscape terminating in the wild mountains of Assynt; but the sheer descent into the gloomy chasm on the other side was rather an awkward thing for any one encased in waders. However, Lionel managed somehow or another to slide and scramble down this zig-zag track on the face of the loose débris; they reached the bottom in safety and crossed the burn; they followed a more secure pathway cut along the precipitous slope overlooking the Aivron; then they got down once more to the river-side, and found themselves walking over velvet-soft turf, in a wood of thinly scattered birch and hazel.

But when they emerged from this wood, passed along by some meadows, and reached the Junction Pool (so called from the Geinig and Aivron meeting here), they found that the sun was much too bright; so they contentedly seated themselves on the bank to wait for a cloud, while old Robert proceeded to consult his fly-book. Neither of them seemed in a very talkative mood; indeed, when you are in front of a Highland river, with its swift-glancing lights, its changing glooms and gleams, its continual murmur and prattle, what need is there of any talk? Talk only distracts the attention. And this part of the stream was especially beautiful. They could hardly quarrel with the sunlight when, underneath the clear water, it sent interlacing lines of gold chasing one another across the brown sand and shingle of the shallows; and if the cloudless sky overhead compelled this unwilling idleness, it also touched each of those dancing ripples with a gleam of most brilliant blue. Farther out those scattered blue gleams became concentrated until they formed glassy sweeps of intensest azure where the deep pools were; and these again gave way to the broken water under the opposite bank, where the swift-running current reflected the golden-green of the overhanging bushes and weeds. Where was the call for any speech between these two? When, at length, Robert admonished the young man to get ready, because a cloud was coming over, and this part of the Aivron had to be waded, Lionel got up with no great good-will; that silent companionship, in the gracious stillness and soothing murmur of the stream, seemed to him to be more profitable to the soul than the lashing of a wide pool with a seventeen-foot rod.

But he buckled to his task like a man; and as he could wade a good distance in, there was no need for him to attempt a long line. Surreptitiously, on many occasions, he had been getting lessons from old Robert; and now, if his casting was not professional in its length, it was at least clean. Moreover, by this time he had learned that the expectant moment in salmon-fishing is not when the fly lights away over at the other side and begins to sweep round in a semicircle, but when it drags in the current before it is withdrawn; and he was in no haste in recovering.

"Why, Mr. Moore, you are casting beautifully," Miss Honnor Cunyngham called to him; and the words were sweet music to his ears, for it may be frankly admitted that this somewhat sensitive novice was playing to the gallery. His diligent and careful thrashing, however, was of no avail. He could not stir anything; and as in time the deepening water drove him ashore, he willingly surrendered his rod to his fair companion, who could now fish from the bank.

Then he sat down to watch—and to dream. He could see that she was getting out more and more line, and throwing beautifully; but he had persuaded himself (or thought he had persuaded himself) into the belief that the singular and constant charm of this river had no association with her, or with the quiet hours these two had passed there together. It was the stream talking to him that had fascinated him as he sat idly and listened. He had grown familiar with every cadence of that mysterious voice—now a whispering and laughing as the water chased over the sunny shallows—then a harsher note where the current, fretting and chafing, as it were, was broken by multitudes of stones—again a low murmur as the black river swept, dark and sullen, through a contracted channel—finally a fiercer tumult as this once-placid Aivron, increasing in pace and volume every moment, flung itself, lion-like, over the masses of rocks—its tawny mane upheaved to the daylight—and then fell, crashing and plunging, into a mighty chasm, the birchwoods around reverberating with its angry roar. Far away is the lonely sea. This friendly river may laugh or brawl as it will, but there is peace for it at last; its varying voices must eventually disappear in the dull, slow tumult of the distant world. And yet it seemed to him to complain as it went by—to appeal to him; and yet why to him, if he, too, was summoned away from this still solitude and sucked into a murmuring ocean still more awful than the sea?

"Well done, Miss Honnor!" old Robert called out.

Suddenly startled from his idle reverie, Lionel beheld the line being swiftly taken across to the other side of the river, sending up a little spurt of spray as it cleft the current.

"A good one this time, Robert, isn't it?" she cried.

"Ay, I'm thinking that's a good fish," old Robert made answer, as he rose from the bank and came down to her side.

"And there's a fair field and no favor," she continued. "Plenty of room for him—and he doesn't seem inclined to tug."

No, this was not a "jiggering" fish; but he was a pretty lively customer, for all that, as they were soon to find out. For, after having rested for a minute or so, he made a wild rush up-stream, still on the other side, that took a dangerous length of line out and kept her running after him, and winding up when possible as well as she was able. Farther and farther he went, until she had arrived at the junction of the Geinig and the Aivron, she being on the Geinig shore, and the fish making up the other stream. Here was a pleasant predicament!

"Mr. Moore," she called out, "take the rod and wade in!—I daren't give him more line—quick, quick, please!"

Her entreaty was quite pathetic in its earnestness; but old Robert was less excited.

"If Mr. Moore was not here you would be in the watter yourself, Miss Honnor," the old man said, with a smile.

However, before the rod could be given into Lionel's hands the salmon had changed his tactics. He came dashing across to the nearer side of the Aivron, so that the nose of land separating the two rivers threatened to come between the fish and his captor; there he lay still.

"Robert," she cried, in despair, "if he goes another yard up-stream he will have the line on that bush! What is to be done?"

Almost at the same moment the fish began to move again—slowly this time—and with agonized anxiety they saw the line, despite all her efforts to keep it off, being quietly drawn into the small hazel-bush. But Robert knew that bush and its ways.

"Take the rod in, sir, as far as you can go," he said to Lionel; and then he himself ran round to a shallow ford of the Geinig, crossed over, went along the bank, and proceeded to get the line cautiously off the twigs and leaves. As soon as he had accomplished that he stealthily withdrew, stooped down, and crept along the Aivron bank until he was a little ahead of the fish, which, indeed, was almost underneath his feet; then he suddenly raised himself to his full height and threw up both arms. That was enough for the salmon. Away to the other side he rushed, leading down-stream; and Lionel had now his work cut out for him, for he was standing in deep water, on a shelving bank of loose shingle, and he had to follow somehow, reeling in as best he might. But ever, as he struggled after that obdurate, unseen creature, he made for shallower water; and at length he reached dry land, and was glad to give the rod into Miss Honnor's hands again—the fish, which had never once shown himself, being now almost opposite her and in mid-channel.

Well, they had a good deal of trouble with this salmon, for he did not exhaust himself with any further rushes, nor did he disport himself in the air; he simply lay low in the water, in a pretty strong current, and awaited events. But here in the open Miss Honnor had regained her confidence and usual composure; and in the end the continuous pressure of the green-heart top was too much for him; he began to yield—fiercely fighting now and again to get away, to be sure; but the climax was a sudden flash of Robert's steel clip, and a heavy-shouldered fifteen-pounder was out on the stones. Old Robert, smiling grimly at the success of his young mistress, but saying nothing, had to "wet" the fish all by himself; for Miss Honnor's drink was water; and as for Lionel, his throat was too valuable and sensitive a possession to be treated to raw spirits at that time of the morning. Then, that ceremony being over, they deposited the salmon in a hole in the bank, to be picked up on their homeward journey, and forthwith set out again, up the valley of the Geinig.

Their surroundings were now becoming more wild and lonely—this, in fact, being the route by which Lionel had travelled the day before when he was after the deer. Down in the glen, it is true, everything was pretty enough—the silver-gray rocks, the rushing brown water, the banks hanging with birches; but far away on those upland heights there was nothing but the monotonous deep purple of the heather, broken here and there, perhaps, by a dark-green pine; and beyond those heights again rose the rounded tops and shoulders of the distant cloud-stained hills. It was after Miss Honnor had industriously but unsuccessfully fished the Horseshoe and the Cormorant Pool that she chanced to be regarding that mountainous line along the sky; and she then perceived that one of those far shoulders was gradually changing from a sombre blue into a soft and pearly gray.

"Do you see the veil that has come over the high peak yonder?" she asked of her companion. "There is rain falling there; and most likely we shall have a shower or two here by and by; and, as you have no waterproof, we may as well push on to a place of shelter where we can have our lunch. I know a pretty little dell up there, just above the Geinig Pool; and it will be quite a new sensation for me to have any one with me, for ordinarily I have my lunch there, in solitary state, and I sit and stare, and sit and stare, until I believe I know every stone in the burn and every spear of grass on the opposite bank."

Even as she spoke there was a slight pattering here in the sunlight, and diamonds began to glitter on the brackan. Then came a cold stirring of wind; there was a sensation of darkness overhead—of impending gloom—of hushed expectancy; finally, just as they reached the little glade, descended into it, crossed the burn, and took refuge beneath some overhanging birch trees, the heavy rattle of the deluge was heard all around them, and they wore glad enough to be under this canopy of trembling leaves. It was only a sharp shower, after all. That universal whir grew fainter; the air became warmer; a kind of watery glow began to show itself in the sky; presently, as they ventured to look up through the dripping, pendulous branches, there was a glimpse of heavenly blue above them; behold, the rain was over and gone!

Then carefully did the handsome old gillie spread out her waterproof on the sloping bank for Miss Honnor to sit on; he brought forth the little parcels neatly tied up in white paper, likewise a bottle of milk and two silver drinking-cups; when he had seen that she was all properly cared for, he handed to Lionel the game-bag which had held the luncheon, so that that might serve as the other seat, if he chose; and then the old man withdrew a few yards down the little hollow, to be within call if he were wanted.

And what had Lionel to say for himself, now that he had been admitted into this secret haunt of the river-maiden? Well, if the truth must be told, he was considerably embarrassed. For one thing, he was mortally afraid that she might suddenly bethink herself of Paul and Virginia, and be annoyed by a situation which was certainly none of his contriving. What was still worse, she might be amused! He could not get it out of his head that there was something dangerously, almost ludicrously, conventional in the whole position; it seemed to suggest some foolish, old-fashioned, sentimental picture. The solitary dell, and the two figures; why, he felt as if blue ribbons were beginning to sprout at his knees; and he feared to turn to his companion lest he should find her with a crook and a kirtle. He did not ask himself why wretched reminiscences of theatrical tradition should thrust themselves upon him here in the lonely wilds of Ross-shire; what he dreaded was that some such idea might occur to her and provoke her resentment—what was still more ghastly, it might make her laugh!

Honnor Cunyngham, for her part, was quietly and contentedly munching her sandwiches of salmon and vinegared lettuce-leaf; and no such idle town-fancies were troubling her. Probably she was thinking that the hot sunlight after the shower made everything intensely vivid—the silver-stemmed birches in this picturesque little dell rising gracefully into the keen blue of the sky; the diamond-starred bracken and grass shining after the wet; the clear, tea-brown water at her feet glancing in the sun; the green and bronze stones and pebbles showing clear at the bottom of the pellucid brook as it chased and danced on its way down to the Geinig. And whatever else she may have been thinking of, she was almost certainly conscious that vinegared lettuce-leaf in a sandwich was a vast improvement.

"Do you come here often?" he said, at length.

"It is my favorite nook," she made answer.

"I confess that I feel horribly like an interloper," he remarked, hesitatingly. "I feel as if I—as if I had no right to be here—as if I were invading a sacred retreat—" and there he stopped; for he would have liked to add, "the sacred retreat of a sylvan goddess or a nymph of the stream," but that he somehow felt that fantastic imagery of that kind would hardly be appropriate.

"You had more need of the shelter than I," said this extremely matter-of-fact young person, "for you had no waterproof, and I had. Come, if you have finished, shall we go up to the Top Pool?—I want you to have a cast over that, for it is an experience; and, though the sun is out, it won't much matter; there is always such a boiling and surging in that caldron."

Old Robert, whose head was just visible above the bracken, was thereupon called to pack up the remains of the simple feast, and then they set forth again—skirting, but not troubling the Geinig Pool, for the sun was too strong. A beautiful pool was this Geinig Pool—the water coming tumbling down over the boulders in masses of chestnut hue and white, then sailing away in a rapid sweep of purplish blue, and then breaking over shallows (whose every ripple was a flashing diamond point) as it went whirling into the rocky channel beyond. The sun lay hot on the steep banks, where not a leaf of the birch-trees stirred now, and on the lichened rocks, and on the long strand of lilac-gray pebbles; altogether a beautiful pool this was, set deep in its cup among the hills, but for their present purposes useless.

The Top Pool, which they presently reached, was altogether a different sort of place; for here the waters plunged into a roaring caldron with a din that stunned the ears; and now it was that Lionel discovered Miss Honnor's intention—he was to have the amusement of throwing a fly over this maelstrom from the side of the sheer bank, while the only foothold afforded him was the stump of an out-projecting pine. Well, he was not going to refuse—and ask a young lady to take his place. He dug his feet into the soft herbage about the roots of the tree; old Robert handed him the rod; he got out some line; and then began to try how he could get a fly down into that raging vortex, while keeping clear of the branches over his head. His first impression was that he might as well attempt to throw a fly to the moon, but presently things began to look more hopeful, and he found at length that, when the fly did get just beyond the downward rush of the fall, it was swept by the current into certain glassy deeps, where he could work it pretty well. Hard as he labored, however, that jerking little gray shrimp (for that was what the fly looked like in the water) could not stir anything. He worked away until even the indefatigable Robert said he had done enough; then he reeled up; and perhaps he was not sorry to regain the top of this sheer precipice, where there was but that single fir-stump and a few loose branches of birch between him and the seething and surging whirlpool below.

He was more fortunate in the Geinig Pool, which Miss Cunyngham also compelled him to take, good-naturedly remarking that she had her fish already, and that he must have its fellow to carry home in the evening. There were some welcome clouds about now, and the rock from which he had to cast over the Geinig Pool afforded him a much better foothold than the fir-roots. At first things did not seem favorable, for he went over all the deep, smooth water without moving a fin; in fact, he had fished almost right to the end of the pool, when, in the very act of recovering his line, he got hold of something. And very soon he found that he had got hold of a very lively something; for the cantrips which this small salmon played were most extraordinary. For a second or two he seemed inclined to go right down the stony channel (which would have instantly settled the matter, as there was no possible means of following him), but the next moment he had dashed right up through the middle of the pool, tearing the water as he went, and frightening the luckless fisherman half out of his wits with this dangerously slackening line. That, however, was soon righted; and now the salmon lay in an eddy just below the fall. Would he attempt to breast that bulk of water in a mad effort to be free of this hateful thing that had got hold of him?—then good-bye to him forever! But no—that was not his fancy; he suddenly sprang into the air—and again sprang—and then savagely beat the surface with body and tail; after which fearsome performance he swerved round and came right in under the rock on which Lionel was standing, where they could see him lying perfectly still in the deep, clear water. He neither tugged nor bored; that olive-green thing (for so he appeared in these depths) lay perfectly motionless—no doubt planning further devilment and only waiting to recover his strength. Meanwhile Lionel had scrambled a bit higher up the rock, so as to get the rod at a safer angle.

"He's a lively fellow, that one!" old Robert said, with a grin. "Ay, sir, and ye hooked him ferry well, too."

"I should say I did!" Lionel exclaimed. "I had no idea there was a fish there—I never saw him coming—I was drawing the line out of the water, and all at once thought I had struck on a log. He's well hooked, I should think; but I didn't hook him—he hooked himself."

"He's not a ferry big one, but he's a salmon whatever," old Robert said; and then he suddenly called out, "Mind, sir!—let him go!—let him go!"

For away went that little wretch again, tearing over to the other side, where he lashed and better lashed the surface; and then, getting tired of that exercise, he somewhat sullenly came sailing into mid-stream, where there was a smooth, dark current, bounded on the side next the fisherman by some brown shelves of rock only a few inches under water. And what must this demon of a fish do but begin boring into the stream, so that every moment the line was being drawn nearer and nearer to the knife-like edge.

"Here, Robert, what am I to do now?" Lionel cried, in dismay. "Another couple of inches, and it's all over! How are we to get him out of that hole?"

"Mebbe he'll no go mich deeper," Robert observed, calmly, but with his gray eyes keenly watching.

"If I lose this fish," Lionel said, between his teeth, "I'll throw myself into the pool after him!"

"You'd better not," said Miss Cunyngham, placidly, "for if Robert has to gaff you, you'll find it a very painful experience."

But now the line was slackening a little; the fisherman reeled in quickly; the salmon made his appearance—undoubtedly yielding; and then, coming over the shallow rocks in obedience to the pressure of the rod, he once more sailed into the black, clear pool just below them. Cautiously old Robert crept down. When he was close to the water, he bared his right arm and grasped the gaff by the handle; then he waited and watched, for the salmon was still too deep. Lionel, meanwhile, had got back a bit on the rock, so that any sudden rush might not snap the top of his rod in two; then he also waited and watched, but somewhat increasing the pressure on the fish. Miss Honnor was probably as interested as either of them, but she only said,

---

"Cautiously old Robert crept down. When he was close to the water, he bared his right arm and grasped the gaff by the handle."

"I think he is well-hooked, and you'll get him, but don't bear too hardly on him for all that."

The conclusion of the fight proved to be a series of rapid and cautious skirmishes between the salmon and old Robert; for, as soon as the former discovered that danger awaited him at the foot of the rock, he made every possible effort to break away, and then, getting more and more exhausted, allowed himself to be led in again. And then at last, on his sailing in almost on his side, so dead beat was he, a firm stroke of the gaff caught him behind the shoulder, and the next moment he was in mid-air, the next again on the bare rock.

Now when you have slain a stag one day, it is not so much of a triumph to kill a salmon the next; nevertheless Lionel was as heartily glad to see that fish ashore as he would have been deeply mortified had it escaped. For was not Honnor Cunyngham looking on? Nay, she was kind enough to say to him,

"You played that fish very well, Mr. Moore."

"I have been watching you so often," said he, modestly, "that I must have learned something. And now you must take all the pools on the way home. I won't touch the rod again unless when wading is absolutely necessary. You see. I have no right to this salmon at all; I consider you have made me a present of him."

"We must try and get another somehow, between us, before getting back to the lodge," said she; and this unconscious coupling of themselves as companions sounded pleasant to his ears.

Moreover, as old Robert had now the fish to carry, Lionel, as usual, made bold to claim Miss Honnor's waterproof, which he slung over his arm; and that also was a privilege he greatly enjoyed. Indeed, his satisfaction as they now proceeded to walk along to the Horseshoe Pool was but natural in the circumstances. This charming companionship secured all to himself—the capture of the salmon—the tribute that had been paid to his skill—the magnetic waterproof hanging over his arm—the prospect of a long ramble home on this beautiful afternoon: all these things combined were surely sufficient to put any young man in an excellent humor. And there was something more in store for him.

"Do you know," he was saying, as they walked along together, "that I have grown quite used to the solitariness of this neighborhood? I don't find it strange, or melancholy, or oppressive any longer. I suppose when I get back to a crowded city, the roar of it will be absolutely bewildering; indeed, I am looking forward with a good deal of interest to seeing something of the world again at Kilfearn—which can't be a very big place either."

"Oh, are you going to the opening of the Kilfearn Town Hall?" she asked.

"Yes," said he, with a little surprise, "I thought everybody was going. Aren't you? I understood the whole world—of Ross-shire—was to be there, and that I was to make a sudden plunge into a perfect whirlpool of human life."

"It will amuse you," she said, with a quiet smile. "You will see all the county families there, staring at one another's guests; and you will hear a lot of songs, like 'My Pretty Jane' and 'Ever of Thee,' sung by bashful young ladies. At the opening of the proceedings my brother Hugh will make a speech; he is their chairman, and I know precisely what he will say. Hugh always speaks to the point. It will be something like this: 'Ladies and gentlemen, I am glad to see you here to-night. We still want £180. We mean to give two more concerts to clear the debt right off. You must all come and bring your friends. I will not longer stand in the way of the performers who have kindly volunteered their services.'"

"And that is a most admirable speech," her companion exclaimed. "It says everything that is wanted and nothing more; I call it a model speech!"

"Mr. Moore," she said, suddenly looking up, "are you going to sing at the concert?"

"I believe so," he answered.

"What are you going to sing?"

"Oh, I don't know yet. Whatever I am asked for. Lady Adela is arranging the programme." And then he added, rather breathlessly, "Is there anything you would care to have me sing?"

"Well, to tell you the truth," said she, quite frankly, "I hardly intended going. But if I thought there was a chance of hearing you sing some such song as 'The Bonnie Earl o' Moray,' I would go."

"'The Bonnie Earl o' Moray?'" he said, eagerly. "The song that Miss Lestrange sang the other night?"

"The song that Miss Lestrange made a fool of the other night," she said, contemptuously. "But if *you* were to sing it, you would make it very fine and impressive. I should like to hear you sing that in a large hall."

"Oh, but certainly I will sing it!" he said, quickly, for he was only too rejoiced that she should prefer this small request, as showing that she did take some little interest in him and what he could do. "I will make a stipulation that I sing it, if I sing anything. Miss Lestrange won't mind, I know."

"I almost think you should go under an assumed name," Miss Honnor said, presently, with a bit of a laugh. "I dare say the people wouldn't recognise you in ordinary dress. And then, when the amateur vocalists had been going on with their Pretty-Janes and Meet-Me-by-Moonlights, when you gave them 'The Bonnie Earl o' Moray,' as you would sing it, I should think amazement would be on most faces. But I dare say Lady Adela has had it announced in the *Inverness Courier* that you are to sing, for they want to make a grand success of the concert, to help to clear off the debt; and of course all the people from the shooting-lodges will be coming, for it isn't every autumn they have a chance of hearing Mr. Lionel Moore in Ross-shire."

Really, she was becoming quite complaisant!—this proud, unapproachable fisher-maiden, who seemed to live, remote and isolated, in a world all of her own. And so she was coming to this amateur concert, merely to hear him sing? Be sure the first thing he did that evening, on entering the drawing-room after dinner, was to go up to Miss Georgie Lestrange with a humble little speech, asking her whether she would object to his borrowing that particular ballad from her repertory. The smiling and gracious young damsel instantly replied that, on the contrary, she would be delighted to play the accompaniment for him. Would he look at the music now? He did look at it; found it simple enough; imagined that the refrain verse might be made rather effective. Would he try it over now? Yes, if she would be so kind. She forthwith went to the piano, he following; and at once there was silence in the long, low-ceilinged drawing-room. Of course this was but a trial, and the room had not been constructed with a view to any acoustic requirements; nevertheless, the fine and penetrating *timbre* of his trained voice told all the same; indeed, it is probable there was a lump in the throat of more than one of those young ladies when he sang the pathetic refrain, with its proud and sonorous finish—

"O lang may his lady-love

    Look frae the Castle Doune,

Ere she see the Earl o' Moray

    Come sounding through the toun."

Simple as the air was, it haunted the ear even of this professional vocalist all the evening; but perhaps that was because he was looking forward to a coming occasion on which he would have to sing the ballad; and well he knew that however numerous his audience might be—though he might be standing before all the Rosses and Frasers, the Gordons and Munroes, the Mackays and Mackenzies of the county—well he knew that he would be singing—that he intended to sing—to an audience of one only. And which would she like to have emphasized the more—the pathetic and hopeless outlook of the lady in the tower, or the proud state and ceremony of the earl himself as he used to "come sounding through the toun"? Well, he would practise a little, and ascertain what he could do with it—on some occasion when he found himself alone away up in the hills, with a silence around him unbroken save for the hushed whisper of the birch-leaves and the distant, low murmur of the Geinig falls.

CHAPTER XI.

THE PHANTOM STAG.

But if he were so anxious about how he should sing (for his audience of one only) that old Scotch ballad, he was not acting very wisely, or else he had a sublime confidence in the soundness of his chest; for on his host's offering him another day's stalking, he cheerfully accepted the same; and that notwithstanding they had now fallen upon a period of extremely rough, cold, and wet weather. Was this another piece of bravado, then— undertaken to produce a favorable impression in a certain quarter—or had the hunter's hunger really got hold of him? On the evening before the appointed raid, even the foresters looked glum; the western hills were ominous and angry, and the wind that came howling down the strath seemed to foretell a storm. But he was not to be daunted; he said he would give up only when Roderick assured him that the expedition was quite impracticable and useless.

"I hear you are going after the deer to-morrow," said the pretty Miss Georgie Lestrange to him, in the drawing-room after dinner, while Lady Sybil was performing her famous fantasia "The Voices of the Moonlight," to which nobody listened but her own admiring self. "And I was told all about that custom of making the stalker a little present on his setting out, for good-luck. It was Honnor Cunyngham who did that for you last time, and I think it should be my turn to-morrow morning."

"Oh, thank you!" said he; but "Thank you for nothing!" he said in his heart; for why should any frivolous trinket—even when presented by this very charming and complaisant young damsel—be allowed to interfere with the prerogative of Miss Cunyngham's sacred talisman?

"I say," continued the bright-eyed, ruddy-haired lass, "what do you and Honnor Cunyngham talk about all day long, when you are away on those fishing excursions? Don't you bore each other to death? Oh, I know she's rather learned, though she doesn't bestow much of her knowledge upon us. Well, I'm not going to say anything against Honnor, for she's so awfully good-natured, you know; she allows her sisters-in-law to experiment on her as an audience, and she has always something friendly and nice to say, though I can guess what she thinks of it all. Now, what *do* you two talk about all day long?"

"Well, there's the fishing," said he, "for one thing."

"Oh, don't tell me!" exclaimed this impertinent young hussy (while "The Voices of the Moonlight" moaned and mourned their mysterious regrets and despairs at the far end of the drawing-room). "Don't tell *me*! Honnor Cunyngham is far too good-looking for you to go talking salmon to her all day long. Very handsome I call her; don't you? She's so distinguished, somehow—so different from any one else. Of course you don't notice it up here so much, where she prides herself on roughing it—you never met her in London?—in London you should see her come into a drawing-room—her walk and manner are simply splendid. She'll never marry," continued this garrulous little person, with the coquettish *pince-nez* perched on her not too Grecian nose. "I'm sure she won't. She despises men—all of them except her brother, Sir Hugh. Lord Rockminster admires her tremendously, but he's too lazy to say so, I suppose. How has she taken such a fancy to you?"

"I was not aware she had," Lionel discreetly made answer, though the question had startled him, and not with pain.

"Oh, yes, she has. Did she think you were lone and unprotected, being persecuted by the rest of us? I am quite certain she wouldn't allow my brother Percy to go fishing a whole day with her; most likely Lord Rockminster wouldn't care to take the trouble. I wonder if she hasn't a bit of a temper? Lady Rosamund is awful sometimes; but she doesn't show that to *you*—catch her! But Honnor Cunyngham—well, the only time I ever went with her on one of her storking expeditions, the water was low, and she thrashed away for hours, and saw nothing. At last a stot happened to come wandering along; and she said, quite savagely, 'I'm going to hook something!' You don't know what a stot is?—it's a young bullock. So she deliberately walked to within twenty yards or so of the animal, threw the line so that it just dropped across its neck, and the fly caught in the thick hair. You should have seen the gay performance that followed! The beast shook its head and shook its head—for it could feel the line, if it couldn't feel the fly; and then, getting alarmed, it started off up the hill, with the reel squealing just as if a salmon were on, and Honnor running after him as hard as she could over the bracken and heather. If it were rage made her hook the stot, she was laughing now—laughing so that when the beast stopped she could hardly reel in the line. And old Robert—I thought he would have had a fit. 'Will I gaff him now, Miss Honnor?' he cried, as he came running along. But the stot didn't mean to be gaffed. Off it set again; and Honnor after it, until at last it caught the line in a birch-bush and broke it; then, just as if nothing had happened, it began to graze, as usual. You should have seen the game that began then—old Robert and Honnor trying to get hold of the stot, so as to take the casting-line and the fly from its mane—it isn't a mane, but you know—and the stot trying to butt them whenever they came near. The end of it was that the beast shook off the fly for itself, and old Robert found it; but I wonder whether it were real rage that made Honnor Cunyngham hook the stot—"

"Of course not!" he said. "It was a mere piece of fun."

"It isn't fun when Lady Rosamund comes down-stairs in a bad temper—after you gentlemen have left," remarked Miss Georgie, significantly; and then she prattled away in this careful undertone. "What horrid stuff that fantasia is; don't you think so? A mixture of Wagner, and Chopin, and 'Home, Sweet Home.' Lady Adela has put you in her novel. Oh, yes, she has; she showed me the last pages this morning. You remember the young married English lady who is a great poetess?—well, she is rescued from drowning in the Bay of Syracuse by a young Greek sailor, and you are the Greek sailor. You'll be flattered by her description of you. You are entirely Greek and godlike—what is that bust?—Alcibiades?—no, no, he was a general, wasn't he?—Alcinous, is it?—or Antinous?—never mind, the bust you see so often in Florence and Rome—well, you're described as being like that; and the young English lady becomes your patron, and you're to be educated, and brought to London. But whether her husband is to be killed off, to make way for you, or whether she is going to hand you over to one of her sisters, I don't know yet. It must be rather nice to look at yourself in a novel, and see what other people think of you and what fate they ordain for you. Lady Adela has got all the criticisms of her last novel—all the nice ones, I mean—cut out and pasted on pages and bound in scarlet morocco. I told her she should have all the unpleasant ones cut out and bound in green—envy and jealousy, don't you see?—but she pretends not to have seen any besides those she has kept. The book is in her own room; I suppose she reads it over every night, before going to bed. And really, after so much praise, it is extraordinary that she is to have no money for the book—no, quite the reverse, I believe. She was looking forward to making Sir Hugh a very handsome present—all out of her own earnings, don't you know—and she wrote to the publishers; but, instead of Sir Hugh getting a present, he will have to give her a check to cover the deficit, poor man! Disappointing, isn't it?—quite horrid, I call it; and every one thought the novel such a success—your friend, Mr. Quirk, was most enthusiastic—and we made sure that the public would be equally impressed. It isn't the loss of the money that Lady Adela frets about; it is the publishers telling her that so few copies have been sold; and we made sure, from all that was said in the papers—especially those that Mr. Quirk was kind enough to send—that the book was going to be read everywhere. Mind you don't say anything of the young Greek sailor until Lady Adela herself shows you the MS.; and of course you mustn't recognize your own portrait, for that is merely a guess of mine. Oh, thank you, thank you!"

The last words were a murmur of gratitude to Lady Sybil Bourne for her kindness in playing this piece of her own composition; and thereafter Miss Georgie's engaging and instructive monologue was not resumed, for the evening was now about to be wound up by a round or two of poker, and at poker Miss Georgie was an eager adept.

All that night it poured a deluge, and the morning beheld the Aivron in roaring spate, the familiar landmarks of the banks having mostly disappeared and also many of the mid-channel rocks; while the blue-black current that came whirling down the strath seemed to bring with it the dull, constant thunder of the distant falls. The western hills looked wild and stormy; there was half a gale of wind tearing along the valley; and, if the torrents of the night had mitigated, there were still flying showers of rain that promised to make of the expedition anything but a pleasure excursion.

"Tell me if it is any use at all!" Lionel insisted, for it must be confessed that the keepers looked very doubtful.

"Well, sir," said the bushy-bearded Roderick, "the deer will be down from the hills—oh, yes—but they'll be restless and moving about—"

"Do you expect I shall have a chance at one—that's all I want to know," was the next demand.

"Oh, yes, there may be that; but you'll get ahfu wet, sir—"

"I'm going," said he, definitely; whereupon the pony was straightway brought up to the door.

And here was Miss Georgie Lestrange, in a charming morning costume, which the male pen may not adequately describe, and she held a small packet in her hands.

"I told Honnor Cunyngham it was my turn," she said, with a kind of bashful smile, as she handed the little present to him, "and she only laughed—I wonder if she thinks she can command all the luck in Ross-shire; has she got a monopoly of it? Well, Mr. Moore, they all say you'll get fearfully wet; and that is a silk handkerchief you must put round your neck; what would the English public say if you went back from the Highlands with a hoarse throat!"

"I'm not thinking of the English public just at present," said he, cheerfully. "I'm thinking of the stag that is wandering about somewhere up in the hills; and I am certain your good wishes will get me a shot at him. How kind of you to get up so early!—good-bye!"

This, it must be admitted, was a most hypocritical speech; for although, as he rode away, he made a pretence of tying the pale pink neckerchief round his throat, it was on the influence of Miss Cunyngham's lucky sixpence—the pierced coin was secretly attached to his watch-chain—that he relied. In fact, before he had gone far from the lodge, he removed that babyish protection against the rain and stuck it in his pocket; he was not going to throw out a red flag to warn the deer.

After all, the morning was not quite so dismal as had been threatened; for now and again, as they went away up the strath, there was a break in the heavy skies; and then the river shone a deep and brilliant purple-blue—save where it came hurling in ale-hued masses over the rocks, or rushed in surging white foam through the stony channels. Sometimes a swift glimmer of sunlight smote down on the swinging current; but these flashes were brief, for the louring clouds were still being driven over from the west, and no one could tell what the day would bring forth.

"What will Miss Honnor do in a spate like that?" Lionel inquired of the head keeper. "Will she go out at all?"

"Oh, ay, Miss Honnor will go out," Roderick made answer; "but she will only be able to fish the tail-ends o' the pools—ay, and it will not be easy to put a fly over the water, unless the wind goes down a bit."

"But do you mean she will go out on a day like this?" he demanded again—as he looked at the wild skies and the thundering river.

"Oh, ay, if there's a chance at ahl Miss Honnor will be out," said Roderick, and he added, with a demure smile, "even if the chentlemen will be for staying at home."

However, Lionel had soon to consider his own attitude towards this swollen stream, when it became necessary to ford it on the hither side of the Bad Step. To tell the truth, when he regarded that racing current, he did not like the look of it at all.

"I don't see how we are to get across," he said, with some hesitation.

"Maggie knaws the weh," Roderick made answer, with a bit of a laugh.

"Yes, that's all very well," said the mounted huntsman. "I dare say she knows the way; but if she gets knocked over in the middle of the current, what is to become of me, or of her either?"

"She'll manage it, sir," said the keeper, confidently, "never fear."

Lionel was just on the point of saying, "Well, you come yourself and ride her across, and I'll go over the Bad Step on foot," but he did not like to show the white feather; so, somewhat apprehensively, he turned the old pony's head to the river-bank. And very soon he found that old Maggie knew much better what she was about than he did; for, as soon as she felt the weight of the water, she did not attempt to go straight across; she deliberately turned her head down-stream, put her buttocks against the force of the current, and thus sideways, and very cautiously, and with many a thrilling stumble and catching up again, she proceeded to ford this whirling Aivron. Never once did she expose herself broadside; her hind-legs were really doing most of the fight; and right gratefully did Lionel clap the neck of this wise beast when he found himself on solid land. The ford farther up was much less dangerous; and so once again the reunited party held on its way.

Then here was the Geinig—no longer the pretty and picturesque river that he knew, but a boiling and surging torrent sweeping in red wrath down its narrow and rocky channel. The farther heights, too, that now came into view, had lost their wonted pale and ethereal hues: there were no soft cloud-stains on the purple slopes of heather—a darkness dwelt over the land. As he gradually got up into that wilder country, the gloom grew more intense, the desolation more awful. The roar of the Geinig was lost now in this dreadful silence. He seemed to have left behind him all human sympathies and associations—to have forsaken his kindred and his kind— to have entered a strange world peopled only with dark phantoms and moving shadows and ghosts. A voiceless solitude, too, save for the moaning of the wind that came sweeping in bitter blasts down from the rainy hills. He did not recognize the features of this melancholy landscape; they had all changed since his last visit; nay, they were changing under his very eyes, as this or that far mountain-top receded behind a veil of gray, or a shadow of greater darkness advanced with stealthy tread along one of those lonely glens. There was something threatening in the aspect of both earth and sky; something louring, conspiring, as if some dread fate were awaiting this intruding stranger; at times he fancied he could hear low-murmuring voices, the first mutterings of distant thunder. What if some red bolt of lightning were suddenly to sever this blackness in twain and reveal its hidden and awful secrets? But no; there was no such friendly or avenging glare; the brooding skies lay over the sombre valleys, and the gloomy phantasmagoria slowly changed and changed in that unearthly twilight, as the mists and the wind and the rain transformed the solid hills and the straths into intermingling vapors and visions. A spectral world, unreal, and yet terrible; apparently voiceless and tenantless; and yet somehow suggesting that there were eyes watching, and vaguely moving and menacing shapes passing hither and thither before him in the gloom.

During these last few days he had been assuring himself that he would enter upon this second stalking expedition without any great tremor. It was only on the first occasion, when everything was strange and unknown to him, that he was naturally nervous. Even the keepers had declared that the shooting of the first stag was everything; that thereafter he would have confidence; that he would take the whole matter as coolly as themselves. And yet, when they now began to proceed more warily (old Maggie having been hobbled some way back) and when every corrie and slope and plateau had to be searched with the glass, he found himself growing not a little anxious at the thought of drawing the trigger; insomuch, indeed, that those sombre fancies of the imagination went out of his head altogether and gave place to the apprehension that on such a day it would be difficult to make a good shot. Their initial difficulty, however, was to find any trace of the "beasts." The wild weather had most likely driven them away from their usual haunts into some place of shelter, the smaller companies joining the main herd; at all events, up to lunch-time the stalkers had seen nothing. It was during this brief rest—in a deep peat-hag, down which trickled a little stream of rain-water—that Lionel discovered two things: first, that he was wet to the skin, and, second, that the wind in these altitudes was of an Arctic keenness. So long as he had been kept going, he had not paid much attention; but now this bitter blast seemed to pierce him to the very marrow; and he began to think that these were very pleasant conditions for a professional singer to be in—for a professional singer whose very existence depended on his voice.

"Here goes for congestion of the lungs," he philosophically observed to himself, as he shiveringly munched his wet sandwiches.

Presently Roderick came along the peat-hag.

"Would you like to wait here, sir, for a while?" said he, in his accustomed undertone. "I'm thinking Alec and me will go aweh up to the top of Meall-Breac and hef a look round there; and if we are seeing nothing, we will come back this weh and go down the Corrie-nam-Miseag—"

"And I am to wait here for you?" Lionel exclaimed. "Not if I know it! By the time you come back, Roderick, you would find me a frozen corpse. I've got to keep moving somehow, and I may as well go on with you. I suppose I cannot have a cigarette before setting out?"

"Aw, naw, sir!" Roderick pleaded. "In this weather, you cannot say where the deer may be—you may happen on them at any moment—and there will be plenty of time for you to smok on the weh hom."

"Very well," Lionel said; and he got up and tried to shake his blood into freer circulation; then he set out with his two companions for the summit of Meall-Breac.

This steep ascent was fatiguing enough; but, at all events, it restored some warmth to his body. He did not go quite to the top; he sat down on a lichened stone, while Roderick proceeded to crawl, inch by inch, until his head and glass were just over the crest of a certain knoll. A long scrutiny followed; then the forester slowly disappeared—the gillie following in his serpent-like track; and Lionel sat on in apathetic patience, slowly getting chilled again. He asked himself what Nina would say to him if she knew of these escapades. He held his back to the wind until he was frozen that way; then he turned his face to the chill blast, folding his arms across his chest. He took a sip from Percy Lestrange's flask; but that was more for employment than anything else, for he discovered there was no real warmth to be got that way. He thought Roderick was never coming back from the top of the hill. He would have started off down the ascent again, but that they might miss him; besides, he might do something fatally wrong. So he sat on this cold stone and shivered, and began to think of Kensal Green.

Suddenly he heard footsteps behind him; he turned and found the two men coming towards him.

"Not a sign of anything, sir," was Roderick's report. "It's awfu' dark and difficult to see, and the clouds are down all along Glen Bhoideach. We'll just step along by the Corrie-nam-Miseag. They very often stop for a while in the corrie when they're crossing over to Achnadruim."

Lionel was not sorry to be again in motion, and yet very soon he found that motion was not an unmixed joy; for these two fellows, who were now going down wind along the route they had come, and therefore walking fearlessly, took enormously long strides and held straight on, no matter what sort of ground they were covering. For the sake of his country, he fought hard to keep up with them; he would not have them say they could outwalk an Englishman—and an Englishman considerably younger than either of them; but the way those two went over this rough and broken land was most extraordinary. And it seemed so easy; they did not appear to be putting forth any exertion; in spite of all he could do, he began to lag a little; and so he thought he would mitigate their ardor by engaging them in a little conversation.

"Roderick," said he, "do you think this neighborhood was ever inhabited?"

"Inhabited?" said Roderick, turning in surprise. "Oh, ay, it was inhabited ahlways—by foxes and eagles."

"Not by human beings?"

"Well, they would be ferry clever that could get a living out of land like this," Roderick said, simply.

"But they say in the House of Commons that the deer-forests are depriving a large portion of the population of a means of subsistence," Lionel observed—rather breathlessly, for these long strides were fearful.

"Ay, do they say that now?" Roderick made answer, with much simplicity. "In the House of Commons? I'm thinking there is some foolish men in the House of Commons. Mebbe they would not like themselves to come here and try to get their living out of rocks and peat-hags."

"But don't you think there may have been people in these parts before the ancient forests rotted down into peat?" Lionel again inquired.

"I do not know about that," Roderick said, discreetly; perhaps he knew that his opinions about prehistoric man were not of great value.

But what Lionel discovered was that talking in no wise interfered with the tremendous pace of the forester; and he was just on the point of begging for a respite from this intolerable exertion when a change in their direction caused both Roderick and the gillie to proceed more circumspectly: they were now coming in view of the Corrie-nam-Miseag, and they had to approach with care, slinking along through hollows and behind mounds and rocks.

By this time, it must be confessed, Lionel was thoroughly dead-beat: he was wet through, icily cold, and miserable to the verge of despair. The afternoon was well advanced; they had seen no sign of a stag anywhere; the gloomy evening threatened to bring darkness on prematurely; and but for very shame's sake, he would have entreated them to abandon this fruitless enterprise, and set out for the far-off region of warmth and reasonable comfort and dry clothes. And yet when Roderick, having crawled up to the top of a small height, suddenly and eagerly signalled for Lionel to follow him, all this hopeless lassitude was instantly forgotten. His heart began to burn, if his limbs were deadly cold; and quickly he was on the ground, too, moving himself up alongside the keeper. The glass was given him, but his trembling fingers could not hold it straight; he put it down, and by and by his natural eyes showed him what he thought were some slightly moving objects.

"There's two of them—two stags," Roderick whispered, "and we can get at them easily if there's no more wandering about that I cannot see. Mebbe the others are over that hull. There's one of them is a fine big beast, but he has only the one horn; the other one, his head is not ferry good. But a stag is a stag whatever; and the evening is wearing on. Now come aweh with me, sir."

What Roderick meant by getting at them easily Lionel was now to find out; he thought he would never have done with this agonizing stooping and crawling and wading through burns. Long before they had got to the neighborhood of the deer, he wished heartily that the night would come suddenly down, or the stags take the alarm and make off—anything, so that he might be released from this unspeakable toil and suffering. And yet he held on, in a sort of blind, despairing fashion; the idea in his head being that if nature gave way he would simply lie down and fall asleep in the heather—whether to wake again or not he hardly cared. But by and by he was to have his reward. Roderick was making for a certain cluster of rocks; and when these were reached, Lionel found, to his inexpressible joy, not only that he was allowed to stand upright, but that the stalk had been accomplished. By peering over one of the boulders, he could see both stags quietly feeding at something like seventy yards' distance. It was going to be an easy shot in every way; himself in ample concealment; a rock on which to rest his rifle; the deer without thought of danger. He would take his time and calm down his nerves.

"Which one?" he whispered to Roderick.

"The one with the one horn is a fine beast," the keeper whispered in return; "and the other one, his head is worth nothing at all."

With extremest caution Lionel put the muzzle over the ledge of the rock, and pushed it quietly forward. He made sure of his footing. He got hold of the barrel with his left hand, and of the stock with his right; he fixed the rifle firmly against his shoulder, and took slow and steady aim. He was not so nervous this time; indeed, everything was in his favor: the stag standing broadside on and hardly moving, and this rock offering so convenient a rest. He held his breath for a moment—concentrated all his attention on the long, smooth barrel—and fired.

"You've got him, sir!" exclaimed Roderick, in an eager whisper, and still keeping his head down; but seeing that the other stag had caught sight of the rifle-smoke and was off at the top of his speed, he rose from his place of concealment and jumped on to the rock that had been hiding him.

"Ay, ay, sir, he'll no go far," he cried to Lionel, who was scrambling up to the same place. "There, he's down again on his knees. Come aweh, sir? we'll go after him. Give me the rifle."

Lionel had just time to get a glimpse of the wounded stag, which was stumbling pitifully along—far behind its now disappearing companion—when he had to descend from the rock in order to follow Roderick. All three ran quickly down the hill and rounded into the hollow where they had last seen the stag, following up his track, and looking out everywhere for his prostrate body. But the farther they went, the more amazed became Roderick and the gillie; there was no sign of the beast that both of them declared could not have run a couple of hundred yards. The track of him disappeared in the bed of a burn and could not be recovered, search as they would; so they proceeded to explore every adjacent hollow and peat-bag, in the certainty that within a very few minutes they must find the lost quarry. The few minutes lengthened out and out; half-hours went by; and yet there was no sign. They went away down the burn; they went away up the burn; they made wider casts, and narrowed in, like so many retrievers; and all to no purpose. And meanwhile darkness and the night were coming on.

"He's lying dead somewhere, as sure as anything can be," Roderick said, looking entirely puzzled and crestfallen; "and we'll hef to bring up a terrier in the morning and search for him. I never sah the like o' that in my life. When he fell where he stood I made sure he was feenished; then he was up again and ran a little weh, and again he went down on his knees—"

"It was then I saw him," Lionel exclaimed, "and I expected him to drop the next moment. Why, he *must* be about here, Roderick, he couldn't vanish into the air—he wasn't a ghost—for I heard the thud of the bullet when it struck him—"

"Ay, and me too," Roderick said, "but we will do no good now, for it is getting so dark; and you hef to cross the two fords, sir—"

"The fords!" said Lionel. "By Jove! I forgot them. I say, we must hurry on. I suppose you are sure to find him in the morning?"

"We will bring up a terrier whatever," Roderick said, doubtfully; for he seemed to have been entirely disconcerted by the disappearance of the phantom stag. "Ay, I hef known them rin a long weh after being wounded—miles and miles they will go—but this wan wass so hard hit, I thought he would drop directly. The teffle tek him—I could hef given him the other barrel myself!"

And still they seemed loath to leave the ground, notwithstanding the gathering darkness. They kept wandering about, examining and searching; until it was quite obvious that even if the stag were lying within easy distance of them they could hardly distinguish it; so finally they withdrew, beaten and baffled, and made away down to the lower country, where the old pony Maggie was probably wondering at their unusual length of absence.

That was a sombre ride home. It was now raining heavily; and all the night seemed to be filled with a murmuring of streams and a moaning of winds among the invisible hills. Roderick walked by the pony's head; and Lionel could just make him out, and no more, so pitch dark it was. Of course he had no idea of the route he was taking or of the nature of the ground they were getting over; but he could guess from Maggie's cautious steps when they were going over rough places, or he could hear the splash of her feet when they were crossing a swamp. Not a word was uttered; no doubt all the forester's attention was bent on making out a path; while as for Lionel, he was too wet and cold and miserable to think of talking to anybody. If he had certainly known that somewhere or other he had left up there a stag, which they could bring down in the morning, that would have consoled him somewhat; but it was just as likely as not that all this privation and fatigue had been endured for nothing. As they trudged along through the gloomy night, the rain fell more heavily than ever, and the bitter wind seemed to search out every bone in his body.

And then when at length they came within sound of the Geinig, that was no longer a friendly voice welcoming them back to more familiar regions; it was an angry and threatening roar; he could see nothing; he could only imagine the wild torrent hurling along through this black desolation.

"Look here, Roderick," he said, "mind you keep away from that river. If we should stumble down one of the steep banks, we should never be heard of again."

"Oh, ay, we're a long distance from the ruvver? and it is as well to keep aweh; for if we were to get into the Geinig to-night, we would be tekken down like straws."

And how welcome was the small red ray that told of the shepherd's cottage just below the juncture of the Geinig and Aivron. It was a cheerful beacon; it spoke of human association and companionship; the moan of the hurrying Aivron seemed to have less of boding in it now. It is true they still had the two fords to encounter, and another long and weary tramp, before they got back to the lodge; but here at least was some assurance that they were out of those storm-haunted solitudes where the night was now holding high revel. That ray of light streaming from the solitary little window seemed to Lionel a blessed thing; it served to dissipate the horrors of this murmuring and threatening blackness all around him; it cheered and warmed his heart; it was a joyful assurance that they were on the right way for home. When they reached the cottage, they knocked at the door; and presently there was a delightful, ruddy glow in the midst of the dark. Would the gentleman not come in and warm himself at the fire and get his clothes dried? No: Lionel said that getting wet through once was better than getting wet through twice; he would go on as he was. But might he have a glass of milk? The shepherd disappeared, and returned with a tumbler of milk and a piece of oatcake; and never in his life had the famous baritone from the far city of London tasted anything sweeter, for he was half-dead with hunger. Greatly refreshed by this opportune bit and sup, the tired and "droukit" rider cheerfully resumed his way; and it was with a stout heart that, after a certain time, he found Roderick cautiously leading the pony down to the water's edge. And then a sudden thought struck him.

"Look here, Roderick," said he, "I suppose I can get across this ford safely enough; but how on earth am I to know when I get to the next one? I can't see a yard in front of the pony's head."

"I'm coming with ye, sir," was the simple answer; and at the same moment there was a general splashing which told him that both Maggie and the tall keeper were in the rushing stream.

"Well, I suppose you can't be wetter than you are," he said.

"Indeed, that's true," Roderick answered, with much composure.

Now this first ford, though a ticklish thing in the pitch darkness, they managed successfully enough; but the next one proved a terrible business. Roderick went by the pony's head, with his hand on the bridle; but whether he helped Maggie, or whether Maggie helped him, it would be hard to say. Lionel could only guess what a mighty floundering there was going on; but Roderick kept encouraging his four-footed companion to hold up; and more than once, when they attained a safe footing, he called a halt to let the faithful Maggie recover her breath.

"Take your feet out o' the stirrups, sir," he said, when they were about half-way across; "there's some nasty sharp ledges the other side, and if she loses her footing you'll chist slip off before she goes over; and it will not tek ye above the waist whatever, so that you can get ashore by yourself."

When they did reach those ledges, Maggie seemed to understand the awkwardness of the situation quite as well as he; she went forward only an inch or two at a time; and if her hind-feet occasionally skated a little, her fore-feet remained firm where she had planted them. As for Lionel, he was, of course, quite helpless; he did not seek to interfere in any way; he was merely ready to slip off the saddle if Maggie rolled over. But presently a sudden red flash revealed to him that they were near land (this was Alec striking a vesuvian to give them a friendly lead); there was some further cautious sliding and stumbling forward; then the uplifting of Maggie's neck and shoulders told him she had gained solid ground and was going up the bank. Never was soft and sure footfall more welcome.

The arrival of this belated and bedrenched little party at the lodge created no little surprise; for it had been concluded that, having been led away by a long stalk, or perhaps following a wounded deer into unexpected regions, and finding themselves overtaken by the dark, they had struck across country for the Aivron-Bridge Inn, to pass the night there. However, Sir Hugh bustled about to have his guest properly looked after; and when Lionel had got into dry clothes and swallowed some bit of warmed-up dinner, he went into the drawing-room, where they were all of them playing poker—all of them, that is to say, except Lord Fareborough, who, in a big easy-chair by the fire, was nursing his five-and-twenty ailments, and no doubt inwardly cursing those people for the chatter they were keeping up. They stopped their game when Lionel entered, to hear the news; and when he had told his heartrending tale, Lady Adela's brother lazily called to her:

"I say, Addie, there's a chance for you to try that terrier of yours. If he's as intelligent as you say, send him out with the Billies to-morrow, and see if he can find the stag for them."

"Why, of course," Lady Adela instantly responded. "Mr. Moore, I have just become possessed of the wisest little terrier in the whole world, I do believe. He only arrived this evening; but he and I have been friends for a long time; I bought him only yesterday from a shepherd down the strath. Oh, I must show you the letter that came with the dog. Georgie, dear, would you mind running into my room and bringing me a letter you will find on the dressing-table?"

Miss Georgie was absent only a couple of seconds; when she returned she handed Lionel the following epistle, which was written on a rather shabby sheet of paper. Its contents, however, were of independent value:

"ALTNASHIELACH. *Tuesday moarning.*

"LADY ADDELA CUNNINGHAM,—

"HONNERD LADY,—I am sendin you the terrier by my sin Jeames that was takking the milk from Bragla to your ladyship's house the last year when he was butten by the red dog and your ladyship so kind as to giv him five shullins the terrier's name is Donacha bit he will soon answer to his English name that is Duncan Honnerd Lady you must be kind to him for he will be a little shy the first time he is awa from home and because he will not understand your languish as he was taught Gealic he got plenty of Blood on the foxes he can warry wan with himself alone let me no how you will be please with him and if he is behaved and obadient I will be glad to have the news

"from your ladyship's humble servant

"MAGNUS ROSS, *Altnashielach*"

"A wee terrier that can worry a fox all by himself must be a gallant little beast, mustn't he?" said Lady Adela, who seemed quite proud of her new acquisition. "And I know he will find that stag for you, Mr. Moore, if he is to be found; for Donacha, or Duncan, is the wisest little creature you ever saw, I wish I could talk Gaelic, just to make him feel at home the first few days." Then she turned to her companions. "Who began this round—Mr. Lestrange? Very well, when it comes to Sybil, I propose we let you gentlemen go off to your cigars in the gun-room; for poor Mr. Moore, I know, hasn't been allowed to smoke all day; and I am sure he must be far too tired to think of playing poker. How many do you want, Rose?"

When this round of poker was finished, the gentlemen did not seem to resent being dismissed to the so-called gun-room, where, round the great blazing peat fire, and with cigars and pipes and whiskey-and-soda to console them in their banishment, Lionel was called upon to give them more minute details regarding his day's adventures. And very various were the opinions expressed as to the chances of that stag being found. Some ominous stories were told of the extraordinary distances deer were known to have run even when mortally wounded; and there were possibilities suggested of his having fallen into a rapid watercourse and been carried down to the rushing river; while Sir Hugh ventured to hint that, if he were not found on the morrow, the probability was that some shepherd, in his remote and lonely shieling just outside the forest, would be feasting on venison for a considerable time to come. Lionel cared less now; heat and food had thawed him into a passive frame of mind; he was tired, worn out, and sleepy; and very glad was he when he was allowed to go to bed.

As a matter of fact, that magic one-horned stag was not found on the next day; no, nor any following day; nor has it ever been heard of since in those parts. And if it vanished from the earth through some evil enchantment, be sure that Lionel—who had picked up some of the superstitions of the neighborhood, and who had profited on a former occasion by the possession of a lucky sixpence—be sure he attributed his cruel ill-fortune, solely and wholly, to that wretched red rag that had been given him by Miss Georgie Lestrange.

CHAPTER XII.

A GLOBE OF GOLD-FISH.

What, then, was the secret charm and fascination exercised over him by this extremely independent, not to say unapproachable, fisher-maiden; why should he be so anxious to win her approval; why should he desire to be continually with her—even when all her attention was given to her salmon-line, and she apparently taking no notice of him whatever? She was handsome, no doubt, and fine-featured and pleasant to look upon; she was good-humored, and friendly in her own way; and she had the education and manners and tact and gentleness of one of her birth and breeding; but there were lots of other women similarly graced and gifted who were only too eager to welcome him and pet him and make much of him, and towards whom he found himself absolutely indifferent. Was he falling in love? Had he been asked the question, he would honestly have answered that he was about the last person in the world to form a romantic attachment. There was no kind of sentimental wistfulness in his nature; his imagination had no poetical trick of investing the face and form of any passably good-looking girl with a halo of rainbow-hues; even as a lad his dreams had concerned themselves more with the possibility of his becoming a great musician than with his sharing his fame and glory with a radiant bride. But, above all, the rhodomontade of simulated passion that he heard in the theatre, and the extravagance of action necessary for stage effect, would of themselves have tended to render him sceptical and callous. He saw too much of how it was done. Did ever any man in his senses swear by the eternal stars in talking to a woman; and did ever any man in his senses kneel at a woman's feet? In former times they may have done so, when fustian and attitudinizing were not fustian and attitudinizing, but common habit and practice; but in our own day did the love-making of the stage, with all its frantic gestures and wild appeals, represent anything belonging to actual life? Of course, if the question had been pushed home, he would have had to admit that love as a violent passion does veritably exist, or otherwise there would not be so many young men blowing out their brains, and young women drowning themselves, out of disappointment; but probably he would have pointed out that in these cases the coroner's jury invariably and charitably certify that the victim is insane.

No; romance had never been much in his way, except the sham romance which he had assumed along with a painted face and a stage costume, and of which he knew the just and accurate value. He had never had time to fall seriously in love, he used to say to Maurice Mangan. And now, in this long spell of idleness in the North, amid these gracious surroundings, if he had had to confess that he found a singular fascination in the society of Honnor Cunyngham, why, he would have discovered a dozen reasons and excuses rather than admit that poetical sentiment had anything to do with it. For one thing, she was different from any woman he had ever met before; and that of itself piqued his curiosity. You had to speak the downright truth to her—when she looked at you with those clear hazel eyes; little make-believes of flattery were of no use at all. Her very tranquillity and isolation were a sort of challenge; her almost masculine independence was like to drive a man to say, "I am as peremptory as she proud-minded." Nevertheless, she was no curst Katherine; her temper was of the serenest; she was almost too bland and placid, Lionel thought—it showed she cared too little about you to be either exacting and petulant, or, on the other hand, solicitous to please.

There came into these silent and reverie-haunted solitudes a letter from the distant and turbulent world without; and of a sudden Lionel felt himself transported back into the theatre again, in the midst of all its struggles and hopes and anxieties, its jealousies and triumphs, its ceaseless clamor and unrest. The letter was from Nina.

"MY DEAR FRIEND LEO,—I have waited now some time that I send you the critiques of my new part, but the great morning newspapers have taken no notice of poor Nina, it is only some of the weekly papers that have observed the change in the part, and you will see that they are very kind to me. Ah, but one—I do not send it—I could not send it to you, Leo—it has made me cry much and much that any one should have such malignity, such meanness, such lying. I forget all the other ones? that one stabs my heart? but Mr. Carey he laughs and says to me You are foolish? you do not know why that is said of you? He is a great ally of Miss Burgoyne, he does not like to see you take her place and be well received by the public. Perhaps it is true; but, Leo, you do not like to be told that you make the part stupid, that there is no life in it, that you are a *machine*, that you sing out of tune. I have asked Mr. Lehmann, I have asked Mr. Carey, and said to them If it is true, let me go? I will not make ridicule of your theatre. But they are so kind to me; and Mrs. Grey also; she says that I have not as much *cheek* as Miss Burgoyne, but that Grace Mainwaring should remember that she is a gentlewoman, and it is not necessary to make her a laughing waitress, although she is in comedy-opera. I cannot please every one, Leo; but if you were here I should not care so much for the *briccone* who *lies*, who *lies*, who hides in the dark, like a thief. You know whether I sing out of tune, Leo. You know whether I am so stupid, so very stupid. Yes, I may not have *cheek*; I wish not to have *cheek*; even to commend myself to a critic. Ah, well, it is no use to be angry; every night I have a reception that you would like to hear, Leo, for *you* have no jealousy; and my heart says *those* people are not under bad influence; they are honest in saying they are pleased; to *them* I sing not out of tune, and am not so very stupid. If I lie awake at night, and cry much, it is then I say to myself that I am stupid; and the next morning I laugh, when Mrs. Grey says some kind thing to me.

"Will you be surprised, most excellent Signor, if you have a visit from Miss Burgoyne? Yes, it is possible. The doctor says she has strained her voice by too long work—but it was a little *reedy* of its own nature, do you not think, Leo?—and says she must have entire rest, and that she must go to the Isle of White; but she said every one was going to Scotland, and why not she, and her two friends, her travelling companions. Then she comes to me and ask your address. I answer—Why to me? There is Mr. Lehmann; and at the stage-door they will know his address, for letters to go. So, you see, you will not be alone in the high-lands, when you have such a *charming visitor* with you, and she will talk to you, not from behind a fan, as on the stage, but all the day, and you will have great comfort and satisfaction. Yes, I see her arrive at the castle. She rings at the gate; your noble friends come out, and ask who she is; they discover, and drive away such a person as a poor cantatrice. But you hear, you come flying out, you rescue her from scorn— ah, it is pitiable, they all weep, they say to you that you are honorable and just, that they did wrong to despise your charming friend. Perhaps they ask her to dine; and she sings to them after; and Leo says to himself, Poor thing; no; her voice is not so reedy. The *dénouement?*—but I am not come to it yet; I have not arranged what will arrive then.

"What is the time of your return, Leo? And you know what will be then? You will find on the stage another Grace Mainwaring, who will sing always out of tune, and be so stupid that you will have fury and will complain to the Manager. Ah, there is now no one to speak with you from behind a fan—only a dull heavy stupid. Misera me! What shall I do? All the poetry departed from Harry Thornhill's singing—there is no more fascination for him—he looks up to the window—he sings 'The starry night brings me no rest'—and he says 'Bother to that stupid Italian girl!—why am I to sing to her?' Poor Leo, he will be disconsolate; but not for long. No; Miss Burgoyne will be coming back; and then he will have some one for to talk with from behind the fan.

"Now, Leo, if you can read any more, I must attend to what you call *beesness*. When Miss Burgoyne returns, I do not go back to be under-study to Miss Girond—no—Mr. Lehmann has said he is pleased with me, and I am to take the part of Miss Considine, who goes into the provincial company. You know it is almost the same consequence as Grace Mainwaring towards the public, and I am, oh, very proud of such an advancement; and I have written to Pandiani, and to Carmela and Andrea, and Mrs. Grey is kinder than ever, and I take lessons always and always, when she has a half-hour from the house-governing. I am *letter perfect*—is it what they say?—in this part as in the other; my bad English does not appear on the stage; I practise and practise always. I am to share in Miss Girond's room, and that will be good, for she is friendly to me, though sometimes a little saucy in her amusement. Already I hear that the theatre-attendant people are coming back—and you—when is your return? You had benevolence to the poor chorus-singer, Signor Leo; and now she is prima-donna do you think she will forget you? No, no! To-day I was going up Regent Street, and in a window behold! a portrait of Mr. Lionel Moore and a portrait of Miss Antonia Ross side by side! I laughed—I said, Leo did not look to this a short time ago. It is the same fotografer; I have had several requests; but only to that one I went, for it is the best one of you he has taken that is seen anywhere. Of course I have to dress as like Miss Burgoyne as possible, which is a pity to me, for it is not too graceful, as I think I could do; but I complain nothing, since Mr. Lehmann gave me the great advancement; and if you will look at the critiques you will see they say I have not a bad appearance in the part. As for the *briccone*—pah!—when I talk like this to you, Leo, I despise him—he is nothing to me—I would not pay twopence that he should praise me.

"Will you write to me, Leo, and say when you return? Have you so much *beesness* that you have only sent me one letter? Adieu!

NINA."

"Your true friend,

Well, this prattling letter from Nina caused him some reflection and some uneasy qualms. He did not so much mind the prospect of having, on his return, to transform his old friend and comrade into his stage-sweetheart, and to make passionate love to her every evening before an audience. That might be a little embarrassing at first; but the feeling would soon wear off; such circumstances were common and well understood in the theatre, where stage-lovers cease their cooing the moment they withdraw into the wings. But this other possibility of finding Miss Burgoyne and her friends in the immediate neighborhood of Strathaivron Lodge? Of course there was no reason why she shouldn't travel through Ross-shire just as well as any one else. She knew his address. If she came anywhere round this way—say to Kilfearn—he must needs go to call on her. Then both Lady Adela Cunyngham and Lord Rockminster had been introduced to Miss Burgoyne in the New Theatre; if he told them, as he ought, on whom he was going to call, might they not want to accompany him and renew the acquaintance? Lady Adela and her sisters considered themselves the naturally appointed patrons of all professional folk whose names figured in the papers; was it not highly probable that Miss Burgoyne and her friends, whosoever these might be, would receive an invitation to Strathaivron Lodge? And then?—why, then might there not be rather too close a resemblance to a band of poor players being entertained by the great people at what Nina imagined to be a castle? A solitary guest was all very well; had Miss Burgoyne preceded or succeeded him, he could not have objected; but a group of strolling players, as it were?—might it not look as if they had been summoned to amuse the noble company? And fancy Miss Burgoyne coming in as a spy upon his mute, and at present quite indefinite, relations with Miss Honnor Cunyngham!—Miss Burgoyne, who was a remarkably sharp-eyed young woman, and had a clever and merry tongue withal, when she was disposed to be humorous.

Then he bethought him of what Honnor Cunyngham, with her firm independence of character, her proud self-reliance, would have said to all these timorous fancies. He knew perfectly well what she would say. She would say, "Well, but even if Miss Burgoyne were to appear at Strathaivron Lodge, how could that affect you? You are yourself; you are apart from her; her visit will be Lady Adela's doing, not yours. And if people choose to regard you as one of a band of strolling players, how can that harm you? Why should you care? The opinion that is of value to you is your own opinion; be right with yourself; and leave others to think what they please. Whoever could so entirely misjudge your position must be a fool; why should you pause for a moment to consider the opinion of a fool or any number of fools? 'To thine own self be true;' and let that suffice."

For he had come to know pretty accurately, during these frequent if intermittent talks and chats along the Aivron banks, how Miss Honnor would regard most things. The wild weather had been succeeded by a period of calm; the river had dwindled and dwindled, until it seemed merely to creep along its channel; where a rushing brown current had come down there now appeared long banks of stones, lilac and silver-gray and purple, basking in the sun; while half-way across the stream in many places the yellow sand and shingle shone through the lazily rippling shallows. Consequently there was little fishing to be done. Honnor Cunyngham went out all the same, for she loved the river-side in all weathers; and as often as he discreetly might, Lionel accompanied her; but as they had frequently to wait for half-hours together until a cloud should come over, he had ample opportunity of learning her views and opinions on a great variety of subjects. For she spoke freely and frankly and simply in this enforced idleness; and, from just a little touch here and there, Lionel began to think that she must have a good deal more of womanly tenderness and sympathy than he had given her credit for. Certainly she was always most considerate towards himself; she seemed to understand that he was a little sensitive on the score of his out-of-door performances; and while she made light of his occasional blunders, she would quietly hint to him that he in turn ought to exercise a generous judgment when those people at the Lodge ventured to enter a province in which he was a past master.

"We are all amateurs in something or another, Mr. Moore," she would say. "And the professionals should not treat us with scorn."

"I wonder in what you show yourself an amateur," said he, bethinking himself how she seemed to keep aloof from the music, art, and literature of her accomplished sisters-in-law. "Everything you do you do thoroughly well."

She laughed.

"You have never seen me try to do anything but cast a line," said she, "and if I can manage that, the credit rests with old Robert."

But the consideration that she invariably extended to her brother's guest was about to show itself in a very marked manner; and the incident arose in this wise. One morning, the weather being much too bright and clear for the shallower pools of the Aivron, they thought they would take luncheon with them, and stroll up to the Geinig, where, in the afternoon, the deeper pools might give them a chance, especially if a few clouds were to come over. Accordingly the three of them went away along the valley, passed over the Bad Step, meandered through the long birch wood, and finally arrived at the little dell above the Geinig Pool, which was Miss Honnor's favorite retreat. They had left somewhat late; the sun was shining from a cloudless sky; luncheon would pass the useless time; so Robert got the small parcels and the drinking-cups out of the bag, and arranged them on the warm turf. It was a modest little banquet, but in the happiest circumstances; for the birch branches above them afforded them a picturesque shelter; and the burn at their feet, attenuated as it was, and merely threading its way down through the stones, flashed diamonds here and there in the light. And then she was so kind as to thank him again for singing "The Bonnie Earl o' Moray"—which had considerably astounded the people assembled at the opening of the Kilfearn Public Hall, or, at least, such of them as did not know that a great singer was among the guests at Strathaivron Lodge.

"I was rather sorry for them who had to follow you," she said; "they must have felt it was hardly fair. It was like Donald Dinnie at the Highland Games: when he has thrown the hammer or tossed the caber, the spectator hardly takes notice of the next competitor. By the way, I suppose you will be going to the Northern meeting at the end of this month?"

"I am sorry I cannot stay so long, though Lady Adela was good enough to ask me," he made answer. "I must go south very soon now."

"Oh, indeed?" she said. "That is a pity. It is worth while being in Inverness then; you see all the different families and their guests; and the balls are picturesque—with the kilt and tartan. It is really the wind-up of the season; the parties break up after that. We come back here and remain until about the middle of October; then we go on to the Braes—worse luck for me. I like the rough-and-tumble of this place; the absence of ceremony; the freedom and the solitude. It will be very different at the Braes."

"Why shouldn't you stop on here, then?" he naturally asked.

"Robert got the small parcels and the drinking-cups out of the bag, and arranged them on the warm turf."

"All by myself?" she said. "Well, I shouldn't mind the loneliness—you see, old Robert is left here, and Roderick, too, and one or two of the girls to keep fires on; but I should have nothing to do but read; the fishing is useless long before that time. And so you are going away quite soon?"

"Yes," said he, and he paused for a second—for there was some wild wish in his heart that she would have just one word of regret. "I must go," he continued, seeing that she did not speak. "I am wanted. And I have had a long holiday—a long and delightful holiday; and I'm sure, when I look back over it, I can't thank you sufficiently for all your kindness to me."

"Thank me, Mr. Moore?" she said, with obvious surprise.

"Oh, yes, indeed," he said, warmly. "If it was only a word now and again, it was always encouragement. I should never have ventured out after the deer if it had not been for you; probably I should never have taken up a gun at all. Then all those delightful days by the river; haven't I to thank you for them? It seems rather hard that I should be so much indebted to you—"

"I am sure you are not at all," she said.

"—without a chance of ever being able to show my gratitude; repayment, of course, is out of the question, for we could never meet again in similar circumstances—in reversed circumstances, rather—I mean, you have had it all your own way in your—your toleration, shall I say?—or your commiseration, of a hopeless duffer. Oh, I know what I'm talking about. Most people in your position would have said, 'Well, let him go and make a fool of himself!' and most people in my position would have said, 'No, I'm not going to make a fool of myself.'"

"I don't quite understand," she said, simply, "why you should care so much for the opinion of other people."

"I suppose there is no chance of my ever seeing you in London, Miss Honnor," he continued, rather breathlessly. "If—if I might presume on the acquaintanceship formed up here, I should like—well, I should like to show you I had not forgotten your kindness. Do you ever come to London?—I think Miss Lestrange said you sometimes did."

"Why, I am in London a great part of every year!" she said. "And this winter I shall be next door to it; for my mother goes to Brighton in November; and she will want me to be with her."

"To Brighton!" he said, quickly and eagerly. "Then, of course, you would be in London sometimes. Would you—would you care to come behind the scenes of a theatre?—or be present at a dress rehearsal, or something of that kind? No, I'm afraid not—I'm afraid that wouldn't interest you—"

"Oh, but it would," she said, pleasantly enough. "It would interest me very much."

And perhaps he would have gone on to assure her how delighted he would be to have the opportunity of showing her, in the great capital, that he had not forgotten her kindness and help in these Northern wilds, but that Miss Honnor, seeing that their frugal meal was over, called for Robert. The handsome old fisherman appeared at once; but she instantly perceived by his face that something was wrong.

"This is ferry strange, Miss Honnor," said he, "that the fly-book is not in the bag. And I could not have dropped it out. I was not thinking of looking for it when we started, for I knew I had put it there—"

"Oh, I know, Robert," she said at once. "Mr. Lestrange asked me this morning for some small Durham Rangers; and I told him to go and take them out of the book. So he has taken the book out of the bag and stupidly forgot to put it back."

"Then I will go aweh down to the Lodge and get it," Robert suggested.

"Is it worth while?" she said. "There is a fly on the casting-line; and there won't be much fishing this afternoon."

"I am not so sure," old Robert made answer. "There might be some clouds; and it is safer to hef the book whatever."

"Very well," said she. "And in that case I will take Mr. Moore over to the other side of the Geinig Pool, and ask him to creep out on the middle rock, and perhaps he will see something. Will there be any gold-fish in the globe, Robert?"

Old Robert grinned.

"Oh, yes, Miss Honnor, the fish will be there, but there is little chance of your getting one out."

"At any rate, Mr. Moore will be pleased to see a globe of gold-fish in the middle of a Highland moor," she said; and, when Robert had picked up the luncheon things, they all set off down the Geinig valley together.

But when they reached a certain wooden foot-bridge across the stream, Robert held on his way, making for the Lodge, while Lionel, well content and asking no questions, followed the young lady. She led the way across the bridge and along the opposite bank until they reached the Geinig Pool, where they scrambled down to the side of the river just above the falls. Here she showed him how to step from one boulder to another, until he found himself on a huge gray rock right in the middle; and forthwith she directed him to crawl out to the edge of the rock, and just put his head over, and see what he could see. As for crawling, he considered himself quite an adept at that now; in an instant he was down on hands and knees, making his way out to the end of the rock. And certainly what he beheld when he cautiously peered over the edge was worth all the trouble. Here, in an almost circular pool, apparently of great depth, the surface of the water was as smooth as glass; for the bulk of the stream tumbled in and tumbled out again along the southern side, leaving this dark hole in an eddy; and the sunlight, striking down into the translucent depths, revealed to him certain slowly moving forms which he recognized at once as salmon. They were not like salmon in color, to be sure; through the dun water their purplish-blue backs showed a dull olive-green; but salmon they undoubtedly were, and of a good size, too. Of course he was immensely excited by such a novel sight. With intensest curiosity he watched them making their slow circles of the pool, exactly like gold-fish in a globe. They seemed to be about four or five feet under the surface. Was it not possible to snatch at one of them with a long gaff? Or was it not possible, on the other hand, to tempt one of them with a fly!

He slowly withdrew his head.

"That is most extraordinary," he called to his companion, who was standing a few yards farther back. "Miss Honnor, won't you put a fly over them?"

"What is the use," said she. "They will look at it, but they won't take it; and I don't think it is well they should know too much about the patterns that Mr. Watson dresses. They know quite enough already. Some of the old hands, I do believe, are familiar with every fly made in Inverness."

"Won't you try?" he pleaded.

"Well, if you would like to see them look at a fly, I'll put it over them," she said, good-naturedly, "but, you know, it is most demoralizing."

So she, also, had to creep out to the edge of the rock; and then she cautiously put out the rod and the short line she had previously prepared. She threw the fly to the opposite side of the pool, let it sink an inch or two, and then quietly jerked it across until it came in the way of the slow-circling salmon. To her it was merely an amusement, but to Lionel it was a breathless excitement, to watch one after another of those big fish, in passing, come up to look at this beautiful, gleaming, shrimp-like object and then sink down again and go on its round. They would not come within two feet of this tempting lure. She tried them in all parts of the pool, sinking the fly well into the plunging fall, and letting it be carried right to the other side before she dragged it across the clear open.

"Won't one of you take it?" she said. "It's as pretty a fly as ever was dressed, though they do call it the Dirty Yellow."

But all of a sudden the circumstances were changed in a most startling manner. A swift, half-seen creature came darting up from out of the plunging torrent, shot into the clear water, snatched at the small object that was floating there, and down went fly and rod until the top was almost touching the surface. The reel had caught in her dress, somehow. But in another second all that was altered—she had got the reel free—she was up on her feet—the line was singing out—the rod raised, with the pliant top yielding to every movement of the fish—and Lionel, quite bewildered by the rapidity of the whole occurrence, wondering what he could do to assist her. Miss Honnor, however, was quite competent to look after herself.

"Who could have expected that?" she said, as the salmon went away down into the deep pool, and deliberately sulked there. "I wasn't fishing, I was only playing; and he very nearly broke me at the first plunge. Really, it all happened so quickly that I could not see what size he was; could you, Mr. Moore?"

"Not I!" he answered. "The creature came out of the rough water like a flash of lightning—I only saw the splash his tail made as he went down again. But what are you going to do, Miss Honnor? Shall I run down the strath and tell old Robert to hurry back?"

"Not at all!—we'll manage him by ourselves," she replied, confidently. "Here, you take him, and I'll gaff him for you."

"I will do nothing of the kind," said he, distinctly. "You have given me too many of your fish. You have been far too generous all the way through. No? I will gaff him for you—but you must tell me how—for I never tried before."

"Oh, it is simple enough," she said. "You've seen old Robert gaff plenty of fish. Only mind you don't strike across the casting-line. Get behind the casting-line—about half-way down the fish—get well over him—and then a sharp, bold stroke will fetch him out."

Accordingly, armed with the gaff, Lionel made his way down to the lowest ridge of the rock, so that he found himself just over the black-brown pool. And, indeed, his services were called upon much sooner than he had expected; for the salmon, grown tired of sulking, now began to swim slowly round and round, sometimes coming up so that they could just catch a glimmer of him, and again disappearing. But the fortunate thing for them was that there were no shallows to frighten the fish; he knew nothing of his danger as he happened to come sailing round Lionel's way; and he was gradually coming nearer and nearer to the surface, until they could watch his every motion as he made his slow rounds. Once or twice Lionel tried to get the gaff over him, and had to withdraw it; but at last Miss Honnor called out,

"This next time, Mr. Moore, as he comes round to you, I will lift him a bit; be ready!"

But what was this amazing thing that happened all in one wild second? Lionel struck at the fish, pinned him securely, dragged him out of the water, and then, to his horror, found that the unexpected weight of this fighting and struggling creature was proving too much for him—he was overbalanced—he could not recover himself—down they all went together—himself, the gaff, and the salmon—into the still, deep pool! As for him, that was nothing; he could swim a little; a few strokes took him to the other side, where he clambered on to the rocks; he managed to recover his cap; and then, with the deepest mortification in his soul, he made his way back to rejoin his companion. What apology could he offer for his unheard-of bungling and stupidity? Would she not look on him as an unendurable ass? Why had he chosen so insecure a foothold and made such a furious plunge at the fish? Over-eagerness, no doubt—

And then the next moment he noticed that her rod was still curved!

"We'll get him yet, Mr. Moore!" she called to him, in the most good-humored fashion. "Come out on to the rock, and you'll see the strangest-looking salmon you ever saw in your life."

And, indeed, that was an odd sight—the big fish slowly sailing round and round the pool, with the gaff still attached and the handle floating parallel with its side.

"It will take some time, though," said she. "I think you'd better go away home and get dry clothes on. I'll manage him by myself."

"I dare say you would manage him better by yourself than with any help of mine," he said, in his bitter chagrin and self-contempt. "I made sure I had lost you the salmon."

"And what then?" she said, with some surprise. "I assure you it wasn't the salmon I was thinking of when I saw you in the water—but the moment you struck out I knew you were safe."

He did not speak any more; he was too humiliated and vexed. It is true that when, at length, the salmon, entirely dead beat, suffered himself to be led in to the side of the rock, Lionel managed to seize the handle of the gaff, and this time, making sure of his foothold, got the fish on land; but this final success in no way atoned for his having so desperately made a fool of himself. In silence he affixed the bit of string she gave him to the head and tail of this very pretty twelve-pounder; and in silence they set out, he carrying the salmon and she the rod over her shoulder.

"It will be a surprise for old Robert when we meet him," she said, cheerfully. "But he will wonder how you came to be so drenched."

"Yes," said he, "it will be a pretty story of tomfoolery for them all to hear. I should like to make a comic drawing of it, if I could. It would have done capitally for John Leech, among the exploits of Mr. Briggs."

She glanced at him curiously. She knew what he was thinking of—of the tale that would be told among the keepers and the gillies of his having soused himself into the Geinig Pool in trying to gaff a fish. And might not the story find its way from the kennels into the gun-room, and thence into the drawing-room?

There was no doubt he was thoroughly ashamed and crestfallen, and angry with himself; and though she talked and chatted just as usual, he was quite taciturn all the way down the side of the Geinig. They reached the Junction Pool.

"Come now, Mr. Moore," she said, with the utmost good-nature, "you make too much of that little mistake. You are far too afraid of ridicule. But I am going to put it all right for you."

What was his astonishment and consternation to see her, after she had laid her rod on the shingle, deliberately walk a yard or two into the shallow water, and then throw herself down into it for a second, while she held out her hand to him.

"Pull me out, Mr. Moore!" she said.

"Good heavens, Miss Honnor!" he exclaimed—but instantly he caught her hand, and she rose to her feet and began to shake the water from her as best she might. "What do you mean?"

"You've pulled me out of the river," said she, laughing, as she shook her dripping sleeves and kicked her skirts; and then she went on, coolly, to explain, "I know you are rather sensitive to ridicule, and you don't like to think of those people telling the story against you as to how you fell into the Geinig Pool. Very well; there needn't be any such story. If any one asks you how you came to be so wet, you can say I got into the water, and you pulled me out. It will sound quite heroic."

"So I am to have the credit of having saved your life?" he said.

"You needn't put it that way," she answered, as she took up the fishing-rod and resumed her homeward walk. "All kinds of accidents are continually happening to people who go salmon-fishing, and no one takes any notice of them. My maid is quite used to getting my things dried—whether they're soaked through with rain or with river-water doesn't much matter to her. And old Robert can take your clothes to the fire in the gun-room long before the gentlemen come back from the hill. So, you see, there will probably be no questions asked; but, if there should be, you have what is quite enough of an explanation."

"Well, Miss Honnor," said he, "I never heard of such a friendly act in all my life—such a gratuitous sacrifice; here you have risked getting your death of cold in order to save my childish vanity from being wounded. Really, I don't know how to thank you—though I wish all the same you had not put me under such a tremendous obligation. But don't imagine that I am going to claim—that I am going to steal—the credit of having saved your life—I am not quite so mean—no, if I am asked, I will tell the whole truth—"

"And make two people ridiculous, instead of one?" she said, with a smile. "No, you can't do that."

However, as it turned out, this Quixotic act of consideration was allowed to remain a dark secret between these two. With the brisk walking and the warm, sunlit air around them, their clothes were already drying; and when old Robert met them, in the dusky chasm at the foot of the Bad Step, he was far too much engaged with the fish to notice their limp and damp garments; while again, as they resumed their march, he, carrying the fish, lagged in the rear, and thus they escaped his keen eyes. Indeed, by the time they reached the Lodge, and as Miss Honnor was about to enter, Lionel said to her that he felt quite warm and comfortable, and proposed to go for a further walk down the strath before dinner; but she peremptorily forbade this and ordered him off to his own room to get a change of clothes.

It is not to be imagined that an incident of this kind could do aught but sink deep into the mind of any young man, and especially into the mind of a young man who had particular reasons for wanting to know how this young lady was affected towards him. She herself had made light of the matter; it had been merely a sudden impulse, born of her own abundant good-nature; probably she would have done as much for Percy Lestrange. But *would* she have done as much for Percy Lestrange? Lionel kept asking himself. He was vain enough to think she would not. Who had been her *protégé* all this time? To whom had she given unobtrusive little hints when she thought these might be useful? In whose exploits and triumphs and failures had she shown an exceptional interest and sympathy? Whom had she permitted to go fishing with her on those long days when the world seemed to belong to the two of them? Whom had she admitted into the little dell above the Geinig Pool which was her chosen and solitary retreat? And he could not but reflect that while there were plenty of women who were eager to present him with silver cigarette-cases, blue and white flower-jars, and things of that kind, there was not one of them, as he believed, who would dip her little finger in a bottle of ink for his sake. More than that, which of them would herself have dared ridicule in order to save him from ridicule? And in what light should he regard this suddenly prompted action on her part, which seemed to him so bewildering at the time, but which she appeared to look on as only a sort of half-humorous freak of friendship?

These speculations only came back to the original question, or series of questions, that had already puzzled him. Why should he set such store by her opinion?—why be so anxious to please her?—why be so proud to think that he had won some small share of favorable regard? It was not his ordinary attitude towards women, who troubled him rather, and interfered with his many interests and the calls of his professional duties. Falling in love?—that could hardly be it; he felt no desire whatever to go down on his knees before her and swear by the eternal stars. Besides, she was so far away from him—living in such a different sphere—among occupations and surroundings and traditions entirely apart from his. Falling in love?—with the isolated, the unapproachable fisher-maiden, the glance of whose calm hazel eyes would be death to any kind of theatrical sentiment? It was all a confusion and a perplexity to him; but at least he was glad to know that he would sit at the same table with her that night at dinner, and, thereafter, perchance, have some opportunity of talking to her in the drawing-room, where a certain incident, known to themselves alone, would serve as a sort of secret tie. And he was cheered to remember that, although he was leaving this still and beautiful neighborhood (where so many strange dreams and fancies and new and welcome experiences had befallen him), he was not bidding good-bye to all of these friends forever. Miss Honnor Cunyngham would be in Brighton in November; and Brighton was not so far away from the great city and the dull, continuous, thunderous roar that would then be all around him.

CHAPTER XIII.

A NEW EXPERIENCE.

Was it possible in the nature of things that Prince Fortunatus should find his spirits dashed with gloom—he whose existence had hitherto been a long series of golden moments, each brighter and more welcome than the other; Even if he had to leave this still and beautiful valley where he had found so much gracious companionship and so many pleasant pursuits, look what was before him; he was returning to be greeted with the applause of enthusiastic audiences, to be sought after and courted and petted in private circles, to find himself talked about in the newspapers, and his portraits exhibited in every other shop-window—in short, to enjoy all the little flatteries and attentions and triumphs attaching to a wide and not ill-deserved popularity. And yet as he sat at this farewell luncheon on the day of his departure, he was the only silent one among these friends of his, who were all chattering around him.

"I'm sure I envy you, Mr. Moore," said his charming hostess, "going away back to the very centre of the intellectual world. It will be such a change for you to find yourself in the very midst of everything—hearing about all that is going on—the new books, the new plays, the new pictures. I suppose that in October there are plenty of pleasant people back in town; and perhaps the dinner-parties are all the more enjoyable when you know that the number of nice people is limited. One really does get tired of this mental stagnation."

"I wish, Mr. Moore," said Lady Rosamund, rather spitefully (considering that her brother was present), "you would take Rockminster with you. He won't go on the hill, and he's no use in the drawing-room. I am certain at this minute he would rather be walking down St. James Street to his club."

"I don't wonder at it!" cried Miss Georgie Lestrange, coming gallantly to the apathetic young man's rescue. "Look how he's situated. There's Sir Hugh and my brother away all day; Lord Fareborough has never come out of his room since the morning he tried deer-stalking; and what can Lord Rockminster find to arouse him in a pack of girls? Oh, I know what he thinks of us," she continued, very placidly. "I remember, if he chooses to forget. Don't you recollect, Rose, the night we were constructing an ideal kingdom by drawing up a list of all the people we should have banished? Every one had his or her turn at saying who should be expelled—people who come late to dinner, people who fence with spiked wire, people who talk in theatres, people who say 'like he does,' and so forth; and when somebody suggested 'all young women who wear red veils,' Lord Rockminster immediately added, 'and all young women who don't wear red veils.' Now you needn't deny it."

"Excuse me, I'm sure I never said anything of the kind; but it's not of the least consequence," Lord Rockminster observed, with perfect composure. "Anything to please you poor dears. You understand well enough why I linger on here—just to give you young creatures a chance of sharpening your wits on me. You wouldn't know what to do without me."

"Rockminster is going to give the world a volume of poems," said Lady Rosamund, who seemed to be rather ill-tempered and scornful this morning. "Nobody could stare at the clouds and hills as he does without being a poet. When he does burst into speech it will be something awful."

"Have you your flask filled?" said that much-bepestered young man, calmly turning to Lionel.

"Oh, yes, thanks."

"When you get to Invershin," his lordship continued, thoughtfully, "you can telegraph to the Station Hotel at Inverness what you want for dinner. No soup; I make it a rule never to take soup in a big hotel; a friendly manager once warned me in confidence. You'll be glad to have a bit of white fish after so much grilse and sea-trout."

"Oh, I'll take my chance," Lionel said; it was not dinner that was occupying his thoughts.

There was a sound of horses' hoofs and carriage wheels; the wagonette was being brought round to the front door.

"I consider it very shabby of Honnor not to have stayed to say good-bye," Lady Adela said to her departing guest. "She might have given up one morning's fishing, I think, especially as you have been such an assiduous attendant—carrying her things for her, and keeping her company on those long excursions—"

"Oh, don't be afraid," said Miss Georgie, with a bit of a covert laugh. "Honnor won't forsake her friend like that. I'll bet you she won't be far from the Horse's Drink when Mr. Moore has to cross the stream."

"If I were you," Lord Rockminster finally said, in a confidential undertone, as they all rose from the table, "I would telegraph about dinner."

How Lionel hated the sight of this open door, and the wagonette, and the portmanteau up beside the coachman!

"Good-bye, Mr. Moore," said the pleasant-mannered young matron to him, as she took his hand for a moment. "I'm afraid it has been awfully dull for you—"

"Lady Adela!" he said.

"But the next time you come we shall try to be less monotonously bucolic. Perhaps by then the phonograph will be able to bring us a whole musical evening from London, whenever we want it—a whole performance of an operetta—"

"Offenbach in a Highland valley!" he exclaimed.

"No," she said, very quietly and graciously; "but perhaps something by the composer of 'The Squire's Daughter'—and there might be in it an air as delightful as that of 'The Starry Night.' Oh, Mr. Moore, don't let them produce any other piece at the New Theatre until we all get back to London again! Well, good-bye—it's so kind of you to have taken pity on us in this wilderness—"

"If you knew how sorry I am to go, Lady Adela!" he said. "And will you say good-bye for me to Miss Cunyngham?"

"You needn't bother to leave a message," said Miss Georgie, with significant eyes. "You'll find she won't be far away from the Horse's Drink."

And as it chanced, Miss Georgie's forecast (whether inspired by a saucy impertinence or not) proved correct. Lionel, having bade farewell to all these friends, got into the wagonette; and away the carriage went—quietly, at first, over the soft turf and stones—to the river. Of course he looked out. Yes, there was Miss Honnor—fishing the Whirl Pool—with old Robert sitting on the shingle watching her. Would she notice?—or would he get down and walk along to her and claim the good-bye she had forgotten? The next moment he was reassured. She caught sight of the approaching wagonette; she carefully placed her rod on the shingle, and then came walking along the river-bank, towards the ford, at which the horses had now arrived.

Even at a distance he could not but admire the grace and ease and dignity of her carriage—the harmonious movement of a perfectly formed figure; and as she drew nearer he kept asking himself (as if the question were necessary) whether he would be able to take away a keen mental photograph of those fine features—the clear and placid forehead, the strongly marked eyebrows, the calm, self-reliant eyes, the proud and yet not unsympathetic lines of the mouth. She came nearer; a smile lit up her face; and there was a kind of radiance there, he thought. He had leaped down from the wagonette: he went forward to meet her; her hand was outstretched.

"I am sorry you are going," she said, frankly.

"And I am far more sorry to have to go," said he, and he held her hand a little longer than there was any occasion for, until she gently withdrew it. "There are so many things I should like to say to you, Miss Honnor; but somehow they always escape you just when they're wanted; and I've told you so often before that I am not likely to forget your kindness to me up here—"

"Surely it is the other way about!" she said, pleasantly. "You have come and cheered up my lonely hours—and been so patient—never grumbled— never looked away up the hill as if you would have given your life to be after the grouse; and in the drawing-room of an evening you've always sung when I asked you—when I was inconsiderate enough to ask you—"

"My goodness! Miss Honnor," he said, "if I had known you looked on it in that light, I should have sung for you constantly, whether you asked or not."

"Well, it's all over now," said she, "and I hope you are taking away with you a pleasant memory of Strathaivron."

"I have spent the happiest days of my life here," he said; and then he hesitated—was about to speak—hesitated again—and finally blurted out, "Is there anything I can do for you in London, Miss Honnor?"

"No, thanks," she said. "By the way, you'll have an hour or two in Inverness. You might go in to Mr. Watson's and ask him to send me out a few more flies—if you have plenty of time, that is."

"I shall be delighted," said he, as if she had conferred the greatest favor on him.

"Well, good-bye—I mustn't keep you late for the train."

"But we shall meet in the South?"

"I hope so," she said, in a very amiable and friendly fashion; and she stood waiting there until he had got into the wagonette, and until the horses had splashed their way across the ford; then she waved her hand to him, and, with a parting smile, turned down the stream again, to rejoin Robert and pick up her rod.

Nor was this quite the last he was to see of those good friends. When the horses had strenuously hauled the carriage up that steep hillside and got into the level highway, he turned to look back at the Lodge, set in the midst of the wide strath, and behold! there was a fluttering of white handkerchiefs there, Lady Adela and her sisters and Miss Georgie still lingering in the porch. Again and again he made response. Then, as he drove on, he caught another glance of Miss Honnor, who, far below him, was industriously fishing the Whirl Pool; when she heard the sound of the wheels, she looked up and waved her hand to him as he went by. Finally there came the crack of a gun across the wide strath; it was a signal from the shooting-party— away on a distant hillside—and he could just make out that they, also, were sending him a telegraphic good-bye. At each opening through the birch-wood skirting the road he answered these farewells, until Strathaivron Lodge was no longer in sight; and then he settled himself in his seat and resigned himself to the long journey.

This was not a pleasant drive. He was depressed with a vague aching and emptiness of the heart that he could not well account for. A schoolboy returning to his tasks after a long holiday would not be quite so profoundly miserable—so reckless, dissatisfied, and ill at ease. But perhaps it was the loss of one of those pleasant companions that was troubling him? Which one, then (he made pretence of asking himself), was he sorriest to part from? Lady Adela, who was always so bright and talkative and cheerful, so charming a hostess, so considerate and gentle a friend? Or the mystic-eyed Lady Sybil, who many an evening had led him away into the wonder-land of Chopin, for she was an accomplished pianist, if her own compositions were but feeble echoes of the masters? Or the more quick-spirited Lady Rosamund, the imperious and petulant beauty, who, in a way most unwonted with her, had bestowed upon him exceptional favor? Or that atrocious little flirt, Miss Georgie Lestrange, with her saucy smiles and speeches, her malicious laugh, and demure, significant eyes?—it was hardly to be wondered at if she made an impression on any young man, for the minx had an abundance of good looks, despite her ruddy hair and pert nose. As for Miss Honnor Cunyngham—oh, no!—she was too far away— she lived remote, isolated, apart—she neither gave nor demanded sympathy or society—she was sufficient unto herself alone. But why ask whether it were this one or that? Soon he would be forgotten by them all. He would be swallowed up in the great city—swept away in the current of its feverish activities—his voice hardly heard above the general din; while they would still be pursuing their various pastimes in this little world of solitude and quiet, or moving on to entertain their friends with the more pompous festivities of the Braes.

It was odd that he should be carrying away with him the seeds of homesickness for a place in which his stay had been counted by weeks. So anxious, indeed, was he to assure himself that his relations with that beautiful valley and its inmates were not entirely severed that, the moment he reached Inverness, instead of going into the Station Hotel and ordering his dinner like a reasonable being, he must needs go straightway off to Mr. Watson's shop.

"I suppose," said he, with a little hesitation—for he did not know whether to mention Miss Cunyngham's name or not—he was afraid he might betray some quite uncalled-for embarrassment—"I suppose you know the flies they use on the Aivron this time of year."

Mr. Watson knew well enough; who better!

"I mean on the Strathaivron Lodge stretch of the water?" Lionel continued.

"Oh, yes; I am often sending flies to Miss Cunyngham," was the answer.

"Oh, Miss Cunyngham?" said Lionel. "It is for her I want some flies."

"Very well, sir, I will make up a small packet, and send it to her? Miss Cunyngham has an account with me—"

"No, no, that isn't what I mean at all," Lionel interposed, hastily. "I want to make Miss Cunyngham a little present. The fact is, I was using her book," he observed, with some importance (as if it could in the least concern a worthy tackle-maker in Inverness to know who had gone fishing with Miss Cunyngham), "and I whipped off a good number, so I want to make amends, don't you see?"

"Very well, sir; how many will I put up?"

"All you've got," was the prompt reply.

Mr. Watson stared.

"Oh, yes," Lionel said. "Miss Cunyngham may as well have a good stock at once. You know the proper kinds—Blue Doctors, Childerses, Jock Scotts, Dirty Yellows, Bishops, Bees—that's about it, isn't it?—and put in plenty of various sizes. Then don't make a parcel of them; put them into those japanned boxes with the cork in them—never mind how many; and if you can't tell me at once how much it will all come to, I will leave you my London address, and you'll send the bill to me. Now if you will be so kind as to give me a sheet of paper and an envelope, I will write a note to accompany the packet."

Mr. Watson probably thought that this young man was daft, but it was not his business to say so; he took down his erratic customer's address and said that all his instructions would be attended to forthwith.

Next Lionel went to a tobacconist's shop, and (for he was a most lavish young man) he ordered a prodigious quantity of "twist," which he had made up into two parcels, the smaller one for Roderick, the larger to be divided equally among the other keepers and gillies. The two parcels he had put into a wooden case, which, again, was filled up with boxes of vesuvians, three or four dozen or so; and it is to be imagined that when *that* small hamper was opened at Strathaivron there was many a chuckle of gratification over the division of the splendid spoil.

Finally—for human nature is but human nature after all; he had been thinking of others so far, and he was now entitled to consider himself a little—he thought he would go along to Mr. Macleay's. When he arrived at the shop, he glanced in at the windows; but among the wild-cats, ptarmigan, black game, mallards, and what not, there was nothing to arrest his attention; it was a stag's head he had in his mind. He went inside, and his first sensation was one of absolute bewilderment. This crowded museum of birds, beasts, and fish—skarts, goosanders, sand-grouse, terns, eagles, ospreys, squirrels, foxes, big-snouted trout, harts, hinds, bucks, does, owls, kestrels, falcons, merlins, and every variety of the common gull shot by the all-pervading Cockney—staring, stuffed, silent, they were a confusion to the eyes, and nowhere could he find his own, his particular, his precious stag. Alas! when Mr. Macleay was so kind as to take him behind into the workshop—which resembled a huge shambles, almost— and when, from among the vast number of heads and horns lying and hanging everywhere around, the Strathaivron head was at last produced, Lionel was horribly shocked and disappointed. Was this, then, his trophy that he hoped to have hung up for the admiration of his friends and his own ecstatic contemplation—this twisted, shapeless, sightless lump of hide and hair, with a great jaw of discolored teeth gleaming from under its flabby folds? It is true that here were the identical horns, for had he not gone lovingly over every tine of them?—but was this rag of a thing all that was left of the splendid stag he had beheld lying on the heather? However, Mr. Macleay speedily reassured him. He was shown the various processes and stages of the taxidermist's art, the amorphous mass of skin and hair gradually taking shape and substance until it stood forth in all its glory of flaming eye and proud nostril and branching antlers; and he was highly pleased to be told that this head he had got in Strathaivron was a fairly good one, as stags now go in the North. So, all his shopping being done, he set off again for the Station Hotel, where he got what he wanted in the shape of dinner, followed by a long and meditative smoke in the billiard-room, with visions appearing among the curls of blue vapor.

What the Highland Railway manages to do with the trains which it despatches from Inverness at 10 P.M. and reproduces the next morning at Perth about 7, it is impossible for the mind of man to imagine; but it is not of much consequence so long as you are snugly ensconced in a sleeping-berth; and Lionel passed the night in profound oblivion. With the new day, however, these unavailing and torturing regrets began again; for now he felt himself more completely than before shut off from the friends he had left; and Strathaivron and all its associations and pursuits had grown distant like a dream. He was lucky enough, on this southward journey, to get a compartment to himself; and here was an excellent opportunity for him to have practised his *vocalises*; but it was not of *vocalises*, nor of anything connected with the theatre, that he was thinking. He was much franker with himself now. He no longer tried to conceal from himself the cause of this vague unrest, this useless looking back and longing, this curious downhearted sense of solitariness. A new experience, truly, and a bewildering one! Indeed, he was ashamed of his own folly. For what was it that he wanted? A mere continuance of that friendly alliance and companionship which he had enjoyed all this time? Was he indulging a sort of sentimental misery simply because he could not walk down to the Aivron's banks and talk to Miss Honnor and watch the sun tracing threads of gold among her tightly braided hair? If that were all, he might get out at the next station, make his way back to the beloved strath, and be sure that Honnor Cunyngham would welcome him just as of old, and allow him to carry her waterproof or ask him to have a cast over the Junction Pool. He had no reason to fear any break in this friendship that had been formed. When he should see her in Brighton, she would be to him as she had been yesterday, when they said good-bye by the side of the river. And were not these the only possible relations between them; and ought he not to be proud and content that he could look forward to an enduring continuance of them?

Yes; but some man would be coming along and marrying her; and where would he be then? What would become of this alliance, this friendly understanding—perhaps, even, some little interest on her part in his affairs—what would become of all these relations, then? It was the way of the world. Their paths would be divided—he would hear vaguely of her—perhaps see her name in the papers as being at a drawing-room or something of the kind. She would have forgotten all those long, still days by the Aivron and the Geinig; no echo would remain in her memory of "The Bonnie Earl o' Morau," as he had sung it for her, with all the passionate pathos of which he was capable; she would be a stranger—moving afar—one heard of only—a remembrance—and no more. So the impalpable future was interwoven with those dreams and not too happy forecasts, as the train thundered on its way, along the wooded banks of the Allan Water and towards the winding Links of Forth.

But there was an alternative that would recur again and again to his fancy, though in rather a confused and breathless way. What if, in the very despair of losing her altogether, at the very moment of parting with her, he had made bold to claim this proud-spirited maiden all for himself? Might not some such sudden and audacious proposal have been the very thing to appeal to her—the very thing to capture her? A challenge—a demand that she should submit—that she should come down from those serene heights of independence and yield herself a willing and gracious helpmeet and companion for life to this daring suitor; might not that have secured for him this wondrous prize? If she had any regard for him at all, she might have been startled into confession. A couple of words—there by the side of the Aivron—might have been enough. No theatrical professions nor mock homage, no kneeling at her feet or swearing by eternal stars; but a look into her eyes—a clasp of the hand—a single question? Something he had indeed meant to say to her, as they stood face to face there for the last time—something, he hardly knew what; and yet his hesitation had been but natural; he might have been hurried into saying too much; he dared not offend. Nay, even as he held her hand, he was unaware of the true state of his feeling towards her; it was this separation—this ever-increasing distance between them—that had enabled him to understand.

And then again his mood changed into one of bitter self-reproach and self-contempt. What miserable folly was this crying for the moon—this picturing of a marriage between the daughter of an ancient and wealthy house—one, too, who was unmistakably proud of her lineage—and a singer in comic opera! Not for nothing had he heard of the twin brothers Cunyngham who fell on Flodden Field. It is true that at the present time he and she mingled in the same society; for he was the pet and plaything of the hour in the fashionable world; but he was not entirely blinded by that favor; he did not wholly mistake his position. And even supposing—a wild conjecture!—that she entertained an exceptional regard for him—that she could be induced to think of marrying him—would she be content that her husband remained on the stage and painted his face every evening and postured before the footlights? On the other hand, apart from the stage, what was he?—a mere nobody, not too-well instructed, having no particular gifts of wit or conversation, without even a well-filled purse—the meanest of qualifications—to recommend him. No doubt they might make a very pretty bargain between them; he might go to her and say,

"Let there be a sacrifice on both sides. I give up the theatre—I give up the applause, the popularity, the opportunities of making pleasant friendships—all the agreeable things of a stage-life; and you on your part give up your pride of birth, and, it may be, something of your place in society. It is a surrender on both sides. Let our motto be, 'All for love, and the world well lost.'" Yes, a very pretty bargain; but as he considered that he was now wandering into the region of romance—a region which he unhesitatingly scorned as having no relation with the facts of the world—

he withdrew from that futile and useless and idle speculation, and took to thinking of Miss Honnor Cunyngham as she actually was, and wondering over which of the Aivron pools the proud-featured fisher-maiden would be casting at this moment.

And here, again, as the hours crept by, was something of a more practical nature to remind him of the now far-distant strath. In order to save him from the hurry of a twenty-minutes' railway-station dinner, Lady Adela had ordered a luncheon-basket to be packed for him, and her skill and forethought in this direction were unequalled, as many a little shooting-party had joyfully discovered. When Lionel leisurely began to explore the contents of the basket, he was proud to think that it was under her own immediate supervision that these things had been put together for him. There was some kind of sentimental interest attaching to the chicken and tongue and galantine, to the salad and biscuits and cake and what not; and he knew that it was no servant who had thought of filling a small tin canister with peaches and grapes, even as he knew that only Lady Adela was aware of his preference for the particular dry Sillery of which a half-bottle here lay in its covering of straw. As he took out the things and placed them on the seat beside him, he could have imagined that a pair of very gentle hands had arranged that repast for him. Then from this much too sumptuous banquet his mind wandered away back to the simple fare that old Robert used to bring forth from the fishing-bag, when Miss Honnor had taken her place among the bracken. Again he was with her in that little dell away among the solitudes of the hills, with the murmur of the Geinig coming up to them from the chasm below. The sunlight flashed on the rippling burn at their feet; the leaves of the birches trembled, and no more than trembled, in the still air; the deep, clear blue of the sky overhead told them to be in no hurry—they would have to wait till the afternoon for clouds. In the perfect silence (for the humming of the bees in the heather was hardly a sound at all) he could hear every soft modulation of her voice—though, to be sure, it was not lovers' talk that passed between them. "Mr. Moore, won't you have the rest of this soda-water?" or, "Yes, one of those brown biscuits, thank you," or, "Please, Mr. Moore, will you crush those bits of paper together and bury them in a hole? Nothing is so horrid as to come upon traces of a pic-nic on a hillside or along a river." Already those long days of constant companionship seemed to be becoming remote. It was the black night-journey between Inverness and Perth that had severed that shining time from the dull and commonplace hours he had now entered upon. He looked out of the window as the train thundered along—Preston—Wigan—Warrington—everywhere squalor, hurry, and noise, with a smoke-laden sky lowering over the sad and dismal country, different, indeed, from that other world he knew of, with its crimson slopes of heather, its laughing waters, its lonely solitudes in their noonday hush, the fair azure of the heavens becoming paler and paler towards the horizon until it touched the distant peaks and shoulders of Assynt. "Muss aus dem Thal jetzt scheiden, wo alles Lust und Klang;" but at least the memory of it would remain with him—a gracious possession.

The long afternoon wore on; Crewe, Stafford, Lichfield, Tamworth went by, as things in a dream, for his thoughts were far away. Sometimes, it is true, he would rebel against this morbid, restless, useless regret that had got hold of him; and he would valiantly attack the newspapers, of which he had an ample supply; but somehow or another the gray columns would fade away, and in their place would come a picture of Strathaivron Lodge, and the valley, and the river, and of an upturned face smiling a last farewell to him as the wagonette rolled on. Was it really only yesterday that he had seen her—talked with her—taken her hand? A yesterday that seemed years away! A vision already growing pale.

Well, London came at last, and all the hurry and bustle of Euston Station; and when he had got his things put on the top of a hansom, and given his address to the driver, there was an end of dreams. No more dreams were possible in this great vortex of a city into which he was now plunged—a turbulent, bewildering, vast black hole it seemed, and yet all afire with its blaze of windows and lamps. In Strathaivron the night was a gentle thing— it came stealing over the landscape as soft as sleep; it brought silence with it and a weight to tired eyes; it bade the woods be still; and to the lonely and darkened peaks of the hills it unveiled its canopy of trembling stars. But here there was no night—there was yellow fire, there were black phantoms unceasingly hurrying hither and thither, and a dull and constant roar more continuous than that of any sea. Tottenham Court Road after Strathaivron! But here at least was actuality; the time for sentimental sorrows, for dumb and hopeless regrets, was over and gone.

And who was the first to greet him on his return to London—who but Nina?—not in person, truly, but by a very graceful little message. The moment he went into his sitting-room his eye fell on the tiny nosegay lying on the table; and when he took the card from the accompanying envelope, he knew whose handwriting he would find there. "*Welcome home—from Nina!*"—that was all; but it was enough to make him rather remorseful. Too much had he neglected his old comrade and ally; he had scarcely ever written to her; she had been but little in his thoughts. Poor Nina!—It was a shame he should treat so faithful a friend so ill; he might have remembered her a little more had not his head been stuffed with foolish fancies. Well, as soon as he had changed his clothes and swallowed a bit of food he would jump into a hansom and go along to the New Theatre; he would be too late to judge of Nina's Grace Mainwaring as a whole, but he would have a little chat with her in the wings.

He was later in getting there than he had expected; indeed, as he made his way to the side of the stage, he discovered that his *locum tenens* had just been recalled and was singing for the second time the well-known serenade, "The Starry Night"—and very well he sang it, too, confound him! Lionel said to himself. And here was Nina, standing on a small platform at the top of a short ladder, and waiting until the passionate appeal of her sweetheart (in the garden without) should be finished. She did not know of the presence of the new-comer. Lionel might have pulled her skirts, it is true, to apprise her of his being there; but that would not have been decorous; besides, he dared not distract her attention from the business of the stage. As soon as the last verse of the serenade had been sung, with its recurring refrain—

"Appear, my sweet, and shame the skies,

That have no splendor

That have no splendor like thine eyes"—

Nina—that is, Grace Mainwaring—carefully opened the casement at which she was supposed to be standing. A flood of moonlight—lime-light, rather—fell on her; but Lionel could not see how she looked the part, because her back was towards him. Very timidly Grace Mainwaring glanced this way and that, to make sure that no one could observe her; she took a rose from her hair, kissed it, and dropped it to her enraptured lover below. It was the end of the act. She had to come down quickly from the platform for the recall that resounded through the theatre; she did not chance to notice Lionel; she was led on and across the stage by Harry Thornhill, she bowing repeatedly and gracefully, he reserving his acknowledgment until he had handed her off. The reception both of them got was most gratifying; there could be no doubt of the sincerity of the applause of this crowded house.

"It seems to me I am not wanted here any more," Lionel said to himself. "Even Nina won't take any notice of the stranger."

The next moment Nina, who was coming across the stage, caught sight of him, and with a little cry of delight she ran towards him—yes, ran; for what cared she about carpenters and scene-shifters?—and caught both his hands in hers.

"Ah, Leo!" she cried, with glad-shining eyes. "Oh, so brown you are!—a hunter!—you are from the forests! And to-day you arrive—and already at the theatre—did you hear the duet—no? Ah, it is good to see you again, after so long!—I could laugh and cry together, it is such a joy to see you—and see you looking so well—"

"I say, Nina," he said, "that fellow Doyle sings tremendously well—he's ever so much improved—they'll be wanting him to take my place altogether and sending me off into the country."

"You, Leo!" she said, with a merry laugh, and still she regarded him with those delighted, welcoming eyes. "Ah, yes, it is likely! Ah, you will see what reception they will give you on Monday. Yes, it is in all the papers already—everywhere I see it; but come—Miss Girond and I, we have Miss Burgoyne's room for the present—you can wait for a few minutes, then I come out to talk to you."

Lionel (feeling very much like a stranger in this place) followed her into Miss Burgoyne's room, where he found Mlle. Girond only too ready to throw away the French novel she was reading. Nina had to disappear into the dressing-room; but this small boy-officer in the gay uniform, with his or her pretty gesticulation and charm of broken English, was quite willing to entertain Mr. Moore, though at times she would forget all about him and walk across to the full-length mirror and twist her small moustache. She chatted to him now and again; she returned to the mirror to touch her eyebrows and adjust her sash; she walked about or flicked the dust from her shining Wellingtons with a silk handkerchief; again she contemplated herself in the glass, and lightly sang,

"En débordant de Saint-Malo

Nos longs avirons battaient l'eau!"

Then she was called away for the beginning of the last act; and Nina, having made the change necessary for her next appearance, came out from the dressing-room and sat down.

"Oh, you are wicked, Leo," she said, as she contentedly crossed her hands in her lap and looked at the young man with those friendly eyes, "that you stayed away so long. I wished to sing the duet with you—but no—you begin Monday—and Miss Burgoyne comes back Monday—"

"Does she? I thought she was ordered a long rest."

Nina laughed.

"She sees in the papers that you come back—it is to be a great occasion—she says to herself, 'Will he sing with that Italian girl? No! Let my throat be well or ill, I am going back;' and she is coming, Leo. Never mind; I am to have the part of Clara; is it not an advancement? And everything is so much more comfortable now; Miss Girond has taken a room with Mrs. Grey; then we go home always together, and she has the use of the piano—"

"Miss Ross, please!" called a voice at the door.

"All right!" she called in reply.

"The chorus is on, miss."

"All right!"

"Ah," she continued, "it is so good to see you back, Leo; yes, yes? London was a stranger city when you were away—there was no one. And it is all you I have to thank, Leo, for my introduction here and my good-fortune—"

"Oh, nonsense, Nina!" he said. "What else could I have done? It isn't you who ought to thank me—it's Lehmann; I consider him precious lucky to have got a substitute for Miss Burgoyne so easily. So Miss Burgoyne is coming back on Monday?"

"Yes," said Nina, as she went to the door. "Shall I see you again, Leo, to-night?"

"Oh, I'm coming to hear you sing 'Now to the dance,'" he said, as he followed her out into the corridor and ascended with her into the wings.

This was a busy act for Nina; and the next time he had an opportunity of talking with her was after she had dressed herself in her bridal robes and was come up ready to go on the stage. Nina looked a little self-conscious when she first encountered him in this attire; perhaps she was afraid of his contrasting her appearance with that of Miss Burgoyne. If he did, it was certainly not to Nina's disadvantage. No; Nina was much more distinguished-looking and refined than the pert little doll-like bride represented by Miss Burgoyne; she wore the gorgeous costume of flowered white satin with ease and grace; and her portentous white wig, with its feathered brilliants and strings of pearls, seemed to add a greater depth and softness and mild lustre to her dark, expressive eyes. For an instant, as she came up to him, those beautiful, liquid eyes were turned to the ground.

"I did not choose anything, Leo," she said, modestly; "I have had to copy Miss Burgoyne."

"Well, there's a difference somehow, Nina," said he, "and I think Miss Burgoyne had better begin and copy you."

For a swift instant she raised her eyes; she was more than pleased. But she said nothing—indeed, she had now to go on the stage. And if he had contrasted her appearance favorably with that of Miss Burgoyne, he was now inclined to give a similar verdict with regard to her acting. It certainly wanted the self-confidence of long experience and also the emphasis and exaggeration of comedy-opera; it was not nearly impudent enough for the upper gallery; but it was graceful and natural to a degree that surprised him. As for her voice, that was incomparably better than Miss Burgoyne's; it was a fresh, sympathetic, finely modulated voice that had been uninjured by excessive training or excessive work. Lionel was quite proud of his *protégée*; unseen, here in the wings, he could applaud as loudly as any; if Nina did not hear, she must have been deaf. And when she came off at the end of the act—or, rather, immediately after the recall, which was as enthusiastic as the soul of actor or actress could desire—there was no stint to his praise; and Nina's heartfelt pleasure on hearing this warm commendation shone through all her stage make-up. He asked if he should wait to act as escort to Miss Girond and herself; but Nina said no; Miss Girond and she went home every night by themselves in a four-wheeled cab; she knew he must be tired after his long journey; and he must go away and get to bed at once. So Lionel shook hands with her and left the theatre, and walked carelessly and absently home to his lodgings in Piccadilly.

Well, he was glad to find his old friend and comrade, Nina, getting on so well and so proud of her success and looking so charming in her new part; and he guessed that she must have written to the grumbling old Pandiani, and sent photographs of herself as Grace Mainwaring to Andrea and Carmela and her other Neapolitan friends. But it was not of Nina that he thought long, as he lay in the easy-chair and smoked, and listened to the heavy murmur of the streets without. He had not got used to London yet. The theatre seemed to him a great, glaring thing; the lime-light an impertinent sham; even the applause of the delighted audience somehow brutal and offensive. There was no repose, no reticence, no self-respect and modesty about the whole affair; it was all too violent; a fanfaronade; a coarse and ostentatious make-believe, that seemed a kind of insult to a quiet mind. He turned away from it altogether. His fancies had fled to the North again; the long railway journey was annihilated; again he was driving out to the still and beautiful valley, where those kind friends were standing at the door of the lodge, fluttering a white welcome to him. He goes down the steep hillside; he crosses the stream at the Horse's Drink; he reaches the hall-door and is shaking hands with this one and that. And if the tall, proud maiden with the fine forehead and the clear, calm hazel eyes is not among this group, be sure she will be here in the evening to add her greeting to the rest. Oh, to think of that next morning—the sweet air blowing down from the hills—the silver lights among the purple clouds—the Aivron swinging along its gravelly bed, a deep, clear bronze where the sunlight strikes the shallows! Farther and farther into the solitudes these two idly wander—away from human ken—until the dogs in the kennels are no longer heard, nor is there even a black-cock crowing in the woods; nothing but the hum of the bees, and the whisper of the birch branches, and the hushed, low thunder of the Geinig falls. He could almost hear it now; or was not the continuous murmur that dazed and dinned his ears a sadly different sound—the muffled roar of cabs and carriages along Piccadilly, bearing home this teeming population from the blare and glare of the crowded theatres? A different sound indeed! He had come into another world; and the Aivron and Geinig, far away, were alone with the darkness and the stars.

CHAPTER XIV.

A MAGNANIMOUS RIVAL.

That Monday night at the New Theatre was a great occasion; for, although there were a few people (themselves not of much account, perhaps) who went about saying there was no one in London, an enormous house welcomed back to the stage those well-known favorites, Miss Burgoyne and Mr. Lionel Moore. And what had become of the Aivron and the Geinig now?—their distant murmurs were easily drowned in the roar of enthusiasm with which the vast audience—a mass of orange-hued faces they seemed across the footlights—greeted the prima-donna and the popular young baritone. Nina was here also, in her subordinate part. And all that Miss Burgoyne could do, on the stage and off the stage, to attract his attention, did not hinder Lionel from watching, with the most affectionate interest, the manner in which his *protégée*, his old comrade Nina, was acquitting herself. Clara was perhaps a little bit too eager and anxious; she anticipated her cues; her parted lips seemed to repeat what was being said to her; lights and shadows of expression chased each other over the mobile features and brightened or darkened her eloquent eyes; and in her passages with Grace Mainwaring she was most effusive, though that other young lady maintained a much more matter-of-fact demeanor.

"Capital, Nina! Very well done!" Lionel exclaimed (to himself) in the wings. "You're on the right track. It is easier to tone down than to brace up. Don't be afraid—keep it going—you'll grow business-like soon enough."

Here Clara had to come tripping off the stage, and Lionel had to go on; he had no opportunity of speaking to her until the end of the act, when they chanced to meet in the long glazed corridor.

"You're a bit nervous to-night, Nina," he said, in a kindly way.

"But so as to be bad?" she said, quickly and anxiously.

"It was very well done indeed—it was splendid—but you almost take too much pains. Most girls with a voice like yours would merely sing a part like that and think the management was getting enough. I suppose you don't know yourself that you keep repeating what the other person is saying to you—as if he weren't getting on fast enough—"

Nina paused for a second.

"Yes, I understand—I understand what you mean," she said, rather slowly; then she continued, in her usual way, "But to-night, Leo, I am anxious—

oh, there are so many things!—this is the first time I act with Miss Burgoyne; and I wish them not to say I am a stick—for your sake, Leo—you brought me here—I must do what I can."

"Oh, Nina, you don't half value yourself!" he said. "You think far too little of yourself. You're a most wonderful creature to find in a theatre. I consider that Lehmann is under a deep obligation to me for giving him the chance of engaging you. By the way, have you heard what he means to do on Sunday week?"

"No—not at all!"

"Saturday week is the 400th night," he continued; "and to celebrate it, Lehmann is going to give the principal members of the company, and a few friends, I suppose, a dinner at the Star and Garter at Richmond. Haven't you heard?—but of course he'll send you a card of invitation. The worst of it is that it is no use driving down at this time of the year; I suppose we shall have to get there just as we please, and meet in the room; but I don't know how all the proper escorts are to be arranged. I was thinking, Nina, I could take you and Miss Girond down, if you will let me."

There was a bright, quick look of pleasure in Nina's eyes—but only for an instant.

"No, no, Leo," she said, with lowered lashes. "That is not right. Miss Burgoyne and you are the two principal people in the theatre—you are on the stage equals—off the stage also you are her friend—you must take her to Richmond, Leo."

"Miss Burgoyne?"

But here the door of Miss Burgoyne's room was suddenly opened, and the voice of the young lady herself was heard, in unmistakably angry tones:

"Oh, bother your headache! I suppose it was your headache made you split my blue jacket in two, and I suppose it was your headache made you smash my brooch last night—I wonder what some women were born for!" And therewithal the charming Grace Mainwaring made her appearance; and not a word—hardly a look—did the indignant small lady choose to bestow on either Lionel or Nina as she brushed by them on her way up to the wings.

Yes, here he was in the theatre again, with all its trivial distractions and interests, and also its larger excitements and ambitions and rewards, not the least of which was the curious fascination he found in holding a great audience hushed and enthralled, listening breathlessly to every far-reaching, passionate note. Then his reappearance on the stage brought him a renewal of all the friendly little attentions and hospitalities that had been interrupted by his leaving for Scotland; for if certain of his fashionable acquaintance were still away at their country houses, there were plenty of others who had returned to town. Club life had begun again, too. But most of all, at this time, Lionel was disposed to enjoy that quiet and gentle companionship with Nina, which was so simple and frank and unreserved. He could talk to her freely, on all subjects save one—and that he was trying to put away from himself in these altered circumstances. He and she had a community of interests; there was never any lack of conversation—whether he were down in Sloane Street, drinking tea and trying over new music with her, or walking in with Miss Girond and her to the theatre through the now almost leafless Green Park. Sometimes, when she was grown petulant and fractious, he had to scold her into good-humor; sometimes she had seriously to remonstrate with him; but it was all given and taken in good part. He was never embarrassed or anxious in her society; he was happy and content and careless, as she appeared to be also. He did not trouble to invent any excuse for calling upon her; he went down to Sloane Street just whenever he had a spare half-hour or hour; and if the morning was bright, or even passable (for it was November now, and even a tolerable sort of day was welcome), and if Miss Girond did not wish to go out or had some other engagement, Nina and he would set off for a stroll by themselves, up into Kensington Gardens, it might be, or along Piccadilly, or through the busy crowds of Oxford Street; while they looked at the shops and the passers-by, and talked about the theatre and the people in it or about old days in Naples. There was no harm; and they thought no harm. Sometimes he could hear her hum to herself a fragment of one of the old familiar canzoni—"Antoniella Antonià!" or "Voca, voca ncas' a mano"—so light-hearted was she; and occasionally they said a word to each other in Neapolitanese—but this was seldom, for Nina considered the practice to be most reprehensible. What she had chiefly to take him to task for, however, was his incurable and inordinate extravagance—wherever she was concerned especially.

"Leo, you think it is a compliment?" she said to him, earnestly. "No, not at all? I am sorry. Why should you buy for me this, that, whatever strikes your eye, and no matter the price? I have everything I desire. Why to me?—why, if you must give, why not to your cousin you tell me of, who is so kind to the sick children in boarding them in the country? There, now, is something worthy, something good, something to be praised—"

"Oh, preach away, Nina!" he answered, with a laugh. "But I've contributed to Francie's funds until she won't take anything more from me—not at present. But why do you always talk about saving and saving? You are an artist, Nina, and you put such value on money!"

"But an artist grows old, Leo," she said.

"Perhaps you have been saving a little yourself, Nina?" he said, at a venture.

"Oh, yes, I have, Leo, a little," she answered, rather shamefacedly.

"What for?" he made bold to ask.

"Oh, how do I know?" she said, with downcast eyes. "Many things might happen: is it not safer? No, Leo, you must not say I love money for itself; it is not fair to me; but—but if a dear friend is ill—if a doctor says to him, 'Suspend all work and go away to Capri, to Algeria, to Eg—Egippo'—is it right?—and perhaps he has been indiscreet—he has been too generous to all his companions—he is in need—then you say, 'Here, take mine—it is between friends.' Then you are proud to have money, are you not?"

"I'm afraid, Nina, that's what they call a parable," said he, darkly. "But I am sure of this, that if that person were to be taken ill, and were so very poor, and were to go to Nina for help, I don't think he would have to fear any refusal. And then, as you say, Nina, you would be proud to have the money—just as I know you would be ready to give it."

It was rarely that Nina blushed, but now her pretty, pale face fairly burned with conscious pleasure; and he hardly dared to look, yet he fancied there was something of moisture in the long, dark lashes, while she did not speak for some seconds. Perhaps he had been too bold in interpreting her parable.

Yes, there was no doubt that this spoiled favorite of the public, who lived amid the excitements, the flatteries, the gratifications of the moment, with hardly a thought of the future, was dreadfully extravagant, though it was rarely on himself that he lavished his reckless expenditure. Nina's protests were of no avail; whenever he saw anything pretty or odd or interesting, that he thought would please her, it was purchased there and then, to be given to her on the first opportunity. One day he was going through Vigo Street, and noticed in a shop-window a pair of old-fashioned, silver-gilt loving-cups—those that interclasp; and forthwith he went in and bought them: "I'll take those; how much are they" being his way of bargaining. In the afternoon he carried them down to Sloane Street.

"Here, Nina, I've brought you a little present; and I'll have to show you how to use it, or you would never guess what it is for."

When he unrolled his pretty gift out of the pink tissue paper, Nina threw up her hands in despair.

"Oh, it is too much of a folly!" she exclaimed. "Why do you do it, Leo? What is the use of old silver to me?"

"Well, it's nice to look at," said he. "And it will help to furnish your house when you get married, Nina."

"Ah, Leo," said she, "if you would only think about yourself! It is always to-day, to-morrow, with you: never the coming years—"

"Yes, I know all about that," he interposed. "Now I'm going to show you how these are used. They're loving-cups, you know, Nina—"

"Loving-cups?" she repeated, rather timidly.

"Yes? and I will show you how the ceremony is performed. Now, will you get me some lemonade, Nina, and a little of the vermouth that I sent to Mrs. Grey?"

She went and got these things for him; and when she returned he poured into one of the tiny goblets about a teaspoonful of the vermouth, filling it up with the lemonade; then he put the other cup on the top of this one, so that they formed a continuous vessel; he shook the contents; then he separated the cups, leaving about half the liquid in each, and one of them he handed to Nina, retaining the other.

"We drink at the same time, Nina—with any kind of wishes you like."

She glanced towards him—and then shyly lowered her eyes—as she raised the small cup to her lips. What were her wishes? Perhaps he did not care to know; perhaps she would not have cared to tell.

"You see, it is a simple ceremony, Nina," he said, as he put the little goblet on the table again. "But at the same time it is very confidential. I mean, you wouldn't ask everybody to go through it with you—it would hardly, for example, be quite circumspect for you to ask any young man you didn't know very well—"

"Leo!"

The sound of her voice startled him; there were tears of indignation in it; he looked up and found she had grown suddenly pale.

"You," she said, with quivering lips, "you and I, Leo—we have drunk together out of these—and you think I allow any one else—any one living in the world—to drink out of them after that?—I would rather have them dashed to pieces and thrown into the sea!"

Her vehemence surprised him—and might have set any other person thinking; but he was used to Nina's proud and wayward moods; so he merely went on to tell her that there was nothing, after all, so very solemn in the ceremony of drinking from a loving-cup; and then he asked her whether she ought not to call Miss Girond, for it was about time they were going down to the theatre.

Of course the forthcoming dinner that Mr. Lehmann was about to give at the Star and Garter created quite a stir behind the scenes, where the routine of life is much more monotonous than the people imagine who sit in the stalls and regard the antics of the merry folk on the stage. There were all kinds of rumors and speculations as to who was going with whom, as to the number and quality of the visitors, and as to the possibility of the manager presenting each of his lady-guests with a little souvenir in honor of the occasion. So when Lionel was summoned to Miss Burgoyne's room one evening, he was not surprised to find her begin to talk of the following Sunday.

"Will you make yourself some tea, Mr. Moore?" she said, from the inner room. "There's some cake on the top of the piano. Then you can bring a chair to the curtain, and I'll talk to you—for I'm not quite finished yet."

He drew a chair to the little opening in the curtain, where he could hear what she had to say, and answer, without any indiscreet prying.

"I am at your service, Miss Grace," said he, lightly.

"How are you going down to Richmond on Sunday?" she asked at once.

"By train, I suppose."

There was a moment's silence—perhaps she was waiting for him to ask a similar question.

"Lord Denysfort is going to drive down," said the voice in the inner room.

"Lord Denysfort!" he said, contemptuously. "What she is the attraction now? I don't like that kind of thing; it gets the theatre a bad name. If I were Lehmann, I wouldn't have a single stranger allowed in the wings."

"Not unless they were your own friends," said the unseen young lady, complacently. "Now I know you're scowling. But I believe you are quite wrong. Lord Denysfort is simply a business acquaintance of Mr. Lehmann's—there are money matters between them, and that kind of thing; and when he was asked to be present at the dinner, it was quite natural that he should offer to drive some of us down. You have no particular detestation of lords, have you? What has become of the tall, handsome young man you brought to us at Henley—the lazy man—and didn't he come to the theatre one night?"

"Lord Rockminster?—he is in Scotland still, I believe."

"Somebody ought to put fireworks in his coat-tail pockets; but he's awfully good-looking—he's just frightfully handsome. He quite fluttered me."

"I say, Miss Burgoyne," Lionel interposed, quickly, "there's a sister-in-law of his coming to town shortly, on her way to Brighton—a Miss Cunyngham—and I should like to have her mother and herself come behind for a little while, some night they were at the theatre—it is interesting to those people, you know—"

"You are the one who would have no strangers in the wings!" said the voice.

"And I want you to be civil to them—"

"Tea and cake? All right. But you haven't told me how you are going down to Richmond."

"Yes, I have. I'm going down by train, most likely."

"Oh, by train. I suppose I ought to accept Lord Denysfort's invitation."

"What's the good of driving at this time of year?" he asked. "It will be pitch dark."

"There will be a full moon, they say."

"You won't see it because of the fog. In fact, the whole thing is a mistake. The dinner should have been given in London."

"Oh, I think it will be great fun dining at a half-deserted hotel—it will be ghostly—and I'm going out on the terrace, if it is as black as midnight."

"And what are you going to do with your gallant warrior—with the furious fire-eater who wanted to bring my humble career to a premature end?"

"I don't know who you mean," said the voice, but with no great decision.

"You don't remember saving my life, then?" he asked. "Have you forgotten the duel that was to have been fought before I went to Scotland, and how you stepped in to protect me? If it hadn't been for you, I might have fallen on the gory field of battle—"

"It's all very well for you to mock," said she, "but there's nothing that young man wouldn't do for my sake; and I don't see anything to laugh at in true esteem and affection. They're too rare nowadays. I know one or two gentlemen who might be improved by a little more devotion and—and chivalry. But it's all persiflage nowadays. Everything is *connu*—"

"Behind the scenes, perhaps; but it's different when you import the fresh, the ingenuous element from the outer world," said he (but what interest had he in the discussion?—he did not wear his heart on his sleeve for Miss Burgoyne to peck at). "Aren't you going to take Mr. Miles down with you?"

"Poor Percy!" said the now muffled voice (perhaps she had a pin in her teeth, or perhaps she was still further touching-up her lips), "I suppose he would come if he were invited; but he doesn't know any of them."

"Why don't you ask Lehmann for an invitation for him?"

"What do you mean, Mr. Moore?" demanded the voice—sharply enough now.

"Oh, nothing."

"I consider you are very impertinent. Why should I ask for an invitation for Mr. Miles? What would that imply? Do you suppose I particularly wish him to be there?"

"Oh, I didn't mean to offend," Lionel said, quite humbly. "Only—you see—the other night you showed me that ingenious dodge of covering the ring you wear with a bit of white india-rubber—and—and I thought it might be an engagement ring—worn on that finger—"

"Then you're quite wrong, Mr. Clever," said the voice. "That ring was given me by a very dear friend, a very, very dear friend—I won't tell you whether a he or a she—and it fits that finger; but all the same I don't want the public to think I am engaged. So there—for your wonderful guessing!"

"I'm sure I beg your pardon," said he; "I didn't mean to be inquisitive."

But at this moment the intervening curtains were thrown open, and here was Grace Mainwaring, in full panoply of white satin and pearls and powdered hair. She was followed by her maid. She went to the long mirror in this larger room, and began to put the finishing touches to the set of her costume and also to her make-up. Then she told Jane to go and get the inner room tidied; and when the maid had disappeared she turned to the young baritone.

"Mr. Moore," said she, rather pointedly, "you are not very communicative."

"In what way?"

"I understand you are going to take Miss Ross and Miss Girond down to Richmond on Sunday; I don't see myself why you should conceal it."

"I never thought of concealing it!" he exclaimed, with a little surprise. "Why should a trifling arrangement like that be concealed—or mentioned either?"

Miss Burgoyne regarded herself in the mirror again, and touched her white wig here and there and the black beauty-spots on her cheek and chin.

"I have been told," she remarked, rather scornfully, "that gentlemen are fond of the society of chorus-girls—I suppose they enjoy a certain freedom there that they don't meet elsewhere."

"Neither Miss Ross nor Miss Girond is a chorus-girl," he said—though he wasn't going to lose his temper over nothing.

"They have both sung in the chorus," she retorted, snappishly.

"That is neither here nor there," he said. "Why, what does it matter how we go down, when we shall all meet there on a common footing? It was an obviously simple arrangement—Sloane Street is on my way, whether I go by road or rail—"

"Oh, pray don't make any apology to *me*—I am not interested in the question," she observed, in a most lofty manner, as she still affected to be examining her dress in the mirror.

"I wasn't making any apology to anybody," he said, bluntly.

"Or explanation," she continued, in the same tone. "You seem to have a strange fancy for foreigners, Mr. Moore; and I suppose they are glad to be allowed to practice talking with any one who can speak decent English."

"Nina—I mean Miss Ross—is an old friend of mine," he said, just beginning to chafe a little. "It is a very small piece of courtesy that I should offer to see her safely down to Richmond, when she is a stranger, with hardly any other acquaintance in London—"

"But pray don't make any excuse to *me*—what have *I* to do with it?" Miss Burgoyne said, sweetly. And then, as she gathered up her long train and swung it over her arm, she added, "Will you kindly open the door for me, Mr. Moore?" And therewith she passed out and along the corridor and up into the wings—he attending her, for he also was wanted in this scene.

Well, Miss Burgoyne might drive down to Richmond with Lord Denysfort or with any one else; he was not going to forsake Nina. On the afternoon appointed, just as it was dark, he called at the house in Sloane Street, and found the two young ladies ready, with nothing but their bonnets to put on. Both of them, he thought, were very prettily dressed; but Nina's costume had a somewhat severe grace, and, indeed, rather comported with Nina's demeanor towards this little French chatterbox, whom she seemed to regard with a kind of grave and young-matronly consideration and forbearance. When they had got into the brougham which was waiting outside for them and had started away for Putney Bridge, it was Mlle. Girond who was merry and excited and talkative; Nina only listened, in good-humored amusement. Mlle. Girond had never been to Richmond, but she had heard of it; she knew all about the beautiful view and the terrace overlooking the river, and she was promising herself the romance and charm of a stroll in the moonlight.

"I don't see much sign of that full moon as yet," Lionel said to her, peering through the window of the brougham, "but I suppose the glare of the gas-lamps would hide it in any case. However, there's a good deal of fog always along the Thames at this time of year; don't be disappointed, Miss Girond, if you have to remain in-doors. Indeed, it is far too cold to go wandering about among statues in the moonlight."

"And if in the dark, they will be all the more mysterieuz, do you not think?" said Mlle. Girond, eagerly. "And there will be surprises—perhaps a laugh, perhaps a shriek—if you run against some one."

"Oh, no, I am not going to allow anything of that kind," said he. "I have to look after you young ladies, and you must conduct yourselves with the strictest decorum."

"Yes, for Nina," Mlle. Girond cried, gayly. "That is for Nina—for me, no! I will have some amusement, or I will run away. Who gave you control of me, monsieur? I thank you, but I do not wish it."

"Estelle!" said Nina, in tones of grave reproach.

"Ah!" said the wilful young lady, and she put out the tips of her fingers as though she would shake away from her these too-serious companions. "You have become English, Nina. Very well. If I have no more gay companion, I go out and seek a statue—I beckon to him—I defy him—ah! he freezes me—he nods his head—it is the Commendatore!" And then she sang, in portentous bass notes—

"Don Giovanni, a cenar teco

M' invitasti—è son venuto!"

Lionel let down the window.

"Do you see that, Miss Girond?"

Far away, above the blue mists and the jet-black trees (for they were out in the country by this time), hung a small, opaque disk of dingy orange.

"It is the moon, Leo!" cried Nina. "Ah, but so dull!"

"That is the fog lying over the low country," he said; "it may be clearer when we get to the top of the hill. It is to be hoped so, at all events. Fancy a theatrical company going out to a rustic festivity and not provided with a better moon than that!"

However, when they finally reached the Star and Garter, they had forgotten about the moon and the aspect of the night; for here were the wide steps and the portico all ablaze with a friendly yellow glow; and just inside stood Mr. Lehmann, with the most shining shirt-front ever beheld, receiving his guests as they arrived. Here, too, was Lord Denysfort, a feeble-looking young man, with huge ears and no chin to speak of, who, however, had shown some sense in engaging a professional whip to drive the four-in-hand down through the fog. Of course there was a good deal of bustle and hurry and confusion—friends anxious about the non-arrival of other friends and so forth—in the midst of which Lionel said to his two companions,

"Dinner will be a long time yet. The ladies who have driven down will be making themselves beautiful for another quarter of an hour. Suppose we go out on the balcony, and see whether any of Miss Girond's statues are visible."

They agreed to this, for they had not taken off their cloaks; so he led them along the hall and round by a smaller passage to a door which he opened; they got outside, and found themselves in the hushed, still night. Below them, on the wide terrace, they could make out the wan, gray, plaster pillars and pediments and statues among the jet-black shrubs; but beyond that all was chaos; the river and the wooded valley were shrouded in a dense mist, pierced only here and there by a small orange ray—some distant window or lamp. They wandered down the wide steps; they crossed to the parapet; they gazed into that great unknown gulf, in which they could descry nothing but one or two spectral black trees, their topmost branches coming up into the clearer air. Then they walked along to the southern end of the terrace; and here they came in sight of the moon—a far-distant world on fire it seemed to be, especially when the sombre golden radiance touched a passing tag of cloud and changed it into lurid smoke. All the side of the vast building looking towards them was dark—save for one window that burned red.

"Is that where we dine?" asked Nina, as they returned.

"Oh, no," Lionel answered. "Our room is at the end of the passage by which we came out—I suppose the shutters are closed. I fancy that is the coffee-room."

"I am going to have a peep in," Mlle. Girond said, as they ascended the steps again; and when they had reached the balcony she went along to the window, leaving her companions behind, for they did not share in this childish curiosity. But the next moment little Capitaine Crépin came back, in a great state of excitement.

"Come, come, come!" she said, breathlessly. "Ah, the poor young gentleman—all alone!—my heart feels for him—Mr. Moore, it is piteous."

"Well, what have you discovered now?" said Lionel, indifferently, for he was getting hungry.

"Come and see—come and see! All alone—no one to say a word—"

Lionel and Nina followed their eager guide along the dark balcony, until they had got near the brilliant red window. They looked in. The room was bright with crimson-shaded lamps, and its solitary occupant they made out clearly enough; it was Mr. Percival Miles—in evening dress, standing before the fireplace, gazing into the coals, his hands in his pockets.

"Ah," said Nina, as she quickly drew back, "that is the young gentleman who sometimes waits for Miss Burgoyne, is it not, Leo? And he is all by himself. It is hard."

"You think it is hard, Nina?" Lionel said, turning to her, as the three spies simultaneously withdrew.

"Oh, yes, yes!" Nina exclaimed.

"Well, you see," continued Lionel, as he opened the glass door to let his companions re-enter the hotel, "an outsider who comes skylarking after an actress, and finds her surrounded by her professional friends and her professional interests, has to undergo a good deal of tribulation. That poor fellow has come down here to dine all by himself, merely to be near her. But, mind you, it was that same fellow who wanted to kill me."

"He, kill you!" Nina said, scornfully. "You allowed him to live—yes?"

"But I don't bear any malice. No, I don't. I'm going to make that boy just the very happiest young man there is in the kingdom of Great Britain this evening."

"Ah, I know, I know!" exclaimed Nina, delightedly.

"Oh, no, you don't know. You don't know anything about it. What you and Miss Girond have got to do now is to go into the cloak-room and leave your things, and afterwards I'll meet you in the dining-room."

"Yes, but you are going to Mr. Lehmann!" said Nina, with a laugh. "I do not know?—yes, I do know. Ah, that is generous of you, Leo—that is noble."

"Noble?—trash!" he said; and he hurried these young people along to the disrobing-room and left them there. Then he went to the manager, who was still in the hall.

"I say," he began, without more ado, "there's a young friend of mine in this hotel whom I wish you'd invite to dine with us."

The manager looked rather startled—then hesitated—then stroked his waxed moustache.

"I—I presume a gentleman friend?"

"Yes, of course," said Lionel, angrily. "It's a Percival Miles—why, you must have heard of Sir Barrington Miles, and this is his eldest son, though he's quite a young fellow—"

"Oh, very well; oh, yes, certainly!" said Mr. Lehmann, apparently very much relieved. "Will you ask him?"

"Well, no, I can't exactly," Lionel said. "But I will send him a formal note in your name—'Mr. Lehmann presents his compliments'—may I?"

"All right; but dinner will be served almost directly. Would you mind telling the waiters to lay another cover?"

About five minutes thereafter, when the company had swarmed into the dining-room—most of them chatting and laughing, but the more business-like looking for their allotted places at table—Mr. Percival Miles put in an appearance, very shy and perhaps a little bewildered, for he knew not to whom he owed this invitation. Lionel had got a seat for him between Mlle. Girond and Mr. Carey, the musical conductor; if he could, and if he had dared, he would have placed him next Miss Burgoyne; but Miss Burgoyne was at the head of the table, between Lord Denysfort and Mr. Lehmann—besides, that fiery young lady might have taken sudden cause of offence. As it was, the young gentleman could gaze upon her from afar; and she had bowed to him—with some surprise clearly showing in her face—just as their eyes had met on his coming into the room. Lionel was next to Nina; he had arranged that.

It was a protracted banquet, and a merry one withal; there was a perfect Babel of noise; and the excellent old custom of drinking healths with distant friends was freely adopted. Miss Girond did her best to amuse the good-looking boy whom she had been instrumental in rescuing from his solitary dinner in the coffee-room; but he did not respond as he ought to have done; from time to time he glanced wistfully towards the head of the table, where Miss Burgoyne was gayly chatting with Lord Denysfort. As for Nina, Nina was very quiet, but very much interested, as her dark, expressive eyes eloquently showed.

"It is so beautiful, Leo," she said. "Every one looks so well; is it the light reflected from the table?" And then she said, in a lower tone, "Do you see

Miss Burgoyne, Leo? She is acting all the time. She is acting to the whole table."

"That Albanian jacket of hers is gorgeous enough, anyway," Lionel responded; he was not much interested apparently in the question of Miss Burgoyne's behavior.

When dinner had been some little time over, the women-folk went away and got wraps and shawls, and the whole company passed outside, the men lighting their cigars at the top of the steps. The heavens overhead were now perfectly clear; the moonlight shone full on the long terrace, with its parapets and pedestals and plaster figures, while all the world below was shut away in a dense fog. Indeed, as the various groups idly walked about or stood and talked—their shadows sharply cut as out of ebony on the white stone—the whole scene was most extraordinary; for it appeared as though these people were the sole occupants of some region in cloud-land—a clear-shining region raised high above the forgotten earth.

"Lehmann is lucky," Lionel said to Nina. "I thought his moonlight effect was going to be a failure."

Miss Girond came up, in an eager and excited fashion.

"Nina!"

"What is it, Estelle?"

"Monsieur of the pretty face," she said, in a whisper, "oh, so sad he was all dinner!—regarding Miss Burgoyne, and she coquetting, oh, frightful, frightful!—but it is all right now—he was at the door when we come out— he takes her hand—'How you do, Miss Burgoyne?'—'Oh, how you do, Mr. Miles?'—and he leads her away before she can go to any one else. And there—away down there—do you see them? He has compensation, do you think?"

She drew Nina a little aside, and sang into her ear—

"—Ce soir, as-tu vu

La fille à notre maître,

D'un air résolu

Guettant à sa fenêtre?

Eh bien! qu'en dis tu?

—Je dis que j'ai tout vu,

Mais je n'ai rien cru;

Je l'aime, je l'aime,

Je l'aime quand même!"

and then she broke into a malicious laugh.

"What are you two conspiring about, now?" Lionel asked—from the bench on which he had carelessly seated himself, the better to enjoy his cigar.

"You must know the consequence of doing a good action, Leo," Nina said to him. "Do you see the black bushes—yonder—and the two figures? Estelle says it is Miss Burgoyne and the young gentleman who would have been all alone but that you intercede. Is he not owing a great deal to you?"

"Well, Nina, if there is any gratitude in woman's bosom, Miss Burgoyne ought to be indebted to me too. She has got her pretty dear. I dare say he would have managed to procure a little interview with her, in some surreptitious way, in any case—I dare say that was his intention in coming down; but now that he is one of the party, one of the guests, she can talk to him before every one. And since I have been the means of bringing the pair of turtle-doves together, I hope they're happy."

"Ah, Leo, you do not understand," Nina said to him—for Miss Girond was now talking to Mr. Carey, who had come up.

"I don't understand what?"

"You do not understand Miss Burgoyne," said Nina.

"What don't I understand about her, then?"

Nina shook her head.

"Why should I say? You will not believe. Perhaps she is grateful to you for bringing in that young man—yes, perhaps—but if she would rather have yourself to go and talk with her and be her companion before all those people? Oh, you do not believe? No, you are too modest—as she is vain and jealous. All during the dinner she was playing coquette, openly, for every one to see; Estelle says it was to pique the young man who came from the other room; no, Leo, it was not—it was meant for you!"

"Oh, nonsense, Nina!—I wasn't thinking anything about her!"

"Does she think that, Leo?" Nina said to him, gently. "Ah, you do not know that woman. She is clever; she is cunning; she wishes to have the fame of being associated with you—even in a photograph for the shop-windows; and you are so blind! The duel?—yes, she would have liked that, too, for the newspapers to speak about it, and the public to talk, and her name and yours together; but then she says, 'No, he will owe more to me if

I interfere and get an apology for him,' It is one way or the other way—anything to win your attention—that you should care for her—and that you should show it to the world—"

"Nina, Nina," said he, "you want to make me outrageously vain. Do you imagine she had a single thought for me when she had Lord Denysfort to carry on with—he hasn't much in his head, poor devil! but a title goes a long way in the theatrical world—and when she could practise on the susceptibilities of her humble adorer who was further down the table? Oh, I fancy Miss Burgoyne had enough to occupy herself with this evening without thinking of me. She was quite busy."

"Ah, you do not understand, Leo," Nina said. "But some day you may understand—if Miss Burgoyne still finds you indifferent, and becomes angry. But before that, she will try much—"

"Nina!"

"You will see, Leo!" Nina said; and that was all she could say just then, for Mr. Lehmann came up to take the general vote as to whether they would rather have tea out there in the moonlight or return to the dining-room.

But any doubt as to the manner in which Miss Burgoyne regarded his intercession on behalf of Mr. Percival Miles was removed, and that in a most summary fashion, by the young lady herself. As they were about to leave the hotel, the men were standing about in the hall, chatting at haphazard or lighting a fresh cigar, while they waited for the women-folk to get ready. Lionel saw Miss Burgoyne coming along the corridor, and was glad of the chance of saying good-night to her before she got on to the front of Lord Denysfort's drag. But it was not good-night that Miss Burgoyne had in her mind.

"Mr. Moore," she said, when she came up, and she spoke in a low, clear, incisive voice that considerably startled him. "I am told it was through you that that boy was invited to the dinner to-night."

He looked at her in amazement.

"Well, what then?" he exclaimed. "What was the objection? I thought he was a friend of yours. That boy?—that boy is a sufficiently important person, surely—heir to the Petmansworth estates—why I should have thought—"

She interrupted him.

"I consider it a gross piece of impertinence," she said, haughtily. "I suppose you thought you were conferring a favor on *me*! How dared you assume that any one—that any one—wished him to be present in that room?"

She turned proudly away from him, without waiting for his reply.

"Lord Denysfort, here I am," said she; and the chinless young man with the large ears gave her his arm and conducted her down the steps. Lionel looked after her—bewildered.

CHAPTER XV.

"LET THE STRUCKEN DEER GO WEEP."

But if Lionel regarded this constant association with Nina—this unreserved discussion of all their private affairs—even the sort of authority and guidance he exercised over her at times—as so simple and natural a thing that it was unnecessary to pause and ask whither it might tend, what about Nina herself? She was quite alone in England; she had more regard for the future than he had; what if certain wistful hopes, concealed almost from herself, had sprung up amid all this intimate and frankly affectionate companionship?

One morning she and Estelle were walking in to Regent Street, to examine proofs of certain photographs that had been taken of them both (for Clara figured in the shop-windows now, as well as Capitaine Crépin). Nina was very merry and vivacious on this sufficiently bright forenoon; and to please Estelle she was talking French—her French being fluent enough, if it was not quite perfect as to accent. They were passing along Piccadilly, when she stopped at a certain shop.

"Come, I show you something," she said.

Estelle followed her in. The moment the shopman saw who it was he did not wait to be questioned.

"It is quite ready, miss; I was just about to send it down."

He brought forward the double loving-cup that Lionel had given to Nina; and as the young lady took it into her hands she glanced at the rim. Yes; the inscription was quite right: "*From Leo to Nina*"—that was the simple legend she had had engraved.

"Here is the cup I spoke of, Estelle; is it not beautiful? And then I would not trouble Lionel to have the inscription made—I told him I would have it done myself and asked him what the words should be—behold it!"

The cup was duly admired and handed back to be sent down to Sloane Street; then Estelle and she left the shop together.

"Oh, yes, it is very beautiful," said the former, continuing to speak in her native tongue, "and a very distinguished present; but there is something still more piquant that he will be buying for you ere long—can you not guess, Nina?—no?—not a wedding-ring?"

The audacity of the question somewhat disconcerted Nina; but she met it with no sham denial, no affected protest.

"He has not spoken to me, Estelle," Nina said, gravely and simply, "And sometimes I ask myself if it is not better we should remain as we are—we are such good friends and companions. We are happy; we have plenty to occupy ourselves with; why undertake more serious cares? Perhaps that is all that Lionel thinks of it; and, if it is so, I am content. And then sometimes, Estelle, I ask myself if it would not be better for him to marry—when he has made his choice, that is to say; and I picture him and his young wife living very happily in a quite small establishment—perhaps two or three rooms only, in one of those large buildings in Victoria Street—and everything very pretty around them, with their music and their occupations and the visits of friends. Would not that be for him a life far more satisfactory than his present distractions—the gayeties and amusements—the invitations of strangers?"

"Yes, yes, yes!" her companion cried, with instant assent. "Ah, Nina, I can see you the most charming young house-mistress—I can see you receive your guests when they come for afternoon music—you wear a tea-gown of brocade the color of wall-flower, with cream-colored lace—you speak French, English, Italian as it is necessary for this one and that—your musical reunions are known everywhere. Will madame permit the poor Estelle to be present?—Estelle, who will not dare to sing before those celebrated ones, but who will applaud, applaud—in herself a prodigious *claque*! And now, behold! Miss Burgoyne arrives—Miss Burgoyne in grand state—and nevertheless you are her dear Nina, her charming friend, although in her heart she hates you for having carried off the handsome Lionel—"

"Estelle," said Nina, gently, "you let your tongue run away. When I picture to myself Lionel in the future, I leave the space beside him empty. Who is to fill it?—perhaps he has never given a thought to that. Perhaps it will always be empty; perhaps one of his fashionable friends will suddenly appear there, who knows? He does not seem ever to look forward; if I remonstrate about his expenditure, he laughs. And why should he give me things of value? I am not covetous. If he wishes to express kindness, is not a word better than any silver cup; If he wishes to be remembered when he is absent, would not the smallest message sent in a letter be of more value than a bracelet with sapphires—"

"Oh, Nina," her companion exclaimed, laughing, "what a thing to say!— that you would rather have a scrap of writing from Lionel Moore than a bracelet with sapphires—"

"No, Estelle, I did not," Nina protested, rather indignantly; "I was talking of the value of presents generally, and of their use or uselessness."

"And yet you seemed very proud of that loving-cup, Nina, and of the inscription on it," Estelle said, demurely; and there the subject ended, for they were now approaching the photographer's.

It was a Saturday night that Honnor Cunyngham and her mother—who had come up from Brighton for a few days—had been induced to fix for their visit to the New Theatre; and as the evening drew near, Lionel became more and more anxious, so that he almost regretted having persuaded them. All his other troubles and worries he could at once carry to Nina, whose cheerful common-sense and abundant courage made light of them and lent him heart; but this one he had to ponder over by himself; he did not care to tell Nina with what concern he looked forward to the impressions that Miss Cunyngham might form of himself and his surroundings when brought immediately into contact with them. And yet he was not altogether silent.

"You see how it is, Nina," he said, in tones of deep vexation. "That fellow Collier has been allowed to gag and gag until the whole piece is filled with his music-hall tomfoolery, and the music has been made quite subsidiary. I wonder Lehmann doesn't get a lot of acrobats and conjurors, and let Miss Burgoyne and you and me stop at home. "The Squire's Daughter" is really a very pretty piece, with some delightful melody running through it; but that fellow has vulgarized it into the lowest burlesque."

"What does it matter to you, Leo?" Nina said. "What he does is separate from you. He cannot vulgarize your singing."

"But he makes all that clowning of his so important—it has become so big a feature of the piece that any friends of yours coming to see the little opera might very naturally say, 'Oh, is this the kind of thing he figures in? This is an intellectual entertainment, truly!'"

"But you do not join in it, Leo!" Nina protested.

"In the most gagging scene of all, I've got to stand and look on the whole time!" he said.

"Oh, no, Leo," Nina said, with mock sympathy, "you can listen to Miss Burgoyne as she talks to you from behind her fan."

"Those two ladies I told you of," he continued, "who are coming on Saturday night—I wonder what they will think of all that low-comedy stuff. I begin to wish I hadn't asked them to come behind, but I thought it might be a sort of inducement. Miss Cunyngham was very kind to me when I was in the Highlands, and this was all I could think of; but I don't think she has much of the frivolous curiosity of her sisters-in-law; and I am not sure that her mother and she would even care much for the honor of having tea in Miss Burgoyne's room. No, I wish I hadn't asked them."

"Do you value their opinion so highly, then, Leo?" Nina asked, gently.

"Oh, yes," he said, with some hesitation—"that is, I shouldn't like them to form any unfavorable impression—to go away with any scornful feeling towards comic opera, and towards the people engaged in it; I should like them to think well of the piece. I suppose I couldn't bribe Collier to leave out the half of his gag, or the whole of it, for that particular night. Did you see what one of the papers said about the 400th performance?—that the fate of "The Squire's Daughter" had for some time been doubtful, but that it had been saved by the increased prominence given to the part played by Mr. Fred Collier!—a compliment to the public taste!—the piece saved by lugging in a lot of music-hall buffoonery!"

"But, Leo," Nina said, "your friends who are coming on Saturday night will not think you responsible for all that."

"People are apt to judge of you by your associates, Nina," he said, absently; he was clearly looking forward to this visit with some compunction, not to say alarm.

Then he went to Miss Burgoyne. Miss Burgoyne had forgiven him for having introduced Percival Miles to the Richmond dinner-party; indeed, she was generally as ready to forgive as she was quick to take offence.

"I wish you would do me a very great favor," he said.

"What is it?" asked Grace Mainwaring, who was standing in front of the tall mirror, adjusting the shining stars and crescents that adorned her powdered hair.

"I suppose you could wear a little nosegay with that dress," he said, "of natural flowers, done up with a bit of white satin ribbon, perhaps, and a silver tube and cord, or something of that kind?"

"Flowers?" she repeated. "Oh, yes, I could wear them—if any one were polite enough to give me them."

"I shall be delighted to send you some every evening for a month, if you'll only do this for me on Saturday," said he. "It is on Saturday night those two ladies are coming to the theatre; and you were good enough to promise to ask them to your room and offer them some tea. The younger of the two—that is, Miss Cunyngham—has never been behind the scenes of a theatre before, and I think she will be very pleased to be introduced to Miss Grace Mainwaring; and don't you think it would be rather nice of Miss Grace

Mainwaring to take those flowers from her dress and present them to the young lady, as a souvenir of her visit?"

She wheeled round, and looked at him with a curious scrutiny.

"Well, this *is* something new!" she said, as she turned to the mirror again. "I thought it was the fortunate Harry Thornhill who received all kinds of compliments and attentions from his lady adorers; I wasn't aware he ever returned them. But do you think it is quite fair, Mr. Moore? If this is some girl who has a love-sick fancy for Harry Thornhill, don't you think you should drop Harry Thornhill and play David Garrick, to cure the poor thing?"

"Considering that Miss Cunyngham has never seen Harry Thornhill," he was beginning, when she interrupted him:

"Oh, only heard him sing in private? Quite enough, I suppose, to put nonsense into a silly school-girl's head."

"When you see this young lady," he observed, "I don't think you will say she looks like a silly school-girl. She's nearly as tall as I am, for one thing."

"I hate giraffes," said Miss Burgoyne, tartly, "Do you put a string round her neck when you go out walking with her?"

He was just on the point of saying something about greenroom manners, but thought better of it.

"Now, Miss Burgoyne," he said to her, "on Saturday night you are going to put on your most winning way—you can do it when you like—and you are going to captivate and fascinate those two people until they'll go away home with the conviction that you are the most charming and delightful creature that ever lived. You can do it easily enough if you like—no one better. You are going to be very nice to them, and you'll send them away just in love with Grace Mainwaring."

Miss Burgoyne altered her tone a little.

"If I give your giraffe friend those flowers, I suppose you expect me to tell lies as well?" she asked, with some approach to good-humor.

"About what?"

"Oh, about being delighted to make her acquaintance, and that kind of thing."

"I have no doubt you will be as pleased to make her acquaintance as she will be to make yours," said he, "and a few civil words never do any harm."

Here Miss Burgoyne was called. She went to the little side-table and sipped some of her home-brewed lemonade; then he opened the door for her, and together they went up into the wings.

"Tall, is she?" continued Miss Burgoyne, as they were looking on at Mr. Fred Collier's buffooneries out there on the stage. "Is she as silent and stupid as her brother?"

"Her brother?"

"Lord Rockminster."

"Oh, Lord Rockminster isn't her brother. You've got them mixed up," said Lionel. "Miss Cunyngham's brother, Sir Hugh, married a sister of Lord Rockminster—the Lady Adela Cunyngham who came to your room one night—don't you remember?"

"You seem to have the whole peerage and baronetage at your fingers' ends," said she, sullenly; and the next moment she was on the stage, smiling and gracious, and receiving her father's guests with that charming manner which the heroine of the operetta could assume when she chose.

Even with Miss Burgoyne's grudgingly promised assistance, Lionel still remained unaccountably perturbed about that visit of Lady Cunyngham and her daughter; and when on the Saturday evening he first became aware—through the confused glare of the footlights—that the two ladies had come into the box he had secured for them, it seemed to him as though he were responsible for every single feature of the performance. As for himself, he was at his best, and he knew it; he sang, 'The starry night brings me no rest' with such a *verve* that the enthusiasm of the audience was unbounded; even Miss Burgoyne—Miss Grace Mainwaring, that is, who was perched up on a bit of scaffolding in order to throw a rose to her lover—listened with a new interest, instead of being busy with her ribbons and the set of her hair; and when she opened the casement in answer to his impassioned appeal, she kissed the crimson-cotton blossom thrice ere she dropped it to her enraptured swain below. This was all very well; but when the comic man took possession of the stage, Lionel—instead of going off to his dressing-room to glance at an evening paper or have a chat with some acquaintance—remained in the wings, looking on with an indescribable loathing. This hideous farcicality seemed more vulgar than ever? what would Honnor Cunyngham think of his associates? He felt as if he were an accomplice in foisting this wretched music-hall stuff on the public. And the mother—the tall lady with the proud, fine features and the grave and placid voice—what would she think of the new acquaintance whom her daughter had introduced to her? Had it been Lady Adela or her sisters, he would not have cared one jot. They were proud to be in alliance with professional people; they flattered themselves that they rather belonged to the set—actors, authors, artists, musicians, those busy and eager amateurs considered to be, like themselves, of imagination all compact. But that he should have asked Honnor Cunyngham to come and look on at the antics of this gaping and grinning fool; that she should know he had to consort with such folk; that she should consider him an aider and abettor in putting this kind of entertainment before the public—this galled him to the quick. The murmur of the Aivron and the Geinig seemed dinning in his ears. If only he could have thrown aside these senseless trappings—if he were an under-keeper now, or a water-bailiff, or even a gillie looking after the dogs and the ponies, he could have met the gaze of those clear hazel eyes without shame. But here he was the coadjutor of this grimacing clown; and she was sitting in her box there—and thinking.

"What is it, Leo?" said Nina, coming up to him rather timidly. "You are annoyed."

"I have made a mistake, that is all," he said, rather impatiently. "I shouldn't have persuaded those two ladies to come to the theatre; I forgot what kind of thing we played in; I might as well have asked them to go to a penny gaff. Collier is worse than ever to-night."

"And you better, Leo," said Nina, who had always comforting words for him. "Did you not hear how enthusiastic the audience were? And if this is the young lady you told me of—who was so friendly in Scotland that she did not fear ridicule for herself in order to save you from the possibility of ridicule—surely she will be so well-wishing to you that she will understand you have nothing to do with the foolishness on the stage."

"If you are thinking of that salmon-fishing incident," he said, rather hastily, "of course you mustn't imagine there was any fear of *her* encountering any ridicule. Oh, certainly not. It was no new thing for her to get wet when she was out fishing—"

"At all events, it was a friendly act to you," said Nina, on whom that occurrence seemed to have made some impression. "And if she is so generous, so benevolent towards you, do you think she will not see you are not responsible for the comic business?"

It was at the end of the penultimate act that an attendant brought round Miss Cunyngham and her mother—the latter a handsome and distinguished-looking elderly lady, with white hair done up *a la Marie Antoinette*—behind the scenes; and Nina, hanging some way back, could see them being presented to Miss Burgoyne. Nina was a little breathless and bewildered. She had heard a good deal about the fisher-maiden in the far North, of her hardy out-of-door life, and her rough and serviceable costume; and perhaps she had formed some mental picture of her—very different from the actual appearance of this tall young Englishwoman, whose clear, calm eyes, strongly marked eyebrows, and proud, refined features were so striking. Here was no simple maiden in a suit of serge, but a young woman of commanding presence, whose long cloak of tan-colored velvet, with its hanging sleeves showing a flash of crimson, seemed to Nina to have a sort of royal magnificence about it. And yet her manner appeared to be very simple and gentle; she smiled as she talked to Miss Burgoyne; and the last that Nina saw of her—as they all left together in the direction of the corridor, Lionel obsequiously attending them—was that the tall young lady walked with a most gracious carriage. Nina made sure that they had all disappeared before she, too, went down the steps; then she made her way to her own room, to get ready for the final act. Miss Girond, of course, was also here; but Nina had no word for Estelle; she seemed preoccupied about something.

Never had Harry Thornhill dressed so quickly; and when, in his gay costume of flowered silk and ruffles, tied wig and buckled shoes, he tapped at Miss Burgoyne's door and entered, he found that this young lady was still in the curtained apartment, though she had sent out Jane to see that her two visitors were being looked after. Lionel, too, helped himself to some tea; and it was with a singular feeling of relief that he discovered, as he presently did, that both Lady Cunyngham and her daughter were quite charmed with the piece, so far as they had seen it. They appeared to put the farcicality altogether aside, and to have been much impressed by the character of the music.

"What a pretty girl that Miss Ross is!" said the younger of the two ladies, incidentally. "But she is not English, is she? I thought I could detect a trace of foreign accent here and there."

"No, she is Italian," Lionel made answer. "Her name is really Rossi— Antonia Rossi—but her intimate friends call her Nina."

"What a beautiful voice she has!" Miss Honnor continued. "So fresh and pure and sweet. I think she has a far more beautiful voice than—"

He quickly held up his hand, and the hint was taken.

"And she puts such life into her part—she seems to be really light-hearted and merry," resumed Miss Honnor, who appeared to have been much taken by Nina's manner on the stage. "Do you know, Mr. Moore, I could not help to-night thinking more than once of "The Chaplet" and my sisters and their amateur friends. The difference between an amateur performance and a performance of trained artists is so marvellous; it doesn't seem to me to be one of degree at all; at an amateur performance, however clever it may be, I am conscious all the time that the people are assuming something quite foreign to themselves, whereas on the stage the people seem to be the actual characters they profess to be. I forget they are actors and actresses—"

"You must be a good audience, Miss Cunyngham," said he (it used to be "Miss Honnor" in Strathaivron, but that was some time ago—*then* he was not decked out and painted for exhibition on the stage).

"Oh, I like to believe," she said. "I don't wish to criticise. I wholly and delightfully give myself up to the illusion. Mother and I go so seldom to the theatre that we are under no temptation to begin and ask how this or that is done, or to make any comparisons; we surrender ourselves to the story, and believe the people to be real people all we can. As for mother, if it weren't a dreadful secret—"

But here the curtains were thrown wide, and out came Miss Burgoyne, obviously conscious of her magnificent costume, profuse in her apologies for not appearing sooner. Something had gone wrong, and the mishap had kept her late; indeed, she had just time to go through the formality of taking a cup of tea with her guests when she was called and had to get ready to go.

"And Nina, hanging some way back, could see them being presented to Miss Burgoyne."

"However, I need not say good-bye just yet," she said to them, as she tucked up her voluminous train. "Wouldn't you like to look on for a little while from the wings? You could have the prompter's chair, Lady Cunyngham, so that you could see the audience or the stage, just as you chose, if Miss Cunyngham wouldn't mind standing about among the gasmen."

"If you are sure we shall not be in the way," said the elder lady, who had, perhaps, a little more curiosity than her daughter.

"Oh, Mr. Moore will show you," said Miss Burgoyne, making no scruple about preceding her visitors along the corridor and up the steps, for she had not too much time.

The prompter's office, now that this piece had been running over four hundred nights, was practically a sinecure, so that there was no trouble about getting Lady Cunyngham installed in the little corner, whence, through a small aperture, she could regard the dusky-hued audience or turn her attention to the stage just as she pleased. Miss Honnor stood close by her, when she was allowed—keeping out of sight of the opposite boxes as much as she could, though she observed that the workmen about her did not care much whether they were visible or not, and that they talked or called to one another with a fine indifference towards what was going forward on the stage. At present a minuet was being danced, and very pretty it was; she could not help noticing how cleverly Miss Burgoyne managed her train. As for her mother, the old lady seemed intensely interested and yet conscious all the time that she herself, in this strange position, was an interloper; again and again she rose and offered to resign her place to the rather shabby-looking elderly man who was the rightful occupant; but he just as often begged her to remain—he seemed mostly interested in the management of the gas-handles just over his head.

And now came in the comic interlude which Lionel had feared most of all—the squire's faithful henchman going through all the phases of getting drunk in double-quick stage-time; and, while those stupidities were going forward, Lionel and Miss Burgoyne were supposed to retire up the stage somewhat and look on. Well, they took up their positions—Grace Mainwaring being seated.

"Your giraffe is rather handsome," she said, behind her fan.

"I believe she is considered to be one of the best-looking women in England," said he, somewhat stiffly.

"Oh, really! Well, of course, tastes differ," Miss Grace Mainwaring said. "I don't think a woman should have blacking-brushes instead of eyebrows. But it's a matter of taste."

"Yes," said he, "and comic opera is the sort of place where one's taste becomes so refined. What do you think of this gag now? Is this what the public like—when they come to hear music?"

"You're very fastidious—you want everything to be super-fine—but you may depend on it that it keeps the piece going with the pit and gallery."

His answer to that was one of this young lady's strangest experiences of the stage: Lionel Moore had suddenly left her, and, indeed, quitted this scene, in which he was supposed to be a chief figure. He walked down the wings until he found himself close to Miss Honnor Cunyngham.

"Miss Cunyngham," he said.

She turned—her eyes somewhat bewildered by the glare of light on the stage.

"Come back, please," he said. "I don't want you to see this scene—it has nothing to do with the operetta—and it is dull and stupid and tedious beyond description."

She followed him two or three steps, wondering.

"You say you like the music," he continued, here in the twilight of the wings, "and the little story is really rather pretty and idyllic; but they *will* go and introduce a lot of music-hall stuff to please the groundlings. I should prefer you not to see it. Won't you rather wait a little, and talk about something?—it isn't often you and I meet. Did you get many salmon after I left Strathaivron?"

"Oh, no," said she, still rather surprised. "Towards the end of the season the red fish are really not worth landing."

"It seems a long time since then," he said. "I find myself sitting up at night and thinking over all those experiences—making pictures of them—and the hours go by in a most astonishing fashion. Here in London, among the November fogs, it seems so strange to think of those splendid days and the long, clear twilights. I suppose it is all so well known to you, you do not trouble to recall it; but I do—it is like a dream—only that I see everything so distinctly—I seem almost to be able to touch each leaf of the bushes in the little dell where we used to have luncheon; do you remember?"

"Above the Geinig Pool?—oh, yes!" she said, smiling.

"And the Junction Pool," he continued, with a curious eagerness, as if he were claiming her sympathy, her interest, on account of that old companionship—"I can make the clearest vision of it as I sit up all by myself at night—you remember the little bush on the opposite side that you used sometimes to catch your fly on, and the shelf of shingle going suddenly down into the brown water—I always thought that was a dangerous place. And how well you used to fish the Rock Pool! Old Robert used to be so proud of you! Once, at the tail of the Rock Pool, you wound up, and said to him, 'Well, I can't do any better than that, Robert;' and then he said, 'No man ever fished that pool better—oh, I beg your pardon, Miss Honnor; no one at all ever fished that pool better.' I suppose Strathaivron is nothing to you—you must be so familiar with it—but to me it is a sort of wonderland, to dream of when I am all by myself at night—"

Alas! it was at this very moment that Nina came up from her room; Clara, the innkeeper's daughter, had to go on immediately after the ball-room scene was over. And Nina, as she came by, caught sight of these two, and for a moment she stood still, her eyes staring. The two figures were in a sort of twilight—a twilight as compared with the glare of the stage beyond them, but there were lights here quite sufficient to illumine their features; it was no imagination on Nina's part—she saw with a startling clearness that Lionel was regarding this tall, English-looking girl with a look she had never seen him direct towards any woman before—a timid, wistful, half-beseeching look that needed no words to explain its meaning. For a second Nina stood there, paralyzed—not daring to breathe—not able to move. Yet was it altogether a revelation to her, or only a sudden and overwhelming confirmation of certain half-frightened misgivings which had visited her from time to time, and which she had striven hard to banish? The next moment Nina had passed on silently, like a ghost, and had disappeared in the dusk behind some scenery.

"When shall you be back in Strathaivron, Miss Honnor?" he asked.

"In the spring, I suppose, for the salmon-fishing," she made answer.

"You will be up there in the clear April days, by the side of that beautiful river, and I shall be playing the mountebank here, among the London gas and fog."

But at this moment the orchestra began the slow music that intimated the resumption of the minuet, and this recalled him to his senses; he had hurriedly to take leave of her, and then he went and rejoined Miss Burgoyne, who merely said, "Well, that's a pretty trick!" as she gave him her hand for the dance.

A still stranger thing, however, happened in the next scene, where the gay young officer, the French prisoner of war, makes love to the innkeeper's daughter. Estelle noticed with great surprise that not only did Nina deliver the English maiden's retorts without any of the saucy spirit that the situation demanded, but also that she was quite confused about the words, stammering and hesitating, and getting through them in the most perfunctory manner. At last, when the little Capitaine Crépin says, "Bewitching maid, say you will fly with me!" Clara's reply is, "You forget I am to be married to-morrow—see, here comes my betrothed;" but Nina only got as far as "married to-morrow"—then she paused—hesitated—she put her hand to her head as if everything had gone from her brain—and at the same moment Estelle, with the most admirable presence of mind, continued, "See, here comes your betrothed," thus giving the lover his cue. The dialogue now remained with Estelle and this husband-elect, so that Nina had time to recover; and in the trio that closes the scene she sang her part well enough. Directly they had left the stage, Estelle ran to her friend.

"Nina, what was the matter?" she exclaimed.

"My head—" said Nina, pressing her hand against her forehead and talking rather faintly—"I do not know—my head is giddy, Estelle—oh, I wish it was all over!—I wish I was home!"

"You have very little more to do now, Nina!" Estelle said quickly to her, in French. "Come, you must have courage, Nina—I will run and get you my smelling-salts, and it will pass away—oh, you must make an effort, Nina—would you let Miss Burgoyne see you break down—no, no, indeed! You will be all right, Nina, I assure you—and I will tell the prompter to be on the watch for you—oh, I wouldn't give way—before Miss Burgoyne—if I were you, no, not for a hundred pounds!"

Therewith the kind-hearted little French officer sped away to her own room, and brought back the smelling-salts and was most eagerly solicitous that Nina should conquer this passing attack of hysteria, as she deemed it. And, indeed, Nina managed to get through the rest of her part without any serious breakdown, to Estelle's exceeding joy.

As they went home together in the four-wheeled cab, Nina did not utter a word. Once or twice Estelle fancied she heard a slight sob; but she merely said to herself,

"Ah, it has come back, that trembling of the nerves? But I will make her take some wine at supper, and she will go to bed and sleep well; to-morrow she will have forgotten all about it."

And Estelle was most kind and considerate when they got down to Sloane Street. She helped Nina off with her things; she stirred up the fire; she put a bottle of white wine on the table, where supper was already laid; she drew in Nina's chair for her. Then Mrs. Grey came up, to see that her children, as she called them, were all right; and she was easily induced to stay for a little while, for a retired actress is always eager to hear news of the theatre; so she and Miss Girond fell to talking between themselves. Nina sat silent; her eyes seemed heavy and tired; she only pretended to touch the food and wine before her.

"Very well, then, Nina," her friend said, when Mrs. Grey had gone, "if you will have nothing to eat or to drink, you must go to bed and see what a sound night's rest will do for you. I am going to sit up a little while to read, but I shall not disturb you."

"Good-night, then, Estelle," said Nina, rather languidly; "you have been so kind to me!"

They kissed each other; then Nina opened the folding-doors, and disappeared into her own room, while Estelle took up her book. It was "Les Vacances de Camille" she had got hold of; but she did not turn the pages quickly; there was something else in her mind. She was thinking of Nina. She was troubled about her, in a vague kind of way. She had never seen Nina look like that before, and she was puzzled and a little concerned.

Suddenly, in this hushed stillness, she heard, or fancied she heard, a slight sound that startled her; it came from the adjoining room. Stealthily she arose and approached the door; she put her ear close and listened; yes, she had not been mistaken—Nina was sobbing bitterly. Estelle did not hesitate a moment; she boldly opened the door and went in; and the first thing she beheld was Nina, just as she had left the other room, now lying prone on the bed, her face buried in the pillow, while in vain she tried to control the violence of her grief.

"Nina!" she cried, in alarm.

Nina sprang up—she thrust out both trembling hands, as if wildly seeking for help, and Estelle was not slow to seize them.

"Nina, what is it?" she exclaimed, frightened by the haggard face and streaming eyes.

"Estelle!—Estelle!" said Nina, in a low voice that simply tore the heart of this faithful friend of hers. "It is nothing! It is only that my life is broken—my life is broken—and I have no mother—*Poverina!*—she would have said to me—"

Her sobs choked her speech; she withdrew her trembling hands; she threw herself again on the bed, face downward, and burst into a wild fit of weeping. Estelle knew not what to do; she was terrified.

"Nina, what has happened?" she cried again.

"It is nothing!—it is nothing!—it is nothing!" she said, between her passionate sobs. "I have made a mistake; I am punished—O God, can you not kill me!—I do not wish to live—"

"Nina!" said Estelle, and the girl bent down and put her cheek close to her friend's, and she tenderly placed both her hands on the masses of beautiful blue-black hair. "Nina—tell me!"

In time the violent sobbing ceased, or partially ceased; Nina rose, but she clung to Estelle's hand and kissed it passionately.

"You have been so kind, so affectionate to me, Estelle! To-morrow you will know—perhaps. I will leave you a letter. I am going away. If you forget me—well, that is right; if you do not forget me, do not think bad of—of poor Nina!"

"I don't know what you mean, Nina," said Estelle, who was herself whimpering by this time; "but I won't let you go away. No, I will not. You do not know what you say. It is madness—to-morrow morning you will reflect—to-morrow morning you will tell me, and rely on me as a friend."

"Yes, to-morrow morning all will be right, Estelle," Nina said, again kissing the hand that she clung to. "Pardon me that I have kept you up—and disturbed you. Go away to your bed, Estelle—to-morrow morning all will be right!"

Very reluctantly Estelle was at length persuaded to leave; and as she left she turned off the gas in the sitting-room. A few minutes thereafter Nina, still dressed as she had come home from the theatre, entered the room, re-lit the gas, and noiselessly proceeded to clear a portion of the table, on which she placed writing materials. Then she went into her bedroom and fetched a little drawer in which she kept her valuables; and the first thing she did was to take out an old-fashioned gold ring she had brought with her from Naples. She put the ring in an envelope, and (while her eyelids were still heavy with tears, and her cheeks wan and worn) she wrote outside—"*For Estelle.*"

CHAPTER XVI.

AN AWAKENING.

London is a dreary-looking city on a Sunday morning, especially on a Sunday morning in November; people seem to know how tedious the hours are going to be, and lie in bed as long as they decently can; the teeming and swarming capital of the world looks as if it had suddenly grown lifeless. When Lionel got up, there was a sort of yellow darkness in the air; hardly a single human being was visible in the Green Park over the way; a solitary saunterer, hands deep in the pockets of his overcoat, who wandered idly along the neglected pavement, had the appearance of having been out all night, and of not knowing what to do with himself, now that what passed for daylight had come. All of a sudden there flashed into the brain of this young man standing by the French window a yearning to get away from this dark and dismal town—there came before him a vision of clear air, of wind-swept waves, with an after-church promenade of fashionable folk in which he might recognize the welcome face of many a friend. He looked at his watch; there was yet time; he would hurry through his breakfast and catch the 10.45 to Brighton.

But was there nothing else prompting this unpremeditated resolve to get away down to Victoria station? Not some secret hope that he might perchance descry Lady Cunyngham and her daughter among the crowd swarming on to the long platform? They had not definitely told him at the theatre that they were returning the next morning; but was it not just possible—or, rather, extremely probable? And surely he might presume on their mutual acquaintance so far as to get into the same railway-carriage and have some casual chatting with them on the way down? He had been as attentive as possible to them on the previous evening; and they had seemed pleased. And he had tried to arouse in Miss Honnor's mind some recollection of the closer relationship which had existed between her and him in the solitudes of far Strathaivron.

When he did arrive at Victoria station he found the people pouring in in shoals; for now was the very height of the Brighton season; besides which there were plenty of Londoners glad to escape, if only for a day, from the perpetual fog and gloom. And yet, curiously enough, although the carriages were being rapidly filled, he took no trouble about securing a seat. After he had gone down the whole length of the train, he turned, and kept watching the new arrivals as they came through the distant gate. The time for departure was imminent; but he did not seem anxious about getting to

Brighton. And at last his patience, or his obstinacy, was rewarded; he saw two figures—away along there—that he instantly recognized; even at a greater distance he could have told that one of these was Honnor Cunyngham, for who else in all England walked like that? The two ladies were unattended by either man or maid; and as they came along they seemed rather concerned at the crowded condition of the train. Lionel walked quickly forward to meet them. There was no time for the expression of surprise on their part—only for the briefest greeting.

"I must try to get you seats," said he, "but the train appears to be very full, and the guards are at their wits' end. I say!" he called to a porter. "Look here; this train is crammed, and the people are pouring in yet; what are they going to do?"

"There's a relief train, sir," said the porter, indicating a long row of empty carriages just across the platform.

"You are sure those are going?"

"Yes, sir."

"Then we can get in now?"

The man looked doubtful; but Lionel soon settled that matter by taking the two ladies along to a Pullman car, where the conductor at once allowed them to pass. It is true that as soon as the public outside perceived that these empty carriages were also going, they took possession without more ado; but in the meantime Lionel and his two companions had had their choice of places, so that they were seated together when the train started.

"It was most fortunate we met you," Lady Cunyngham said, bending very friendly eyes on the young man. "I do so hate a crowded train; it happens so seldom in travelling in England that one is not used to it. Are you going down to Brighton for any time, Mr. Moore?"

"Mother," said Honnor Cunyngham, almost reproachfully, "you forget what Mr. Moore's engagements are."

"Yes," said he, with a smile, "it is rather a cruel question. My glimpses of the sea and sky are few and far between. The heavens that I usually find over my head are made of canvas; and the country scenes I wander through are run on wheels."

"But don't you think," said Miss Honnor to him (and it seemed so cheerful to be away from the London gloom and out here in the clearer air; to find himself sitting so near this young lady, able to regard her dress, listening to her voice, sometimes venturing to meet the straightforward glance of her calm eyes—all this was a wondrous and marvellous thing)—"don't you think you enjoy getting away from town all the more keenly? I shall never forget you in Strathaivron; *you* were never bored like some of the other gentlemen."

"Each and every day was one to be marked by a white stone," he said, with an earnestness hardly befitting railway-carriage conversation.

"The wet ones, too?" she asked, pleasantly.

"Wet or dry, what was the difference?" he made bold to say. "What did I care about the rain if I could go down to the Aivron or away up to the Geinig with you and old Robert?"

"You certainly were very brave about it," she said, in the most friendly way; "you never once grumbled when the sandwiches got damp—not once."

And so the three of them kept gayly and carelessly talking and chatting together, as the long train thundered away to the south; while ever and anon they could turn their eyes to that changing phantasmagoria of the outer world that went whirling by the windows. It was rather a wild-looking day, sometimes brightening with a wan glare of sunlight, but more often darkening until the country looked like a French landscape, in its sombre tones of gray and black and green. Yet, nevertheless, there was a sort of picturesqueness in the brooding sky, the russet woods, the purple hedges, and the new-ploughed furrows; while now and again a distant mansion, set on a height, shone a fair yellow above its terraced lawn. Scattered rooks swept down the wind and settled in a field. The moorhens had forsaken the ruffled water of the ponds and sought shelter among the withered sedge. Puffs of white steam from the engine flew across and were lost in the leafless trees. Embankments suddenly showed themselves high in the air, and as suddenly dipped again; then there were long stretches of coppice, with red bracken, and a sprinkling of gold on the oaks. To Lionel the time went by all too quickly; before he had said the half of what he wanted to say, behold! here they were at Preston Park.

"You are at least remaining over until to-morrow?" Lady Cunyngham asked him.

"Well, no," said he, "I did not think of coming down until this morning, and so I had made no arrangements. I should think it hardly likely there would be a vacant bedroom at the Orleans Club at this time of year—no, in any case, I must get back by the 8.40 to-night."

"And in the meantime," she asked again, "have you any engagement?"

"None. I dare say I shall have a stroll along the sea-front, and then drop in for lunch at the Orleans."

"You might as well come down now and lunch with us," said she, simply.

Lionel's face brightened up amazingly; he had been looking forward to saying good-bye at the station with anything but joy.

"I should be delighted—if I am not in the way," was his prompt answer.

"Oh, Honnor and I are entirely by ourselves at present," said this elderly lady with the silver-white hair. "We are expecting Lady Adela and her sisters this week, however; and perhaps my son will come down later on."

"Are they back from Scotland?"

"They arrive to-morrow, I believe."

"And Lady Adela's novel?"

"Oh, I don't know anything about that," said she, with a good-humored smile. "Surely she can't have written another novel already!"

When they got into the station, a footman was awaiting them, but they had no bags or baggage of any description; they walked a little way along the platform and entered the carriage; presently they were driving away down to the sea-front. What Honnor Cunyngham thought of the arrangement, it is impossible to say, but the invitation was none of her giving: no doubt it was merely a little compliment in acknowledgment of Mr. Moore's kindness of the preceding night. However, when the barouche pulled up in front of a house in Adelaide Crescent, Mr. Moore had his own proposal to make.

"It seems so pleasant down there," said he, looking towards the wide stretches of greensward and the promenade along the sea-wall, where the people, just come out of church, were strolling to and fro; "every one appears to be out—don't you think we should have a little walk before going in?"

Honnor Cunyngham said nothing; it was her mother who at once and good-naturedly assented; and when they had descended from the carriage they forthwith made their way down to mix in this idle throng. It was quite a bright and pleasant morning here—a stiff southwesterly breeze blowing—a considerably heavy sea thundering in and springing with jets of white spray into the air—the sunlight shining along the yellow houses of Brunswick Terrace, where there were cheerful bits of green here and there in the balconies. Then the crowd was rather more gayly dressed than an English crowd usually is; for women allow themselves a little more latitude in the way of color during the Brighton season, and on such a morning there was ample excuse for a display of sunshades. And was it merely a wish to breathe the fresh-blowing wind and to listen to the hissing withdrawal and recurrent roar of the waves that had induced Lionel to ask his two companions to join in this slow march up and down? Young men have their little vanities and weaknesses, like other folk. Rumor had on more than one occasion coupled his name with that of some fair damsel; what if he were to say now, "Well, if you will talk, here is one worth talking about." He was conscious on this shining morning that Miss Cunyngham— the more beautiful daughter of a beautiful mother—was looking superb; he remembered what Miss Georgie had said about Honnor's proud and graceful carriage. He knew a good many of the people in this slow-moving assemblage; and he was not sorry they should see him talking to this tall and handsome young Englishwoman—who also appeared to have a numerous acquaintanceship.

"Why, you seem to know everybody, Mr. Moore?" she said to him, with a smile.

"You would think all London was here this morning—it's really astonishing!" he made answer.

Occasionally they stopped to have a chat with more particular friends; and then Lionel would remain a little bit aside; though once or twice Lady Cunyngham chose to introduce him, and that pleased him, he hardly knew why. But at last she said,

"Well, I think we must be getting home. Properly speaking we have no right to be in the prayer-book brigade at all, for we have not been to church this morning."

Not unlikely the squire of these two ladies was rather loath to leave this gay assemblage; but he was speedily consoled, for, to his inexpressible joy, he found, when they got in-doors, that there was no one else coming to lunch—these three were to be quite by themselves. And of what did they not talk during this careless, protracted, idling meal? Curiously enough, it was Nina, not Miss Burgoyne, who appeared to have chiefly impressed the two visitors on the preceding evening; and when Lady Cunyngham discovered that she was an old companion and fellow-student of Lionel's, she was much interested, and would have him tell her all about his experiences in Naples. And again Miss Honnor recurred to the difference between amateur and professional acting, that seemed to have struck her so forcibly the previous night.

" 'Why, you seem to know everybody, Mr. Moore!' she said to him, with a smile."

"Really, Mr. Moore," said she, "you must have an astonishing amount of good-nature and tolerance. If I had complete command of any art, and saw a band of amateurs attempting something in it and not even conscious of their own amateurishness, I don't know whether I should be more inclined to laugh or to be angry. I used to be amused, up there in Strathaivron, with the confidence Georgie Lestrange showed in singing a duet with you—"

"Ah, but Miss Lestrange sings very well," said he. "And, you know, if Lady Adela and her sisters perform a piece like "The Chaplet"—well, that is a Watteau-like sort of thing—Sèvres china—force or passion of any kind isn't wanted—it's all artificial, and confessedly so. And then, when the professional actor finds himself acting with amateurs, I dare say he modifies himself a little—"

"Becomes an amateur, in short," she said.

"In a measure. Otherwise he would be a regular bull in a china shop. And surely, when you get a number of people in a remote place like Strathaivron, the efforts of amateurs to amuse them should be encouraged and approved. I thought it was very unselfish of them—very kind—though they generally succeeded in sending Lord Fareborough to bed. By the way, Miss Cunyngham, did Lord Fareborough ever get a stag?"

For it was observable that this young man, whenever he got the chance, was anxious to lead away the conversation from the theatre and all things pertaining thereunto, and would rather talk about Strathaivron and salmon-fishing and Miss Honnor's plans with regard to the coming year.

"Oh, no," she said, "he never went out but that once, and then he nearly killed himself, according to his own account. We never quite knew what happened; there was some dark mystery that Roderick wouldn't explain; and, you know, Lord Fareborough himself is rather short-tempered. He ought not to have gone out—a man who has imagined himself into that hypochondriacal state. However, it has given him an excuse for thinking himself a greater invalid than ever; and he has got it into his head now that we all of us persuaded him to try a day's stalking—a conspiracy, as it were, to murder him. There was some accident at one of the fords, I believe. He came home early. I never heard of his having fired at a stag at all." And then she added, with a smile. "Mr. Moore, what made you send me such a lot of salmon-flies?"

"Oh, well," he said, "I thought you ought to have a good stock." How could he tell her of his vague hope that the Jock Scotts and Blue Doctors might serve for a long time to recall him to her memory?

"I suppose you have got the stag's head by now?" she asked.

"Oh, yes, indeed; and tremendously proud of it I am," he responded, eagerly. "You know I should never have gone deer-stalking but for you. I made sure I was going to make a fool of myself—"

"I remember you were rather sensitive, or anxious not to miss, perhaps," she said, in a very gentle way. "I thought of it again last night, when I saw you so completely master in your own sphere—so much at home—with everything at your command—"

"Oh, yes, very much at home," he answered her, with just a touch of bitterness. "Perhaps it is easy to be at home—in harlequinade—though you may not quite like it." And then once more he refused to talk of the theatre. "I am going to send old Robert some tobacco at Christmas," said he.

"I heard of what you did already in that way," she said, smiling. "Do you know that you may spoil a place by your extravagance? I should think all the keepers and gillies in Strathaivron were blessing your name at this very moment."

"And you go up in the spring, you said?"

"Yes. That is the real fishing-time. My brother Hugh and I have it all to ourselves then; Lady Adela and the rest of them prefer London."

And then it was almost in his heart to cry out to her, "May not I, too, go up there, if but for a single week—for six clear-shining days in the springtime?" Ben More, Suilven, Canisp—oh, to see them once again!—and the windy skies, and Geinig thundering down its rocky chasm, and Aivron singing its morning song along the golden gravel of its shoals! what did he want with any theatre?—with the harlequinade in which he was losing his life? Could he not escape? Euston station was not so far away—and Invershin? It seemed to him as though he had already shaken himself free—that a gladder pulsation filled his veins—that he was breathing a sweeter air. The white April days shone all around him; the silver and purple clouds went flying overhead; here he was by the deep, brown pools again, with the gray rocks and the overhanging birch-woods and the long shallows filling all the world with that soft, continuous murmur. As for his singing?—oh, yes, he could sing—he could sing, if needs were,

"O lang may his lady-love

    Look frae the Castle Doune,

Ere she see the Earl o' Moray

    Come sounding through the toun"—

but there is no gaslight here—there are no painted faces—he has not to look on at the antics of a clown, with shame and confusion in his heart—

The wild fancy was suddenly snapped in twain; Lady Cunyngham rose; the two younger people did likewise.

"Now, I know you gentlemen like a cigar or cigarette after luncheon," she said to Lionel, "and we are going to leave you quite by yourself—you will find us in the drawing-room when you please."

Of course he would not hear of such a proposal; he opened the door for them, and followed them up-stairs; what were cigars or cigarettes to him when he had such a chance of listening to Honnor Cunyngham's low, modulated voice, or watching for a smile in the calmly observant hazel eyes? Indeed, in the drawing-room, as Miss Honnor showed him a large collection of Assiout ware which had been sent her by an English officer in Egypt (by what right or title, Lionel swiftly asked himself, had any English officer made bold to send Miss Cunyngham a hamperful of these red-clay idiotcies?), this solitary guest had again and again to remind himself that he must not outstay his welcome. And yet they seemed to find a great deal to talk about; and the elder of the two ladies was exceedingly kind to him; and there was a singular fascination in his finding himself entirely *en famille* with them. But alas! Even if he or they had chosen to forget, the early dusk of the November afternoon was a sufficient warning; the windows told him he had to go. And go he did at last. He bade them good-bye; with some friendly words still dwelling in his ears he made his way down the dim stairs and had the door opened for him; then he found himself in this now empty and hopeless town of Brighton, that seemed given over to the low, multitudinous murmur of that wide waste of waves.

He did not go along to the Orleans Club; his heart and brain were too busy to permit of his meeting chance acquaintances. He walked away towards Shoreham till a smart shower made him turn. When he got back to the town the lamps were lit, throwing long, golden reflections on the wet asphalt, but the rain had ceased; so he continued to pace absently along through this blue twilight, hardly noticing the occasional dark figures that passed. What was the reason, then, of this vague unrest—this unknown longing—this dissatisfaction and almost despair? Had he not been more fortunate than he could have hoped for? He had met Miss Honnor and her mother in the morning, and had been with them all the way down; they had been most kind to him; he had spent the best part of the day with them; they had parted excellent friends; looking back, he could not recall a single word he would have liked unsaid. Then a happy fancy struck him: the moment he got up to town he would go and seek out Maurice Mangan. There was a wholesome quality in Mangan's saturnine contempt for the non-essential things of life; Mangan's clear penetration, his covert sympathy, his scorn or mock-melancholy, would help him to get rid of these vapors.

When Lionel returned to town a little after ten o'clock that night he walked along to Mangan's rooms in Victoria Street, and found his friend sitting in front of the fire alone.

"Glad you've looked in, Linn."

"Well, you don't seem to be busy, old chap; who ever saw you before without a book or a pipe?"

"I've been musing, and dreaming dreams, and wishing I was a poet," said this tall, thin, languid-looking man, whose abnormally keen gray eyes were now grown a little absent. "It's only a fancy, you know—perhaps something could be made of it by a fellow who could rhyme—"

"But what is it?" Lionel interposed.

"Well," said the other, still idly staring into the fire before him, "I think I would call it 'The Cry of the Violets'—the violets that are sold in bunches at the head of the Haymarket at midnight. Don't you fancy there might be something in it—if you think of where they come from—the woods and copses, children playing, and all that—and of what they've come to—the gas-glare and drunken laughter and jeers. I would make them tell their own story—I would make them cry to Heaven for swift death and oblivion before the last degradation of being pinned on to the flaunting dress." And then again he said: "No, I don't suppose there's any thing in it; but I'll tell you what made me think of it. This morning, as we were coming back from Winstead church—you know how extraordinarily mild it has been of late, and the lane going down to the church is very well sheltered—I found a couple of violets in at the roots of the hedge—within a few inches of each other, indeed—and I gave them to Miss Francie, and she put them in her prayer-book and carried them home. I thought the violets would not object to that, if they only knew."

"So you went down to Winstead this morning?"

"Yes."

"And how are the old people?"

"Oh, very well."

"And Francie?"

"Very busy—and very happy, I think. If she doesn't deserve to be, who does?" he continued, rousing himself somewhat from his absent manner. "I suppose, now, there is no absolutely faultless woman; and yet I sometimes think it would puzzle the most fastidious critic of human nature to point out any one particular in which Miss Francie could be finer than she is; I think it would. It is not my business to find fault; I don't want to find fault; but I have often thought over Miss Francie—her occupations, her theories, her personal disposition, even her dress—and I've wondered where the improvement was to be suggested. You see, she might be a very good woman, and yet have no sense of humor; she might be very charitable, and also a little vainglorious about it; she might have very exalted ideas of duty, and be a trifle hard on those who did not come up to her standards; but in Miss Francie's case these qualifications haven't to be put in at all. She always seems to me to be doing the right thing, and just in the right way— with a kind of fine touch that has no namby-pambiness about it. Oh, she can be firm, too; she can scold them well enough, those children—when she doesn't laugh and pat them on the shoulder the minute after."

"This is, indeed, something, as coming from you, Maurice!" Lionel exclaimed. "Has it been left for you to discover an absolutely perfect human being?"

"It isn't for you to find fault with her, anyway," the other said, rather sharply. "She's fond enough of you."

"Who said I was finding fault with her?—not likely I am going to find fault with Francie!" Lionel replied, with sufficient good-humor. "Well, now that you have discovered an absolutely faultless creature, you might come to the help of another who is only too conscious that he has plenty of faults, and who is so dissatisfied with himself and his surroundings that he is about sick of life altogether."

Notwithstanding the light tone in which he introduced the subject, Mangan looked up quickly, and regarded the younger man with those penetrating gray eyes.

"Where have you been to-day, Linn?"

"Brighton."

"Among the dukes and duchesses again? Ah, you needn't be angry—I respect as much as anybody those whom God has placed over us—I haven't forgotten my catechism—I can order myself lowly and reverently to all my betters. But tell me what the matter is. You sick of life?—I wonder what the gay world of London would think of that!"

And therewithal Lionel, in a somewhat rambling and incoherent fashion, told his friend of a good many things that had happened to him of late—of his vague aspirations and dissatisfactions—of Miss Cunyngham's visit to the theatre, and his disgust over the music-hall clowning—of his going down to Brighton that day, and his wish to stand on some other footing with those friends of his—winding up by asking, to Mangan's surprise, how long it would take to study for the bar and get called, and whether his training—the confidence acquired on the stage—might not help in addressing a jury.

"So the idol has got tired of being worshipped," Mangan said, at last. "It is an odd thing. I wonder how many thousands of people there are in London—not merely shop-girls—who consider you the most fortunate person alive—in whose imagination you loom larger than any saint or soldier, any priest or statesman, of our own time. And I wonder what they would say if they knew you were thinking of voluntarily abdicating so proud and enviable a position. Well, well!—and the reason for this sacrifice? Of course, you know it is a not uncommon thing for women to give up their carriages and luxuries and fine living, and go into a retreat, where they have to sweep out cells, and even keep strict silence for a week at a time, which, I suppose, is a more difficult business. The reason in their case is clear enough; they are driven to all that by their spiritual needs; they want to have their souls washed clean by penance and self-denial. But you," he continued, in no unfriendly mood, but with his usual uncompromising sincerity, "whence comes your renunciation? It is simply that a woman has turned your head. You want to find yourself on the same plane with her; you want to be socially her equal; and to do that you think you should throw off those theatrical trappings. You see, my dear Linn, if I have remembered my catechism, you have not; you have forgotten that you must learn and labor truly to get your own living, and do your duty in that state of life unto which it has pleased God to call you. You want to change your state of life; you want to become a barrister. What would happen? The chances are entirely against your being able to earn your own living—at least for years; but what is far more certain is that your fashionable friends—whose positions and occupations you admire—would care nothing more about you. You are interesting to them now because you are a favorite of the public, because you play the chief part at the New Theatre. What would you be as a briefless barrister? Who would provide you with salmon-fishing and deer-stalking then? If you aspired to marry one of those dames of high degree, what would be your claims and qualifications? You say you would almost rather be a gillie in charge of dogs and ponies. A gillie in charge of dogs and ponies doesn't enjoy many conversations with his young mistress; and if he made bold to demand any closer alliance Pauline would pretty soon have that Claude kicked off the premises—and serve him right. If you had come to me and said, 'I am too well off; I am being spoiled and petted to death; the simplicity and dignity of life is being wholly lost in all this fashionable flattery, this public notoriety and applause; and to recover myself a little—as a kind of purification—I am going to put aside my trappings; I will go and work as a hod-carrier for three months or six months; I will live on the plainest fare; I will bear patiently the cursing the master of the gang will undoubtedly hurl at me; I will sleep on a straw mattress'—then I could have understood that. But what is it you renounce?—and why? You think you would recommend yourself better to your swell friends if you dropped the theatre altogether—"

"Don't you want to hire a hall?" said Lionel, gloomily.

"Oh, nobody likes being preached at less than I do myself," Mangan said, with perfect equanimity, "but you see I think I ought to tell you, when you ask me, how I regard the situation. And, mind you, there is something very heroic—very impracticably heroic, but magnanimous all the same—in your idea that you might abandon all the popularity and position you have won as a mere matter of sentiment. Of course you won't do it. You couldn't bring yourself to become a mere nobody—as would happen if you went into chambers and began reading up law-books. And you wouldn't be any nearer to salmon-fishing and deer-forests that way, or to the people who possess these by birth and inheritance. The trouble with you, Linn, my boy, as with most of us, is that you weren't born in the purple. It is quite true that if you were called to the bar you could properly claim the title of esquire, and you would find yourself not further down than the hundred and fiftieth or hundred and sixtieth section in the tables of precedence; but if you went with this qualification to those fine friends of yours, they would admit its validity, and let you know at the same time you were no longer interesting to them. Harry Thornhill, of the New Theatre, has a free passport everywhere; Mr. Lionel Moore, of the Middle Temple, wouldn't be wanted anywhere."

"You are very worldly-wise to-night, Maurice."

"I don't want to see you make a sacrifice that wouldn't bring you what you expect to gain by it," Mangan said. "But, as I say, you won't make any such sacrifice. You have had your brain turned by a pretty pair of eyes—perhaps by an elegant figure—and you have been troubled and dissatisfied and dreaming dreams."

"If that is your conclusion and summing-up of the whole matter," Lionel said, with studied indifference, "perhaps you will offer me a drink, and I'll have a cigarette, and we can talk about something on which we are likely to agree."

"I'm sure I beg your pardon," Mangan said, with a laugh; and he went and brought forth what modest stores he had, and he was quite willing that the conversation should flow into another channel.

And little did Lionel know that at this very moment there was something awaiting him at his own rooms that would (far more effectually than any reasoning and plain speaking) banish from his mind, for the moment at least, all those restless aspirations and vague regrets. When eventually he arrived in Piccadilly and went up-stairs, he was not expecting any letters, this being Sunday; and as there was on the table only a small parcel, he would probably have left that unheeded till the morning (no doubt it was a pair of worked slippers, or a couple of ivory-backed brushes, or something of the kind) but that in passing he happened to glance at the note on the top of it, and he observed that the handwriting was foreign. He took it up carelessly and opened it; his carelessness soon vanished. The message was from Mlle. Girond, and it was in French:

"DEAR MR. MOORE,—To-day Mrs. Grey and I have called twice at your apartments, but in vain, and now I leave this letter for you. It is frightful, what has happened. Nina has gone, no one knows where; we can hear nothing of her. This morning when I came down to her room she was gone; there was a letter for me, one for Mr. Lehmann, one for Miss Constance, asking her to be ready to sing to-morrow night, another for Mrs. Grey, with money for the apartments until the end of the month, and also there was this little packet for you. In her letter to me she asks me to see them all delivered. During the night she must have made these arrangements; in the morning she is gone! I am in despair; I know not what to do. Will you have the goodness to come down to-morrow as soon as possible?

"ESTELLE."

And then mechanically he drew a chair to the table, and sat down and pulled the small package towards him; perhaps the contents might help to explain this extraordinary thing that had occurred. But the moment that he took the lid off the pasteboard box he was more bewildered than ever; for the first glimpse told him that Nina had returned to him all the little presents he had made to her in careless moments.

"Nina!" he said, under his voice, in a tone of indignant reproach.

Yes, here was every one of them, from the enclasped loving-cup to the chance trinkets he had purchased for her just as they happened to attract his eye. He took them all out; there was no letter, no message of any kind. And then he asked himself, almost angrily, what sort of mad freak was this. Had the wayward and petulant Nina—forgetting all the suave and gracious demeanor she had been teaching herself since she came to England—had she run away in a fit of temper, breaking her engagement at the theatre, and causing alarm and anxiety to her friends, all about nothing? For he and she had not quarrelled in any way whatsoever, as far as he knew. One fancy, at least, never occurred to him—or, if it occurred to him, it was dismissed in a moment—that Nina might have had a secret lover; that she had honestly wished to return these presents before making an elopement. It was quite possible that Nicolo Ciana, if he had heard of Nina's success in England, might have pursued her, and sought to marry so very eligible a helpmeet; but if the young man with the greasy hair and the sham jewelry and the falsetto voice had really come to England, Lionel knew who would have been the first to bid him return to his native shores and his *zuccherelli*. Had not Nina indignantly denied that he had ever dared to address her as "Nenna mia," or that his perpetual "Antoniella, Antonià," in any way referred to her? No; Lionel did not think that Nicolo Ciana had much to do with Nina's disappearance.

And then, as he regarded this little box of useless jewelry, another wild guess flashed through his brain, leaving him somewhat breathless, almost frightened. Was it possible that Nina had mistaken these gifts for love-gifts, had discovered her mistake, and, in a fit of wounded pride, had flung them back and fled forever from this England that had deceived her? He was not vain enough to think there could be anything more serious, that Nina might be breaking her heart over what had happened to her; but it was quite enough if he had unconsciously led her to believe that he was paying her attentions. He looked at that loving-cup with some pricking of conscience; he had to confess that such a gift was capable of misconstruction. It had never occurred to him that she might regard it as some kind of mute declaration—as a pledge of affection between him and her that necessitated no clearer understanding. He had seen the two tiny goblets in a window; he had been taken by the pretty silver-gilt ornamentation; he had been interested in the old-fashioned custom; and he had lightly imagined that Nina would be pleased—that was all. And now that he thought of it, he had to confess that he had been indiscreet. It is true he had given Nina those presents from time to time in a careless and haphazard fashion that ought not to have been misunderstood—only, as he had to remind himself, Nina must have perceived that he did not give similar presents to Miss Burgoyne, or Estelle Girond, or anybody else in the theatre. And was Nina now thinking that he had treated her badly?—Nina, who had been always his sympathizing friend, his gentle adviser, and kind companion. Was there any one in the world that he less wished to harm? He supposed she must have been angry when she returned these jewels and gew-gaws; clearly she was too proud to send him any other message. And now she would be away somewhere, where he could not get hold of her to pet her into a reconciliation again; no doubt there was some hurt feeling of injury in her heart—perhaps she was even crying.

"Poor Nina!" he said to himself, little dreaming of the true state of affairs. "I hope it isn't so? but if it is so, here have I, through mere thoughtlessness, wounded her pride, and, what is more, interfered with her professional career. I suppose she'll go right away back to old Pandiani; and they'll be precious glad to get her now at Malta, after her success in England. Perhaps some day we shall hear of her coming over here again, as a famous star in grand opera; that will be her revenge. But I never thought Nina would want to be revenged on me."

And yet he was uneasy; there was something in all this he did not understand. He began to long for the coming of the next day, that he might go away down to Sloane Street and hear what Miss Girond had to tell him. Why, for example, he asked himself, had Nina taken this step so abruptly— so entirely without warning? How and when had she made the discovery that she had mistaken the intention of those friendly little acts of kindness and his constant association with her? Then he tried to remember on what terms he had last parted from her. It was at the theatre, as he patiently summoned up each circumstance. It was at the theatre, on the preceding night. She had come to him in the wings, observing that he looked rather vexed, and she had given him comforting and cheerful words, as was her wont. Surely there was no anger in her mind against him then. But thereafter? Well, he had seen no more of Nina. When Miss Cunyngham had come behind the scenes, he had forgotten all about Nina. And then suddenly he remembered that he must have been standing close by the prompter's box, absorbed in talking to Miss Cunyngham, when Nina would have to come up to go on the stage. Had she passed them? Had she suspected? Had she, in her proud and petted way, resented this intimacy, and resolved to throw back to him the harmless little gifts he had bestowed on her? Poor Nina! she had always been so wilful—so easily pleased, so easily offended—but of late he had rather forgotten that, for she had been bearing herself with what she regarded as an English manner; and indeed their friendship had been so constant and unvarying, so kind and considerate on both sides, that there had been no opportunity for the half-vexed, half-laughing quarrels of earlier days. He would seek out this spoiled child (he said to himself) and scold her into being good again. And yet, even as he tried to persuade himself that all would still be well, he could not help recalling the fierce vehemence with which Nina had repudiated the suggestion that perhaps she might let some one else drink out of this hapless loving-cup that now lay before him. "I would rather have it dashed to pieces and thrown into the sea!" she had said, with pale face and quivering lips and eyes bordering on tears. He remembered that he had been a little surprised at the time—not thinking what it all might mean.

CHAPTER XVII.

A CRISIS.

When he went down to Sloane Street in the morning, he found Estelle eagerly awaiting him. She received him in Nina's small parlor; Mrs. Grey had just gone out. A glance round the room did not show him any difference, except that a row of photographs (of himself, mostly, in various costumes) had disappeared from the mantelshelf.

"Well, what is all this about?" he said, somewhat abruptly.

"Ah, do not blame me too quick!" Estelle said, with tears springing to her clear blue eyes. "Perhaps I am to blame—perhaps when I see her in such trouble on Saturday night, I should entreat her to tell me why; but I said, 'To-night I will not worry her more; to-morrow morning I will talk to her; we will go for a long walk together? Nina will tell me all her sorrow.' Then the morning comes, and she is gone away; what can I do? Twice I go to your apartment—"

"Oh, I am not blaming you at all, Miss Girond," he said, at once and quite gently. "If anybody is to blame, I suppose it's myself, for I appear to have quarrelled with Nina without knowing it. Of course you understood that that packet you left yesterday contained the various little presents I have given her from time to time—worthless bits of things—but all the same her sending them back shows that Nina has some ground of offence. I'm very sorry; if I could only get hold of her I would try to reason with her; but she was always sensitive and proud and impulsive like that. And then to run away because of some fancied slight—"

Estelle interrupted him with a little gesture of impatience, almost of despair.

"Ah, you are wrong, you are wrong," she said. "It is far more serious than that. It is no little quarrel. It is a pain that stabs to the heart—that kills. You will see Nina never again to make up a little quarrel. She has taken her grief away with her. I myself, when I first saw her troubled at the theatre, I also made a mistake—I thought she was hysteric—"

"At the theatre?" said he, with some sudden recalling of his own surmise.

"You did not regard her, perhaps, towards the end of her part, on Saturday night?" said Estelle. "I thought once she would fall on the stage. On the way home I think she was crying—I did not look. Then she is in this room—oh, so silent and miserable—as one in despair, until I persuade her to go to sleep until the morning, when she would tell me her sorrow. Then I was reading; I heard something; I went to the door there—it was Nina crying, oh, so bitterly; and when I ran to her, she was wild with her grief. 'My life is broken, Estelle, my life is broken!' she said—"

But here Estelle herself began to sob, and could not get on with her story at all; she rose from her chair and began to pace up and down.

"I cannot tell you—it was terrible—"

And terrible it was for him, too, to have this revelation made to him. Now he knew it was no little quarrel that had sent Nina away; it was something far more tragic than that; it was the sudden blighting of a life's hopes.

"Estelle," said he, quite forgetting, "you spoke of a letter she had left for you; will you show it to me?"

She took it from her pocket and handed it to him. There was no sign of haste or agitation in these pages; Nina's small and accurate handwriting was as neat and precise as ever; she even seemed to have been careful of her English, as she was leaving this her last message, in the dead watches of the night:

"DEAR ESTELLE" [Nina wrote],—"Forgive me for the trouble I cause you; but I know you will do what I ask, for the sake of our friendship of past days. I leave a letter for Mr. Lehmann, and one for Miss Constance, and a packet for Mr. Moore; will you please have them all sent as soon as possible? I hope Mr. Lehmann will forgive me for any embarrassment, but Miss Constance is quite perfect in the part, and if she gets the letter to-day it will be the longer notice. I enclose a ring for you, Estelle; if you wear it, you will sometimes think of Nina. For it is true what I said to you when you came into my room to-night—I go away in the morning. I have made a terrible mistake, an illusion, a folly, and, now that my eyes are opened, I will try to bear the consequences as I can; but I could not go on the stage as well; it would be too bad a punishment; I could not, Estelle. I must go, and forget—it is so easy to say forget! I go away without feeling injured towards any one; it was my own fault, no one was in fault but me. And if I have done wrong to any one, or appear ungrateful, I am sorry; I did not wish it. Again I ask you to say to Mr. Lehmann, who has been so kind to me in the theatre, that I hope he will forgive me the trouble I cause; but I *could not* go on with my part just now.

"Shall I ever see you again, Estelle? It is sad, but I think not; it is not so easy to forget as to write it. Perhaps some day I send you a line—no, perhaps some day I send you a message; but you will not know where I am; and if you are my friend you will not seek to know. Adieu, Estelle! I hope you will always be happy, as you are good; but even in your happiest days you will sometimes give a thought to poor Nina."

He sat there looking at the letter, long after he had finished reading it; there was nothing of the petulance of a spoiled child in this simple, this heartbroken farewell. And Nina herself was in every phrase of it—in her anxiety not to be a trouble to any one—her gratitude for very small kindnesses—her wish to live in the gentle remembrance of her friends.

"But why did no one stop her?—why did no one remonstrate?" he asked, in a sort of stupefaction.

"Who could, then?" said Mlle. Girond, returning to her seat and clasping her hands in front of her. "As soon as the housemaid appears in the morning, Nina asks her to come into the room; the money is put into an envelope for Mrs. Grey; the not great luggage is taken quiet down the stair, so that no one is disturbed. Everything is arranged; you know Nina was always so—so business-like—"

"Yes, but the fool of a housemaid should have called Mrs. Grey!" he exclaimed.

"But why, Mr. Moore?" Estelle continued. "She only thought that Nina was so considerate—no one to be awakened—and then a cab is called, and Nina goes away—"

"And of course the housemaid didn't hear what direction was given to the cabman!"

"No; it is a misfortune," said Estelle, with a sigh. "It is a misfortune, but she is not so much in fault. She did not conjecture—she thought Nina was going to catch an early train—that she did not wish to disturb any one. All was in order; all natural, simple; no one can blame her. And so poor Nina disappears—"

"Yes, disappears into the world of London, or into the larger world, without friends, without money—had she any money, Miss Girond?"

"Oh, yes, yes!" Estelle exclaimed. "You did not know? Ah, she was so particular; always exact in her economies, and sometimes I laughed at her; but always she said perhaps some day she would have to play the part of the—the—benevolent fairy to some poor one, and she must save up—"

"Had she a bank account?"

Estelle nodded her head.

"Then she could not have got the money yesterday, if she wished to withdraw it; she must have been in London this morning!"

"Perhaps," said Estelle. "But then! Look at the letter. She says if I am her friend, I will not seek to know where she is."

"But that does not apply to me," he retorted—while his brain was filled with all kinds of wild guesses as to whither Nina had fled.

"You are not her friend?" Estelle said, quietly.

"If I could only see her for three minutes!" he said, in his despair, as he rose and went to the window. "Why should she go away from her friends if she is in trouble? Besides ourselves and the people in the theatre, she knows no one in this country. If she goes away back to her acquaintances in Italy, she will not say a word; she will have no sympathy, no distraction of any kind; and all the success she has gained here will be as good as lost. It is like Nina to say she blames no one; but her sending me back those bits of jewelry tells me who is to blame—"

Estelle hesitated.

"Can I say?" she said, in rather low tones, and her eyes were cast down. "Is it not breaking confidence? But Nina was speaking of you—she took me into the shop in Piccadilly to show me the beautiful gold cup—and when I said to her, 'It is another present soon—it is a wedding-ring soon he will give you—'"

"Then it is you who have been putting those fancies into her head!" he said, turning to her.

"I? Not I!" answered Estelle, with a quick indignation. "It is you! Ah, perhaps you did not think—perhaps you are accustomed to have every ones—to have every one—give homage to the great singer—you amuse the time—what do you care? I put such things into her head? No!—not at all! But you! You give her a wishing-cup—what is the wish? You come here often—you are very kind to her—oh, yes, very kind, and Nina is grateful for kindness—you sing with her—what do you call them?—songs of love. Ah, yes, the *chansons amoureuses* are very beautiful—very charming—but sometimes they break hearts."

"I tell you I had no idea of anything of the kind," he said—for to be rated by the little boy-officer was a new experience. "But I am going to try to find Nina—whatever you may choose to do."

"I respect her wish," said Mlle. Girond, somewhat stiffly. However, the next moment she had changed her mood. "Mr. Moore, if you were to find her, what then?" she asked, rather timidly.

"I should bring her back to her friends," he answered, simply enough.

"And then?"

"I should want to see her as happy and contented as she used to be—the Nina we used to know. I should want to get her back to the theatre, where she was succeeding so well. She liked her work; she was interested in it; and you know she was becoming quite a favorite with the public. Come, Miss Girond," he said, "you needn't be angry with me; that won't do any good. I see now I have been very thoughtless and careless; I ought not to have given her that loving-cup; I ought not to have given her any of those trinkets, I suppose. But it never occurred to me at the time; I fancied she would be pleased at the moment, that was all."

"And you did not reflect, then," said Estelle, regarding him for a second, "what it was that may have brought Nina to England at the beginning?— no?—what made her wish to play at the New Theatre? Ah, a man is so blind!"

"Brought Nina to England?" he repeated, rather bewildered.

"But these are only my conjectures," she said, quickly. "No, I have no secrets to tell. I ask myself what brings Nina to England, to the New Theatre, to the companionship with her old friend—I ask myself that, and I see. But you—perhaps it is not your fault that you are blind; you have so many ladies seeking for favor you have no time to think of this one or that, or you are grown indifferent, it may be. Poor Nina! she that was always so proud, too; it is herself that has struck herself; a deep wound to her pride; that is why she goes away, and she will never come back. No, Mr. Moore, she will never come back. I asked you what you would do if you were to find her—it is useless. She will never come back; she is too proud."

Estelle looked at her watch.

"Soon I must go in to the theatre. There was a note from Mr. Lehmann this morning; he wishes me to go over some parts with Miss Constance, to make sure."

"What hour have you to be there?" he said, taking up his hat.

"Half-past eleven."

"I will walk in with you, if you like," he said; "there will be time. And I want to see that Lehmann isn't put to any inconvenience; for, you know, I introduced Nina to the New Theatre."

On their way into town Estelle was thoughtful and silent; while Lionel kept looking far ahead, as if he expected to descry Nina coming round some street-corner or in some passing cab. But at last his companion said to him,

"You had no quarrel, then, with Nina, on the Saturday night?"

"None. On the contrary, the last time she spoke to me was in the most kindly way," he said.

"Then why does she resolve to send you back those presents?" Estelle asked. "Why is it she knows all at once that her life is broken? You have no conjecture at all?"

"Well," said he, with a little hesitation, "it is a difficult thing to speak of. If Nina were looking forward as you think—if she mistook the intention of those trinkets I gave her—well, you know, there was a young lady and her mother, two friends of mine, who came to the theatre on Saturday night, and I dare say Nina passed while I was talking to the young lady in the wings—and—and Nina may have imagined something. I can only guess—it is possible—"

"Now I know," said Estelle, rather sadly. "Poor Nina! And still you think she would come back if you could find her? Her pride makes her fly from you; and you think you would persuade her? Never, never! She will not come back—she would drown herself first."

"Oh, don't talk like that!" he said, with frowning brows; and both relapsed into silence and their own thoughts.

Mr. Lehmann did not seem much put about by this defection on the part of one of his principal singers.

"It is a pity," he said to Lionel. "She had a fresh voice; she was improving in her stage-business; and the public liked her. What on earth made her go off like this?"

"She left no explanation with me," Lionel said, honestly enough. "But in her letter to Miss Girond she hopes you won't be put to any inconvenience. By the way, if Miss Ross owes you any forfeit, I'll settle that up with you."

"No, there's no forfeit in her agreement; it wasn't considered necessary," the manager made answer. "Of course I am assuming that it's all fair and square; that she hasn't gone off to take a better engagement—"

"You needn't be afraid of that," Lionel said, briefly; and, as Miss Constance here made her appearance, he withdrew from the empty stage, and presently had left the building.

He thought he would walk up to the Restaurant Gianuzzi in Rupert Street, and make inquiries there. But he was not very hopeful. For one thing, if Nina were desirous of concealment or of getting free away, she would not go to a place where, as he knew, she had lodged before; for another, he had disapproved of her living there all by herself, and Nina never forgot even his least expression of opinion. When he asked at the restaurant if a young lady had called there on the previous day to engage a room, he was answered that they had no young-lady visitor of any kind in the house; he was hardly disappointed.

But as he walked along and up Regent Street (here were the well-remembered shops that Nina and he used to glance into as they passed idly on, talking sometimes, sometimes silent, but very well content in each other's society) he began to ask himself whether in truth he ought to seek out Nina and try to intercept her flight, even if that were yet possible. Estelle's questions were significant. What would he do, supposing he could induce Nina to come back? At present, he vaguely wished to restore the old situation—to have Nina again among her friends, happy in her work at the theatre, ready to go out for a stroll with him if the morning were fine, he wanted his old comrade, who was always so wise and prudent and cheerful, whom he could always please by sending her down a new song, a new waltz, an Italian illustrated journal, or some similar little token of remembrance. But if Estelle's theory were the true one, *that* Nina was gone forever, never to return; her place was vacant now, never to be refilled; and somewhere or other—perhaps hidden in London, perhaps on her way back to her native land—there was a woman, proud, silent, and tearless, her heart quivering from the blow that he had unintentionally dealt. How could he face *that* Nina? What humble explanations and apologies could he offer? To ask her to come back would of itself be an insult. Her wrongs were her defence? she was sacred from intrusion, from expostulation and entreaty.

At the theatre that evening he let the public fare as it liked, so far as his part in the performance was concerned. He got through his duties mechanically. The stage lacked interest; the wings were empty; the long, glazed corridor conveyed a mute reproach. As for the new Clara, Miss Constance did fairly well; she had not much of a voice, but she was as bold as brass, and her "cheek" seemed to be approved by the audience. At one point Estelle came up to him.

"Is it not a change for no Nina to be in the theatre? But there is one that is glad—oh, very glad! Miss Burgoyne rejoices!"—and Estelle, as she passed on, made use of a phrase in French, which, perhaps fortunately, he did not understand.

After the performance, he went up to the Garden Club—he did not care to go home to his own rooms and sit thinking. And the first person he saw after he passed into the long coffee-room was Octavius Quirk, who was seated all by himself devouring a Gargantuan supper.

"This is luck," Lionel said to himself. "Maurice's Jabberwock will begin with his blatherskite nonsense—it will be something to pass the time."

But on the contrary, as it turned out, the short, fat man with the unwholesome complexion was not at this moment in the humor for frothy and windy invective about nothing; perhaps the abundant supper had mollified him; he was quite suave.

"Ah, Moore," said he, "haven't seen you since you came back from Scotland. It was awfully kind of Lady Adela to send me a haunch of venison."

"It would serve you for one meal, I suppose," Lionel thought; he did not say so.

"I dine with them to-morrow night," continued Mr. Quirk, complacently.

"Oh, indeed," said Lionel? Lady Adela seemed rather in a hurry, immediately on her return to town, to secure her tame critic.

"Very good dinners they give you up there at Campden Hill," Mr. Quirk resumed, as he took out a big cigar from his case. "Excellent—excellent—and the people very well chosen, too, if it weren't for that loathsome brute, Quincey Hooper. Why do they tolerate a fellow like that—the meanest lick-spittle and boot-blacker to any Englishman who has got a handle to his name, while all the time he is writing in his wretched Philadelphia rag every girding thing he can think of against England. Comparison, comparison, continually—and far more venomous than the foolish, feeble sort of stuff which is only Anglophobia and water; and yet Hooper hasn't the courage to speak out either—it's a morbid envy of England that is afraid to declare itself openly and can only deal in hints and innuendoes. What can Lady Adela see in a fellow like that? Of course he writes puffing paragraphs about her and sends them to her; but what good are they to her, coming from America? She wants to be recognized as a clever woman by her own set. She appeals to the *dii majorum gentium*; what does she care for the verdict of Washington or Philadelphia or New York?"

Well, Lionel had no opinion to express on this point; on a previous occasion he had wondered why these two augurs had not been content to agree, seeing that the wide Atlantic rolled between their respective spheres of operation.

"I have been favored," resumed Mr. Quirk, more blandly, "with a sight of some portions of Lady Adela's new novel."

"Already?"

"Oh, it isn't nearly finished yet; but she has had the earlier chapters set up in type, so that she could submit them to—to her particular friends, in fact. You haven't seen them?" asked Mr. Quirk, lifting his heavy and boiled-gooseberry eyes and looking at Lionel.

"Oh, no," was the answer. "My judgment is of no use to her; she is aware of that. I hope you were pleased with what you saw of it. Her last novel was not quite so successful as they had hoped, was it?"

"My dear fellow!" Mr. Quirk exclaimed, in astonishment (for he could not have the power of the log-rollers called in question). "Not successful? Most successful!—most successful! I don't know that it produced so much money—but what is that to people in their sphere?"

"Perhaps not much," said Lionel, timidly (for what did he know about such esoteric matters?). "I suppose the money they might get from a novel would be of little consideration—but it would show that the book had been read."

"And what, again, do they care for vulgar popularity?—the approbation of the common herd—of the bovine-headed multitude? No, no, it is the verdict of the polished world they seek—it is fame—*éclat*—it is recognition from their peers. It may be only *un succès d'estime*—all the more honorable! And I must say Lady Adela is a very clever woman; the pains she takes to get 'Kathleen's Sweethearts' mentioned even now are wonderful. Indeed, I propose to give her an additional hint or two to-morrow. Of course you know —— is doomed?" asked Mr. Quirk, naming a famous statesman who was then very seriously ill.

"Really?"

"Oh, yes. Gout at the heart; hopeless complications; he can't possibly last another ten days. Very well," continued Mr. Quirk, with much satisfaction, as if Providence were working hand in hand with him, "I mean to advise Lady Adela to send him a copy of 'Kathleen's Sweethearts.' Now do you understand? No? Why, man, if there's any luck, when he dies and all the memoirs come out in the newspapers, it will be mentioned that the last book the deceased statesman tried to read was Lady Adela Cunyngham's well-known novel. Do you see? Good business? Then there's another thing she must absolutely do with her new book. These woman-suffrage people are splendid howlers and spouters; let her go in for woman-suffrage thick and thin—and she'll get quoted on a hundred dozen of platforms. That's the way to do it, you know! Bless you, the publishers' advertisements are no good at all nowadays!"

Lionel was not paying very much heed; perhaps that was why he rather indifferently asked Mr. Quirk whether he himself was in favor of extending the suffrage to women.

"I?" cried Mr. Quirk, with a boisterous horse-laugh. "What do I care about it? Let them suffer away as much as ever they like!"

"Yes, they're used to that, aren't they?" said Lionel.

"What I want to do is to put Lady Adela up to a dodge or two for getting her book talked about; that's the important and immediate point, and I think I can be of some service to her," said Mr. Quirk? and then he added, more pompously, "I think she is willing to place herself entirely in my hands."

Happily at this moment there came into the room two or three young gentlemen, intent upon supper and subsequent cards, who took possession of the farther end of the table; and Lionel was glad to get up and join the new-comers, for he felt he could not eat in the immediate neighborhood of this ill-favored person. He had his poached eggs and a pint of hock in the company of these new friends; and, after having for some time listened to their ingenuous talk—which was chiefly a laudation of Miss Nellie Farren—he lit a cigarette and set out for home.

So it was Octavius Quirk who was now established as Lady Adela's favorite? It was he who was shown the first sheets of the new novel; it was he who was asked to dinner immediately on the return of the family from Scotland; it was he who was to be Lady Adela's chief counsellor throughout the next appeal to the British public? And perhaps he advised Lady Sybil, also, about the best way to get her musical compositions talked of; and might not one expect to find, in some minor exhibition, a portrait of Octavius Quirk, Esq., by Lady Rosamund Bourne? It seemed a gruesome kind of thing to think of these three beautiful women paying court to that lank-haired, puffy, bilious-looking baboon. He wondered what Miss Georgie Lestrange thought of it; Miss Georgie had humorous eyes that could say a good deal. And Lord Rockminster—how did Lord Rockminster manage to tolerate this uncouth creature?—was his good-natured devotion to his three accomplished sisters equal even to that?

Lionel did not proceed to ask himself why he had grown suddenly jealous of a man whom he himself had introduced to Lady Adela Cunyngham. Yet the reason was not far to seek. Before his visit to Scotland, it would have mattered little to him if any one of his lady friends—or any half dozen of them, for the matter of that—had appeared inclined to put some other favorite in his place; for he had an abundant acquaintance in the fashionable world; and, indeed, had grown somewhat callous to their polite attentions. But Lady Adela and her two sisters were relations of Honnor Cunyngham; they were going down to Brighton this very week; he was anxious (though hardly knowing why) to stand well in their opinion and be of importance in their eyes. As he now walked home he thought he would go and call on Lady Adela the following afternoon; if she were going down to that house in Adelaide Crescent, there would be plenty of talk among the women-folk; his name might be mentioned.

Next morning there was no further word of Nina. When he had got his fencing over, he went along to Sloane Street, but hardly with any expectation of news. No, Estelle had nothing to tell him; Nina had gone away—and wished to remain undiscovered.

"Poor Nina!" said Estelle, with a sigh.

Somewhat early in the afternoon he went up to Campden Hill. Lady Adela was at home. He noticed that the man-servant who ushered him into the drawing-room was very slow and circumspect about it, as if he wished to give ample warning to those within; and, indeed, just as he had come into the hall, he had fancied he heard a faint shriek, which startled him not a little. When he now entered the room he found Miss Georgie Lestrange standing in the middle of the floor, while Lady Adela was seated at a small writing-table a little way off. They both greeted him in the most friendly fashion; and then Miss Georgie (a little embarrassed, as he imagined) went towards the French window and looked out into the wintry garden.

"You have come most opportunely, Mr. Moore," said Lady Adela, in her pleasant way. "I'm sure you'll be able to tell us: how high would a woman naturally throw her arms on coming suddenly on a dead body?"

He was somewhat staggered.

"I—I'm sure I don't know."

"You see, Georgie has been so awfully kind to me this morning," Lady Adela continued. "I have arrived at some very dramatic scenes in my new story, and she has been good enough to act as my model; I want to have everything as vivid as possible; and why shouldn't a writer have a model as well as a painter; I hope to have all the attitudes strictly correct—to describe even the tone of her shriek when she comes upon the dead body of her brother. Imagination first, then actuality of detail; Rose tells me that Mr. Mellord, after he has finished a portrait, won't put in a blade of grass or a roseleaf without having it before him. If there's to be a crust of bread on the table, he must have the crust of bread."

"Yes, but Mr. Moore," said Miss Georgie, coming suddenly back from the window—and she was blushing furiously, up to the roots of her pretty golden-red hair, and covertly laughing at the same time, "my difficulty is that I try to do my best as the woman who unexpectedly sees her dead brother before her; but I've got nothing to come and go on. I never saw a dead body in my life; and it would hardly do to try it with a real dead body—"

"Georgie, don't be horrid!" Lady Adela said, severely. "Here is Mr. Moore, who can tell you how high the hands should be held, and whether they should be clenched or open."

"Well, Lady Adela," he said, in his confusion (for he was in mortal terror lest she should ask him to get up and posture before her), "the fact is that on the stage there are so many ways of expressing fear or dismay that no two people would probably adopt the same gestures. Would you have her hands above her head? Wouldn't it be more natural for her to have them about the height of her shoulders—the elbows drawn tightly back—her palms uplifted as if to shut away the terrible sight?—"

"Yes, yes!" said Lady Adela, eagerly; and she quickly scribbled some notes on the paper before her. "The very thing!—the very thing!"

"But don't you think," he ventured to say, "that that would look rather mechanical—rather stagey, in fact? I know nothing about writing; but I should think you would want to deal mostly with the expression of the woman's face—"

"I want to have it all!" the anxious authoress exclaimed. "I want to have attitudes—gestures—everything; to make the picture vivid. I must have the actual tone of her shriek—"

"Which Mr. Moore heard as he came in," Miss Georgie said, as a kind of challenge.

"Yes, I thought I heard a slight cry," he admitted, gravely.

"Thank you so much, Mr. Moore," said Lady Adela, with her most charming smile, as she began to fold up her notes. "The little piece of realism you have suggested will come in admirably; and I think I've done enough for to-day—thanks to Georgie here, who has just been an angel of patience."

Tea followed, and some idle talk, during which Lionel learned that Lady Adela and her sisters were going down to Brighton the following day. He incidentally mentioned Octavius Quirk's name; whereupon his hostess, who was a sharp and a shrewd woman when she was not dabbling in literature, instantly and graciously explained to him that she had been corresponding a good deal with Octavius Quirk of late, over her new work. She informed him, further, that Octavius Quirk was coming to dine there that evening— what a pity it was that Mr. Moore was engaged every evening at the theatre! When Lionel left, she had persuaded him that he was just as much a favorite as ever; he could very well understand that she had cultivated Octavius Quirk's acquaintance only in his capacity as a kind of pseudo-literary person.

Day after day of this lonely week passed; Lionel, all unknown to himself, was marching onward to his fate. On the Saturday there were two performances of "The Squire's Daughter;" at night he felt very tired—which was unusual with him; that, or some other palpable excuse, was sufficient to take him down to Victoria station on the Sunday morning. He had forgotten, or put aside, all Maurice Mangan's cool-blooded presentation of his case; undefined longings were in his brain; the future was to be quite different from the past—and somehow Honnor Cunyngham was the central figure in these mirage-like visions. He had formed no definite plans; he had prepared no persuasive appeal; the only and immediate thing he knew was that he wished to be in the same place with her, breathing the same air with her, with the chance of catching a distant glimpse of her, even if he were himself to remain unseen. Would she be out walking along the sea-front after church? Surely so, when she had Lady Adela and her sisters as her guests. And if not, he would call in the afternoon; how well he remembered the rather dusky drawing-room and its curious scent of sweet-briar or some similar perfume. A hushed half-hour there would be something to be treasured up and conned over again and again in subsequent recollection. Would she be sitting near the window, half-shadowed by the curtains? Or standing in front of the fire, perhaps, absently gazing into it, her tall and elegant figure outlined by the crimson flames?

When he arrived at Brighton he walked rapidly away down to the King's Road, and there he moderated his pace, keeping his eyes alert. The people were beginning to come out from the various churches and many of them, before going in-doors, joined that slow promenade up and down the greensward farther west. But, look where he might, there was no sign of Lady Cunyngham and her daughter, nor of Lady Adela and her two sisters. They would have been easily distinguishable, he thought. That they were in Brighton, he had no doubt; but apparently they were nowhere in this throng; so, rather downhearted, he retraced his steps to the Orleans Club, where he passed an hour or two with such acquaintances as he met there.

He was more fortunate in the afternoon. When he went along to Adelaide Crescent, Lady Cunyngham and her daughter were both at home; and it was with a sense of joyous relief—and yet with a touch of disquietude too—that he found himself ascending the soft-carpeted stairs. When he was shown into the drawing-room, he found only one occupant there—it was Honnor Cunyngham herself, who was standing by a big portfolio set on a brass stand, and apparently engaged in arranging some large photographs. She turned and greeted him very pleasantly and without any surprise; she went to two low settles coming out at right angles from the fireplace and sat down, while he took a seat opposite her; if he was rather nervous and bewildered, at finding himself thus suddenly face to face with her and alone with her, she was quite calm and self-possessed.

"Mother has just gone up-stairs; she will be here presently," Miss Honnor said. "But what a pity my sisters did not know you were coming down. After church they all went off to visit an old lady, a great friend of theirs, who can't get out-of-doors nowadays; and so I suppose they stayed on so as to keep her company. However, I have no doubt they will be here before long. What a pleasant thing it must be for you," she added, "to be able to run down to Brighton for a day after a week's hard work at the theatre."

"Yes," he answered, in a half-bitter kind of fashion. "It is a pleasant thing to get away from the theatre—anywhere. I think I am becoming rather sick of the theatre and all its associations."

"Really, Mr. Moore," she said, with a smile, "it is surprising to hear you say so—you of all men."

"What comes of it? You play the fool before a lot of idle people, until—until—your nature is subdued to what it works in, I suppose. What service do you do to any human being?—of what use are you in the world?"

"Surely you confer a benefit on the public when you provide them with innocent amusement," she ventured to say—she had not considered this subject much, if at all.

"But what comes of it? They laugh for an hour or two and go home. It is all gone—like a breath of wind—"

"But isn't mere distraction a useful and wholesome thing?" she remonstrated again, "I know a great philosopher who is exceedingly fond of billiards, and very eager about the game too; but he doesn't expect to gain any moral enlightenment from three balls and a bit of stick. Distraction, amusement, is necessary to human beings; we can't always be thinking of the problems of life."

"They talk of the divine power of song!" he continued. "Well, what I want to do is this. I can sing a little; and I want to know that this gift I have from Nature hasn't been entirely thrown away—scattered to the winds and lost. Here in Brighton they are always getting up morning or afternoon concerts for charitable purposes; and I wish, Miss Honnor, when you happen to be interested in any of these, you would let me know; I should be delighted to run down and volunteer my services. I should be just delighted. It would be something saved. If I were struck down by an illness, and had to lie thinking, I could say to myself that I had done this little scrap of good—not much for a man to do, but I suppose all that could be expected from a singer."

She could not understand this strange disparagement of himself and his profession; and she may have been vaguely afraid of the drift of these confidences; at all events, when she had thanked him for his generous offer, she rose and went to the portfolio.

"There are some things here that I think will interest you, Mr. Moore," she said. "They only arrived last night, and I was just putting them away when you came in."

He went to the portfolio; she took out two or three large photographs and handed them to him; the first glance showed him what they were—pictures of the Aivron and the Geinig valleys, with the rocks and pools and overhanging woods he knew so well. He regarded them for an instant or two.

"Do you know what first made me long to get away from the theatre?" he said, in a low voice. "It was those places there. It was Strathaivron—and you."

"I, Mr. Moore?"

And now he had to go on; he had taken his fate in his hands; there was some kind of despairing recklessness in his brain; his breath came and went quickly and painfully as he spoke.

"Well, I must tell you now, whatever comes of it. I must tell you the truth—you may think it madness—I cannot help that. What I want to do is to give up the theatre altogether. I want to let all that go, with a past never to be regretted—never to be recalled. I want to make for myself a new future—if you will share it with me."

"Mr. Moore!"

Their eyes met; hers frightened, his eagerly and tremblingly expectant.

"There, now you know the truth. Will you say but one word? Honnor—may I hope?"

He sought to take her hand, but she shrank back a step—not in anger, but apparently quite stupefied.

"Oh, no, no, Mr. Moore," she said, piteously. "What have I done? How could I imagine you were thinking of any such thing? And—and on my account—that you should dream of making such a sacrifice—giving up your reputation and your position—"

Where was his acting now?—where the passionate appeal he would have made on the stage? He stood stock-still—his eyes bent earnestly on hers—and he spoke slowly:

"It is no sacrifice. It is nothing. I wish for another life—but with you—with you. Have you one word of hope to give me?"

He saw his answer already.

"I cannot—I cannot," she said, with downcast eyes, and obviously in such deep distress that his heart smote him.

"It is enough," said he. "I—I was a fool to deceive myself with such imaginings—that are far beyond me. You will forgive me, Miss Honnor; I did not wish to cause you any pain; why, what harm is done except that I have been too presumptuous and too frank—and you will forget that. Tell me you forgive me!"

He held out his hand; she took it for a moment; and for another moment he held hers in a firm grasp.

"If I could tell you," he said, in a low voice, "what I thought of you—what every one thinks of you—you might perhaps understand why I have dared to speak."

She withdrew her hand quickly; her mother was at the door. When Lady Cunyngham came into the room, her daughter was apparently turning over those photographs and engravings. Lionel went forward to the elder lady to pay his respects; there was a brief conversation, introduced by Miss Honnor, about Mr. Moore's generous proposal to sing at any charitable concert they might be interested in; and then, as soon as he could, Lionel said good-bye, left the house, and passed into the outer world—where the dusk of the December afternoon was coming down over the far wastes of sea.

CHAPTER XVIII.

AN INVOCATION.

All his vague, wild, impracticable hopes and schemes had suddenly received their death-blow; but there was nothing worse than that; he himself (as he imagined) had been dealt no desperate wound. For one thing, flattered and petted as this young man had been, he was neither unreasoning nor vain; that a woman should have refused to marry him did not seem to him a monstrous thing; she was surely within her right in saying no; while, on the other hand, he was neither going to die of chagrin nor yet to plan a melodramatic revenge. But the truth was that he had never been passionately in love with Honnor Cunyngham. Passionate love he did not much believe in; he associated it with lime-light and crowded audiences and the odor of gas. Indeed, it might almost be said that he had been in love not so much with Honnor Cunyngham as with the condition of life which she represented. He had grown restless and dissatisfied with his present state; he had been imagining for himself another sort of existence—but always with her as the central figure of those fancied realms; he had been dreaming dreams—of which she had invariably formed part. And now he had been awakened (somewhat abruptly, perhaps, but that may have been his own fault); and there was nothing for it but to summon his common-sense to his aid, and to assure himself that Honnor Cunyngham, at least, was not to blame.

And yet sometimes, in spite of himself, as he smoked a final cigarette at midnight in those rooms in Piccadilly, a trace of bitterness would come into his reveries.

"I have been taught my place, that's all," he would say to himself. "Maurice was right—I had forgotten my catechism. I wanted to play the gardener's son, or Mordaunt to Lady Mabel; and I can't write poetry, and I'm not in the House of Commons. I suppose my head was a little bewildered by the kindness and condescension of those excellent people. They are glad to welcome you into their rooms—you are a sort of curiosity—you sing for them—they're very civil for an hour or two—but you must remember to leave before the footmen proceed to shut the hall-door. Well, what's to be done? Am I to rush away to the wars, and come back a field-marshal? Am I to make myself so obnoxious in Parliament that the noble earl will give me his daughter in order to shut my mouth? Oh, no; they simplify matters nowadays; 'as you were' is the word of command; go back to the theatre; paint your face and put on your finery; play the fool along with the rest of the comic people, and we'll come and look at you from the stalls; and if you will marry, why, then, keep in your own sphere, and marry Kate Burgoyne!"

For now—when he was peevish and discontented and restless, or even sick at heart, he hardly knew why—there was no Nina to solace and soothe him with her gentle companionship, her wise counsel, her bright and cheerful and wayward good-humor. Apparently he had as many friends and acquaintances as before, and yet he was haunted by a curious sense of solitude. Of a morning he would go out for a stroll along the familiar thoroughfares—Bond Street, Conduit Street, Regent Street, where he knew all the shops at which Nina used to linger for a moment, to glance at a picture or a bonnet—and these seemed altogether different now. He could not have imagined he should have missed Nina so much. Instead of dining in his rooms at five o'clock and thereafter walking down to Sloane Street to have a cup of tea with Nina and Mlle. Girond before they all three set out for the theatre, he spent most of his afternoons at the Garden Club, where there was a good deal of the game of poker being played by young gentlemen in the up-stairs rooms. And sometimes he returned thither after the performance, seeking anew the distraction of card-playing and betting, until he became notorious as the fiercest plunger in the place. Nobody could "bluff" Lionel Moore; he would "call" his opponent if he himself had nothing better than a pair of twos; and many a solid handful of sovereigns he had to pay for that privilege of gazing.

Day after day went by, and still there was no word of Nina; at times he was visited by sudden sharp misgivings that terrified him. The heading of a paragraph in a newspaper would startle his eyes; and then he would breathe again when he found that this poor wretch who had grown weary of the world was unknown to him. Every evening, when Mlle. Girond came into the theatre, she was met by the same anxious, wondering question; and her reply was invariably the same.

"Don't you think it very strange?" he asked of Estelle. "Nina said she would write to you or send you a message—I suppose as soon as all her plans were made. I hope nothing has happened to her," he added, as a kind of timid expression of his own darker self-questionings.

"Something—something terrible?" said Estelle. "Ah, no. We should hear. No; Nina will make sure we cannot reach her—that she is not to be seen by you or me—then perhaps I have a message. Oh, she is very proud; she will make sure; the pain in her heart, she will hide it and hide it—until some time goes, and she can hold up her head, with a brave face. Poor Nina!—she will suffer—for she will not speak, no, not to any one."

"But look here, Miss Girond," he exclaimed, "if she has gone back to her friends in Italy, that's all right; but if she is in this country, without any occupation, her money will soon be exhausted—she can't have had so very much. What will become of her then? Don't you think I should put an advertisement in the papers—not in my name, but in yours—your initials—begging her at least to let you know where she is?"

Estelle shook her head.

"No, it is useless. Perhaps I understand Nina a little better than you, though you know her longer. She is gentle and affectionate and very grateful to her friends; but under that there is firmness—oh, yes. She has firmness of mind, although she is so loving; when she has decided to go away and remain, you will not draw her back, no, not at all! She will remain where she wishes to be; perhaps she decides never to see any of us again. Well, well, it is pitiable, but for us to interfere, that is useless."

"Oh, I am not so sure of that," he said. "As you say, I have known Nina longer than you have; if I could only learn where she is, I am quite sure that I could persuade her to come back."

"Very well—try!" said Estelle, throwing out both hands. "I say no—that she will not say where she is. And your London papers, how will they find her? Perhaps she is in a small English village—perhaps in Paris—perhaps in Naples—perhaps in Malta. For me, no. She said, 'If you are my friend, you will not seek to discover where I have gone.' I am her friend; I obey her wish. When she thinks it is right, she will send me a message. Until then, I wait."

But if Nina had gone away—depriving him of her pleasant companionship, her quick sympathy, her grave and almost matron-like remonstrances—there was another quite ready to take her place. Miss Burgoyne did not at all appear to regret the disappearance from the theatre of Antonia Rossi. She was kinder to this young man than ever; she showered her experienced blandishments upon him, even when she rallied him about his gloomy looks or listless demeanor. All the time he was not on the stage, and not engaged in dressing, he usually spent in her sitting-room; there were cigarettes and lemonade awaiting him; and when she herself could not appear, at all events she could carry on a sort of conversation with him from the inner sanctuary; and often she would come out and finish her make-up before the large mirror while she talked to him.

"They tell me you gamble," she said to him on one occasion, in her blunt way.

"Not much," he said.

"What good do you get out of it?" she asked again.

"Oh, well, it is a sort of distraction. It keeps people from thinking."

"And what have you to think about?" continued Grace Mainwaring, regarding herself in the glass. "What dreadful crimes have you to forget? You want to drown remorse, do you? I dare say you ought; but I don't believe it all the same. You men don't care what you do, and poor girls' hearts get broken. But gambling! Well, I imagine most men have one vice or another, but gambling has always seemed to me the stupidest thing one could take to. Drink kills you, but I suppose you get some fun out of it. What fun do you get out of gambling? Too serious, isn't it? And then the waste of money. The fact is, you want somebody to take care of you, Master Lionel; and a fine job she'll have of it, whoever undertakes it!"

"Why should it be a she," he asked, "assuming that I am incapable of managing my own affairs?"

"Because it is the way of the world," she answered, promptly. "And you, of all people, need somebody to look after you. Why should you have to take to gambling, at your time of life? You're not shamming *ennui*, are you, to imitate your swell acquaintances? *Ennui!* I could cure their *ennui* for them, if they'd only come to *me!*" she added, somewhat scornfully.

"A cure for *ennui?*" he said. "That would be valuable; what is it?"

"I'd tell them to light a wax match and put it up their nostril and hold it there till it went out," she answered, with some sharpness.

"It would make them jump, anyway, wouldn't it?" he said, listlessly.

"It would give them something to claim their very earnest attention for at least a fortnight," Miss Burgoyne observed, with decision; and then she had to ask him to open the door, for it was time for her to get up to the wings.

Christmas was now close at hand, and one evening when Harry Thornhill, attired in his laced coat and ruffles, silken stockings and buckled shoes, went as usual into Miss Burgoyne's room, he perceived that she had, somewhere or other, obtained a piece of mistletoe, which she had placed on the top of the piano. As soon as Grace Mainwaring knew he was there, she came forth from the dressing-room and went to the big mirror, kicking out her resplendent train of flounced white satin behind her, and proceeding to judge of the general effect of her powder and patches and heavily-pencilled eyebrows.

"Where are you going for Christmas?" she asked.

"Into the country," he answered.

"That's no good," said the brilliant-eyed white little bride, still contemplating herself in the glass, and giving a finishing touch here and there. "The country's too horrid at this time of year. We are going to

Brighton, some friends and I, a rather biggish party; and a whole heap of rooms have been taken at a hotel. That will be fun, I promise you. A dance in the evening. You'd better come; I can get you an invitation."

"Thanks, I couldn't very well. I am going to play the good boy, and pass one night under the parental roof. It isn't often I get the chance."

"I wish you would tell me where to hang up that piece of mistletoe," she said, presently.

"I know where I should like to hang it up," he made answer, with a sort of lazy impertinence.

"Where?"

"Just over your head."

"Why?"

"You would see."

She made a little grimace.

"Oh, no, I shouldn't see anything of the kind," she retorted, confidently. "I should see nothing of the kind. You haven't acquired the right, young gentleman. On the stage Harry Thornhill may claim his privileges—or make believe; but off the stage he must keep his distance."

That significant phrase about his not having acquired the right was almost a challenge. And why should he not say, "Well, give me the right!" What did it matter? It was of little concern what happened to him. As he lay back in his chair and looked at her, he guessed what she would do. He imagined the pretty little performance. "Well, give me the right, then!" Miss Burgoyne turns round from the mirror. "Lionel, what do you mean?"

"You know what I mean: let us be engaged lovers off the stage as well as on." She hangs down her head. He goes to her and kisses her—without any mistletoe; she murmurs some doubt and hesitation, in her maiden shyness; he laughingly reassures her; it is all over, in half a dozen seconds. And then? Why, then he has secured for himself a sufficiently good-natured life-companion; it will be convenient in many ways, especially when they are engaged at the same theatre; he will marry in his own sphere, and everybody be satisfied. If he has to give up his bachelor ways and habits, she will probably look after a little establishment as well as another; where there is no frantic passion on either side, there will be no frantic jealousy; and, after all, what is better than peace and quiet and content?

Was he too indolent, then, to accept this future that seemed to be offered to him?

"Isn't it rather odd to go to a Brighton hotel for Christmas?" he said, at random.

"It's the swagger thing to do, don't you know?" said Miss Burgoyne, whose phraseology sometimes made him wince. "It's the latest fad among people who have no formal family ties. I can imagine it will be the jolliest thing possible. Instead of the big family gathering, where half the relations hate the sight of the other half, you have all nice people, picked friends and acquaintances; and you go away down to a place where you can have your choice of rooms, where you have every freedom and no responsibility, where you can have everything you want and no trouble in getting it. Instead of foggy London, the sea; and at night, instead of Sir Roger de Coverley with a lot of hobbledehoys, you have a charming little dance, on a good floor, with capital partners. Come, Master Lionel, change your mind; and you and I will go down together on Christmas morning in the Pullman. Most of the others are there already; it's only one or two poor professionals who will have to go down on Christmas-day."

But Lionel shook his head.

"Duty—duty," he murmured.

"Duty!" said she, contemptuously. "Duty is a thing you owe to other people, which no one ever thinks of paying to you." And therewith this profound moralist and epigrammatist tucked up her white satin train and waited for him to open the door, so that she might make her way to the stage, he humbly following.

On the Christmas morning the display of parcels, packets, and envelopes, large and small, spread out on the side-table in his sitting-room was simply portentous; for the fashionable world of London had had no intimation yet that their favorite singer was ill-disposed towards them, and had even at times formed sullen resolutions of withdrawing altogether from their brilliant rooms. As he quite indifferently turned the packages and letters over, trying to guess at the name of the sender by the address, he said to himself,

"They toss you those things out of their bounty as they fling a shilling to a crossing-sweeper because it is Christmas-day."

But here was one that he opened, recognizing the handwriting of his cousin Francie; and Francie had sent him a very pretty pair of blue velvet slippers, with his initials worked by herself in thread of gold. That was all right, for he had got for Miss Francie a little present that he was about to take down with him—a hand-bag in green lizard-skin that might be useful to her when she was going on her numerous errands. It was different with the next packet he opened (also recognizing the writing), for this was a paperweight—an oblong slab of crystal set in silver, with a photograph of the sender showing through, and the inscription at the foot, "To Lionel Moore, from his sincere friend, K.B." And he had never thought of getting anything for Miss Burgoyne! Well, it was too late now; he would have to atone for his neglect of her when he returned to town. Meanwhile he recollected that just about now she would be getting down to Victoria station *en route* to Brighton; and, indeed, had it not been for the duty he owed the old people, he would have been well content to be going with her. The last time he had been in a Pullman car on the way to Brighton it was with other friends—or acquaintances; he knew his place now, and was resigned. So he continued opening these parcels and envelopes carelessly and somewhat ungratefully, merely glancing at the various messages, until it was time to bethink him of setting forth.

But first of all, when the cab had been summoned and his portmanteau put on the top, he told the man to drive to a certain number in Sloane Street; he thought he would call for a minute on Mrs. Grey and Miss Girond and wish them a pleasant Christmas. Estelle, when she made her appearance, knew better what had brought him hither.

"Ah, it is so kind of you to send me the pretty work-case—thank you, thank you very much; and Mrs. Grey is so proud of the beautiful lamp—she will tell you in a moment when she comes in. And if there is something we might have liked better—pardon, it is no disfavor to the pretty presents, not at all—it is what you would like, too, I am sure—it is a message from Nina. Yes, I expected it a little—I was awake hour after hour this morning—when the postman came I ran down the stairs—no! no word of any kind."

He stood silent for a minute.

"I confess I had some kind of fancy she might wish to send you just a line or a card—any sort of reminder of her existence—on Christmas-day; for she knows the English custom," he said, rather absently. "And there is nothing—nothing of any kind, you say. Well, I have written to Pandiani."

"Ah, the *maestro?*—yes?"

"You see, I knew it was no use writing to her friends," he continued, "for, if she were with them, she would tell them not to answer. But it is different with Pandiani. If she has got any musical engagement in Naples, or if she has gone to Malta, he would know. It seems hard that at Christmas-time we should be unable to send a message to Nina."

"Perhaps she is sure that we think of her," Estelle said, rather sadly. "I did not know till she was gone that I loved her so much and would miss her so much; because sometimes—sometimes she reproved me—and we had little disagreements—but all the same she was so kind—and always it was for your opinion I was corrected—it was what you would think if I did this or that. Ah, well, Nina will take her own time before she allows us to know. Perhaps she is not very happy."

Nor had Mrs. Grey any more helpful counsel or conjecture to offer; so, rather downheartedly, he got into the hansom again and set out for Victoria station, where he was to meet Maurice Mangan.

Maurice he found in charge of a bewildering number of variously sized packages, which seemed to cause him some anxiety, for there was no sort of proper cohesion among them.

"Toys for Francie's children, I'll bet," said Lionel.

"Well, how otherwise could I show my gratitude?" Mangan said. "You know it's awfully good of your people, Linn, to ask a poor, solitary devil like me to join their Christmas family party. It's almost too much—"

"I should think they were precious glad to get you!" Lionel made answer, as he and his friend took their seats in one of the carriages.

"And I've got a little present for Miss Francie herself," continued Mangan, opening his bag, and taking therefrom a small packet. He carefully undid the tissue-paper wrappers, until he could show his companion what they contained; it was a copy of "Aurora Leigh," bound in white vellum, and on the cover were stamped two tiny violets,-green-stemmed and purple-blossomed.

"'Aurora Leigh,'" said Lionel—not daring, however, to take the dainty volume in his hands. "That will just suit Miss Savonarola. And what are the two violets, Maurice—what do they mean?"

"Oh, that was merely a little device of my own," Mangan said, evasively.

"You don't mean to say that these are your handiwork?" Lionel asked, looking a little closer.

"Ob, no. I merely drew them, and the binder had them stamped in color for me."

"And what did that cost?"

"I don't know yet."

"And don't care—so long as it's for Francie. And yet you are always lecturing me on my extravagance!"

"Oh, well, it's Christmas-time," Mangan said; "and I confess I like Christmas and all its ways. I do. I seem to feel the general excitement throughout the country tingling in me too; I like to see the children eagerly delighted, and the houses decorated with evergreens, and the old folk pleased and happy with the enthusiasm of the youngsters. If I've got to drink an extra glass of port, I'm there; if it's Sir Roger de Coverley, I'm there; I'll do anything to add to the general *Schwärmerei*. What the modern *littérateur* thinks it fine to write about Christmas being all sham sentiment is simply insufferable bosh. Christmas isn't in the least bit played out—though the magazinist may be, or may pretend to be. I think it's a grand thing to have a season for sending good wishes, for recollection of absent friends, for letting the young folk kick up their heels. I say, Linn, I hope there's going to be some sunlight down there. I am longing to see a holly-tree in the open air—the green leaves and scarlet berries glittering in the sunlight. Oh, I can tell you an autumn session of Parliament is a sickening thing—when the interminable speeches and wranglings drag on and on until you think they're going to tumble over into Christmas-day itself. There's fog in your brain as well as in your throat, and you seem to forget there ever was an outer world; you get listless and resigned, and think you've lived all your life in darkness. Well, just a glimmer of sunshine, that's all I bargain for—just a faint glimmer—and a sight of the two holly-trees by the gate of the doctor's house."

What intoxication had got into the head of this man? Whither had fled his accustomed indifference and indolence, his sardonic self-criticism? He was like a school-boy off for the holidays. He kept looking out of the window—with persistent hope of the gray sky clearing. He was impatient of the delay at the various stations. And when at length they got out and found the doctor's trap awaiting them, and proceeded to get up the long and gradual incline that leads to Winstead village, he observed that the fat old pony, if he were lent for a fortnight to a butcher, would find it necessary to improve his pace.

When they reached the doctor's house and entered, they found that only the old lady was at home; the doctor had gone to visit a patient; Miss Francie was, as usual, away among her young convalescents.

"It has been a busy time for Francie," Mrs. Moore said. "She has been making so many different things for them. And I don't like to hear her sewing-machine going so late at night."

"Then why do you let her do it?" Lionel said, in his impetuous way. "Why don't you get in somebody to help her? Look here, I'll pay for that. You call in a seamstress to do all that sewing, and I'll give her a sovereign a week. Why should Francie have her eyes ruined?"

"Lionel is like the British government, Mrs. Moore," Mangan said, with a smile. "He thinks he can get over every difficulty by pulling out his purse.

But perhaps Miss Francie might prefer carrying out her charitable work herself."

So Maurice Mangan was arrogating to himself, was he, the right of guessing Francie's preferences?

"Well, mother, tell me where I am likely to find her. I am going to pull her out of those fever-dens and refuges for cripples. Why, she ought to know that's all exploded now. Slumming, as a fad, had its day, but it's quite gone out now—"

"Do you think it is because it is fashionable, or was fashionable, that Miss Francie takes an interest in those poor children?" Maurice asked, gently.

Lionel was nearly telling him to mind his own business; why should he step in to defend Cousin Francie?

"She said she was going across the common to old Widow Jackson's," his mother answered him, "and you may find her either there or on the way to the village."

"Widow Jackson's?" he repeated, in doubt.

"Oh, I know it," Mangan said, cheerfully. And again Lionel was somewhat astonished. How had Maurice Mangan acquired this particular knowledge of Francie's surroundings? Perhaps his attendance at the House of Commons had not been so unintermittent as he had intimated?

There were still further surprises in store for Master Lionel. When at length they encountered Miss Francie—how pretty she looked as she came along the pathway through the gorse, in her simple costume of dark gray, with a brown velvet hat and brown tan gloves!—it was in vain that he tried to dissuade her from giving up the rest of the afternoon to her small *protégés*. In the most natural way in the world she turned to Maurice Mangan—and her eyes sought his in a curiously straightforward, confiding fashion that caused Lionel to wonder.

"On Christmas-day, of all the days of the year!" she said, as if appealing to Maurice. "Surely, surely, I must give up Christmas-day to them! Oh, do you know, Mr. Mangan, there never was a happier present than you thought of for the little blind boy who got his leg broken—you remember? He learned almost directly how to do the puzzle; and he gets the ring off so quickly that no one can see how it is done; and he laughs with delight when he finds that any neighbor coming in can only growl and grumble—and fail. I'm going there just now; won't you come? And mind you be very angry when you can't get the ring off; you may use any language you like about your clumsiness—poor little chap, he has heard plenty of that in his time."

Maurice needed no second invitation; this was what he had come for; he had found the sunlight to lighten up the Christmas-day withal; his face, that was almost beautiful in its fine intellectuality, showed that whenever she spoke to him. Lionel, of course, went with them.

And again it was Maurice Mangan whom Miss Francie addressed, as they walked along to the village.

"Do you know, in all this blessed place, I can't find a copy of Mrs. Hemans's poems; and I wanted you to read 'The Arab to his Horse'—is that the title?—at my school-treat to-morrow. They would all understand that. Well, we must get something else; for we're to make a show of being educational and instructive before the romping begins. I think the 'Highland Schottische' is the best of any for children who haven't learned dancing; they can all jump about somehow—and the music is inspiriting. The vicar's daughters are coming to hammer at the piano. Oh, Mr. Mangan," she continued, still appealing to him, "do you think you could tell them a thrilling folk-story?—wouldn't that be better?"

"Don't you want me to do something, Francie?" said Lionel, perhaps a little hurt.

"Do you mean—"

"The only thing I'm fit for—I'll sing them a song, if you like. 'My Pretty Jane'—no, that would hardly do—'The Death of Nelson' or 'Rule Britannia'—"

"Wouldn't there be rather a risk, Lionel? If you were to miss your train—and disappoint a great audience in London?" she said, gently.

"Oh, I'll take my chance of that? I'm used to it," he said, "I'll have Dick and the pony waiting outside. Oh, yes, I'll sing something for them."

"It will be very kind of you," she said.

And again, as they went to this or that cottage, to see that the small convalescent folk were afforded every possible means of holding high holiday (how fortunate they were as compared with thousands of similar unfortunates, shivering away the hopeless hours in dingy courts and alleys, gin clutching at every penny, that might have got food for their empty stomachs or rags for their poor shrunken limbs!), it was to Maurice Mangan that Francie chiefly talked, and, indeed, he seemed to know all about those patient little sufferers, and the time they had been down here, and when they might have to be sent back to London to make way for their successors. There was also a question as to which of their toys they might be permitted to carry off with them.

"Oh, I wouldn't deprive them of one," Mangan said, distinctly. "I've brought down a heap more this morning."

"Again—again?" she said, almost reproachfully; but the gentle gray eyes looked pleased, notwithstanding.

Well, that Christmas evening was spent in the doctor's house with much quiet enjoyment; for the old people were proud to have their only son with them for so long a time; and Francie seemed glad to have the various labors of the day over; and Maurice Mangan, with quite unwonted zest, kept the talk flowing free. Next morning was chiefly devoted to preparations for the big entertainment to be given in the school-room; and in due course Lionel redeemed his promise by singing no fewer than four songs—at the shyly proffered request of the vicar's pretty daughters; thereafter, leaving Maurice to conduct the gay proceedings to a close, he got out and jumped into the trap and was driven off to the station. He arrived at the New Theatre in plenty of time; the odor of consumed gas was almost a shock to him, well as he was used to it, after the clear air of Winstead.

And did he grudge or envy the obvious interest and confidence that appeared to have sprung up between his cousin and his friend? Not one bit. Maurice had always had a higher appreciation of Francie and her aims and ideals than he himself had, much as he liked her; and it was but natural she should turn to the quarter from which she could derive most sympathy and practical help. And if Maurice's long-proclaimed admiration for Miss Savonarola should lead to a still closer bond between those two—what then?

It was not jealousy that had hold of Lionel Moore's heart just at this time; it was rather a curious unrest that seemed to increase as day by day went by without bringing any word of Nina. Had she vouchsafed the smallest message, to say she was safe and well, to give him some notion of her whereabouts, it might have been different; but he knew not which way to turn, north, south, east, or west; at this season of kindly remembrance he could summon up no sort of picture of Nina and her surroundings. If only he had known, he kept repeating to himself. He had been so wrapped up in his idle dreams and visions that, all unwittingly, he had spurned and crushed this true heart beating close to his side. And as for making amends, what amends could now be made; He only wanted to know that Nina was alive—and could forgive.

As he sat by himself in the still watches of the night, plunged in silent reverie, strange fancies began to fill his brain. He recalled stories in which he had read of persons separated by great distances communicating with each other by some species of spiritual telegraphy; and a conviction took possession of him that now, if ever—now as the old year was about to go out and the new year come in—he could call to Nina across the unknown void that lay between them, and that she would hear and perchance respond. Surely, on New-Year's Eve, Nina would be thinking of her friends in London; and, if their earnest and anxious thoughts could but meet her half-way, might there not be some sudden understanding, some recognition, some glad assurance that all was well? This wild fancy so grew upon him that when the last day of the year arrived it had become a fixed belief; and yet it was with a haunting sense of dread—a dread of he knew not what—that he looked forward to the stroke of twelve.

He got through his performance that night as if he were in a dream, and hurried home; it was not far from midnight when he arrived. He only glanced at the outside of the letters awaiting him; there was no one from her; not in that way was Nina to communicate with him, if her hopes for the future, her forgiveness for what lay in the past, were to reach him at all. He drew a chair to the table and sat down, leaving the letters unheeded.

The slow minutes passed; his thoughts went wandering over the world, seeking for what they could not find. And how was he to call to Nina across the black gulf of the night, wheresoever she might be? Suddenly there leaped into his recollection an old German ballad he used to sing. It was that of the three comrades who were wont to drink together, until one died, and another died, and nevertheless the solitary survivor kept the accustomed tryst, and still, sitting there alone, he had the three glasses filled, and still he sang aloud, "*Aus voller Brust.*" There came an evening; as he filled the cups, a tear fell into his own; yet bravely he called to his ghostly companions, "I drink to you, my brothers—but why are you so mute and still?" And behold! the glasses clinked together; and the wine was slowly drunk out of all the three, "*Fiducit! du wackerer Zecher!*"—it was the loyal comrade's last draught. And now Lionel, hardly knowing what he was doing—for there were such wild desires and longings in his brain—went to a small cabinet hard by and brought forth the loving-cup he had given to Nina. They two were the last who had drunk out of it. And if now, if once again, on this last night of all the nights of the year, he were to repeat his challenge, would she not know? He cared not in what form she might appear—Nina could not be other than gentle—silent she might be, but surely her eyes would shine with kindness and forgiveness. He was not aware of it, but his fingers were trembling as he took the cup in twain, and put the two tiny goblets on the table and filled them with wine. Nay, in a sort of half-dazed fashion he went and opened the door and left it wide— might there not be some shadowy footfall on the empty stair! He returned to the table and sat down; it was almost twelve; he was shivering a little— the night was cold.

All around him the silence appeared to grow more profound; there was only the ticking of a clock. As minute after minute passed, the suspense became almost unendurable; something seemed to be choking him; and yet his eyes would furtively and nervously wander from the small goblets before him to the open door, as if he expected some vision to present itself there, from whatsoever distant shore it might come.

The clock behind him struck a silver note, and instantly this vain fantasy vanished; what was the use of regarding the two wine-filled cups when he knew that Nina was far and far away? He sprang to his feet and went to the window, and gazed out into the black and formless chaos beyond.

"Nina!" he called, "Nina!—Nina!" as if he would pierce the hollow distance with this passionate cry.

Alas! how could Nina answer? At this moment, over all the length and breadth of England, innumerable belfries had suddenly awakened from their sleep, and ten thousand bells were clanging their iron tongues, welcoming in the new-found year. Down in the valleys, where white mists lay along the slumbering rivers; far up on lonely moorlands, under the clear stars; out on the sea-coasts, where the small red points of the windows were face-to-face with the slow-moaning, inarticulate main; everywhere, over all the land, arose this clamor of joy-bells; and how could Nina respond to his appeal? If she had heard, if she had tried to answer, her piteous cry was swallowed up and lost; heart could not speak to heart, whatever message they might wish to send, through this universal, far-pulsating jangle and tumult.

But perhaps she had not heard at all? Perhaps there was something more impassable between her and him than even the wide, dark seas and the night?

He turned away from the window. He went back to the chair; he threw his arms on the table before him—and hid his face.

CHAPTER XIX.

ENTRAPPED.

There were two young gentlemen standing with their backs to the fire in the supper-room of the Garden Club. They were rather good-looking young men, very carefully shaven and shorn, gray-eyed, fair-moustached; and, indeed, they were so extremely like each other that it might have been hard to distinguish between them but that one chewed a toothpick and the other a cigarette. Both were in evening dress, and both still wore the overcoat and crush-hat in which they had come into the club. They could talk freely, without risk of being overheard; for the members along there at the supper-table were all listening, with much laughter, to a professional entertainer, who, unlike the proverbial clown released from the pantomime, was never so merry and amusing as when diverting a select little circle of friends with his own marvellous adventures.

"It's about time for Lionel Moore to make his appearance," said one of the two companions, glancing at the clock.

"I would rather have anybody else, if it comes to that," said the other, peevishly. "Moore spoils the game all to bits. You never know where to have him—"

"Yes, that's just where he finds his salvation," continued he of the toothpick. "Mind you, that wild play has its advantages. He gets caught now and again, but he catches you at times. You make sure he is bluffing, you raise him and raise him, then you call him—and find he has three aces! And I will say this for Moore—he's a capital loser. He doesn't seem to mind losing a bit, so long as you keep on. You would think he was a millionaire; only a millionaire would have an eye on every chip, I suppose. What salary do they give him at the New Theatre?"

"He threw his arms on the table before him, and hid his face"

"Fifty pounds a week, I've heard say; but people tell such lies. Even fifty pounds a week won't hold out if he goes on like that. What I maintain is that it isn't good poker. For one thing, I object to 'straddling' altogether; it's simply a stupid way of raising the stakes; of course, the straddler has the advantage of coming in last, but then look at the disadvantage of having to bet first. No, I don't object to betting before the draw; that's sensible; there's some skill and judgment in that; but straddling is simply stupid. You ought to make it easy for every one to come in; that's the proper game; frighten them out afterwards if you can." And then he added, gloomily, "That fellow Moore is a regular bull in a china-shop."

"I suspect he has been raking over a few of your chips, Bertie," his companion said, with a placid grin.

Just as he was speaking, Lionel entered the room, and, having ordered some supper, took a seat at the table. One of those young gentlemen, throwing away his toothpick, came and sat down opposite him.

"Big house to-night, as usual?" he asked.

"Full," was the answer. "I dare say when the archangel blows his trump, "The Squire's Daughter" will still be advertised in the bills all over the town. I don't see why it should stop before then."

"It would be a sudden change for the company, wouldn't it?" the young man on the other side of the table said. "Fancy, now, a music-hall singer— no disrespect to you, Moore—I mean a music-hall comic—fancy his finding himself all at once in heaven; don't you think he'd feel deuced awkward? He wouldn't be quite at home, would he?—want to get back to Mr. Chairman and the chorus in the gallery, eh, what?—'pon my soul, it would make a capital picture if you could get a fellow with plenty of imagination to do it—quite tragic, don't you know—you'd have the poor devil's face just full of misery—not knowing where to go or what to do—"

"The British public would be inclined to rise and rend that painter," said Lionel, carelessly; this young man was useful as a poker-player, but otherwise not interesting.

Two or three members now came in; and by the time Lionel had finished his frugal supper there was a chosen band of five ready to go up-stairs and set to work with the cards. There was some ordering of lemon-squashes and further cigarettes; new packs were brought by the waiter; the players took their places; and the game was opened. With a sixpenny "ante" and a ten-shilling "limit," the amusement could have been kept mild enough by any one who preferred it should remain so.

But the usual thing happened. Now and again a fierce fight would ensue between two good hands, and that seemed to arouse a spirit of general emulation and eagerness; the play grew more bold; bets apart from the game were laid by individual players between themselves. The putting up of the "ante" became a mere farce, for every one came in as a matter of course, even if he had to draw five cards; and already the piles of chips on the table had undergone serious diminution or augmentation—in the latter case there was a glimmer of gold among the bits of ivory. There was no visible excitement, however; perhaps a player caught bluffing might smile a little—that was all.

Lionel had been pretty fortunate, considering his wild style of play; but then his very recklessness stood him in good stead when he chanced to have a fair hand—his reputation for bluffing leading on his opponents. And then an extraordinary bit of luck had befallen him. On this occasion the first hand dealt him contained three queens, a seven, and a five. To make the other players imagine he had either two pairs or was drawing to a flush, he threw away only one of the two useless cards—the five, as it chanced; but his satisfaction (which he bravely endeavored to conceal) may be imagined when he found that the single card dealt him in its place was a seven—he therefore had a full hand! When it came to his turn, instead of beginning cautiously, as an ordinary player would have done, he boldly raised the bet ten shillings. But that frightened nobody. His game was known; they imagined he had either two pairs or had failed to fill his flush and was merely bluffing. When, however, there was another raise of ten shillings from the opposite side of the table, that was a very different matter; one by one the others dropped out, leaving these two in. And then it went on:

"Well, I'll just see your ten shillings and raise you another ten."

"And another ten."

"And another ten."

"And another ten."

Of course, universal attention was now concentrated on this duel. Probably four out of five of the players were of opinion that Lionel Moore was bluffing; that, at least, was certainly the opinion of his antagonist, who kept raising and raising without a qualm. At length both of them had to borrow money to go on with; but still the duel continued, and still the pile of gold and chips in the middle of the table grew and increased.

"And another ten."

"And another ten."

Not a word of encouragement or dissuasion was uttered by any one of the onlookers; they sat silent and amused, wondering which of the two was about to be smitten under the fifth rib. And at last it was Lionel's opponent who gave in.

"On this occasion," said he, depositing his half-sovereign, "I will simply gaze; what have you got?"

"Well, I have got a full hand," Lionel answered, putting down his hand on the table.

"That is good enough," the other said, stolidly. "Take away the money."

After this dire combat, the game fell flat a little; but interest was soon revived by a round of Jack-pots; and here again Lionel was in good luck. Indeed, when the players rose from the table about three o'clock, he might have come away a winner of close on £40 had not some reckless person called out something about whiskey poker. Now whiskey poker is the very stupidest form of gambling that the mind of man has ever conceived, though at the end of the evening some folk hunger after it as a kind of final fillip. Each person puts down a certain sum—it may be a sovereign, it may be five sovereigns; poker hands are dealt out, the cards being displayed face upwards on the table; there is no drawing; whoever has the best hand simply annexes the pool. It looks like a game, but it is not a game; it is merely cutting the cards; but, as the stakes can be doubled or trebled each round, the jaded appetite for gambling finds here a potent and fiery stimulant just as the party breaks up. Lionel was not anxious to get away with the money he had won. It was he who proposed to increase the stakes to £10 from each player—which the rest of them, to their credit be it said, refused to do. In the end, when they went to get their hats and coats before issuing into the morning air, some one happened to ask Lionel how he had come off on the whole night; and he replied that he did not think he had either won or lost anything to speak of. He hardly knew. Certainly he did not seem to care.

The dawn was not yet. The gas-lamps shone in the murky thoroughfares as he set out for Piccadilly—alone. The others all went away in hansoms; he preferred to walk. And even when he reached his rooms, he did not go to bed at once; he sat up thinking, a prey to a strange sort of restlessness that had of late taken possession of him. For this young man's gay and happy butterfly-life was entirely gone. The tragic disappearance of Nina, followed by the sudden shattering of all his visionary hopes in connection with Honnor Cunyngham, had left him in a troubled, anxious, morbid state that he himself, perhaps, could not well have accounted for. Then the sense of solitariness that he had experienced when he found that Nina had so unexpectedly vanished from his ken had been intensified since he had taken to declining invitations from his fashionable friends, and spending his nights in the aimless distraction of gambling at the Garden Club. Was there a touch of hurt pride in his withdrawal from the society of those who in former days used to be called "the great"? At least he discovered this, that if he did wish to withdraw from their society, nothing in the world was easier. They did not importune him. He was free to go his own way. Perhaps this also wounded him; perhaps it was to revenge himself that he sought to increase his popularity with the crowd; at night he sang with a sort of bravado to bring down the house; in the day-time it comforted him to perceive from a distance in that or the other window a goodly display of his photographs, which he had learned to recognize from afar. But in whatever direction these wayward moods drew him or tossed him, there was ever this all-pervading disquiet, and a haunting regret that almost savored of remorse, and a sick impatience of the slow-passing and lonely hours.

He had given up all hopes of hearing from Nina now or of gaining any news of her. Pandiani had nothing to tell him. The Signorina Antonia Rossi had not written to any of her Neapolitan friends, so far as could be ascertained, since the previous December; certainly she had not presented herself here in Naples to seek any engagement. The old *maestro*, in praying his illustrious and celebrated correspondent to accept his respectful submissions, likewise begged of him, should anything be learned with regard to the Signorina Rossi, to communicate farther. There was no hope in that quarter.

But one morning Estelle made a new suggestion.

"There is something I have recalled; yes, it is perhaps of not great importance; yet perhaps again," she said. "One day Nina and I, we were speaking of this thing and the other, and she said it was right and proper that a young lady should have a *dot*—what is the English?—no matter. She said the young lady should bring something towards the—the management; and she asked how she or I could do that. Then comes her plan. She was thinking of it before she arrives in England. It was to go to America—to be engaged for concerts—oh, they pay large, large salaries, if you have a good voice—and Nina would take engagements for all the big cities, until she got over to San Francisco, and from there to Australia—a great tour—a long time—but at the end, then she has the little fortune, and she is independent, whatever happens. Marriage?—well, perhaps not, but she is independent. Yes, it was Nina's plan to go away on that long tour; but she comes to England—she is engaged at the New Theatre—she practises her little economies—but not so as it would be in America, and now, now if she wishes to go away for a long, long time, is it not America? She goes on the long voyage; she forgets—what she wishes to forget. Her singing, it is constant occupation; she must work; and they welcome a good voice there—she will have friends. Do you consider it not possible? Yes, it is possible—for that is to go entirely away, and there is no danger of any one interfering."

"It's just frightful to think of," he said, "if what you imagine is correct. Fancy her crossing the Atlantic all by herself—landing in New York unknown to any human being there—"

"Ah, but do you fear for Nina?" Estelle cried. "No, no—she has courage—she has self-reliance, even in despair—she will have made preparations for all. Everywhere she has her passport—in her voice. 'I am Miss Ross, from the New Theatre, London,' she says. 'How do we know that you are Miss Ross?' 'Give me a sheet of music, then.' Perhaps it is in a theatre or a concert-room. Nina sings. 'Thank you, mademoiselle, it is enough; what are the terms you wish for an engagement?' Then it is finished, and Nina has all her plans made for her by the management; and she goes from one town to the other, far away perhaps; perhaps she has not much time to think of England. So much the better; poor Nina!"

And for a while he took an eager interest in the American newspapers. Such of them as he could get hold of he read diligently—particularly the columns in which concerts and musical entertainments were announced or reported. But there was no mention of Miss Ross, or of any new singer whom he could identify with her. Gradually he lost all hope in that direction also. He did not forget Nina. He could not; but he grew to think that—whether she were in America, or in Australia, or in whatever far land she might be—she had gone away forever. Her abrupt disappearance was no momentary withdrawal; she had sundered their familiar association, their close comradeship, that was never to be resumed; according to the old and sad refrain, it was "Adieu for evermore, my dear, and adieu for evermore!" Well, for him there were still crowded houses, with their dull thunders of applause; and there were cards and betting to send the one feverish hour flying after the other; and there were the lonely walks through the London streets in the daytime—when the hours did *not* fly so quickly. He had carefully put away those trinkets that Nina had returned to him; he would fain have forgotten their existence.

And then there was Miss Burgoyne. Miss Burgoyne could be very brisk and cheerful when she chose; and she now seemed bent on showing Mr. Lionel Moore the sunnier side of her character. In truth, she was most assiduously kind to the young man, even when she scolded him about the life he was leading. Her room and its mild refreshments were always at his disposal. She begged for his photograph, and, having got it, she told him to write something very nice and pretty at the foot of it; why should formalities be used between people so intimately and constantly associated? On more than one occasion she substituted a real rose (which was not nearly so effective, however) for the millinery blossom which Grace Mainwaring had to drop from the balcony to her lover below; and of course Lionel had to treasure the flower and keep it in water, until the hot and gassy atmosphere of his dressing-room killed it. Once or twice she called him Lionel, by way of pretty inadvertence.

There came an afternoon when the fog that had lain all day over London deepened and deepened until in the evening the streets were become almost impassable. The various members of the company, setting out in good time, managed to reach the theatre—though there were breathless accounts of adventures and escapes as this one or that hurried through the wings and down into the dressing-room corridor; but the public, not being paid to come forth on such a night, for the most part preferred the snugness and safety of their own homes, so that the house was but half filled, and the faces of the scant audience were more dusky than ever—were almost invisible—beyond the blaze of the footlights. And as the performance proceeded, Miss Burgoyne professed to become more and more alarmed. Dreadful reports came in from without. All traffic was suspended. It was scarcely possible to cross a street. Even the policemen, familiar with the thoroughfares, hardly dared leave the pavement to escort a bewildered traveller to the other side.

When Lionel, having dressed for the last act, went into Miss Burgoyne's room, he found her (apparently) very much perturbed.

"Have you heard? It's worse than ever!" she called to him from the inner apartment.

"So they say."

"Whatever am I to do?" she exclaimed, her anxiety proving too much for her grammar.

"Well, I think you couldn't do better than stop where you are," Harry Thornhill made answer, carelessly.

"Stop where I am? It's impossible! My brother Jim would go frantic. He would make sure I was run over or drowned or something, and be off to the police-stations."

"Oh, no, he wouldn't? he wouldn't stir out on such a night, if he had any sense."

"Not if he thought his sister was lost? That's all you know. There are some people who do have a little affection in their nature," said Miss Burgoyne, as she drew aside the curtain and came forth, and went to the tall glass. "But surely I can get a four-wheeled cab, Mr. Moore? I will give the man a sovereign to take me safe home. And even then it will be dreadful. I get so frightened in a bad fog—absolutely terrified—and especially at night. Supposing the man were to lose his way? Or he might be drunk? I wish I had asked Jim to come down for me. There's Miss Constance's mother never misses a single night; I wonder who she thinks is going to run away with that puny-faced creature!"

"Oh, if you are at all afraid to make the venture alone, I will go with you," said he. "I don't suppose I can see farther in a fog than any one else; but if you are nervous about being alone, you'd better let me accompany you."

"Will you?" she said, suddenly wheeling round, and bestowing upon him a glance of obvious gratitude. "That is indeed kind of you! Now I don't care for all the fogs in Christendom. But really and truly," she added—"really and truly you must tell me if I am taking you away from any other engagement."

"Not at all," he said, idly. "I had thought of going up to the Garden Club for some supper, but it isn't the sort of night for anybody to be wandering about. When I've left you in the Edgeware Road, I can find my way to my rooms easily. Once in Park Lane, I could go blindfold."

And very proud and pleased was Miss Burgoyne to accept his escort—that is to say, when he had, with an immense amount of trouble, brought a four-wheeled cab, accompanied by two link-boys with blazing torches, up to the stage-door. And when they had started off on their unknown journey through this thick chaos, she did not minimize the fears she otherwise should have suffered; this was thanking him by implication. As for the route chosen by the cabman, or rather by the link-boys, neither he nor she had the faintest idea what it was. Outside they could see nothing but the gold and crimson of the torches flaring through the densely yellow fog; while the grating of the wheels against the curb told them that their driver was keeping as close as he could to the pavement. Then they would find themselves leaving that guidance, and blindly adventuring out into the open thoroughfare to avoid some obstacle—some spectral wain or omnibus got hopelessly stranded; while there were muffled cries and calls here, there, and everywhere. They went at a snail's pace, of course. Once, at a corner, the near wheels got on the pavement; the cab tilted over; Miss Burgoyne shrieked aloud and clung to her companion; then there was a heavy bump, and the venerable vehicle resumed its slow progress. Suddenly they beheld a cluster of dim, nebulous, phantom lights high up in air.

"This must be Oxford Circus, surely," Lionel said.

He put his head out of the window and called to the cabman.

"Where are we now, cabby?"

"Blessed if I know, sir!" was the husky answer, coming from under the heavy folds of a cravat.

"Boy," he called again, "where are we? Is this Oxford Circus?"

"No, no, sir," responded the sharp voice of the London *gamin.* "We ain't 'alf way up Regent Street yet!"

He shut the window.

"At this rate, goodness only knows when you'll ever get home," he said to her. "You should have stopped at the theatre."

"Oh, I don't mind," said she, cheerfully. "It's an adventure. It's something to be talked of afterwards. I shouldn't wonder if the theatrical papers got hold of it—just the kind of paragraph to go the round—Harry Thornhill and Grace Mainwaring lost in a fog together. No, I don't mind. I'm very well off. But fancy some of those poor girls about the theatre, who must be trying to get home on foot. No four-wheeled cabs for them; no companion to keep up their spirits. I sha'n't forget your kindness, Mr. Moore."

Indeed, Lionel was much more anxious than she was. He would rather have done without that paragraph in the newspapers. All his senses were on the rack; and yet he could make out absolutely nothing of his whereabouts in this formless void of a world, with its opaque atmosphere, its distant calls, inquiries, warnings, its murky lamp-lights that only became visible when they were over one's head. Miss Burgoyne seemed to be well content, to be amused even. She liked to see her in the newspapers. There would be a pretty little paragraph to get quoted in gossippy columns, even if she and her more anxious fellow-adventurer did not reach home till breakfast-time.

The link-boys certainly deserved the very substantial reward that Lionel bestowed on them; for when, after what seemed interminable hours—with all kinds of stoppages and inquiries in this Egyptian darkness—the cab came to a final halt, and when Miss Burgoyne had been piloted across the pavement, she declared that here, indubitably, was her own door. Indeed, at this very moment it was opened, and there was a glimmer of a candle in the passage.

"No, Mr. Moore," she said, distinctly, when Lionel came back after paying the cabman, "you are not going off like that, certainly not. You must be starving; you must come up-stairs and have something to eat and drink." "Jim," she said, addressing her brother, who was standing there, candle in hand, "have you left any supper for us?"

"I haven't touched a thing yet," said he. "I've been waiting for you I don't know how long."

"There's a truly heroic brother!" exclaimed the young lady, as she pulled Lionel into the little lobby and shut the door. "What's enough for two is enough for three. Come along, Mr. Moore; and now you've got safely into a house, I think you'd much better have Jim's room for the night—or the morning, rather? I'm sure Jim won't mind taking the sofa."

"I? Not I!" said her brother, blowing out the candle as they entered the lamp-lit room.

It was a pretty room, and, with its blazing fire, looked very warm and snug after the cold, raw night without. Miss Burgoyne threw off her cloak and hat, and set to work to supplement the supper that was already laid on the central table. Her brother Jim—who was a dawdling, good-natured-looking lad of about fifteen, clad in a marvellous costume of cricketing trousers, a "blazer" of overpowering blue and yellow stripes, and an Egyptian fez set far back on his forehead—helped her to explore the contents of the cupboard; and very soon the three of them were seated at a comfortable and most welcome little banquet. Indeed, the charming little feast was almost sumptuous; insomuch that Lionel was inclined to ask himself whether Miss Burgoyne, who was an astute young lady, had not foreseen the possibility of this small supper-party before leaving home in the afternoon. The ousters, for example: did Miss Burgoyne order a dozen ousters for herself alone every evening?—for her brother declared that he never touched, and would not touch, any such thing. Lionel observed that his own photograph, which he had recently given her, had been accorded the place of honor on the mantel-shelf; another portrait of him, which she had bought, stood on the piano. But why these trivial suspicions, when she was so kind and hospitable and considerate? She pressed things on him; she herself filled up his glass; she was as merry as possible, and talkative and good-humored.

"Just to think we've known each other so long, and you've never been in my house before!" she said. "That's a portrait of my younger sister you're looking at—isn't she pretty? It's a pastel—Miss Corkran's. Of course she is not allowed to sit up for me; only Jim does that; he keeps me company at supper-time, for I couldn't sit down all by myself, could I, in the middle of the night? Oh, yes, you must have some more. I know gentlemen are afraid of champagne in a house looked after by a woman; but that's all right; that was sent me as a Christmas present by Mr. Lehmann."

"It is excellent," Lionel assured her, "but I must keep my head clear if I am to find my way into Park Lane; after that, it will be easy enough getting home."

"But there's Jim's room," she exclaimed.

"Oh, no, thank you," he said; "I shall get down there without any trouble."

And then she went to a cabinet that formed part of a book-case, and returned with a cigar-box in her hand.

"I am not so sure of these," she said. "They are some I got when papa was last in town, and he seemed to think them tolerable."

"Oh, but I sha'n't smoke, thanks; no, no, I couldn't think of it!" he protested. "You'll soon be coming down again to breakfast."

"To please me, Mr. Moore," she said, somewhat authoritatively. "I assure you there's nothing in the world I like so much as the smell of cigars."

What was she going to say next? But he took a cigar and lit it, and again she filled up his glass, which he had not emptied; and they set to talking about the Royal Academy of Music, while she nibbled Lychee nuts, and her brother Jim subsided into a French novel. Miss Burgoyne was a sharp and shrewd observer; she had had a sufficiently varied career, and had come through some amusing experiences. She talked well, but on this evening, or morning, rather, always on the good-natured side; if she described the foibles of any one with whom she had come in contact, it was with a laugh. Lionel was inclined to forget that outer world of thick, cold fog, so warm and pleasant was the bright and pretty room, so easily the time seemed to pass.

However, he had to tear himself away in the end. She insisted on his having a muffler of Jim's to wrap round his throat; both she and her brother went down-stairs to see him out; and then, with a hasty good-bye, he plunged into the dark. He had some difficulty in crossing to the top of Park Lane, for there were wagons come in from the country waiting for the daylight to give them some chance of moving on; but eventually he found himself in the well-known thoroughfare, and thereafter had not much trouble in getting down to his rooms in Piccadilly. This time he went to bed without sitting up in front of the fire in aimless reverie.

This was not the last he was to hear of that adventure. Two days afterwards the foreshadowed paragraph appeared in an evening paper; and from thence it was copied into all the weekly periodicals that deal more or less directly with theatrical affairs. It was headed "'The Squire's Daughter' in Wednesday Night's Fog," and gave a minute and somewhat highly colored account of Miss Burgoyne's experiences on the night in question; while the fact of her having been escorted by Mr. Lionel Moore was pointed to as another instance of the way in which professional people were always ready to help one another. That this account emanated in the first place from Miss Burgoyne herself, there could be no doubt whatever; for there were certain incidents—as, for example, the cab wheels getting up on the pavement and the near upsetting of the vehicle—which were only known to herself and her companion; but Lionel did not in his own mind accuse her of having directly instigated its publication. He thought it was more likely one of the advertising tricks of Mr. Lehmann, who was always trying to keep the chief members of his company well before the public. It was the first time, certainly, that he, Lionel, had had his name coupled (unprofessionally) with that of Miss Burgoyne in the columns of a newspaper; but was that of any consequence? People might think what they liked. He had grown a little reckless and careless of late.

"And again she filled up his glass, which he had not emptied."

But a much more important event was now about to happen which the theatrical papers would have been glad to get for their weekly gossip, had the persons chiefly concerned thought fit. Just at this time there was being formed in London, under distinguished patronage, a loan-collection of arms and embroideries of the Middle Ages, and there was to be a Private View on the Saturday preceding the opening of the exhibition to the public. Among others, Miss Burgoyne received a couple of cards of invitation, whereupon she came to Lionel, told him that her brother Jim was going to see some football match on that day, explained that she was very anxious to have a look at the precious needle-work, and virtually asked him to take her to the show. Lionel hung back; the crowd at this Private View was sure to include a number of fashionable folk; there might be one or two people there whom he would rather not meet. But Miss Burgoyne was gently persuasive, not to say pertinacious; he could not well refuse; finally it was arranged he should call for her about half past one o'clock on the Saturday, so that they might have a look round before the crush began in the afternoon.

Trust an actress to know how to dress for any possible occasion! When he called for her, he found her attired in a most charming costume; though, to be sure, when she was at last ready to go, he may have thought her furs a trifle too magnificent for her height. They drove in a hansom to Bond Street. There were few people in the rooms, certainly no one whom he knew; she could study those gorgeous treasures of embroidery from Italy and the East, he could examine the swords and daggers and coats of mail, as they pleased. And when they had lightly glanced round the rooms, he was for getting away again; but she was bent on remaining until the world should arrive, and declared that she had not half exhausted the interest of the various cases.

As it chanced, the first persons he saw whom he knew were Miss Georgie Lestrange and her brother; and Miss Georgie, not perceiving that any one was with him (for Miss Burgoyne was at the moment feasting her eyes on some rich-hued Persian stuffs), came up to him.

"Why, Mr. Moore, you have quite disappeared of late," the ruddy-haired damsel said, quite reproachfully. "Where have you been? What have you been doing?"

"Don't you ever read the newspapers, Miss Lestrange?" he said. "I have been advertised as being on view every night at the New Theatre."

"Oh, I don't mean that. Lady Adela says you have quite forsaken her."

"Is Lady Adela to be here this afternoon?" he asked, in an off-hand way.

"Oh, certainly," replied Miss Georgie. "She is going everywhere just now, in order to put everything into her new novel. It is to be a perfectly complete picture of London life as we see it around us."

"That is, the London between Bond Street and Campden Hill?"

"Oh, well, all London is too big for one canvas. You must cut it into sections. I dare say she will take up Whitechapel in her next book."

Miss Burgoyne turned from the glass case to seek her companion, and seemed a little surprised to find him talking to these two strangers. It was the swiftest glance; but Miss Georgie divined the situation in an instant.

"Good-bye for the present," she said, and she and her brother passed on.

And now he was more anxious than ever to get away. If Lady Adela and her sisters were coming to this exhibition, was it not highly probable that Honnor Cunyngham might be of the party? He did not wish to meet any one of them; especially did he not care to meet them while he was acting as escort to Miss Burgoyne. There were reasons which he could hardly define; he only knew that the clicking of the turnstile on the stair was an alarming sound, and that he regarded each new group of visitors, as they came into the room, with a furtive apprehension.

"Oh, very well," Miss Burgoyne said, at length, "let us go." And on the staircase she again said: "What is it? Are you afraid of meeting the mamma of some girl you've jilted? Or some man to whom you owe money for cards? Ah, Master Lionel, when are you going to reform and lead a steady and respectable life?"

He breathed more freely when he was outside; here, in the crowd, if he met any one to whom he did not wish to speak, he could be engaged with his companion and pass on without recognition. He proposed to Miss Burgoyne that they should walk home, by way of Piccadilly and Park Lane, and that young lady cheerfully assented. It was quite a pleasant afternoon, for London in midwinter. The setting sun shone with a dull-copper lustre along the fronts of the tall buildings, and over the trees of the Green Park hung clouds that were glorified by the intervening red-hued mists. The air was crisp and cold—what a blessing it was to be able to breathe!

Lionel was silent and absorbed; he only said, "Yes?" "Really!" "Indeed!" in answer to the vivacious chatter of his companion, who was in the most animated spirits. His brows were drawn down; his look was more sombre than it ought to have been, considering who was with him. Perhaps he was thinking of the crowded rooms they had recently left, and of the friends who might now be arriving there, from whom he had voluntarily isolated himself. Had they, had any one of them, counselled him to keep within his own sphere? Well, he had taken that advice; here he was—walking with Miss Burgoyne!

All of a sudden that young lady stopped and turned to the window of a jeweller's shop; and of course he followed. No wonder her eyes had been attracted; here were all kinds of beautiful things and splendors—tiaras, coronets, necklaces, pendants, bracelets, earrings, bangles, brooches—set with all manner of precious stones, the clear, radiant diamond, the purple amethyst, the sea-green emerald, the mystic opal, the blue-black sapphire, the clouded pearl. Her raptured vision wandered from tray to tray, but it was a comparatively trifling article that finally claimed her attention—a tiny finger-ring set with small rubies and brilliants.

"Oh, do look at this!" she said to her companion. "Did you ever see such a love of a ring?—what a perfect engagement-ring it would make!"

Then what mad, half-sullen, half-petulant, and wholly reckless impulse sprang into his brain!

"Well, will you wear that as an engagement-ring, if I give it to you?" he asked.

She looked up, startled, amused, but not displeased.

"Why, really—really—that *is* a question to ask!" she exclaimed.

"Come along in and see if it fits your finger—come along!" and therewith Miss Burgoyne, a little bewildered and still inclined to laugh, found herself at the jeweller's counter. Was it a joke? Oh, certainly not. Lionel was quite serious and matter of fact. The tray was produced. The ring was taken out. For a moment she hesitated as to which finger to try it on, but overcame that shyness and placed it on the third finger of her left hand and said it fitted admirably.

"Just keep it where it is, then," he said; and then he added a word or two to the jeweller, whom he knew; and he and his companion left the shop.

"Oh, Lionel, what an idea!" said Miss Burgoyne, with her eyes bent modestly on the pavement. "If I had fancied you knew that man, do you think I would ever have entered the place? What must he think? What would any one think?—an engagement in the middle of the streets of London!"

"Plenty of witnesses to the ceremony, that's all," said he, lightly.

Nay, was there not a curious sense of possession, now that he walked alongside this little, bright person in the magnificent furs? He had acquired something by this simple transaction; he would be less lonely now; he would mate with his kind. But he did not choose to look far into the future. Here he was walking along Piccadilly, with a cheerful and smiling and prettily costumed young lady by his side who had just been so kind as to accept an engagement-ring from him, and what more could he want?

"Lionel," she said, still with modestly downcast eyes, "this mustn't be known to any human being—no, not to a single human being—not yet, I mean. I will get a strip of white india-rubber to cover the ring, so that no one shall be able to see it on the stage."

Perhaps he recalled the fact that recently she had been wearing another ring similarly concealed from the public gaze; or perhaps he had forgotten that little circumstance. What did it matter? Did anything matter? He only knew he had pledged himself to marry Kate Burgoyne—enough.

CHAPTER XX.

IN DIRER STRAITS.

Now, when a young man, in whatever wayward mood of petulance or defiance or wounded self-love, chooses to play tricks with his own fate, he is pretty sure to discover that sooner or later he has himself to reckon with—his other and saner self that will arise and refuse to be silenced. And this awakening came almost directly to Lionel Moore. Even as he went down to the theatre that same evening, he began to wonder whether Miss Burgoyne would really be wearing the ring he had given her. Or would she not rather consider the whole affair a joke?—not a very clever joke, indeed, but at least something to be put on one side and forgotten. She had been inclined to laugh at the idea of two people becoming engaged to each other in the middle of the London streets. A life-pledge offered and accepted in front of a window in Piccadilly!—why, such was the way of comic opera, not of the actual world. Jests of that kind were all very well in the theatre, but they were best confined to the stage. And would not Miss Burgoyne understand that on a momentary impulse he had yielded to a fit of half-sullen recklessness, and would she not be quite ready and willing to release him?

But when, according to custom, he went into her room that evening, he soon became aware that Miss Burgoyne did not at all treat this matter as a jest.

"See!" she said to him, with a becoming shyness—and she showed him how cleverly she had covered her engagement-ring with a little band of flesh-tinted india-rubber, "No one will be able to see it? and I sha'n't have to take it off at all. Why, I could play Galatea, and not a human being would notice that the statue was wearing a ring!"

She seemed very proud and pleased and happy, though she spoke in an undertone, for Jane was within earshot. As for him, he did not say anything. Of course he was bound to stand by what he had done and suffer the consequences, whatever they might be. When he left the room and went up-stairs into the wings, it was in a vague sort of stupefaction; but here were the immediate exigencies of the stage, and perhaps it was better not to look too far ahead.

But it was with just a little sense of shame that he found, when the piece was over, and they were ready to leave the theatre, that Miss Burgoyne expected him to accompany her on her way home. If only he had had sufficient courage, he might have said to her,

"Look here; we are engaged to be married, and I'm not going to back out; I will fulfil my promise whenever you please. But for goodness' sake don't expect me to play the lover—off the stage as well as on. Sweethearting is a silly sort of business; don't we have enough every evening before the footlights? Let us conduct ourselves as rational human creatures—when we're not paid to make fools of ourselves. What good will it do if I drive home with you in this hansom? Do you expect me to put my arm round your waist? No, thanks; there isn't much novelty in that kind of thing for Grace Mainwaring and Harry Thornhill."

And when eventually they did arrive in Edgeware Road, she could not induce him to enter the house and have some bit of supper with herself and her brother Jim.

"What are you going to do to-morrow, then?" she asked. "Will you call for me in the morning and go to church with me?"

"I don't think I shall stir out to-morrow," he said, "I feel rather out of sorts; and I fancy I may try what a day in bed will do."

"How can you expect to be well if you sit up all night playing cards?" she demanded, with reason on her side. "However, there's to be no more of that now. So you won't come in—not for a quarter of an hour?"

She rang the bell.

"Oh, Lionel, by the way, do you think Jim should know?" she asked, with her eyes cast down in maiden modesty.

"Just as you like," he answered.

"Why, you don't seem to take any interest!" she exclaimed, with a pout. "I wonder what Percy Miles will say when he hears of it. Oh, my goodness, I'm afraid to think!"

"What he will say won't matter very much," Lionel remarked, indifferently.

"Poor boy! I'm sorry for him," she said, apparently with a little compunction, perhaps even regret.

The door was opened by her brother.

"Sure you won't come in?" she finally asked. "Well, I shall be at home all to-morrow afternoon, if you happen to be up in this direction. Good-night!"

"Good-night," said he, taking her outstretched hand for a second; then he turned and walked away. There had not been much love-making—so far.

But he did not go straight to his lodgings. He wandered away aimlessly through the dark streets. He felt sick at heart—not especially because of this imbroglio into which he had walked with open eyes, for that did not seem to matter much, one way or the other. But everything appeared to have gone wrong with him since Nina had left; and the worst of it was that he was gradually ceasing to care how things went, right or wrong. At this moment, for example, he ought to have been thinking of the situation he had created for himself, and resolving either to get out of it before more harm was done, or to loyally fulfil his contract by cultivating what affection for Miss Burgoyne was possible in the circumstances. But he was not thinking of Miss Burgoyne at all. He was thinking of Nina. He was thinking how hard it was that whenever his fancy went in search of her—away to Malta, to Australia, to the United States, as it might be—he could not hope to find a Nina whom he could recognize. For she would be quite changed now. His imagination could not picture to himself a Nina grown grave and sad-eyed, perhaps furtively hiding her sorrow, fearing to encounter her friends. The Nina whom he had always known was a light-hearted and laughing companion, eagerly talkative, a smile on her parted lips, affection, kindliness ever present in her shining, soft, dark eyes. Sometimes silent, too; sometimes, again, singing a fragment of one of the old familiar folk-songs of her youth. What was that one with the refrain, "*Io te voglio bene assaje, e tu non pienz' a me*"?—

"La notta tutte dormeno,

    E io che buò dormire!

    Pensanno a Nenna mia

    Mme sent' ascevolì.

Li quarte d' ora sonano

    A uno, a doje e tre...

    Io te voglio bene assaje,

    E tu non pienz' a me!"

—Look, now, at this beautiful morning—the wide bay all of silver and azure—Vesuvius sending its column of dusky smoke into the cloudless sky—the little steamer churning up the clear as it starts away from the quay. Ah, we have escaped from you, good Maestro Pandiani? there shall be no grumblings and incessant repetitions to-day? no, nor odors of onions coming up the narrow and dirty stairs: here is the open world, all shining, and the sweet air blowing by, and Battista trying to sell his useless canes, and the minstrels playing "Santa Lucia" most sentimentally, as though they had never played it before. Whither, then, Nina? To Castellamare or Sorrento, with their pink and yellow houses, their terraces and gardens, their vine-smothered bowers, or rather to the filmy island out yonder, that seems to move and tremble in the heat? A couple of words in their own tongue suffice to silence the importunate coral-girls; we climb the never-ending steps; behold, a cool and gracious balcony, with windows looking far out over the quivering plain of the sea. Then the soup, and the boiled corn, and the *caccia-cavallo*—you Neapolitan girl!—and nothing will serve you but that orris-scented stuff that you fondly believe to be honest wine. You will permit a cigarette? Then shall we descend to the beach again, and get into a boat, and lie down, and find ourselves shot into the Blue Grotto—find ourselves floating between heaven and earth in a hollow-sounding globe of azure flame?... Dreams—dreams! *"Io te voglio bene assaje, e tu non pienz' a me!"*

During the first period of Miss Burgoyne's engagement to Lionel Moore, all went well. Jane, her dresser, had quite a wonderful time of it; her assiduous and arduous ministrations were received with the greatest good-nature; now she was never told, if she hurt her mistress in lacing up a dress, that she deserved to have her face slapped. Miss Burgoyne was amiability itself towards the whole company, so far as she had any relations with them: and at her little receptions in the evening she was all brightness and merriment, even when she had to join in the conversation from behind the heavy *portière*. Whether this small coterie in the theatre guessed at the true state of affairs, it is hard to say; but at least Miss Burgoyne did not trouble herself much about concealment. She called her affianced lover "Lionel," no matter who chanced to be present; and she would ask him to help her to hand the tea, just as if he already belonged to her. Moreover, she told him that Mr. Percival Miles had some suspicion of what had happened.

"Not that I would admit anything definite," said the young lady. "There will be time enough for that. And I did not want a scene. But I'm sorry. It does seem a pity that so much devotion should meet with no requital."

"Devotion!" said Lionel.

"Oh, of course you don't know what devotion is. Your fashionable friends have taught you what good form is; you are *blasé*, indifferent; it's not women, it's cards, that interest you. You have no fresh feeling left," continued this *ingénue* of the greenroom. "You have been so spoiled—"

"I see he's up at the Garden Club," said Lionel, to change the subject.

"Who?"

"The young gentleman you were just speaking of."

"Percy Miles? What does he want with an all-night club?"

"I'm sure I don't know."

"Ah, well, I suppose he is not likely to get in," she said, turning to the tall mirror. "Percy is very nice—just the nicest boy I know—but I'm afraid he is not particularly clever. He has written some verses in one or two magazines—of course you can't expect me to criticise them severely, considering who was the 'only begetter' of them—"

"Oh, that has nothing to do with it," Lionel interrupted again. "He is sure to get in. There's no qualification at the Garden, so long as you're all right socially. There are plenty such as he in the club already."

"But why does he want to get in?" she said, wheeling round. "Why should he want to sit up all night playing cards? Now tell me honestly, Lionel, it isn't your doing! You didn't ask him to join, did you? You can't be treasuring up any feeling of vengeance—"

"Oh, nonsense; I had nothing to do with it. I saw his name in the candidates' book quite by accident. And the election is by committee—he'll get in all right. What does he want with it?—oh, I don't know. Perhaps he has been disappointed in love and seeks for a little consolation in card-playing."

"Yes, you always sneer at love—because you don't know anything about it," she said, snappishly. "Or perhaps you are an extinct volcano. I suppose you have sighed your heart out like a furnace—and for a foreigner, I'll be bound!"

Nay, it was hardly to be wondered at that Miss Burgoyne should be indignant with so lukewarm and reluctant a lover, who received her coy advances with coldness, and was only decently civil to her when they talked of wholly indifferent matters. The mischief of it was that, in casting about for some key to the odd situation, she took it into her head to become jealous of Nina; and many were the bitter things she managed to say about foreigners generally, and about Italians in particular, and Italian singers, and so forth. Of course Miss Ross was never openly mentioned, but Lionel understood well enough at whom these covert innuendoes were hurled; and sometimes his eyes burned with a fire far other than that which should be in a lover's eyes when contemplating his mistress. Indeed, it was a dangerous amusement for Miss Burgoyne to indulge in. It was easy to wound; it might be less easy to efface the memory of those wounds. And then there was a kind of devilish ingenuity about her occult taunts. For example, she dared not say that doubtless Miss Nina Ross had gone away back to Naples, and had taken up with a sweetheart, with whom she was now walking about; but she described the sort of young man calculated to capture the fancy of an Italian girl.

"The seedy swell of Naples or Rome—he is irresistible to the Italian girl," she said, on one occasion. "You know him; his shirt open at the neck down almost to his chest—his trousers tight at the knee and enormously wide at the foot—a poncho-looking kind of cloak, with a greasy Astrachan collar— a tall French hat, rather shabby—a face the color of paste—an odor of cigarettes and garlic—dirty hands—and a cane. I suppose the theatre is too expensive, so he goes to the public gardens, and strolls up and down, and takes off his hat with a sweep to people he pretends to recognize; or perhaps he sits in front of a *café*, with a glass of cheap brandy before him, an evening journal in his hands, and a toothpick in his mouth."

"You seem to have made his very particular acquaintance," said he, with a touch of scorn. "Did he give you his arm when you were walking together in the public gardens?"

"Give *me* his arm?" she exclaimed. "I would not allow such a creature to come within twenty yards of me! I prefer people who use soap."

"What a pity it is they can't invent soap for purifying the mind!" he said, venomously; and he went out, and spoke no more to her during the rest of that evening.

Matters went from bad to worse: for Miss Burgoyne, finding nothing else that could account for his habitual depression of spirits, his occasional irritability and obvious indifference towards herself, made bold to assume that he was secretly, even if unconsciously, fretting over Nina's absence; and her jealousy grew more and more angry and vindictive, until it carried her beyond all bounds. For now she began to say disparaging or malicious things about Miss Ross, and that without subterfuge. At last there came a climax.

She had sent for him (for he did not invariably go into her room before the beginning of the last act, as once he had done), and, as she was still in the inner apartment, he took a chair, and stretched out his legs, and flicked a spot or two of dust from his silver-buckled shoes.

"What hour did you get home *this* morning?" she called to him, in rather a saucy tone.

"I don't know exactly."

"And don't care. You are leading a pretty life," she went on, rather indiscreetly, for Jane was with her. "Distraction! Distraction from what?

You sit up all night; you eat supper at all hours of the morning; you get dyspepsia and indigestion; and of course you become low-spirited—then there must be distraction. If you would lead a wholesome life you wouldn't need any distraction."

"Oh, don't worry!" he said, impatiently.

"What's come over that Italian friend of yours—that Miss Ross?"

"I don't know."

"You've never heard anything of her?"

"No—nothing."

"Don't you call that rather cool on her part? You introduce her to this theatre, you get her an engagement, you befriend her in every way, and all of a sudden she bolts, without a thank you!"

"I presume Miss Ross is the best judge of her own actions," said he, stiffly.

"Oh, you needn't be so touchy!" said Grace Thornhill, as she came forth in all the splendor of her bridal array, and at once proceeded to the mirror. "But I can quite understand your not liking having been treated in that fashion. People often are deceived in their friends, aren't they? And there's nothing so horrid as ingratitude. Certainly she ought to have been grateful to you, considering the fuss you made about her—the whole company remarked it!"

He did not answer; he did not even look her way; but there was an angry cloud gathering on his brows.

"No; very ungrateful, I call it," she continued, in the same dangerously supercilious tone. "You take up some creature you know nothing about and befriend her, and even make a spectacle of yourself through the way you run after her, and all at once she says, 'Good-bye? I've had enough of you'—and that's all the explanation you have!"

"Oh, leave Miss Ross alone, will you?" he said, in accents that might have warned her.

Perhaps she was unheeding; perhaps she was stung into retort; at all events, she turned and faced him.

"Leave her alone?" she said, with a flash of defiance in her look. "It is you who ought to leave her alone! She has cheated you—why should you show temper? Why should you sulk with every one, simply because an Italian organ-grinder has shown you what she thinks of you? Oh, I suppose the heavens must fall, because you've lost your pretty plaything—that made a laughing-stock of you? You don't even know where she is—I can tell you!—wandering along in front of the pavement at Brighton, in a green petticoat and a yellow handkerchief on her head, and singing to a concertina! That's about it, I should think; and very likely the seedy swell is waiting for her in their lodgings—waiting for her to bring the money home!"

Lionel rose; he said not a word; but the pallor of his face and the fire in his eyes were terrible to see. Plainly enough she saw them; but she was only half-terrified; she seemed aroused to a sort of whirlwind of passion.

"Oh, say it!" she cried. "Why don't you say it? Do you think I don't see it in your eyes? '*I hate you!*—that's what you want to say; and you haven't the courage—you're a man, and you haven't the courage!"

That look did not depart from his face; but he stood in silence for a second, as if considering whether he should speak. His self-control infuriated her all the more.

"Do you think I care?" she exclaimed, with panting breath. "Do you think I care whether you hate me or not—whether you go sighing all day after your painted Italian doll? And do you imagine I want to wear this thing—that it is for this I will put up with every kind of insult and neglect? Not I!"

She pulled the bit of india-rubber from her finger; she dragged off the engagement-ring and dashed it on the floor in front of his feet—while her eyes sparkled with rage, and the cherry-paste hardly concealed the whiteness of her lips.

"Take it—and give it to the organ-grinder!" she called, in the madness of her rage.

He did not even look whither the ring had rolled. Without a single word he quite calmly turned and opened the door and passed outside. Nay, he was so considerate as to leave the door open for her; for he knew she would be wanted on the stage directly. He himself went up into the wings—in his gay costume of satin and silk and powdered wig and ruffles.

Had the audience only known, during the last act of this comedy, what fierce passions were agitating the breasts of the two chief performers in this pretty play, they might have looked on with added interest. How could they tell that the gallant and dashing Harry Thornhill was in his secret heart filled with anger and disdain whenever he came near his charming sweetheart? how could they divine that the coquettish Grace Mainwaring was not thinking of her wiles and graces at all, but was on the road to a most piteous repentance? The one was saying to himself, "Very well, let the vixen go to the devil; a happy riddance!" and the other was saying, "Oh, dear me, what have I done?—why did he put me in such a passion?" But the public in the stalls were all unknowing. They looked on and laughed, or looked on and sat solemn and stolid, as happened to be their nature; and then they slightly clapped their pale-gloved hands, and rose and donned their cloaks and coats. They had forgotten what the piece was about by the time they reached their broughams.

Later on, at the stage-door, whither a four-wheeler had been brought for her, Miss Burgoyne lingered. Presently Lionel came along. He would have passed her, but she intercepted him; and in the dusk outside she thrust forth her hand.

"Will you forgive me, Lionel? I ask your forgiveness," she said, in an undertone that was suggestive of tears. "I don't know what made me say such things—I didn't mean them—I'm very sorry. See," she continued, and in the dull lamp-light she showed him her ungloved hand, with the engagement-ring in its former place—"I have put on the ring again. Of course, you are hurt and offended; but you are more forgiving than a woman—a man should be. I will never say a word against her again; I should have remembered how you were companions before she came to England; and I can understand your affection for her, and your—your regret about her going away. Now will you be generous?—will you forgive me?"

"Oh, yes, that's all right," he said—as he was bound to say.

"But that's not enough. Will you come now and have some supper with Jim and me, and we'll talk about everything—except that one thing?"

"No, thanks, I can't; I have an engagement," he made answer.

She hesitated for a moment. Then she offered him her hand again.

"Well, at all events, bygones are to be bygones," she said. "And to-morrow I'm going to begin to knit a woollen vest for you, that you can slip on before you come out. Good-night, dearest!"

"Good-night," he said; and he opened the door of the cab for her and told the cabman her address; then—rather slowly and absently—he set out for the Garden Club.

The first person he beheld at the Garden Club was Octavius Quirk—of course at the supper-table.

"Going to Lady Adela's on the 3d?" said the bilious-looking Quirk, in a gay manner.

"I should want to be asked first," was Lionel's simple rejoinder.

"Ah!" said the other, complacently, "I heard you had not been much there lately. A charming house—most interesting—quite delightful to see people of their station so eagerly devoted to the arts. Music, painting, literature—all the elegancies of life—and all touched with a light and graceful hand. You should read some of Lady Adela's descriptions in her new book—not seen it?—no?—ah, well, it will be out before long for the general world to read. As I was saying, her descriptions of places abroad are simply charming—charming. There's where the practised traveller comes in; no heavy and laborious work; the striking peculiarities hit off with the most delicate appreciation: the *fine fleur* of difference noted everywhere. Your bourgeois goes and rams his bull's head against everything he meets; he's in wonderment and ecstacy almost before he lands; he stares with astonishment at a fisherwoman on Calais pier and weeps maudlin tears over the masonry of the Sainte Chapelle. Then Lady Adela's style—marvellous, marvellous. I give you my word as an expert! Full of distinction; choice; fastidious; penetrated everywhere by a certain *je ne sais quoi* of dexterity and aptitude; each word charged with color, as a critic might say. You have not seen any of the sheets?" continued Mr. Quirk, with his mouth full of steak and olives. "Dear me! You haven't quarrelled with Lady Adela, have you? I did hear there was some little disappointment that you did not get Lady Sybil's 'Soldiers' Marching Song' introduced at the New Theatre; but I dare say the composer wouldn't have his operetta interfered with. Even you are not all-powerful. However, Lady Adela is unreasonable if she has taken offence: I will see that it is put right."

"I wouldn't trouble you—thanks!" said Lionel, rather coldly; and then, having eaten a biscuit and drank a glass of claret and water, he went up-stairs to the card-room.

There were two tables occupied—one party playing whist, the other poker; to the latter Lionel idly made his way.

"Coming in, Moore?"

"Oh, yes, I'll come in. What are you playing?"

"Usual thing: sixpenny ante and five-shilling limit."

"Let's have it a shilling ante and a sovereign limit," he proposed, as they made room for him at the table, and to this they agreed, and the game began.

At first Lionel could get no hands at all, but he never went out; sometimes he drew four cards to an ace or a queen, sometimes he took the whole five; while his losses, if steady, were not material. Occasionally he bluffed, and got a small pot; but it was risky, as he was distinctly in a run of bad luck. At last he was dealt nine, ten, knave, queen, ace, in different suite. This looked better.

"How many?" asked the dealer.

"I will take one card, if you please," he said, throwing away the ace.

He glanced at the card, as he put it into his hand: it was a king; he had a straight. Then he watched what the others were taking. The player on his left also asked for one—a doubtful intimation. His next neighbor asked for two—probably he had three of a kind. The dealer threw up his cards. The age had already taken three—no doubt he had started with the common or garden pair.

It was Lionel's turn to bet.

"Well," said he, "I will just go five shillings on this little lot."

"I will see your five shillings and go a sovereign better," said his neighbor.

"That's twenty-five shillings for me to come in," said he who had taken two cards. "Well, I'll raise you another sovereign."

The age went out.

"Two sovereigns against me," said Lionel "Very well, then, I'll just raise you another."

"And another."

This frightened the third player, who incontinently retired. There were now left in only Lionel and his antagonist, and each had drawn but one card. Now the guessing came in. Had the player been drawing to two pairs, or to fill a flush or a straight; had he got a full hand; or was he left with his two pairs; or, again, had he failed to fill, and was he betting on a perfectly worthless lot? At all events the two combatants kept hammering away at each other, until there was a goodly pile of gold on the table, and the interest of the silent onlookers was proportionately increased. Were both bluffing and each afraid to call the other? Or was it that cruel and horrible combination—a full hand betting against four of a kind?

"I call you," said Lionel's enemy, at length, as he put down the last sovereign he had on the table.

"A straight," was Lionel's answer, as he showed his cards.

"Not good enough, my boy," said the other, as he calmly ranged a flush of diamonds before him.

"Take away the money, Johnny," said Lionel, as if it were a matter of no moment. "Or wait a second; I'll go you double or quits."

But here there was an almost general protest.

"Oh, what's the use of that, Moore? It was the duke who brought that nonsense in, and it ought to be stopped; it spoils the game. Stick to the legitimate thing. When you once begin that stupidity, there's no stopping it."

However, the player whom Lionel had challenged had no mind to deny him.

"For the whole pot, or for what you put in?" he asked.

"Either—whichever you like," Lionel said, carelessly.

"We'll say the whole pot, then: either I give you what's on the table, or you double it," the lucky young gentleman made answer, as he proceeded to count the sovereigns and chips—there was £28 in all. "Will you call to me? Very well. What do you say this is?"—spinning a sovereign.

"I say it's a head," Lionel replied.

"You've made a mistake, then—very sorry," said the other, as he raked in his own money.

"I owe you twenty-eight pounds, Johnny," Lionel said, without more ado; and he took out his note-book and jotted it down. Then they went on again.

Now the game of poker is played in calm; happy is he who can preserve a perfectly expressionless face through all its vicissitudes. But the game of whiskey-poker (which is no game) is played amid vacuous excitement and strong language and derisive laughter—especially towards four in the morning. The whole of this little party seemed ready to go; in fact, they had all risen and were standing round the table; but nevertheless they remained, while successive hands were dealt, face upwards. At first only a sovereign each was staked, then two, then three, then four, then five—and there a line was drawn. But in staking five sovereigns every time, with four to one against you, a considerable amount of money can be lost; and Lionel had been in ill-luck all the sitting. He did not, however, seem to mind his losses, so long as the fierce spirit of gambling could be kept up; and it was with no desperate effort at recovering his money that he was always for increasing the stakes. He would have sat down at the table and gone on indefinitely with this frantic plunging, but that his companions declared they must go directly; at last three of them solemnly swore they would have only one round more. There were then left in only Lionel and the young fellow who had won his £28 early in the evening.

"Johnny, I'll go you once for twenty pounds," Lionel said.

"Done with you."

"I say, you fellows," protested one of the bystanders, "you'll smash up this club—you'll have the police shutting it up as a gambling-hell. Besides, you're breaking the rules; you'll have the committee expelling you."

"What rules?" Lionel's opponent asked, wheeling round.

"The amount of the stakes, for one thing; and playing after three o'clock, for another," was the answer.

"I'll bet you ten pounds there's no limit as to time in the rules of this club— I mean as regards card-playing," the young man said, boldly.

"I take you."

The bell was rung; a waiter was sent to fetch a List of Members; and then he who had accepted the bet read out these solemn words:

"Rule XIX. No higher stakes than guinea points shall ever be played for, nor shall any card or billiard playing be permitted in the club after 3 A.M."

"There's your confounded money; what a fool of a club to let you stay here all night if you like, and to stop card-playing at three!" He turned to Lionel. "Well, Moore, what did you say: twenty pounds? I'll just make it thirty, if you like, and see if I can't get back that ten."

"Right with you, Johnny."

The young man dealt the two hands: he found he had a pair of fours, Lionel nothing but a king. The winner took over the loser's I.O.U. for the £30, and then said,

"Well, now, I'll go you double or quits."

"Oh, certainly," said Lionel, "if you like. But I don't think you should. You are the winner; stick to what you've got."

"Oh, I'll give you a chance to get it all back," the young man said; and this time Lionel dealt the cards. And again the latter lost—having to substitute an I.O.U. for £60 for its predecessor.

"Well, now, I'll give you one more chance," the winner said, with a laugh.

"I'm hanged if you shall, Johnny!" said one of the bystanders; and he had the courage to intervene and snatch up the cards. "Come away to your beds, boys, and stop that nonsense! You've lost enough, Moore; and this fellow would go on till Doomsday."

But that insatiate young man was not to be beaten, after all. When they were separating in the street below he drew Lionel aside.

"Look here, old man, why should we be deprived of our final little flutter? I want to give you a chance of getting back the whole thing."

"Not at all, my good fellow," Lionel said, with a smile. "Why don't you keep the money and rest content? Do you think I grudge it to you?"

"Come—an absolutely last double or quits," said the other, and he pulled out a coin from his pocket and put it between his two palms. "Heads or tails?—and then go home happy!"

"Well, since you challenge me, I'll go this once more, and this once more only. I call a tail."

The upper hand was removed: in the dull lamp-light the dusky gold coin was examined.

"It's a head," said Lionel, "so that's all right, and it's you who are to go home happy. I'll settle up with you to-morrow evening. Do you want this hansom?—I don't: I think I'd rather walk. Good-night, Johnny."

It was a long price to pay for a few hours of distraction and forgetfulness; still, he had had these; and the loss of the money, *per se*, did not affect him much. He walked away home. When he reached his rooms, there were some letters for him lying on the table; he took them and looked at them; he noticed one handwriting that used to be rather more familiar. This letter he opened first.

AIVRON LODGE, CAMPDEN HILL, *Feb.* 23.

"MY DEAR MR. MOORE,—It is really quite shocking the way you have neglected us of late, and I, at least, cannot imagine any reason. Perhaps we have both been in fault. My sisters and I have all been very busy, in our several ways; and then it is awkward you should have only the one Sunday evening free. But there, let *bygones* be *bygones*, and come and dine with us on Sunday, March 3, at 8. Forgive the short notice; I've had some trouble in trying to secure one, or two people whom I don't know very well, and I couldn't fix earlier. The fact is, I want it to be an *intellectual* little dinner; and who could represent music and the drama so fitly as yourself? I want only people with brains at it—perhaps you wouldn't include Rockminster in that category, but I must have him to help me, as my husband is away in Scotland looking after his beasts. Now do be good-natured, dear Mr. Moore, and say you will come.

"And I am going to try your goodness another way. You remember speaking to me about a friend of yours who was connected with newspapers, and who knew some of the London correspondents of the provincial journals? Could you oblige me with his address and the correct spelling of his name? I presume he would not consider it out of the way if I wrote to him as being a friend of yours, and enclosed a card of invitation. I want to have *all* the *talents*—that is, all of them I can get to come and honor the house of a mere novice and beginner. I did not catch either your friend's surname or his Christian name.

ADELA CUNYNGHAM."

Ever yours sincerely,

He tossed the letter on to the table.

"I wonder," he said to himself, "how much of that is meant for me, and how much for Maurice Mangan and newspaper paragraphs."

But it was high time to get to bed; and that he did without any serious fretting over his losses at the Garden Club. These had amounted, on the whole gamble, to nearly £170; which might have made him pause. For did he not owe responsibilities elsewhere? If he went on at this rate (he ought to have been asking himself) whence was likely to come the money for the plenishing of a certain small household—an elegant little establishment towards which Miss Kate Burgoyne was no doubt now looking forward with pleased and expectant eyes.

CHAPTER XXI.

IN A DEN OF LIONS, AND THEREAFTER.

When Maurice Mangan, according to appointment, called at Lionel's rooms on the evening of Lady Adela Cunyngham's dinner-party, he was surprised to find his friend seated in front of the fire, wrapped up in a dressing-gown.

"Linn, what's the matter with you?" he exclaimed, looking at him. "Are you ill? What have you been doing to yourself?"

"Oh, nothing," was the answer. "I have been rather worried and out of sorts lately, that is all. And I can't go to that dinner to-night, Maurice. Will you make my excuses for me, like a good fellow? Tell Lady Adela I'm awfully sorry—"

"I'm sure I sha'n't do anything of the sort," Mangan said, promptly. "Do you think I am going to leave you here all by yourself? You know why I accepted the invitation: mere curiosity; I wanted to see you among those people—I wanted to describe to Miss Francie how you looked when you were being adored—"

"My dear chap, you would have seen nothing of the sort," Lionel said. "To-night there is to be a shining galaxy of genius, and each particular star will be eager to absorb all the adoration that is going. Authors, actors, painters, musicians—that kind of people; kid-gloved Bohemia."

"Come, Linn; rouse yourself, man," his friend protested. "You'll do no good moping here by the fire. There's still time for you to dress; I came early in case you might want to walk up to Campden Hill. And you shouldn't disappoint your friends, if this is to be so great an occasion."

"I suppose you're right," Lionel said, and he rose wearily, "though I would twenty times rather go to bed. You can find a book for yourself, Maurice; I sha'n't keep you many minutes," and with that he disappeared into his dressing-room.

A four-wheeler carried them up to Campden Hill; a welcome glow of light shone forth on the carriage-drive and the dark bushes. As they entered and crossed the wide hall, they were preceded by a young lady whose name was at the same moment announced at the door of the drawing-room—"Miss Gabrielle Grey."

"Oh, really," said Mangan to his companion, as they were leaving their coats and hats. "I always thought 'Gabrielle Grey' was the pseudonym of an elderly clergyman's widow, or somebody of that kind."

"But who is Miss Gabriel Grey?"

"You mean to say you have never even heard of her? Oh, she writes novels—very popular, too, and very deservedly so, for that kind of thing— excellent in tone, highly moral, and stuffed full of High-Church sentiment; and I can tell you this, Linn, my boy, that for a lady novelist to have plenty of High-Church sentiment at her command is about equivalent to holding four of a kind at poker—and that's an illustration you'll understand. Now come and introduce me to my hostess, and tell me who all the people are."

Lady Adela received both Lionel and his friend in the most kindly manner.

"What a charming photograph that is of you in evening dress," she said to Lionel. "Really, I've had to lock away my copy of it; girls are such thieves nowadays; they think nothing of picking up what pleases them and popping it in their pockets." And therewith Lady Adela turned to Mr. Quirk, with whom she had been talking; and the new-comers passed on, and found themselves in a corner from whence they could survey the room.

The first glance revealed to Lionel that, if all the talents were there, the "quality" was conspicuously absent.

"I know hardly anybody here," he said, in an undertone, to Mangan.

"Oh, I know some of them," was the answer, also in an undertone. "Rather small lions—I think she might have done better with proper guidance. But perhaps this is only a beginning. Isn't your friend Quirk a picture? Who is the remarkably handsome girl just beyond?"

"That's Lady Adela's sister, Lady Sybil."

"The composer? I see; that's why she's talking to that portentous old ass, Schweinkopf, the musical critic. Then there's Miss Gabrielle Grey—poor thing! she's not very pretty—'I was not good enough for man, and so am given to'—publishers. By Jove, there's Ichabod—standing by the door; don't you know him?—Egerton—but they call him Ichabod at the Garrick. Now, what could our hostess expect to get out of Ichabod? He has nothing left to him but biting his nails like the senile Pope or Pagan in the 'Pilgrim's Progress.'"

"What does he do?"

"He is a reviewer, *et prœterea nihil*. Some twenty years ago he wrote two or three novels, but people wouldn't look at them, and so he became morose about the public taste and modern literature. In fact, there has been no English literature—for twenty years; this is his wail and moan whenever an editor allows him to lift up his voice. It was feeble on the part of your friend to ask Ichabod; she won't get anything out of him. I can see a reason for most of the others—those whom I know; but Ichabod is hopeless."

Mangan suddenly ceased these careless comments; his attention was arrested by the entrance of a tall young lady who came in very quietly—without being announced even.

"I say, who's that?" he exclaimed, under his breath.

And Lionel had been startled too; for he had convinced himself ere he came that Honnor Cunyngham was certain to be in Scotland. But there she was, as distinguished-looking, as self-possessed as ever; her glance direct and simple and calm, though she seemed to hesitate for a moment as if seeking for some one whom she might know in the crowd. From the fact of her not having been announced, Lionel guessed that she was staying in the house; perhaps, indeed, she had been in the drawing-room before. He hardly knew what to do. He forgot to answer his friend's question. If dinner were to be happily announced now, would it not save her from some embarrassment if he and she could go in their separate ways without meeting? and thereafter he could leave without returning to the drawing-room. Yet, if she were staying in the house, she must have known that he was coming?

All this swift consideration was the work of a single second; the next second Miss Honnor's eyes had fallen upon the young man; and immediately and in the most natural way in the world she came across the room to him. It is true that there was a slight touch of color visible on the gracious forehead when she offered him her hand; but there was no other sign of self-consciousness; and she said, quite quietly and simply,

"It is some time since we have met, Mr. Moore; but, of course, I notice your name in the papers frequently."

"I hardly expected to see you here to-night," he said, in reply. "I thought you would be off to Scotland for the salmon-fishing."

"I go to-morrow night," she made answer.

At the same moment Lord Rockminster came up, holding a bit of folded paper furtively in his hand; the faithful brother looked perplexed, for he had to remember the names of these various strangers; but here at least were two whom he did know.

"Mr. Moore, will you take Miss Cunyngham in to dinner?" he murmured, as he went by; so that Lionel found there would have been no escape for him in any case. But now that the first little awkwardness of their meeting was over, there was nothing else. Miss Cunyngham spoke to him quite pleasantly and naturally—though she did not meet his eyes much.

Meantime dinner was announced, and Lord Rockminster led the way with a trim little elderly lady whom Lionel afterwards discovered to be (for she told him as much) the London correspondent of a famous Parisian journal devoted to fashions and the *beau monde*.

And here he was, seated side by side with Honnor Cunyngham, talking to her, listening to her, and with no sort of perturbation whatever. He began to ask himself whether he had ever been in love with her—whether he had not rather been in love with her way of life and its surroundings. He was thinking not so much of her as her departure on the morrow, and the scenes that lay beyond. Why had he not £10,000 a year—£5000—nay, £1000 a year—and freedom? Why could he not warm his soul with the consciousness that the salmon-rods were all packed and waiting in the hall; that new casting-lines had been put in the fly-book; that only the short drive up to Euston and a single black night lay between him and all the wide wonder of the world that would open out thereafter? Forth from the darkness into a whiter light—a larger day—a sweeter air; for now we are among the russet beech-hedges, the deep-green pines, the purple hills touched here and there with snow; and the far-stretching landscape is shining in the morning sun; and the peewits are wheeling hither and thither in the blue. Then we are thundering through rocky chasms and watching the roaring brown torrent beneath; or panting or struggling away up the lonely altitudes of Drumouchter; and again merrily racing and chasing down into the spacious valley of the Spey. And what for the end?—the long, still strath after leaving Invershin—the penetration into the more secret solitudes—the peaks of Coulmore and Suilven in the west—and here the Aivron making a murmuring music over its golden gravel! There is a smell of peat in the air; there are children's voices about the keepers' cottages; and here is the handsome old Robert, rejoiced that the year has opened again and Miss Honnor come back! "Well, Robert, you must come in and have a dram, and I will show you the tackle I've brought with me." "I am not wishing for a dram, Miss Honnor, so much as I am glad to see you back again, ay, and looking so well!"

"Mr. Moore," she said (and she startled him out of his reverie), "do you ever give a little dinner-party at your rooms?"

"Well, seldom," he said. "You see, I have only the one evening in the week; and I have generally some engagement or other."

"There was a slight touch of color visible on the gracious forehead when she offered him her hand."

"I should like to send you a salmon, if it would be of any use to you," she went on to say.

"Thank you very much; I would rather see you hook and land it than have the compliment of its being sent to me twenty times over. I was thinking this very minute of the Aivron, and your getting down to the ford the day after to-morrow, and old Robert being there to welcome you. I envy him—and you. Are you to be all by yourself at the lodge?"

"For the present, yes," Miss Honnor said. "My brother and Captain Waveney come at the beginning of April. Of course it is rather hazardous going just now; the river might be frozen over for a fortnight at a time; but that seldom happens. And in ordinarily mild weather it is very beautiful up there—the most beautiful time of the year, I think; the birch-woods are all of the clearest lilac, and the brackens turned to deep crimson; then the bent grass on the higher hills—what they call deer's hair—is a mass of gold. And I don't in the least mind being alone in the evening—in fact, I enjoy it. It is a splendid time for reading. There is not a sound. Caroline comes in from time to time to pile on more peats and sweep the hearth; then she goes out again; and you sit in an easy-chair with your back to the lamp; and if you've got an interesting book, what more company do you want? Then it's very early to bed in Strathaivron; and I've got a room that looks both ways—across the strath and down; and sometimes there is moonlight making the windows blue; or if there isn't, you can lie and look at the soft red light thrown out by the peat, until the silence is too much for you, and you are asleep before you have had time to think of it. Now tell me about yourself," she suddenly said. "I hope the constant work and the long and depressing winter have not told on you. It must have been very unpleasant getting home so late at night during the fogs."

He would rather she had continued talking about the far Aivron and the Geinig; he did not care to come back to the theatre and Kate Burgoyne.

"One gets used to everything, I suppose," he said.

"But still it must be gratifying to you to be in so successful a piece—to be aware of the delight you are giving, evening after evening, to so many people," Miss Honnor reminded him. "By the way, how is the pretty Italian girl—the young lady you said you had known in Naples?"

"She has left the New Theatre," he said, not lifting his eyes.

"Oh, really. Then I'm sure that must have been unfortunate for the operetta; for she had such a beautiful voice—she sang so exquisitely—and besides that there was go much refinement and grace in everything she did. I remember mother was so particularly struck with her; we have often spoken of her since; her manner on the stage was so charming—so gentle and graceful—it had a curious fascination that was irresistible. And I confess I was delighted with the little touch of foreign accent; perhaps if she had not been so very pretty, one would have been less ready to be pleased with everything. And where is she now, Mr. Moore?"

"I'm sure I don't know," Lionel said, rather unwillingly; he would rather not have been questioned.

"And is that how friendships in the theatre are kept up?" Miss Honnor said, reproachfully. "But it is all very well for us idle folk to talk. I suppose you are all far too busy to give much time to correspondence."

"No, we have not much time for letter-writing," he said, absently.

Indeed, it was well for him that he had this companion who could talk to him in her quiet, low tones; for he was out of spirits and inclined to be silent; and certainly he had no wish to join in the frothy discussion which Octavius Quirk had started at the upper end of the table. Mr. Mellord, the famous Academician, had taken in Lady Adela to dinner; but she had placed Mr. Quirk on her left hand; and from this position of authority he was roaring away like any sucking-dove and challenging everybody to dispute his windy platitudes. Lord Rockminster, down at the other end, mute and in safety, was looking on at this motley little assemblage, and probably wondering what his three gifted sisters would do next. It was hard that he had no Miss Georgie Lestrange to amuse him; perhaps Miss Georgie had been considered ineligible for admission into this intellectual coterie. Poor man!—and to think he might have been dining in solitary comfort at his club, at a quiet little table, with two candles, and a Sunday paper propped up by the water-bottle! But he betrayed no impatience; he sat and looked and meditated.

However, when dinner was over and the ladies had left the room, he had to go and take his sister's place, so that he found himself in the thick of the babble. Mr. Quirk was no longer goring spiders' webs; he was now attacking a solid and substantial subject—nothing less than the condition of the British army; and a pretty poor opinion he seemed to have of it. As it chanced, the only person who had seen service was Lord Rockminster (at Knightsbridge), but he did not choose to open his mouth, so that Mr. Quirk had it all his way—except when Maurice Mangan thought it worth while to give him a cuff or a kick, just by way of reminding him that he was mortal. Ichabod, in silence, stuck to the port wine. Quincey Hooper, the American journalist, drew in a chair by the side of Lord Rockminster and humbly fawned. And meanwhile Quirk, head downward, so to speak, charged rank and file, and sent them flying; arose again and swept the heads off officers; and was just about to annihilate the volunteers when Mangan interrupted him.

"Oh, you expect too much," he said, in his slow and half-contemptuous fashion. "The British soldier is not over well-educated, I admit; but you needn't try him by an impossible standard. I dare say you are thinking of ancient days when a Roman general could address his troops in Latin and make quite sure of being understood; but you can't expect Tommy Atkins to be so learned. And our generals, as you say, may chiefly distinguish themselves at reviews; but the reviews they seem to me to be too fond of are those published monthly. As for the volunteers—"

"You will have a joke about them, too, I suppose," Quirk retorted. "An excellent subject for a joke—the safety of the country! A capital subject for a merry jest; Nero fiddling with Rome in flames—"

"I beg your pardon? Nero never did anything of the kind," Mangan observed, with a perfectly diabolical inconsequence, "for violins weren't invented in those days."

This was too much for Mr. Quirk; he would not resume argument with such a trifler; nor, indeed, was there any opportunity; for Lord Rockminster now suggested they should go into the drawing-room—and Ichabod had to leave that decanter of port.

Now, if Maurice Mangan had come to this house to see how Lionel was feted and caressed by "the great"—in order that he might carry the tale down to Winstead to please the old folk and Miss Francie—he was doomed to disappointment. There were very few of "the great" present, to begin with; and those who were paid no particular attention to Lionel Moore. It was Octavius Quirk who appeared to be the hero of the evening, so far as the attention devoted to him by Lady Adela and her immediate little circle was concerned. But Maurice himself was not wholly left neglected. When tea was brought in, his hostess came over to where he was standing.

"Won't you sit down, Mr. Mangan?—I want to talk to you about something of very great importance—importance to me, that is, for you know how vain young authors are. You have heard of my new book?—yes, I thought Mr. Moore must have told you. Well, it's all ready, except the title-page. I am not quite settled about the title yet; and you literary gentlemen are so quick and clever with suggestions—I am sure you will give me good advice. And I've had a number of different titles printed, to see how they look in type; what do you think of this one? At present it seems to be the favorite; it was Mr. Quirk's suggestion—"

She showed him a slip with "North and South" printed on it in large letters.

"I don't like it at all," Mangan said, frankly. "People will think the book has something to do with the American civil war. However, don't take my opinion at all. My connection with literature is almost infinitesimal—I'm merely a newspaper hack, you know."

"What you say about the title is *quite* right? and I am *so* much obliged to you, Mr. Mangan," Lady Adela said, with almost pathetic emphasis. "The American war, of course; I never thought of that!"

"What is Ichabod's choice?—I beg your pardon, I mean have you shown the titles to Mr. Egerton?"

"I'm afraid he doesn't approve of any of them," said Lady Adela, sadly turning over the slips.

"No, I suppose not; good titles went out with good fiction—when he ceased to write novels a number of years ago. May I look at the others?"

She handed him the slips.

"Well, now, there is one that in my poor opinion would be rather effective—'Lotus and Lily'—a pretty sound—"

"Yes—perhaps," said Lady Adela, doubtfully, "but then, you see, it has not much connection with the book. The worst of it is that all the novel is printed—all but the three title-pages. Otherwise I might have called my heroine Lily—"

"But I fear you could not have called your hero Lotus," said Mangan, gravely. "Not very well. However, it is no use speculating on that now, as you say. What is the next one?—'Transformation.' Of course you know that Hawthorne wrote a book under that title, Lady Adela?"

"Yes," said she, cheerfully. "But there's no copyright in America; so why shouldn't I take the title if it suits?"

He hesitated; there seemed to be some ethical point here; but he fell back on base expediency.

"It is a mistake for two authors to use the same title—I'm sure it is," said he. "Look at the confusion. The reviewers might pass over your novel, thinking it was only a new edition of Hawthorne's book."

"Yes, that's quite true," said Lady Adela, thoughtfully.

"Well, here is one," he continued. "'Sicily and South Kensington;' that's odd; that's new; that might take the popular fancy."

"Do you know, that is a favorite of my own," Lady Adela said, with a slight eagerness, "for it really describes the book. You understand, Mr. Mangan, all the first part is about the South of Italy; and then I come to London and try to describe everything that is just going on round about us. I have put *everything* in; so that really—though I shouldn't praise myself—but it isn't praise at all, Mr. Mangan, it is merely telling you what I have aimed at—and really any one taking up my poor little book some hundred years hence might very fairly assume that it was a correct picture of all that was going on in the reign of Queen Victoria. I do not say that it is well done; not at all; that would be self-praise; but I do think it may have some little historical value. Modern life is so busy, so hurried, and so complex that it is difficult to form any impression of it as a whole; I take up book after book, written by living authors with whom I shouldn't dream of comparing myself, and yet I see how small a circle their characters work in. You would think the world consisted of only eight or ten people, and that there was hardly room for them to move. They never get away from one another; they don't mix in the crowd; there is no crowd. But here in my poor way I am trying to show what a panorama London is; always changing; occupations, desires, struggles following one another in breathless rapidity; in short, I want to show modern life as it is, not as it is dreamed of by clever authors who live in a study. Now that is my excuse, Mr. Mangan, for being such a dreadful bore; and I am *so* much obliged to you for your kind advice about the title; it is so easy for clever people to be kind—just a word, and it's done. Thank you," said she, as he took her cup from her and placed it on the table; and then, before she left him, she ventured to say, with a charming modesty, "I'm sure you will forgive me, Mr. Mangan, but if I were to send you a copy of the book, might I hope that you would find ten minutes to glance over it?"

"I am certain I shall read it with very great interest," said he; and that was strictly true, for this Lady Adela Cunyngham completely puzzled him; she seemed so extraordinary a combination of a clever woman of the world and an awful fool.

And Lionel? Well, he had got introduced to Miss Gabrielle Grey, whom he found to be a very quiet, shy, pensive sort of creature, not posing as a distinguished person at all. He dared not talk to her of her books, for he did not even know the names of them; but he let her understand that he knew she was an authoress, and it seemed to please her to know that her fame had penetrated into the mysterious regions behind the footlights. She began to question him, in a timid sort of way, about his experiences—whether stage-fright was difficult to get over—whether he thought that the immediate and enthusiastic approbation of the public was a beneficial stimulant—whether the continuous excitement of the emotional nature tended to render it callous, or, on the other hand, more sensitive and sympathetic—and so forth. Was she dimly looking forward to the conquest of a new domain, where the young ladies of the rectory and the vicarage might be induced fearfully to follow her? But Lionel did not linger long in that drawing-room. He got Maurice Mangan away as soon as he could; they slipped out unobserved—especially as there were plenty of new-comers now arriving. When they had passed down through the back garden to the gate, the one lit a cigarette, and the other a pipe; and together they wended their way towards Kensington Road and Piccadilly.

"Why," said Mangan, "I shall have quite a favorable report to carry down to Winstead. I did not see you treated with any of that unwholesome adulation I have heard so much of!"

"I am almost a stranger in the house now," Lionel said, briefly.

"Why?"

"Oh, various circumstances, of late."

"They did not even ask you to sing," his friend said, in accents of some surprise.

"They dared not. Didn't you see that most of the people were strangers? How could Lady Adela be sure that she was not wounding somebody's susceptibilities by having operatic music on a Sunday evening? She knew nothing at all about half those people; they were merely names to her, that she had collected round her in order that she might count herself in among the arts."

"That ill-conditioned brute Quirk seemed to me to be dominating the whole thing," said Mangan, rather testily. "It's an awful price to pay for a few puffs. I wonder a woman like that can bear him to come near her, but she pets the baboon as if he were a King Charles spaniel. Linnie, my boy, you're no longer first favorite. I can see that; self-interest has proved too strong; the flattering little review, the complimentary little notice, has ousted you. It isn't you who are privileged to meet my Lady Morgan in the street—

'And then to gammon her, in the *Examiner*,

With a paragraph short and sweet.'

Well, now, tell me about that very striking-looking girl, or woman, rather, whom you took in to dinner. I asked you who she was when she came into the room."

"That was Miss Honnor Cunyngham."

"Not the salmon-fishing young lady I have heard you speak of?"

"Yes."

"Why, she didn't look like that," said Mangan, thoughtfully. "Not the least. She has got a splendid forehead—powerful and clear—and almost too much character about the square brows and the calm eyes. I should have taken her to be a strongly intellectual woman, of the finer and more reticent type. Well, well, a salmon-fisher!"

"Why shouldn't she be both?"

"Why, indeed?" said Maurice, absently; and therewith he relapsed (as was frequently his wont) into silence, and in silence the two friends pursued their way eastwards to Lionel's rooms.

But when they had arrived at their destination, when soda-water had been produced and opened, and when Mangan was lying back in an easy-chair, regarding his friend, he resumed the conversation.

"I should have thought going to see those people to-night would have brightened you up a little," he began, "but you seem thoroughly out of sorts, Linn. What is the matter? Overwork or worry? I should not think overwork; I've never seen your theatre-business prove too much for you. Worry? What about, then?"

"There may be different things," Lionel said, evasively, as he brought over the spirit case. "I haven't been sleeping well of late—lying awake even if I don't go to bed till three or four; and I get a singing in my ears sometimes that is bothersome. Oh, never mind me; I'm all right."

"But I'm going to mind you, for you are not all right. Is it money?"

"No, no."

"What, then? There is something seriously worrying you."

"Oh, there are several things," Lionel exclaimed, forced at last into confession. "I can't think what has become of Nina Ross, that's one thing; if I only knew she was safe and well, I don't think I should mind the other things. No, not a bit. But there was something about her going away that I can't explain to you, only I—I was responsible in a sort of way; and Nina and I were always such good friends and companions. Well, it's no use talking about that. Then there's another little detail," he added, with an air of indifference: "I'm engaged to be married."

Mangan stared at him.

"Engaged to be married?" he repeated, as if he had not heard aright. "To whom?"

"Miss Burgoyne."

"Miss Burgoyne—of the New Theatre?"

"The same."

"Are you out of your senses, Linn!" Maurice cried, angrily.

"No, I don't think so," he said, and he went to the mantelpiece for a cigarette.

"How did it come about?" demanded Maurice, again.

"Oh, I don't know. It isn't of much consequence, is it?" Lionel answered, carelessly.

Then Maurice instantly reflected that, if this thing were really done, it was not for him to protest.

"Of course I say nothing against the young lady—certainly not. I thought she was very pleasant the night I was introduced to her, and nice-looking too. But I had no idea you were taken in that quarter, Linn; none—hence the surprise. I used to think you were in the happy position which Landor declared impossible. What were the lines? I haven't seen them for twenty years, but they were something like this:

'Fair maiden, when I look on thee,

 I wish that I were young and free;

 But both at once, ah, who could be?'

I thought you were 'both at once'—and very well content. But supposing you have given up your freedom, why should that vex and trouble you? The engagement time is said to be the happiest period of a man's life; what is wrong in your case?"

Lionel took a turn or two up and down the room.

"Well, I will tell you the truth, Maurice," he blurted out, at last. "I got engaged to her in a fit of restlessness or caprice, or some such ridiculous nonsense, and I don't regret it; I mean, I am willing to stand by it; but that is not enough for her, and I can look forward to nothing but a perpetual series of differences and quarrels. She expects me to play Harry Thornhill off the stage, I suppose."

Mangan looked at him for some time.

"Even between friends," he said, slowly, "there are some things it is difficult to talk about with safety. Of course you know what an outsider would say: that you had got into a devil of a mess; that you had blundered into an engagement with a woman whom you find you don't want to marry."

"Well, is there anything uncommon in that?" Lionel demanded. "Is that an unusual experience in human life? But I don't admit as much, in my case. I am quite willing to marry her, so long as she keeps her temper, and doesn't expect me to play the fool. I dare say we shall get on well enough, like other people, after the fateful deed is done. In the meantime," he added, with a forced laugh—"in the meantime, I find myself now and again wishing I was a sailor brave and bold, careering round the Cape of Good Hope in a gale of wind, and with no loftier aspiration in my mind than a pint of rum and a well-filled pipe."

"Faith, I think that's just where you ought to be," said Mangan, dryly, "instead of in this town of London, at the present moment. I declare you've quite bewildered me. If you had told me you were engaged to that tall salmon-fishing girl—you used to talk about her a good deal, you know—or to that fascinating young Italian creature—and I've seen before now how easily the gentle friend and companion can be transformed into a sweetheart—I should have been ready with all kinds of pretty speeches and good wishes. But Miss Burgoyne of the New Theatre? Linn, my boy, I've discovered what's the matter with you, and I can prescribe an absolutely certain cure."

"What is it?"

"The cure? You have partly suggested it yourself. You must go at once and take your passage in a sailing ship for Australia. You can stay there for a time and examine the colony; of course you'll write a book about it, like everybody else. Then you make your way to San Francisco, and accept a three-months' engagement there. You come on to New York, and accept a three-months' engagement there. And when you return to England you will find that all your troubles have vanished, and that you are once again the Linn Moore we all of us used to know."

A wild fancy flashed through Lionel's brain; what if in these far wanderings he were suddenly to encounter Nina? In vain—in vain; Nina had become for him but a shadow, a ghost, with no voice to call to him from any sphere.

"You would have me run away?—I don't see how I can do that," he said, quietly; and then he abruptly changed the subject. "What did you think of Lady Adela?"

"Well, to tell you the truth, I've been wondering whether she were at the same time a smart and clever woman and an abject fool, or whether she were simply smart and clever and thought me an abject fool. It must be either one or the other. She played the literary *ingénue* very well—a little too openly, perhaps. I'm curious about her book—"

"Oh, don't judge of her by her book!" Lionel exclaimed. "That isn't fair. Her book you may very likely consider foolish—not at all. I suppose her head is a little bit turned by the things that Quirk and those fellows have been writing about her; but that's only natural. And if she showed her hand a little too freely in trying to interest you in her novel, you must remember how eager she is to succeed. You'll do what you can for her book—won't you, Maurice?"

Maurice Mangan, on his way home that night, had other things to think of than Lady Adela's poor little book. He saw clearly enough the embroilment into which Lionel had landed himself; but he could not see so clearly how he was to get out of it. One question he forgot to ask: what had induced that mood of petulance or recklessness, or both combined, in which Lionel had wilfully and madly pledged all his future life? However, the thing was done; here was his friend going forward to a *mariage de convenance* (where there was very little *convenance*, to be sure) with a sort of careless indifference, if not of bravado; while his bride, on the other hand, might surely be pardoned if she resented, and indignantly resented, his attitude towards her. What kind of prospect was this for two young people? Maurice thought that on the very first opportunity he would go away down to Winstead and talk the matter over with Francie; who than she more capable of advising in aught concerning Lionel's welfare?

Notwithstanding his intercession with Maurice on behalf of Lady Adela's forthcoming novel, Lionel did not seem disposed to resume the friendly relations with the people up at Campden Hill which had formerly existed. He did not even call after the dinner-party. If Mr. Octavius Quirk were for the moment installed as chief favorite, he had no wish to interfere with him; there were plenty of other houses open, if one chose to go. But the fact is, Lionel now spent many afternoons and nearly every evening at the Garden Club; whist before dinner, poker after supper, being the established rule. Moreover, a new element had been introduced, as far as he was concerned. Mr. Percival Miles had been elected a member of the club, and had forthwith presented himself in the card-room, where he at once distinguished himself by his bold and intrepid play. The curious thing was that, while openly professing a kind of cold acquaintanceship, it was invariably against Lionel Moore that he made his most determined stand; with the other players he might play an ordinarily discreet and cautious game; but when Moore could be challenged, this pale-faced young man never failed promptly to seize the opportunity. And the worst of it was that he had extraordinary luck, both in the run of the cards and in his manœuvres.

"What is that young whipper-snapper up to?" Lionel said to himself, after a particularly bad night (and morning) as he sat staring into the dead ashes of his fireplace. "He wanted to take my life—until my good angel interfered and saved me. Now does he want to break me financially? By Jove! they're coming near to doing it among them. I shall have to go to Moss to-morrow for another £250. Well, what does it matter? The luck must turn some time. If it doesn't?—if it doesn't?—then there may come the trip before the mast, as the final panacea, according to Maurice. Australia?—there would be freedom there, and perhaps forgetfulness."

As he was passing into his bedroom he chanced to observe a package that was lying on a chair, and for a second he glanced at the handwriting of the address. It was Miss Burgoyne's. What could she want with him now? He cut the string, and opened the parcel; behold, here was the brown-and-scarlet woollen vest that she had knitted for him with her own fair hands. Why these impatiently down-drawn brows? A true lover would have passionately kissed this tender token of affection, and bethought him of all the hours and half-hours and quarters of an hour during which she had been employed in her pretty task, no doubt thinking of him all the time. Alas! the love-gift was almost angrily thrown on to the chair again—and he went into his own room.

CHAPTER XXII.

PRIUS DEMENTAT.

When Maurice Mangan left the train at Winstead, and climbed out of the deep chalk cutting in which the station is buried, and emerged upon the open downs, he found himself in a very different world from that he had left. Far away behind him lay the great city (even now the dusky dome of St. Paul's was visible across the level swathes of landscape), with its miry ways and teeming population and continuous thunder of traffic; while here were the windy skies of a wild March morning and swaying trees and cawing rooks and air that was sweet in the nostrils and soft to the throat. As he light-heartedly strode away across the undulations of blossoming gorse, fragments of song from his favorite poets chased one another through his brain; and somehow they were all connected with the glad opening out of the year—"And then my heart with pleasure fills, and dances with the daffodils"—"Along the grass sweet airs are blown, our way this day in spring"—"And in the gloaming o' the wood, the throssil whistled sweet"—Mangan could sing no more than a crow; but he felt as if he were singing; there was a kind of music in the long stride, the quick pulse, the deep inhalations of the delicious air. For all was going to be well now; he was about to consult Francie as to Lionel's sad estate. He did not stay to ask himself whether it were likely that a quiet and gentle girl, living in this secluded neighborhood, could be of much help in such a matter; it was enough that he was going to talk it all over with Miss Francie; things would be clearer then.

Now, as you go up from Winstead Station to Winstead Village, there is a strip of coppice that runs parallel with one part of the highway; and through this prolonged dingle a pathway meanders, which he who is not in a hurry may prefer to the road. Of course Mangan chose this pleasanter way, though he had to moderate his pace now because of the briars; and right glad was he to notice the various symptoms of the new-born life of the world—the pale anemones stirred by the warm, moist breeze, the delicate blossoms of the little wood-sorrel, the budded raceme of the wild hyacinth; while loud and clear a blackbird sang from a neighboring bough. He did not expect to meet any one; he certainly did not expect to meet Miss Francie Wright, who would doubtless be away at her cottages. But all of a sudden he was startled by the apparition of a rabbit that came running towards him, and then, seeing him, bolted off at right angles; and as this caused him to look up from his botanizings, here, unmistakably, was Miss Francie, coming along through the glade. Her pale complexion showed a little color as she drew near; but there was not much embarrassment in the calm, kind eyes.

"This is indeed a stroke of good-fortune," he said, "for I came down for the very purpose of having a talk with you all by yourself—about Lionel. But I did not imagine I should meet you here."

"I am going down to the station," she said. "I expect a parcel by the train you must have come by; and I want it at once."

"May I go with you and carry it for you?" he said, promptly; and of course she could not refuse so civil an offer. The awkward part of the arrangement was that they had to go along through this straggling strip of wood in single file, making a really confidential chat almost an impossibility; whereupon he proposed, and she agreed, that they should get out into the highway; and thereafter they went on to the station by the ordinary road.

But this task he had undertaken proved to be a great deal more difficult and delicate than he had anticipated. To have a talk with Francie—that seemed simple enough; it was less simple, as he discovered, to have to tell Lionel's cousin that the young man had gone and engaged himself to be married. Indeed, he beat about the bush for a considerable time.

"You see," he said, "a young fellow at his time of life, especially if he has been petted a good deal, is very apt to be wayward and restless, and likely to get into trouble through the mere impulsiveness, the recklessness of youth—"

"Mr. Mangan," Miss Francie said, with a smile in the quiet gray eyes, "why do you always talk of Linn as if he were so much younger than you? There is no great difference. You always speak as if you were quite middle-aged."

"I am worse than middle-aged—I am resigned, and read Marcus Aurelius," he said. "I suppose I have taken life too easily. Youth is the time for fighting; there is no fight left in me at all; I accept what happens. Oh, by the way, when my book on Comte comes out, I may have to buckle on my armor again; I suppose there will be strife and war and deadly thrusts; unless, indeed, the Positivists may not consider me worth answering. However, that is of no consequence; it's about Linn I have come down; and really, Miss Francie, I fear he is in a bad way, and that he is taking a worse way to get out of it."

"I am very sorry to hear that," she said, gravely.

"And then he's such a good fellow," Mangan continued. "If he were selfish or cruel or grasping, one might think that a few buffets from the world might rather be of service to him; but as it is I don't understand at all how he has got himself into such a position—or been entrapped into it; you see, I don't know Miss Burgoyne very well—"

"Miss Burgoyne?" she repeated, doubtfully.

"Miss Burgoyne of the New Theatre."

Then Mangan watched his companion, timidly and furtively—which was a strange thing for him, for ordinarily his deep-set gray eyes were singularly intense and sincere.

"Perhaps I ought to tell you at once," he said, slowly, "that—that—the fact is, Lionel is engaged to be married to Miss Burgoyne."

"Lionel—engaged to be married?" she said, quickly, and she looked up. He met her eyes and read them; surely there was nothing there other than a certain pleased curiosity; she had forgotten that this engagement might be the cause of her cousin's trouble; she only seemed to think it odd that Linn was about to be married.

"Yes; and now I am afraid he regrets his rashness, and is in terrible trouble over it—or perhaps that is only one of several things. Well, I had made other forecasts for him," Mangan went on to say, with a little hesitation. "I could have imagined another future for him. Indeed, at one time, I thought that if ever he looked out for a wife it would be—a little nearer home—"

Her eyes were swiftly downcast; but the next instant she had bravely raised them and was regarding him.

"Do you mean me, Mr. Mangan?" she asked.

He did not answer; he left her to understand. Miss Francie shook her head, and there was a slight smile on her lips.

"No, no," she said. "That was never possible at any time. Where was your clear sight, Mr. Mangan? Of course I am very fond of Linn; I have been so all my life; and there's nothing I wouldn't do to save him trouble or pain. But even a stupid country girl may form her ideal—and in my case Lionel never came anywhere near to that. I know he is good and generous and manly—he is quite wonderful, considering what he has come through; but on the other hand—well—oh, well, I'm not going to say anything against Linn—I will not."

"I am sure you will not," said Mangan, quietly; and here they reached the station.

The parcel had not arrived; there was nothing for it but to retrace their steps; and on their way across the common they returned to Lionel and his wretched plight.

"Surely," said Miss Francie, with a touch of indication in her voice—"surely, if Miss Burgoyne learns that he is fretting over this engagement, she will release him at once. No woman could be so shameless as to keep him to an unwilling bargain—"

"I am not so sure about that," Mangan made answer. "She may think she has affection for two, and that all will be well. It is a good match for her. His position in his profession and in society will be advantageous to her. Then she may be vain of her conquest—so many different motives may come in. But the chief point is that Linn doesn't want to be released from this engagement; he declares he will abide by it—if only she doesn't expect him to be very affectionate. It is an extraordinary imbroglio altogether; I am beginning to believe that all the time he has been in love with that Italian girl whom he knew in Naples, and who was in the New Theatre for a while, and that now he has made the discovery, when it is too late, he doesn't care what happens to him. She has gone away; he has no idea where she is; here he is engaged to Miss Burgoyne, and quite willing to marry her; and in the meantime he plays cards heavily to escape from thinking. In fact, he is not taking the least care of himself, and you would be surprised at the change in his appearance already. It isn't like Linn Moore to talk of going to bed when he ought to be setting out for a dinner-party; and the worst of it is, he won't pay any heed to what you say to him. But something must be done; Linn is too good a fellow to be allowed to go to the mischief without some kind of protest or interference."

"If you like," said Miss Francie, slowly, "I will go to Miss Burgoyne. She is a woman; she could not but listen. She cannot want to bring misery on them both."

"No," said he, with a little show of authority. "Whatever we may try—not that. I have heard that Miss Burgoyne has a bit of a temper."

"I am not afraid," said his companion, simply.

"No, no. If that were the only way, I should propose to go to Miss Burgoyne myself," he said. "But, you see, the awkward thing is that neither you nor I have any right to appeal to her, so long as Linn is willing to fulfil the engagement. We don't know her; we could not remonstrate as a friend of her own might. If we were to interfere on his behalf, she would immediately turn to him; and he is determined not to back out."

"Then what is to be done, Mr. Mangan?" she exclaimed, in despair.

"I—I don't quite see at present," he answered her. "I thought I would talk it over with you, Miss Francie. I thought there might be something in that; that the way might seem clearer. But I see no way at all, unless you were to go to him yourself. He would listen to you. Or he might even listen to me, if I represented to him that you were distressed at the condition of affairs. At present he doesn't appear to care what happens to him."

They had crossed the common; they had come to the foot of the wood; and they did not go on to the highway, for Miss Francie suggested that the sylvan path was the more interesting. And so they passed in among the trees, making their way through the straggling undergrowth, while the soft March wind blew moist and sweet all around them, and the blackbirds and thrushes filled the world with their silver melody, and in the more distant woods the ringdoves crooned. Maurice Mangan followed her—in silence. Perhaps he was thinking of Lionel; perhaps he was thinking of the confession she had made in crossing the common; at all events, he did not address her; and when she stooped to gather some hyacinths and anemones he merely waited for her. But as they drew near to the farther end of the coppice the path became clearer, and now he walked by her side.

"Miss Francie," he said (and it was *his* eyes that were cast down now), "you were speaking of the ideals that girls in the country may form for themselves—and girls everywhere, I dare say; but don't you think it rather hard?"

"What is?"

"Why, that you should raise up an impossible standard, and that poor common human beings, with all their imperfections and disqualifications, are sent to the right about."

"Oh, no," Miss Francie said, cheerfully. "You don't understand at all. A girl does not form her ideal out of her own head. She is not clever enough to do that; or, rather, she is not stupid enough to try to do that. She takes her ideal from some one she knows—from the finest type of character she has met; so that it is not an impossible standard, for one person, at least, has attained to it."

"And, for the sake of that one, she discards all those unfortunates who, by their age or appearance or lack of position or lack of distinction, cannot hope to come near," he said, rather absently. "Isn't that hard? It makes all sorts of things so hopeless, so impossible. You put your one chosen friend on this pedestal; and then all the others, who might wish to win your regard, they know what the result of comparison would be, and they go away home and hide their heads."

"I don't see, Mr. Mangan," she said, in a somewhat low voice, and yet a little proudly too, "why you should fear comparison with any one—no, not with any one; or imagine that anything could—could displace you in the regard of your friends."

He hesitated again—anxious, eager, and yet afraid. At last he said, rather sadly,

"I wish I knew something of your ideals, and how far away beyond human possibility they are."

"Oh, I can tell you," she said, plucking up heart of grace, for here was an easy way out of an embarrassing position. "My ideal woman is Sister Alexandra, of the East London Hospital. She was down here last Sunday—sweeter, more angelic than ever. That is the noblest type of woman I know. And I was so glad she enjoyed her rare holiday; and when she went away in the evening we had her just loaded with flowers for her ward."

"And the ideal man?"

"Oh," said Miss Francie, hurriedly, "I hardly know about that. Of course, when I—when I spoke of Linn a little while ago, I did not wish to say anything against him—certainly not—no one admires his better qualities more than I do—but—but there may be other qualities—"

They were come to the wooden gate opening on to the highway; he paused ere he lifted the latch.

"Francie," said he, "do you think that some day you might be induced to put aside all your high standards and ideals, and—and—in short, accept a battered old journalist, without money, position, distinction, without any graces, except this, that gratitude might add something to his affection for you?"

Tears sprang into her eyes, and yet there was a smile there, too; she was not wholly frightened—perhaps she had known all along.

"Ah, and you don't understand yet, Maurice!" she said, and she frankly gave him her hand, and her eyes were kind even through her tears. "You don't understand what I have been saying to you, that a girl's ideal is one particular person—her ideal is the man or woman whom she admires and loves the most. Can you not guess?"

"Francie, you will be my wife?" he said to her, drawing her closer to him, his hands clasped round her head.

She did not answer. She was silent for a second or two. And then she said, with averted eyes,

"You spoke of gratitude, Maurice. I know who has the most reason to be grateful—and who will try the hardest to show it."

So that betrothal was completed; and when they passed out from the coppice into the whiter air, behold! the wild March skies had parted somewhat, and there was a shimmer of silver sunlight along the broad highway between the hedges. It was an auspicious omen—or, at least, their full hearts may have thought so; and then, again, there was a wedding chorus all around them from the birds—from the bright-eyed robin perched on the crimson bramble-spray; from the speckled thrush on the swaying elm; from the lark far-hovering over a field of young corn. But in their own happiness they had thought of others; Francie soon came back to Lionel again and his grievous misfortunes; and she was listening with meekness to this tall, clear-eyed man, who could now claim a certain gentle authority over her. They were a long time before they got to the doctor's house.

That same evening Miss Kate Burgoyne invited Lionel to come to her room for a cup of tea when he had dressed for the last act; and accordingly, when he was ready, he strolled along the corridor, rapped with his knuckles, and entered. It turned out that the prima-donna had other visitors: a young lady whom he had never seen before and Mr. Percival Miles. The young gentleman, in faultless evening dress, seemed a little surprised at the easy manner in which Lionel had lounged into the place; and perhaps Lionel was also a little surprised—for this was Mr. Miles's first appearance in the room; but each man merely nodded to the other, in a formal-acquaintance style, as they were in the habit of doing at the Garden Club. At the same moment Miss Burgoyne opened a portion of the curtain, so that she could address her guests.

"Mr. Moore, let me introduce you to my friend, Miss Ingram. Mr. Miles I think you know."

And Lionel was glad enough to turn to the young lady and enter into conversation with her, for the pale young man with the slight yellow moustache was defiantly silent, and had even something fierce about his demeanor. It was no business of Lionel's to provoke a quarrel with this truculent fire-eater, especially in Miss Burgoyne's room. To quarrel about Kate Burgoyne?—the irony of events could go no further than that.

And of course, as the most immediate topic, they spoke of the gale that had been blowing across London all the afternoon and evening; for the southerly winds that had prevailed in the morning had freshened up and increased in violence until a veritable hurricane was now raging, threatening roofs, chimneys, and lamp-posts, to say nothing of the whirled and driven and bewildered foot-passengers.

"I hear there has been a bad accident in Oxford Street," Lionel said to the young lady. "Some scaffolding has fallen—a lot of people hurt. I'm afraid there will be a sad tale to tell from the sea; even now, while we are secure in this big building, thinking only of amusement, I suppose there is many a ship laboring in the gale, or going headlong on to the rocks. Have you far to get home?" he asked.

"Oh, I am going home with Miss Burgoyne," the young lady answered.

But here Miss Burgoyne herself appeared, coming forth in the full splendor of Grace Mainwaring's bridal attire and with all her radiant witcheries of make-up, and the poor lad sitting there, who had never before been so near this vision of delight, seemed quite entranced by its (strictly speaking) superhuman loveliness. He could not take his eyes away from her. He did not think of joining in the conversation. He watched her at the mirror; he watched her making tea; he watched her munching a tiny piece of bread and butter (which was imprudent on her part, after the care she had bestowed on her lips); and always he was silent and spellbound. Miss Burgoyne, on the other hand, was talkative enough.

"Isn't it an awful night!" she exclaimed. "I thought the cab I came down in would be blown over. And they say it's getting worse and worse. I hear there has been a dreadful accident; some of the men were telling Jane about it; have you heard, Mr. Moore?—something about a scaffold. I suppose this theatre is safe enough; I don't feel any shaking. But I know I shall be so nervous going home to-night—I dread it already—"

"Miss Ingram says she is going home with you," Lionel pointed out, carelessly.

"But that is worse!" the prima-donna cried. "Two women are worse than one—they make each other nervous; no, what you want is a man's bluntness of perception—his indifference—and the sense of security you get from his being there. Two frightened women; how are they going to keep each other's courage up?"

It was clearly an invitation; almost a challenge. Lionel only said,

"Why, what have you to fear! The blowing over of a cab is about the last thing likely to happen. If you were walking along the pavement, you might be struck by a falling slate; but you are out in the middle of the road. If you go home in a four-wheeled cab, you will be as safe as you are at this minute in this room."

She turned away from him; at the same moment the pale young gentleman said, rather breathlessly,

"Miss Burgoyne, if you would permit me to accompany you and Miss Ingram home, I should esteem it a great honor—and—and pleasure."

She whipped round in an instant.

"Oh, thank you, Percy—Mr. Miles, I mean," she added, in pretty confusion. "That will be so kind of you. We shall be delighted, I'm sure—very kind of you indeed."

No more was said at the moment, for Miss Burgoyne had been called; and Lionel, as he wended his way to the wings, could only ask himself,

"What is she up to now? She calls me Mr. Moore before her friends, and him Percy, and she contrives to put him into the position of rescuing two distressed damsels. Well, what does it matter? I suppose women are like that."

But Mr. Percival Miles's accompanying those two young ladies through the storm did matter to him, in another way, and seriously. When, the performance being over, he got into evening dress and drove along in a hansom to the Garden Club, he found there two or three of the young gentlemen who were in the habit of lounging about the supper-room, glancing at illustrated papers or chewing toothpicks, until the time for poker had arrived.

"Johnny," he said to one of them, "somehow I feel awfully down in the mouth to-night."

"That's unusual with you, then," was the cheerful reply. "For you are the pluckiest loser I ever saw. But I must say your luck of late has been just something frightful."

"Well, I'm down altogether—in luck, in finances, and spirits; and I'm going to pull myself up a peg. Come and keep me company. I'm going to order a magnum of Perrier Jouet of '74, and I only want a glass or two; you must help me out, or some of those other fellows."

"That's a pretty piece of extravagance!" the other exclaimed. "A magnum— to get a couple of glasses out of it; like an otter taking a single bite from a salmon's shoulder. Never mind, old chap; I'm in. I hate champagne at this time of night; but I don't want you to kill yourself."

As they sat at supper, with this big bottle before them, Lionel said,

"It will be a bad thing for me if young Miles doesn't show up to-night."

"I should have thought it would have been an excellent thing for you if Miles had never entered this club," his companion observed.

"That's true," said Lionel, rather gloomily. "But my only chance now is to get some of my property back, and I can only get it back from him. You fellows are no use to me—not if I were winning all along the line."

"Look here, Moore," said the young man, in a more serious tone, "you may say it's none of my business; but the way you and that fellow Miles have been going on is perfectly awful. If the committee should hear about it, there will be a row, and no mistake!"

"My dear boy," Lionel protested, as he pushed the unnecessary bottle to his neighbor, "the committee have nothing to do with understandings that are settled outside the club. You don't see Miles or me handing checks for £200 or £300 across the table. How can the committee expel you for holding up three fingers or nodding your head?"

"Well, then, you'll excuse me saying it, but he's a young ass, to gamble in that fashion," Johnny remarked, bluntly. "What fun does he get out of it? And it's quite a new thing with him—that's the odd business. I know a man who was at Merton with him; and certainly Miles got into a devil of a scrape—which cut short his career there; but it had nothing to do with gambling. He never was that way inclined at all; it's a new development, since he joined this club. Well, I suppose he can do what he likes. The heir to a baronetcy and such a place as Petmansworth can get just as much as he wants from the Jews."

"My good man, he doesn't need to go to the Jews," said Lionel, with grim irony.

"Where does he get all that money from? Do you think his father is fool enough to encourage him in such extravagance? I should hope not! At the same time I wish I had a father tarred with something of that same brush."

"Where does he get all the money from? So far he has got it from me," Lionel said, with a bit of a shrug. "He doesn't need to go to his father, or to the Jews either, when he can plunder me. And such a run of luck as he has had is simply astounding—"

"It isn't luck at all," the other interrupted. "It's your play. You play too bold a game—too bold when you know he is going to play a bolder. Twice running he caught you last night bluffing on no hand at all; and I don't know what fabulous stakes were up—with your nods and signs. It's no use your trying to bluff that fellow. He won't be bluffed."

"The thing is as broad as it's long, man," Lionel said, impatiently. "If he is determined to see me every time, he must be caught when I have a good hand—it stands to reason. The only thing is that my luck has been so confoundedly bad of late."

"Yes; and when the luck's against you, you go betting on no hands at all— with Miles waiting for you!" his companion exclaimed. "All right; every man must play the game his own way. You don't seem to have found it profitable so far."

"Profitable!" Lionel said, with a dark look in his eyes. "I can tell you I am in a tight corner, and I reckoned on to-night to settle it one way or the other—not with you fellows, I can't get anything worth while out of you, but with Miles. And now he's gone away home with—"

He stopped in time; ladies' names are not mentioned in clubs—at least, not in such clubs as the Garden.

"The odd thing is," continued Johnny, as he lit a cigarette, and definitely refused to have any more of the wine, "the extremely odd thing is that he doesn't seem to care to win from the rest of us. He lets us share our modest little pots as if they weren't worth looking at. It's you he goes for, invariably."

"And he's gone for me to some purpose," Lionel said, morosely. "I'm just about broke—broke five or six times over, if it comes to that—and by that pennyworth of yellow ribbon!"

"You needn't call him names," said Johnny, as he lay back in his chair. "Upon my soul I think Miles is somebody in disguise—a priest—an Inquisitor—somebody with a mission—to punish the sin of gambling. What does he care about the game? Nothing—I'll swear it! He's only watching for you. He's an avenger. He has been sent by some superior power—"

"Then it must have been by the devil," said Lionel, with a sombre expression, "for he has got the devil's own luck at his back. Wait till I get four of a kind when he is betting on a full hand—and then you'll see his corpse laid out!" This was all he could say just then; for here was the young man himself, who must have come back from the Edgeware Road in a remarkably swift hansom.

Almost directly there was an adjournment to the card-room; and the players took their places.

"I propose we have in the joker,"[2] Lionel called aloud, as the cards were dealt for deal.

"I don't see the fun of it," objected the young man who had been Lionel's companion at the supper-table. "You never know where you are when the joker is in. What do you say, Miles?"

"Oh, have it in by all means," Percival Miles said, with his eyes fixed on the table.

And perhaps it was that Lionel was anxious and nervous (for much depended on the results of this night's play), but he seemed to feel that the pale young man who sat opposite him appeared to be even more cold and implacable in manner than was usual with him. He began to have superstitious fears—like most gamblers. That was an uncanny suggestion his recent companion had put into his head—that here was an avenger—a deputed instrument—an agent to inflict an awarded punishment. At the same time he tried to laugh at the notion. Punishment—from this stripling of a boy! It was a ludicrous idea, to be sure. When Lionel had in former days accepted his challenge to fight, it was with some kind of impatient resolve to teach him a wholesome lesson and brush him aside. And he had regarded his running after Miss Burgoyne with a sort of good-natured toleration and contempt; there were always those young fools in the wake of actresses. But that he, Lionel, should be afraid of this young idiot? What was there to be afraid of? He was no swashbuckler—this pallid youth with the thin lips, who concentrated all his attention on the cards, and had no word or jest for his neighbors. How could there be anything baleful in the expression of eyes that were curiously expressionless? It was a pretty face (Lionel had at one time thought), but now it seemed capable of a good deal of relentless determination. Lionel had heard of people shivering when brought into contact with the repellent atmosphere that appeared to surround a particular person; but what was there deadly about this young man?

The game at first was not very exciting, though now and again the joker played a merry trick, appearing in some unexpected place, and laying many a good hand low. Indeed, it almost seemed as if Lionel had resolved to recoup himself by steady play; and so far there had been no duel between him and young Miles. That was not distant, however. On this occasion Lionel, who was seated on the left of the dealer—in other words, he being age—when the cards were dealt found himself with two pairs in his hand, aces and queens. It was a pretty show. When the time came for him to declare his intention, he said,

"Well, I'm just going to make this another ten shillings to come in."

That frightened no one; they all came in; what caused them to halt and reflect was that, on Lionel being subsequently asked how many cards he wished to have, he said,

"None, thank you."

Not a syllable was uttered; there were surmises too occult for words. The player on Lionel's left bet an humble two shillings. The next player simply came in. So did the third—who was Mr. Percival Miles. Likewise the dealer;

in fact, they were all prepared to pay that modest sum to inspect the age's hand. But Lionel wanted a higher price for that privilege.

"I'm coming in with the little two shillings," said he, "and I will raise you a sovereign."

That promptly sent out the player on his left; his neighbor also retired. Not so the pallid young man with the thin lips.

"And one better," he said, depositing another sovereign.

The dealer incontinently fled. There only remained Lionel and his enemy; and the position of affairs was this—that while Lionel had taken no additional cards, and was presumably in possession of a straight or a flush (unless he was bluffing), Miles had taken one card, and most likely had got two pairs (unless he was finessing). Two pairs against two pairs, then? But Lionel had aces and queens.

"And five better," Lionel said, watching his enemy.

"And five better," said the younger man, stolidly.

And now the onlookers altered their surmises. No one but a lunatic would challenge a player who had declined to take supplementary cards unless he himself had an exceptionally strong hand, or unless he was morally certain that his opponent was bluffing. Had Miles "filled," then, with his one card; and was a straight being played against a straight, or a flush against a flush? Or had the stolid young man started with fours? The subdued excitement with which this duel was now being regarded was enthralling; they forgot to protest against the wild raising of the bets; and when Lionel and his implacable foe, having exhausted all their money, had recourse of nods— merely marking their indebtedness to the pool on a bit of paper lying beside them—the others could only guess at the amount that was being played for. It was Lionel who gave in; clearly that insatiate bloodsucker was not to be shaken off.

"I call you."

"Three nines," was the answer, and Miles laid down on the table a pair of nines and the joker. The other two were worthless; clearly, he had taken the one card as a blind.

"That is good enough—take away the money," Lionel said, calmly; and the younger man, with quite as expressionless a face, raked over the pile of gold, bank-notes, and counters.

There was a general sense of relief; that strain had been too intense.

"Very magnificent, you know," said the player who was next to Lionel, as he placed his ante on the table, "but it isn't poker. I think if you fix a limit you should stick to it. Have your private bets if you like; but let us have a limit that allows everybody to see the fun."

"Oh, certainly, I agree to that," Lionel said, at once. "We will keep to the sovereign limit; and Mr. Miles and I will understand well enough what we are betting when we happen to play against each other."

Thereafter the game went more quietly, though Lionel was clearly playing with absolute carelessness; no doubt his companions understood that he could not hope to retrieve his losses in this moderate play. He seemed tired, too, and dispirited; frequently he threw up his cards without drawing— which was unusual with him.

"Have a drink, old man, to wake you up?" his neighbor said to him, about half-past two.

"No, thanks," he answered, listlessly looking on at the cards.

"A cigarette, then?"

"No, thanks. I think I must give up smoking altogether—my throat isn't quite right."

But an extraordinary stroke of good-luck aroused him. On looking at his cards he found he had been dealt four aces and a ten. Surely the hour of his revenge had sounded at last; for with such a hand he could easily frighten the others out, while he knew that Percival Miles would remain in, if he had anything at all. Accordingly, when it came to his turn he raised before the draw—raised the pool a sovereign; and this caused two of the players to retire, leaving himself, Miles, and the dealer. He took one card—to his astonishment and concealed delight he found it was the joker. Five aces!— surely on such a hand he might bet his furniture, his clothes, his last cigarette. Five aces!—it was nothing but brute force; all that was wanted was to pile on the money; he could well afford to be reckless this time. He saw that Miles also asked for one card, and that the dealer helped himself to two; but what the took was a matter of supreme indifference to him.

It was Percival Miles's turn to bet.

"I will bet a sovereign," said he.

"And I'll stay in with you," remarked the dealer, depositing the golden coin.

"One better," said Lionel.

"And one better," said Miles.

Here the dealer retired, so that these two were left in as before—well, not as before, for Lionel had five aces in his hand! And now they made no pretence of keeping to the limit that had been imposed; their bets were registered on the bit of paper which each had by him; and pertinaciously did these two gladiators hack and slash at each other. Lionel was quite reckless. His enemy had taken one card. Very well. Supposing he had "filled" a flush or a straight, so much the better. Supposing he also had got fours—that, too, was excellent well; for he could have nothing higher than four kings. Strictly speaking, there was only one hand that could beat Lionel's—a straight flush; but then a straight flush is an uncommonly rare thing; and, besides, the appearance of five aces in one's hand seems to convey a sense of quite unlimited power. That five aces are no better than four aces does not strike the possessor of them; he regards the goodly show—and strives to conceal his elation.

But even the onlookers, intensely interested as they were in this fell combat, began to grow afraid when they guessed at the sum that was now in the imaginary pool. The story might get about the club; the committee might shut up the card-room; there might be a talk of expulsion. As for Lionel, he kept saying to himself, "Well, this is a safe thing; and I could go on all night; but I won't take a brutal advantage. As soon as I think I have got back about what this young fellow has already taken from me since he came into the club, I will stop. I don't want to break him. I don't want to send him to the money-lenders."

As for the pale young man across the table, his demeanor was that of a perfect poker-player. The only thing that could be noticed was a slight contraction of his pupils, as if he were concentrating his eyes on the things immediately around him and trying to leave his face quite inscrutable. There was no eagerness in his betting—nor was there any affected resignation; it was entirely mechanical; like clock-work came the raised and raised bet.

"I call you," said Lionel, at last, amid a breathless silence.

Without a word Percival Miles laid his cards on the table, arranging them in sequence; they were five, six, seven, eight, and nine of clubs—not an imposing hand, certainly, but Lionel knew his doom was sealed. He rose from his chair, with a brief laugh that did not sound very natural.

"I think I know when I've had enough," he said. "Good-night!" And "Good-night!" came from one and all of them—though there was an ominous pause until the door was shut behind him.

He went down below, to the supper-room, which was all deserted now; he drew in a chair to a small writing-table and took a sheet of note-paper. On it he scrawled, with rather a feverish hand:

"As I understand it, I owe you £800 on this evening, with £300 from yesterday—£1100 in all. I will try to let you have it to-morrow. L.M."—and that he put in an envelope, which he addressed to "Percival Miles, Esq.," and sent up-stairs by one of the servants. Then he went and got his coat and hat, and left. It was raining hard, and there was a blustering wind, but he called no hansom; the wet and cold seemed grateful to him, for he was hot and excited. And then, somewhat blindly, and bare-throated, he passed through the streaming thoroughfares—caring little how long it took him to reach Piccadilly.

[2]

The joker is a fifty-third card, of any kind of device, which is added to the pack; the player to whom it is dealt can make it any card he chooses. For example, if the other four cards he holds are two queens and two sevens, he can make the joker card a third queen, and thus secure for himself a full hand.

CHAPTER XXIII.

A MEMORABLE DAY.

"...But do you know, dear Maurice, that you propose marrying a beggar; and, more than that, a most unabashed beggar, as you will be saying to yourself presently? The fact is, immediately after you left this afternoon, the post brought me a letter from Sister Alexandra, who tells me that two of her small children, suffering from hip-disease, must be sent home, for the doctors say they are getting no better, and the beds in the ward are wanted. They are not fit to be sent home, she writes; then all the country holiday money collected last summer has been spent, and what is she to do? Well, I have told her to send them on to me, and I shall take my chance of finding the £5 that will be necessary. The fact is, I happen to know one of the poor little things—Grace Wilson her name is, the dearest little mite. But the truth is, dear Maurice, I haven't a penny? for I have overdrawn the small allowance that comes to me quarterly, and spent it all. Now don't be vexed that I ask you, *so soon*, for a little help; a sovereign will do, if Linn will give another; and Linn has always been very good to me in this way, though for some time back I have been ashamed to take anything from him. The doctor grumbles, but gives me five shillings whenever I ask him; Auntie will give me the same; and the rest I can get from our friends and acquaintances about here. Don't be impatient with me, dear Maurice; and some day I will take you down to Whitechapel and show you the very prettiest sight in the whole world—and that is Sister Alexandra with her fifty children...."

Maurice Mangan read this passage as he was driving in a hansom along Pall Mall, on his way to call on Lionel. The previous portion of the letter, which more intimately concerned herself and himself, he had read several times over before coming out, studying every phrase of it as if it were an individual treasure, and trying to listen for the sound of her voice in every sentence. And as for this more practical matter, why, although he was rather a poor man, he thought he was not going to allow Frances to wander about in search of grudging shillings and half-crowns so long as he himself could come to her aid; so at the foot of St. James Street he stopped the hansom, went into the telegraph-office, and sent off the following message: "Five pounds will reach you to-morrow morning. You cannot refuse my first gift in our new relationship.—Maurice." And thereafter he went on to Piccadilly—feeling richer, indeed, rather than poorer.

When he rang the bell at Lionel's lodgings, it was with no very clear idea of the message or counsel he was bringing with him; but the news he now received put all these things out of his head. The house-porter appeared, looking somewhat concerned.

"Yes, sir, Mr. Moore is up-stairs; but I'm afraid he's very unwell."

"What is the matter?" Maurice asked, instantly.

"He must have got wet coming home last night, sir; and he has caught a bad cold. I've just been for Dr. Whitsen, and he will be here at twelve."

"But Dr. Whitsen is a throat doctor."

"Yes, sir; but it is always his throat Mr. Moore is most anxious about; and when he found himself husky this morning, he would take nothing but a raw egg beaten up and a little port-wine negus; and now he won't speak— he will only write on a piece of paper. He is saving himself for the theatre to-night, sir, I think that is it; but would you like to go up and see him?"

"Oh, yes, I will go up and see him," Mangan said; and without more ado he ascended the stairs and made his way into Lionel's bedroom.

He found his friend under a perfect mountain of clothes that had been heaped upon him; and certainly he was not shivering now—on the contrary, his face was flushed and hot, and his eyes singularly bright and restless. As soon as Lionel saw who this new-comer was, he made a sign that a block of paper and a pencil lying on the table should be brought to him; and, turning slightly, he put the paper on the pillow and wrote:

"I'm nursing my voice—hope to be all right by night—are you busy to-day, Maurice?"

"No; there is no House on Saturday," Maurice made answer.

"I wish you would stay by me," Lionel wrote, with rather a shaky hand. "I'm in dreadful trouble. I undertook to pay Percival Miles £1100 and Lord Rockminster £300 to-day without fail; and I haven't a farthing, and don't know where to send or what to do."

"Oh, never mind about money!" Maurice said, almost impatiently, for there was something about the young man's appearance he did not at all like. "Why should you worry about that? The important business is for you to get well."

"I tell you I *must* pay Rockminster to-day," the trembling pencil scrawled. "He was the only one of them who stood my friend. I tell you I *must* pay him—if I have to get up and go out and seek for the money myself."

"Nonsense!" Mangan exclaimed. "What do people care about a day or two, when they hear you are ill? However, you needn't worry, Linn. As for that other sum you mention, well, that is beyond me—I couldn't lay my hands on it at once; but as for the three hundred pounds, I will lend you that—so set your mind at rest on that point."

"And you'll give it into Lord Rockminster's own hands—*this day?*"

"Surely it will be quite the same if I send the check by a commissionaire; he must get it sooner or later."

The earnest, restless eyes looked strangely supplicating.

"Into his own hands, Maurice!"

"Very well, very well," Mangan had just time to say, for here was the doctor.

Dr. Whitsen examined his patient with the customary professional calm and reticence; asked a few questions, which Lionel answered with such husky voice as was left him; and then he said,

"Yes, you have caught a severe chill, and your system is feverish generally; the throat is distinctly congested—"

"But to-night, doctor—the theatre—to-night!" Lionel broke in, excitedly. "Surely by eight o'clock—"

"Oh, quite impossible; not to be thought of," the doctor responded, with decision.

"Why can't you do something to tide me over, for the one night?" the young man said, with appealing and almost pathetic eyes. "I've never disappointed the public once before, never once; and if I could only get over to-night, there's the long rest to-morrow and Monday."

"Come, come," said the doctor, soothingly, "you must not excite yourself about a mere trifle. You know it is no uncommon thing, and the public don't resent it; they would be most unreasonable if they did. Singers are but mortal like themselves. No, no, you must put that out of your mind altogether."

Lionel turned to Maurice.

"Maurice," he said, in that husky voice, and yet with a curious, subdued eagerness, "telegraph to Lehmann at once—at once. Doyle is all right; he has sung the part often enough. And will you send a note to Doyle; he can go into my dressing-room and take any of my things he wants; Lingard has the keys. And a telegram to mother, in case she should see something in the newspapers; tell her there is nothing the matter—only a trifling cold—"

"Really, Mr. Moore," said the doctor, interposing, "you must have a little care; you must calm yourself. I am sure your friend will attend to all these matters for you, but in the meantime you must exercise the greatest self-control, or you may do your throat some serious injury. Why should you be disturbed by so common an incident in professional life? Your substitute will do well enough, and the public will greet you with all the greater favor on your return."

"It never happened before," the young man said, in lower tones. "I never had to give in before."

"Now tell me," Dr. Whitsen continued. "Dr. Ballardyce is your usual medical attendant, is he not?"

"I know him very well; he is an old friend of mine, but I've never had occasion to trouble him much," was the answer, given with some greater care and reserve.

"I will call on him as I go by, and if possible we will come down together in the afternoon," the doctor said; and then Maurice fetched him writing materials from the other room, and he sat down at the little table. Before he went, he gave some general directions; then the two friends were left alone.

Lionel took up the pencil again, and turned to the block of paper.

"The £300, Maurice," his trembling fingers scrawled, showing how his mind was still torturing itself with those obligations.

"Oh, that's all right," Maurice answered, lightly. "You give me Lord Rockminster's address, and I'll take the check to him myself as soon as the doctors have been here in the afternoon. Don't you worry about that, Linn, or about anything; for you know you mustn't increase that feverishness, or we shall have you a right-down, *bona-fide* patient on our hands; and then when will you get back to the theatre again? I am going out now to telegraph to Lehmann. But I don't think I need alarm the Winstead people; you see, they don't read the Sunday papers; and, indeed, if I send a note now to Francie, she will get it the first thing in the morning. Linn," he continued, after a moment's hesitation, "are you too much upset by your own affairs to listen to a bit of news? I came with the intention of telling you, but perhaps I'd better wait until you get over these present troubles."

Lionel looked at him, with those bright, restless eyes, for a second or two, as if to gather something from his expression; and then he wrote:

"Is it about Francie?"

Maurice nodded; it was enough. Lionel stretched out his hot hand and took that of his companion.

"I am glad," he said, in a low voice. And then, after a moment or two's thinking, he turned to his writing again: "Well, it *is* hard, Maurice. I have been looking forward to this for many a day, and have been wondering how I should congratulate you both. And I get the news now—when I'm ruined. I haven't enough money even to buy a wedding-present for Francie!"

"Do you think she will mind that?" Mangan said, cheerfully. "But I'm going to send her your good wishes, Linn—now, when I write. And look here, if she should come up to see you, or your father and mother—for it is quite possible the doctors may insist on your giving your voice a rest for a considerable while—well, if they should come up from Winstead, mind you say nothing about your monetary troubles. They needn't be mentioned to anybody, nor need they worry you; I dare say I shall be able to get something more done; it will be all right. Only, if the Winstead people should come up, don't you say anything to them about these monetary affairs, or connect me with them; for it might put me into an awkward position—you understand?"

And the last words Lionel wrote on the block of paper before Mangan went out to execute his various commissions were these:

"You are a good friend, Maurice."

When the doctors arrived in the afternoon, Mangan had come back. They found Lionel complaining of acute headache and a burning thirst; his skin hot and dry; pulse full and quick; also, he seemed drowsy and heavy, though his eyes retained their restless brightness. There could be no doubt, as they privately informed Maurice, he was in the first stages of a violent fever; and the best thing that could be done was to get in a professional nurse at once. Yes, Mr. Mangan might communicate with his friends; his father, being himself a doctor, would judge whether it were worth while coming up just then; but, of course, it would be inadvisable to have a lot of relations crowding the sick-room. Obviously, the immediate cause of the fever was the chill caught on the previous night, but there might have been predisposing causes; and everything calculated to excite the mind unduly was to be kept away from him. As for the throat, there were no dangerous symptoms as yet; the simple congestion would probably disappear, when the fever abated, with a return to health; but the people at the theatre might as well know that it would be a long time before Mr. Moore could return to his duties. Dr. Ballardyce would see at once about having a professional nurse sent; meanwhile, quiet, rest, and the absence of mental disturbance were the great things. And so the two augurs departed.

The moment that Mangan returned to Lionel's room, the latter glanced at him quickly and furtively.

"Are they gone, Maurice?" he whispered.

"Yes."

"And the check—for Lord Rockminster?"

"There it is, already drawn out," was the answer, as the slip of lilac paper was unfolded; "but I can't take it to him until the nurse comes—certainly not."

"She may be an hour, Maurice," Lionel said, restlessly. "I don't want anybody to wait on me. If you think it necessary, call up Mrs. Jenkins, and she can sit in the next room; the bell here is enough. Oh, my head!—my head!"—and he turned away, wearily.

Maurice saw well enough that he would never rest until this money was paid, so he called up the house-porter's wife and gave her some instructions, and forthwith set off for the address in Palace Gardens Terrace which Lionel had given him. When he arrived there, he was informed that his lordship was not at home. He pressed his inquiries; he said his business was of the utmost importance; and at last he elicited, after considerable waiting, that, though no one in the house could say whither Lord Rockminster had gone, it was understood that he was dining at the Universities Club that evening. With this information Mangan returned to Piccadilly. He found the nurse already arrived and installed. He pacified Lionel with the news; for, if he went along to the Universities Club at half-past eight, he must surely be able to place the money in Lord Rockminster's own hands.

"Maurice, you're awfully kind," his friend murmured. "And you've had nothing to eat all day. Tell Mrs. Jenkins to get you something—"

"Oh, that's all right," Mangan said, carelessly. "I'll just scribble a line to Francie, to tell her what the doctors have said; and I'll take that down to the post myself. Then I'll get something to eat and come back here; and at half-past eight I'm going along to Pall Mall, where I'm certain to catch Lord Rockminster—so that it's all quite right and straight, you see."

But, as it chanced, when he went along to the Universities that evening, he found he had missed his man—by only a minute or two. He was surprised and troubled; he knew how Lionel would fret. The hall-porter did not know whither Lord Rockminster had gone; that is to say, he almost certainly did know, but it was not his business to tell. Luckily, at this same moment, there was a young fellow leaving the club, and, as he was lighting his cigar, he heard Maurice's inquiries—and perhaps was rather struck by his appearance, which was certainly not that of a sheriff's officer.

"I think I can tell you where they have gone, sir," said the young man, good-naturedly. "Some of them had an early dinner to-night, to go up to the billiard handicap at the Palm-Tree; I fancy Lord Rockminster was of the party, and that you will find him there."

This information proved correct. Mangan went up to the Palm-Tree Club in St. James Street and sent in his card. Almost directly he was invited to step up-stairs to the billiard-room. Just as he entered the door, he saw Lord Rockminster leave the raised bench where he had been seated by the side of a very artificial-looking palm-tree stem, and the next moment the two men were face to face.

"How do you do, Mr. Mangan?" Lord Rockminster said, in his usual impassive way. "You remember I had the pleasure of meeting you at my sister's. What is the matter with your friend Mr. Moore?—I see by the evening paper he is not to appear to-night."

"He is far from well—a chill followed by a fever," Mangan answered. "I have just come from him, with a message for you."

"Oh, really," said the young nobleman. "Ah, I dare say I know; but I assure you it is quite unnecessary. Tell him not to mind. When a fellow's ill, why should he be troubled?"

Maurice had taken out his pocket-book, and was searching for the lilac slip.

"But here is the check, Lord Rockminster; and nothing would do him but that I must give it into your own hands."

"Oh, really."

Lord Rockminster took the check, and happened to glance at it.

"Ah, I see this is drawn out by yourself, Mr. Mangan," he said. "I presume—eh—that you have lent Mr. Moore the money?"

Maurice hesitated, but there was no prevarication handy.

"If you ask the question, it is so. However, I suppose it is all the same."

"All the same?—yes," Lord Rockminster said, slowly; "with only this difference, that before he owed me the money, and now he owes it to you. I don't see any necessity for that arrangement. I haven't asked him for it; I sha'n't ask him for it until he is quite ready and able to pay; why, therefore, should he borrow from you? Take back your check, Mr. Mangan; I understand what you were willing to do for your friend; I assure you it is quite uncalled for."

But Maurice refused. He explained all the circumstances of the case—Lionel's feverish condition, his fretting about the debt, the necessity for keeping his mind pacified, and so on; and at last Lord Rockminster said,

"Very well; you can tell him you have given me the check. At the same time you can't compel me to pay it into my bankers'; and I don't see why I should take three hundred pounds of your money when you don't owe me any. When Mr. Moore gets perfectly well again, you can tell him he still owes me three hundred pounds—and he can take his own time about paying it." And with that Maurice took his leave, Lord Rockminster going down the stair with him and out to the hall-door, where he bade him good-bye.

When he returned to Piccadilly, he said to the nurse,

"I suppose you can sleep at a moment's notice?"

"Pretty well, sir," she answered, with a demure professional smile.

"Then you'd better find out this room that Mrs. Jenkins has got for you, and lie down for a few hours. I sha'n't be leaving until after midnight—perhaps one or two o'clock. Then, when I go, you can have this sofa here; and I shall be back early in the morning, to give you another rest."

"Thank you, sir."

He went into the adjoining room.

"Headache any better, Linn, my boy?" he asked, stooping over the bed.

There was no answer for a second or two; then the eyes were opened, showing a drowsy, pained expression.

"Did you see him, Maurice?"

"Oh, yes, that's all settled," Mangan said, cheerfully. "I can't say there is much of the grasping creditor about your friend. I could hardly persuade him to take the check at all, after I had hunted him from place to place. What made you so desperately punctilious, Linn? You don't imagine he would have talked about it to any women-folk, even supposing you had not paid up? Is that it? No, no, you can't imagine he would do anything of that kind; I should call him a thoroughly good fellow, if one might be so familiar with his betters. However, I don't want you to say anything; you mustn't speak; I'm going to talk to you." He drew in a chair to the bedside and sat down. "Now I wish you to understand. You've got a mortal bad cold, which may develop into a fever; and you have a slightly congested throat; altogether you must consider yourself an invalid, old man; and it may be some time before you can get back to the theatre. Now the first thing for you is peace of mind; you're not to worry about anything; you've got to dismiss every possible care and vexation."

"It's all you know, Maurice," the sick man said, with a wearied sigh.

"Oh, I know more than you think. We'll just take one thing at a time. About this eleven hundred pounds for example. You are aware I am not, strictly speaking, a Crœsus, yet I have made my little economies, and they are tied up in one or two fairly safe things. Well, now—Oh, be quiet, Linn, and let me have it out! Something happened to me yesterday that more than ever convinced me of the worthlessness of riches. You know the coppice that goes up from Winstead station. At the farther end there is a gate. At that gate yesterday I heard a dozen words—twenty or thirty, perhaps—that were of more value to me than Pactolus in full flood or all the money heaped up in Aladdin's cave. And now I am so puffed up with joy and pride that I am going still further to despise my wealth—my hoards and vast accumulations; and on Monday, if I can, I am going to get you that eleven hundred pounds, just as sure as ever was—"

"Maurice—you have to think of Francie," Lionel said, in his husky, low voice. And here Mangan paused for a second or two.

"Well," said he, more thoughtfully, "what happened yesterday certainly involves responsibilities; but these haven't been assumed yet; and the nearest duty is the one to be considered. I don't know whether I shall tell Francie; I may, or I may not; but I am certain that if I do she will approve—certain as that I am alive."

"I won't rob Francie," said Lionel, with a little moan of weariness or pain.

"You can't rob her of what she hasn't got," Mangan said, promptly. "I know this, that if Francie knew you were in these straits and worrying about it, she would instantly come up and offer you her own little money—which is not a very large fortune, as I understand; and I also know that you would refuse it."

"A dose of prussic acid first," Lionel murmured, to himself.

"Prussic acid!—Bosh!" said Maurice. "What is the use of talking rubbish! Well, I'm not going to let you talk at all. I'm going to read you the news out of the evening papers until you go to sleep."

When Dr. Ballardyce called next morning, he found that the fever had gained apace; all the symptoms were aggravated—the temperature, in especial, had seriously increased. The sick man lay drowsily indifferent, now and again moaning slightly; but sometimes he would waken up, and then there was a curiously anxious and restless look in his eyes. The nurse said she was afraid he had not been asleep at all, though occasionally he had appeared to be asleep. When the doctor left again, she was sent to bed, and Maurice Mangan took her place in the sitting-room.

That was an extraordinary Sunday, long to be remembered. Anything more hopelessly dismal than the outlook from those Piccadilly windows it was impossible to imagine. The gale of Friday had blown itself out in rain; and that had been followed by stagnant weather and a continuous drizzle; so that the trees in the Green Park opposite looked like black phantoms in the vague gray mist; while everything seemed wet and clammy and cold. Maurice paced up and down the room, his feet shod in noiseless slippers; or he gazed out on that melancholy spectacle until he thought of suicide; or again he would go into the adjoining apartment, to see how his friend was getting on or whether he wanted anything. But as the day wore on, matters became a little brisker; for there were numerous callers, and some of them waited to have a special message sent down to them; while others, knowing Mangan, and learning that he was in charge of the invalid, came up to have a word with himself. Baskets of flowers began to arrive, too; and these, of course, must have come from private conservatories. No one was allowed to enter the sick-room; but Maurice carried thither the news of all this kindly remembrance and sympathy, as something that might be grateful to his patient.

"You've got a tremendous number of friends, Linn, and no mistake," he said. "Many a great statesman or poet might envy you."

"I suppose it is in the papers?" Lionel asked, without raising his head.

"In one or two of the late editions last evening, and in most of to-day's papers; but to-morrow it will be all over the country. I have had several London correspondents here this afternoon."

"All over the country?" Lionel repeated, absently, and then he lay still for a second or two. "No use—no use!" he moaned, in so low a voice that Mangan could hardly hear. And then again he looked up wearily.

"Come here, Maurice. I want to—to ask you something. If—if I were to die—do you think—they would put it in any of the papers abroad?"

"Nonsense—what are you talking about?" Maurice exclaimed, in a simulated anger. "Talking of dying—because you've got a feverish cold; that's not like you, Linn! You're not going to frighten your people when they come up from Winstead, by talking like that?"

"Don't let them come up," was all he said, and shut his eyes again.

Among the callers that afternoon who, learning that Mr. Mangan was up-stairs, came personally to make inquiries, was Miss Burgoyne, who was accompanied by her brother.

"What is the matter?" she said, briefly, to Maurice. "One never can trust what is in the newspapers."

He told her.

"Serious?"

"That depends," he said, in a low voice, as they stood together at the window. "I hope not. But I suppose the fever will have to run its course."

"It will be some time before he can be back at the theatre?"

"It will be a very long time. There is some slight congestion of the throat as well. When he pulls through with the fever, he will most likely be sent abroad, for rest to his throat."

She considered for a second or two; then she said, with a matter-of-fact air:

"They needn't make a fuss about that. His throat will be all right. It is only repeated congestions that seriously affect the membrane; and he has been exceptionally lucky—or exceptionally strong, perhaps. Who is his doctor?"

"Dr. Ballardyce."

"Don't know him."

"Then there's Dr. Whitsen."

"Oh, *that's* all right—*he'll* do. It's the voice that's the important thing; the general system must take its chance. Well, tell him I'm very sorry. I suppose there's nothing one can send him?"

"Thank you, I don't think there is anything. Look at the flowers and grapes and things there—already—and this is Sunday."

She glanced at those gifts with open disdain.

"Very easy for rich folks to show their sympathy by sending an order to their head-gardener!"

"I will tell him that you called, and left kind messages for him."

"Yes, tell him that. And tell him Doyle does very well—fairly well—though he's as nervous as a pantomime-girl hoisted in a transformation-scene. If I were you," continued this extremely practical young lady, "I wouldn't tell any of the newspaper men that it may be a considerable time before Mr. Moore is back. Nobody likes to lose touch of the public more than he can help, you know; and if they're always expecting you back, that's something. Good-bye!"

Maurice accompanied her down-stairs and to the door; then he returned to the sitting-room and to his private meditations. For this brief interview had been of the keenest interest to him; he had studied every expression of her face, listened to every intonation of her voice; almost forced, in spite of himself, to admire her magnificent nerve. But now, of course, in recalling all these things, he was thinking of Francie; as a man invariably does when he places the one woman of the world on a pedestal, that all the rest of her sex may be compared with her; and even his extorted admiration of the prima-donna's coolness and self-possession and business-like tact did not prevent his rejoicing at the thought that Francie and Miss Burgoyne were poles asunder.

That evening Maurice was startled. He had gone very quietly into the sick-room, just to see how his patient was getting on, and found him breathing heavily and also restlessly muttering to himself. Perhaps even the slight noise of his entrance had attracted the notice of one abnormally sensitive; at all events, Lionel opened his eyes, which were no longer drowsy, but eager and excited, and said,

"Maurice, have you not sent for Nina yet?"

"For Nina?"

"Oh, yes, yes," Lionel went on, as quickly as his laboring breath would allow. "How can I go abroad without saying good-bye to Nina? Tell Jenkins to go down to Sloane Street at once—at once, Maurice—before she leaves for the theatre. I have been waiting for her all day—I heard the people coming up—one after another—but not Nina. And I cannot go without saying good-bye. I want to tell her something. She must make friends with Miss Burgoyne, now she has got into the theatre. Lehmann will give her a better part by and by—oh, yes, I'll see to that for Nina—and I must write to Pandiani, to tell him of her success—"

"Oh, but that's all settled, Linn," his friend broke in, perceiving the situation at once. "Now you just keep quiet, and it will be all perfectly arranged—perfectly. Of course I know you are glad your old friend and companion has got a place in the theatre."

"Yes, she was my friend—she was my friend once," he said, and he looked appealingly at Maurice? "but—but I sometimes think—sometimes it is my head—that there is something wrong. Can you tell me, Maurice? There is something—I don't know what—but it troubles me—I cannot tell what it is. When she was here to-day, she would not speak to me. She came and looked. She stood by the door there. She had on the black dress and the crimson bonnet—but she had forgotten her music. I thought, perhaps, she was going down to the theatre—but why wouldn't she speak to me, Maurice? She did not look angry—she looked like—like—oh, just like

Nina—and I could not ask her why she would not say anything—my throat was so bad—"

"Yes, I know that, Linn," Maurice said, gently, "and that is why you mustn't talk any more now. You must lie still and rest, so that you may take your place in the theatre again—"

"But haven't they told you I am never going to the theatre again?" he said, eagerly. "Oh, no; as soon as I can I am going away abroad—I am going away all over the world—to find some one. You said she was my friend and my good comrade—do you think I could let her be away in some distant place, and all alone? I could not rest in my grave! It may be Malta, or Cairo, or Australia, or San Francisco; but that is what I am set on. I have thought of it so long that—that I think my head has got tired, and my heart a little bit broken, as they say, only I never believed in that. Never mind, Maurice, I am going away to find Nina—ah, that will be a surprise some day—a surprise just as when she first came here—into the room—in the black dress and the crimson bonnet—*la cianciosella*, she was going away again!— she was always so proud and easily offended—always the *cianciosella*!"

He turned a little, and moaned, and lay still; and Maurice, fearing that his presence would only add to this delirious excitement, was about to slip from the room, when his sick friend called him back.

"Maurice, don't forget this now! When she comes again, you must stand by her at the door there, and tell her not to be frightened: I am not so very ill. Tell Nina not to be frightened. She used not to be frightened. Ask her to remember the afternoons when I had the broken ankle—she and Sabetta Debernardi used to come nearly every day—and Sabetta brought her zither—and Nina and I played dominoes. Maurice, you never heard Nina sing to herself—just to herself, not thinking—and sometimes Sabetta would play a *barcarola*—oh, there was one that Nina used to sing sometimes—'*Da la parte de Castelo—ziraremo mio tesoro—mio tesoro!—la passara el Bucintoro—per condur el Dose in mar*'—I heard it last night again—but—but all stringed instruments—and the sound of wind and waves—it was so strange and terrible—when I was listening for Nina's voice. I think it was at Capri—along the shores—but it was night-time—and I could not hear Nina because of the wind and the waves. Oh, it was terrible, Maurice! The sea was roaring all round the shores—and it was so black—only I thought if the water were about to come up and drown me, it might—it might take me away somewhere—I don't know where—perhaps to the place where Nina's ship went down in the dark. Why did she go away, Maurice?—why did she go away from us all?—the poor *cianciosella*!"

These rambling, wearied, broken utterances were suddenly arrested: there was a tapping at the outer door—and Lionel turned frightened, anxious eyes on his friend.

"I'll go and see who it is," Mangan said, quietly. "Meanwhile you must lie perfectly quiet and still, Linn, and be sure that everything will come right."

In the next room, at the open door, he found the reporter of a daily newspaper which was in the habit of devoting a column every Monday morning to music and musicians. He was bidden to enter. He said he wished to have the last authentic news of the condition of the popular young baritone, for of course there would be some talk, especially in "the profession," about Mr. Moore's non-appearance on the preceding night.

"Well," said Maurice, in an undertone, "don't publish anything alarming, you know, for he has friends and relatives who are naturally anxious. The fever has increased somewhat; that is the usual thing; a nervous fever must run its course. And to-night he has been slightly delirious—"

"Oh, delirious?" said the reporter, with a quick look.

"Slightly—slightly—just wandering a little in his feverishness. I wouldn't make much of it. The public don't care for medical details. When the crisis of the fever comes, there will be something more definite to mention."

"If all goes well, when do you expect he will be able to return to the New Theatre?"

"That," said Maurice, remembering Miss Burgoyne's hint, "it is quite impossible to say."

"Thanks," said the reporter. "Good-night." And therewith Mangan returned to the sick-room.

He found that Lionel had forgotten all about having been startled into silence by the tapping at the outer door. His heated brain was busy with other bewildering possibilities now.

"Maurice—Maurice!" he said, eagerly. "It is near the time—quick, quick!— get me the box—behind the music—on the piano—"

"Look here, Linn," said his friend, with some affectation of asperity, "you must really calm yourself and be silent, or I shall have to go and sit in the other room. You are straining your throat every time you speak, and exciting yourself as well."

"Ah, and it is my last chance!" Lionel said, piteously, and with burning eyes. "If you only knew, Maurice, you would not refuse!"

"Well, tell me quietly what you want," Mangan said.

"The box—on the top of the piano," Lionel made answer, in a low voice, but his eyes were tremblingly anxious. "Quick, Maurice!"

Mangan went and without any difficulty found the box that held Nina's trinkets, and returned with it.

"Open it!" Lionel said, clearly striving to conceal his excitement. "Yes, yes—put those other things aside—yes, that is it—the two cups—take them separate; it isn't twelve yet, is it? No, no; there will be time; now put them on the table by the window there—yes, that is it—now pour some wine into them—never mind what, Maurice, only be quick!"

Well, he could not refuse this appeal; he thought that most likely the yielding to these incoherent wishes would prove the best means of pacifying the fevered mind; so he went into the next room and brought back some wine, and half filled the two tiny goblets.

"Now, wait, Maurice," Lionel said, slowly, and in a still lower voice, though his eyes were afire. "Wait and watch—closely, closely—don't breathe or speak. It is near twelve. Watch! Do not take your eyes off them; and at twelve o'clock, when you see one of the cups move, then you must seize it—seize it, and seize Nina's hand!—and hold her fast! Oh, I can tell you she will not leave us any more—not when I have spoken to her and told her how cruel it was of her to go away. I do not know where she is now; but at twelve, all of a sudden, there will be a kind of trembling of the air— that is Nina—for she has been here before; how long to twelve now, Maurice?" he asked, eagerly.

"Oh, it is a long time till twelve yet," his friend said. "I think, if I were you, I would try to sleep for an hour or two; and I'll go into the other room so as not to disturb you."

"No, no, Maurice," Lionel said, with panting vehemence. "You must not stir! It is quite near, I tell you—it is close on twelve—watch the cups, Maurice, and be ready to spring up and seize her hand and hold her fast. Quite near twelve—surely I hear something—it is something outside the window—like stringed instruments—and waves, dark waves—no, no! Maurice, Maurice! it is in the next room!—it is some one sobbing!—it is Nina!—Nina!"

He uttered a loud shriek and struggled wildly to raise himself; but Maurice, with gentle pressure and persuasive words, got him to lie still.

"It is past twelve now, Linn; and you see there has been nothing. We must wait; and some day we will find out all about Nina for you. Of course you would like to know about your old companion. Oh, we'll find her, rest assured!"

Lionel had turned away, and was lying moaning and muttering to himself. The only phrase his companion could make out was something about "a wide, wide sea—and all dark."

But Maurice, finding him now comparatively quiet, stealthily put back the various trinkets into the box and carried it into the other room. And then, hearing no further sound, he remained there—remained until the nurse came down to take his place.

He told her what had occurred; but she was familiar with these things, and doubtless knew much better than himself how to deal with such emergencies. At the street-door he paused to light his pipe—his first smoke that day, and surely well-earned. Then he went away through the dark thoroughfares down to Westminster, not without much pity and sadness in his mind, also perhaps with some curious speculations—as to the lot of poor, luckless mortals, their errors and redeeming virtues, and the vagrant and cruel buffetings of fate.

CHAPTER XXIV.

FRIENDS IN NEED.

On the Monday morning matters were so serious that Mangan telegraphed down to Winstead; but the old doctor and his wife and Francie were already on their way to town. When they arrived in Piccadilly, and went into the sick-room, Lionel did not know them; most likely he merely confused them with the crowding phantoms of his brain. He was now in a high state of fever, but the delirium was not violent; he lay murmuring and moaning, and it was only chance phrases they could catch—about some one being lost— and a wide and dark sea—and so forth. Sometimes he fancied that Nina was standing at the door, and he would appeal piteously to her, and then sink back with a sigh, as if convinced once more that it was only a vision. The Winstead people took apartments for themselves at a hotel in Half-Moon Street; but of course they spent nearly all their time in this sitting-room, where they could do little but listen to the reports of the doctors, and wait and hope.

In the afternoon Mangan said,

"Francie, you're not used to sitting in-doors all day; won't you come out for a little stroll in the Park over there?"

"And I'm sure you want a breath of fresh air as much as any one, Mr. Mangan," the old lady said. "What would my boy have done without you all this time?"

Francie at once and obediently put on her things, and she and Maurice went down-stairs and crossed the street and entered the Park, where they could walk up and down the unfrequented ways and talk as they pleased.

"I suppose you will be going down to the House of Commons almost directly?" she asked.

"Oh, no," he answered. "I've begged off. I could not think of getting to work while Linn is so ill as that."

"Do you know what I have been thinking all day, Maurice?" she said, gently. "When I saw you with the doctors, and when I heard of all you have done since Saturday morning—well, I could not help thinking that there must be something fine about Lionel to have secured him such a friend."

He looked at her with some surprise.

"But you have been his friend—all these years!" he said.

"Ah, that's different; we were brought up together. Tell me—the Nina he is always talking about—I suppose that is the Italian girl who was at the theatre, and whom he knew in Naples—he used to write home about her—"

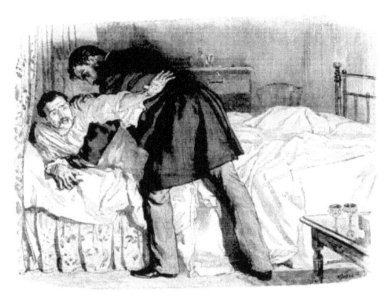

"He uttered a loud shriek, and struggled wildly to raise himself."

"Yes," he said; "and it is only now I am beginning to understand something of the situation. I do believe mental distress has had as much to do with bringing on this fever as anything else; the chill may have been only an accident that developed it. I told you when I saw him, before he was struck down, how he seemed to be all at sixes and sevens with himself— everything wrong—worried, harassed, and sick of life, though he would hardly explain anything; he was always too proud to ask for pity. Well, now, I am piecing together a story, out of these incoherent appeals and recollections that come into his delirium; and if I am right, it is a sad enough one, for it seems to me so hopeless. I believe he was all the time in love with that Nina—Miss Ross—and did not know it; for their association, their companionship, was so constant, so like an intimate friendship. Then there seems to have been some misunderstanding, and she went away unexpectedly—there is a box of jewels and trinkets on the top of the piano, and I am certain these were what she sent back to him when she left. I don't think he has the slightest idea where she is; and that is troubling him more than anything else—"

"But, Maurice," said Francie, instantly, "could we not find out where she is?—surely she would come and see him and pacify his mind; it would just make all the difference! Surely we could find out where she is!"

Mangan hesitated; it was not the first time this idea had occurred to himself.

"I am afraid," said he, "that, even if we knew where she was, it would be rather awkward to approach her. There may have been something about her going away that prevented Linn from trying to find her out. For one thing, his engagement to Miss Burgoyne. I believe he blundered into that in a sort of reckless despair; but there it is; and there it is likely to be, unfortunately—"

"But surely, surely, Maurice," said Francie, "Miss Ross would not make that any obstacle if she knew that her coming would give peace and rest to one who is dangerously ill. Surely she would not think of such a thing at such a time—"

"And then again," he said, "the chances are all against our finding her, if she wishes to remain concealed, or even absent. Linn talks of Malta, of Australia, of San Francisco, and so on; but I don't believe he has the slightest idea where she is. No, I'm afraid it's no use thinking of it; the crisis of the fever will be here before any such thing could be tried."

Then he said, presently,

"I had a visit from Miss Burgoyne yesterday afternoon."

"I suppose she was terribly distressed," Francie said, naturally enough.

"Oh, no. On the contrary, she was remarkably cool and composed. I almost admired her self-possession. She does not think Lionel's throat will suffer; and no doubt she trusts to his sound constitution to pull him through the fever; so perhaps there is not much reason that she should betray any anxiety. Oh, yes, she was very brave about it—and—and business-like. At the same time I confess to a sort of prejudice in favor of feminine women. I think a little touch of femininity might improve Miss Burgoyne, for example. However, she knows she is in possession; and if Linn pulls through all right, there she is, waiting for him."

It seemed to Francie that her companion had managed to form a pretty strong dislike towards that young lady, considering how little he could possibly know of her.

"I suppose one ought not to contemplate such things," he continued, "but if Linn were to come out of the fever with the loss of his voice, I suspect he would have little trouble in freeing himself from that engagement with Miss Burgoyne."

"But surely a woman could not be so base as to keep a man to an unwilling engagement!" Francie protested, as she had protested before.

"I don't know about that," her companion said. "As I told you, Miss Burgoyne is a business-like person. Linn, with his handsome figure and his fine voice, with his popularity and social position, is a very desirable match for her; but Linn become a nobody—his voice gone—his social success along with it—would be something entirely different. At the same time, Dr. Whitsen agrees with her in thinking there won't be any permanent injury; it is the fever that is the serious thing."

They went back to the house; the reports were no better. And all that night Lionel's fevered imaginings did not cease. He was haunted now by visions of cruelties and sufferings being inflicted on some one he knew in a far-distant land; he pleaded with the torturers; he called for help; sometimes he said she was dead and released, and there was no more need for him to go away in a ship to seek for her. The wearied brain could get no rest at all. Daylight came, and still he lay there, moaning and murmuring to himself. But help was at hand.

Between ten and eleven, Dr. Ballardyce, who had paid his usual morning visit, was going away, and Maurice, as his custom was, went down-stairs with him to hear the last word. He said good-bye to the doctor and opened the door for him; and just as he did so he found before him a young woman who was about to ring the bell. She glanced up with frightened eyes; he was no less startled; and then, with a hurried "I beg your pardon," she turned to go away. But Maurice was by her side in a moment—bareheaded as he was.

"Miss Ross!" he exclaimed—for surely, surely, he could not have mistaken the pale olive face and the beautiful, soft, dark, lustrous eyes; nay, he made bold to put his hand on her arm, so determined was he to detain her.

"I—I only wished to hear how he was—but—but not that he should know," Nina said (she was all trembling, and her lips were pale).

"Oh, yes," Mangan said. "But you must not go away—I have something to tell you—come in-doors! You know he is seriously ill—you cannot refuse!"

There was but an intervening step or two; she timidly followed and entered the little hall; and he closed the door after them.

"Is he so very ill?" she said, in a low voice. "I saw it in the newspapers—I could not wait—but he is not to know that I came—"

"But—but I have something to say to you," he answered her, somewhat breathlessly, for he was uncertain what to do; he only knew that she must not go. "Yes, he is very ill—and distressed—his brain is excited—and we want to calm him. Surely you will come and speak to him—"

She shrank back involuntarily, and there was a pathetic fear in the large, timid eyes.

"Me? No—no!" she said. "Ah, no, I could not do that! Is he so very ill?"

Tears stood in the long, black lashes, and she turned her head away.

"But you don't understand," Maurice said, eagerly. "All the way through this illness, it is about you he has been grieving; you have never been out of his thoughts; and if you saw his distress, I know you would do anything in your power to quiet him a little. It is what his cousin said yesterday. 'If we could only find Miss Ross,' she said, 'that would be everything; that would bring him rest; he would be satisfied that she was well, and remembering him, and not gone away forever.' I never expected to see you; I thought it was useless trying to find you; but now—now—you cannot be so cruel as to refuse him this comfort! You would be sorry if you saw him. Perhaps he might not recognize you—probably not. But if you could persuade him that you really were in London—that you would come some other day soon to see him again—I know that would pacify him, just when peace of mind is all-important. Now, can you refuse?"

"No, no," Nina said, in a low voice; "you will do with me what you like. It is no matter—what it is to me. Do with me as you please." And then again she turned her large, dark eyes upon him, as if to make sure he was not deceiving her. "Did you say that—that he remembered me—that he had asked for me?"

"Remember you! If you only could have heard the piteous way he has talked of you—always and always—and of your going away. I have such a lot I could tell you! He had those loving-cups filled one night—there was some fancy in his head he could call you back—"

She was sobbing a little; but she bravely dried her tears, and said,

"Tell me what I am to do."

But that was precisely what he did not know himself—for a moment. He considered.

"Come up-stairs," he said. "His family are there. I will tell him a visitor has called to see him. He often thinks you are there, but that you won't speak to him. Well, you will just say a few words, to convince him, and as quietly as you can, and come out again. Perhaps he will take it all as a matter of course; and that will be well; and I will tell him you will come again, after he has had some sleep. Of course you must be very calm too; there must be no excitement."

"No, no," Nina murmured, in the same low voice, and she followed him up-stairs.

On entering the sitting-room she glanced apprehensively at those strangers; but Francie, divining in an instant who she was and why Maurice had brought her hither, immediately came to her and pressed her hand, in silence.

Maurice went into the sick-room.

"Linn," said he, cheerfully, "I've brought you a visitor; but she can't stay very long; she will come again some other time. You've always been asking about Miss Ross, and why she didn't come to see you; well, here she is!"

Lionel slowly opened his tired eyes and looked towards the door; but he seemed to take no interest in the girl who was standing there, pale, trembling, and quite forgetting all she had been enjoined to do. Lionel, with those restless, fatigued eyes, regarded her for but a second—then he turned away, shaking his head. He had seen that illusory phantom so often!

"Linn," said his friend, reproachfully, "when Miss Ross comes to see you, are you not going to say a word to her?"

It was Nina herself who interrupted him. She uttered a little cry of appeal and pity—"Leo!" She went quickly forward, and threw herself on her knees by the bedside, and seized his hand, and bathed it with her hot tears. "Leo, do you not know me! I am Nina! If you wish me to come back—see! see!— I am here! I kiss your hand—it is Nina!"

He looked at her strangely, and turned with bewildered eyes to Maurice.

"Maurice, is it twelve o'clock? Has she really come this time? Did you hear her speak just now? Is it Nina—at last! at last!"

With her head still bowed down, and her whole frame shaken with her sobbing, but still clasping his hand, she murmured to him some phrase— Maurice guessed it was in the familiar Neapolitan dialect; for Lionel presently said to her—slowly, because of his heavy breathing:

"Ah, you are still *la cianciosella*!—but you have come back—and not to go away. I have forgotten so many things. My head is not well. But wait a little while, Nina—wait a little while—"

"Oh, yes, Leo," she said, and she rose and dried her eyes, with her head turned aside somewhat. "I will wait until you have plenty of time to tell me. I shall come and see you whenever you want me."

She looked at Maurice humbly for directions; his eyes plainly said—yes, it was time she should withdraw. She went into the other room—rather blindly, as it seemed to her—and she sank into a chair, still trembling and exhausted; but Francie was by her side in a moment.

"Did he know you?" she asked in an undertone.

"Yes, I think," Nina answered. "But oh, he looks so strange—so different. He has suffered. It is terrible; but I am glad that I came—"

"It is so kind of you—for I see you are so tired!" said Francie, in her gentle way. "Perhaps you have been travelling?"

"Only last night—but I did not sleep any—"

"Shall I get you some tea?" was the next inquiry.

But here the old doctor, who had been stealthily moving about the room, interfered, and produced a biscuit-box and a decanter of port wine and a glass; while the old lady begged Miss Ross to take off her cloak and remain with them a little while. At this moment Mangan came out from the sick-room.

"Doctor," said he in a whisper, "you must go in presently; I think you'll see a difference. He is quite pleased and content—talking to himself a little, but not complaining any more. Twice he has said, 'Maurice, Nina has spoken at last.'"

There was a tinkle of a bell; Maurice answered it with the swiftness of a nurse in a hospital. He returned in a minute, looking a little puzzled.

"He wants to make quite sure you have been here," he said to Nina, in the same undertone; "and I told him you were in the next room, but that you were tired, and could not see him just now. No, I don't think it would do for you to go back at present—what do you say, doctor?—he seems so much more tranquil, and it would be a pity to run any risk. But if you could just let him know you were here—he might hear your talking to us—that would be no harm—"

"She threw herself on her knees by the bedside and seized his hand."

"I know how to tell Leo that I am here," Nina said, simply; and she went to the piano and opened it. Then, with the most exquisite softness, she began to play some familiar Neapolitan airs—slowly and gently, so that they must have sounded in the sick-chamber like mere echoes of song coming from across wide waters. And would he not understand that it was Nina who was speaking to him; that she was only a few yards from him; and not the ghostly Nina who had so often come to the sick-room door and remained there strangely silent, but the wilful, gentle, capricious, warm-hearted *cianciosella* who had kissed his hand but a little while ago, and wept over it, amid her bitter sobs. These were love-songs for the most part that she was playing; but that was neither here nor there; the soft, rippling notes were more like the sound of a trickling waterfall in some still summer solitude. "*Cannetella, oje Cannetè!*" "*Chello che tu me dice, Nenna, non boglio fà.*" "*Io te voglio bene assaje, e tu non pienz' a me!*" He would know it was Nina who was playing for him—until slowly and more slowly, and gently and more gently, the velvet-soft notes gradually ceased, and at length there was silence.

Old Mrs. Moore went over to the girl and patted her affectionately on the shoulder and kissed her.

"Lionel has told us a great deal about you," the old lady said; "even when he was in Naples we seemed to know you quite well; and now I hope we shall be friends."

And Nina made answer, with downcast eyes:

"Whenever you wish it, madame, I shall be glad to come and play a little—if he cares to hear the Neapolitan airs that he used to know in former days."

Yes, there was no doubt that this opportune visit had made a great difference in Lionel's condition; for, though the fever did not abate—and could not be expected to abate until the crisis had been reached, there were no more of those agonized pleadings and murmurings that showed such deep distress of mind. Frequently, indeed, he seemed to know nothing of what had occurred; he would talk of Nina as being in Naples or as having gone down to the theatre; but all the same he was more tranquil. As for Nina, she said she would do just as they wished. She had arrived in London that morning, and had gone to Mrs. Grey's, in Sloane Street, and engaged a room. She could go down there now, and wait until she was sent for, if they thought it would please Lionel to know that one of his former companions had come to see him. She put it very prettily and modestly; it was only as an old ally and comrade of Lionel's that she was here; perhaps he might be glad to know of her presence. Or, if they thought that might disturb him, she would not come back at all; she would be content to hear, from time to time, how the fever was going on, if she might be permitted to call and ask the people below.

It was Maurice who answered her.

"If you don't mind, Miss Ross," said he, "I should like you to be here just as much as ever you found convenient. I keep telling Lionel you are in the next room; and that, at any moment he wants, you will play some of those Neapolitan airs for him; and he seems satisfied. It has been the worst part of his delirium that he fancied you were away in some distant place and were being cruelly ill-used, and he has excited himself dreadfully about it. Well, we don't want that to come back; and if at any moment I can say, 'But look!—here is Nina'—I beg your pardon!" said Mangan, blushing furiously, and looking as sheepish as a caught school-boy. "I mean if I could say to him, 'Look! here is Miss Ross, perfectly safe and well,' that would pacify him."

"And if you are fatigued after your journey," said Dr. Moore, who was a firm believer in the fine, old-fashioned fortifying theory, "we shall be having our midday meal by and by, in a room up-stairs, and I'm sure we'll make you heartily welcome."

"And I think, my dear," said the mother, rising from her chair and taking the girl kindly by the hand, "that if you and I and Francie were to go up there now we should be more out of the way; and there would be no chance of our talking being heard."

It was at this plain but substantial midday meal, served in an up-stairs room, that Nina incidentally told them something of her adventures and experiences during the past six months, though, of course, nothing was said about her reasons for leaving London. Maurice happened to inquire where it was that she had heard of Lionel's illness.

"In Glasgow," said Nina. "I saw about it in a newspaper yesterday; I came up by the train last night, because—because—" here some slight color appeared in the pale, clear complexion—"because if an old friend is very ill one wishes to be near." And perhaps it was to escape from this little embarrassment that she proceeded to say: "Oh, they are so kind, the Glasgow people; I have never seen such domesticity." She glanced at Maurice, as if to see whether the word was right; then she went on. "When I was engaged by the director of the Saturday Evening Concerts he told me that they had to change their singers frequently; that if I wished to remain in Glasgow or Edinburgh I must sing at private concerts and give lessons to have continual employment. And there was not much difficulty; oh, they are so enthusiastic, the Scotch people, about music!—to sing in the St. Andrew's Hall or the City Hall—and especially if you sing one of their own Scotch songs—the enthusiasm, the applause—it is like fire going through the nerves. Well, it is very pleasant, but it is not enough employment, even though I get one or two other engagements, like the Edinburgh Orchestral Festival. No, it is not enough; but then I began to sing at musical evenings, in the fashionable private houses, and also to give lessons in the daytime; and then it was I began to know the kindness of that people, their consideration, their benignitance to a stranger, their good-humor, and good wishes to you. Oh, a little brusque sometimes, the father of a family, perhaps; the lady of the house and her daughters—never! More than once a lady has said to me, 'What, are you all alone in this big town?—my daughters will call for you to-morrow and take you to the Botanic Gardens; and after you will come back to tea.' Or, again, they have shown me photographs of a beautiful large house—like a castle, almost—on the side of a hill, among trees; and they say, 'That is our house in the summer; it is by the sea; if you are here in the summer, you must come and stay with us, and you will play lawn-tennis with the girls and go boating with them and fishing all day; then every evening we will have a little concert—'"

"I beg your pardon," interposed the blunt-tongued doctor, "but do you call that Scotch hospitality, Miss Ross?—to invite a professional singer to their houses and get her services for nothing?"

"Ah, no, no, you mistake," said Nina, putting up the palm of her right hand for a second. "You mistake. I was offered terms as well—generous, oh, yes, very generous; but it was not that that impressed me—it was their kindness—their admitting me into their domesticity—I have found the mother as kind to me as to her own daughters. No airs of patronage; they did not say, 'You are a foreigner; we cannot trust you;' they said, 'You are alone; come into our family, and be friends with us.' But not at once; no, no; for at first I did not know any one—"

"I should think it would be easy for you to make friends anywhere," said Francie, in her gentle fashion.

They did not linger long over that meal; it was hardly a time for feasting; indeed, Maurice had gone down before the others, to hear the nurse's report. She had nothing to say; the sick-room had been so still, she had not even ventured in, hoping the patient was asleep.

That afternoon there were many callers; and Mangan, who went down to such of them as wanted to have special intelligence, was pleased in a way. "Well," he would say to himself, as he went up and down the stairs, "the public have a little gratitude, after all, and even mere acquaintances do think of you occasionally. It is something. But if you should go under, if you should drop out from amid the universal forward-hurrying throng, what then? If you have done something that can be mentioned, in art or letters or science, the newspapers may toss you a paragraph; or if you have been a notorious criminal or charlatan or windbag, they may even devote a leader to you; but the multitude—what time have they to think? A careless eye glances at the couple of obituary lines that have been paid for by relatives; then onwards again. Perhaps, here and there, one solitary heart is struck deep, and remembers; but the ordinary crowd of one's acquaintances— what time have they? Good-bye, friend!—but we are in such a hurry!" Nevertheless, he was glad to tell Lionel of these callers, and of their flowers and cards and messages and what not.

On this Tuesday afternoon Miss Burgoyne also called; but, hearing that there were some relations come, she would not go up-stairs. Maurice went down to see her.

"What brought on this fever?" she asked, after the usual inquiries.

"A variety of causes, I should imagine," he answered. "The immediate one was a severe chill."

"They say he has lost all his money and is deeply in debt," she observed.

"Who says?" he demanded—too sharply, for he did not like this woman.

"Oh, I have heard of it," she answered.

"It is not true then. I don't know of his being in debt at all; if he is, he has friends who will see him through until he gets all right again."

"Oh, well," she said, apparently much relieved, "it is of no great consequence, so long as his voice is not touched. With his voice he can always retrieve himself and keep well ahead. They do tell such stories. Thank you, Mr. Mangan. Good-bye."

"Good-bye," said he, with unnecessary coldness; why should a disciple of Marcus Aurelius take umbrage at any manifestation of our common human nature?

She turned for a moment as he opened the door for her.

"Tell him I called; and that his portrait and mine are to appear in this week's *Footlights*—in the same number."

"Very well."

"Good-bye!"

When Dr. Ballardyce came that evening to make his usual examination, his report was of a twofold character: the fever was still ravaging the now enfeebled constitution—the temperature, in especial, being seriously high; but the patient seemed much calmer in mind.

"Indeed," said the doctor to Maurice, at the foot of the stairs, as he was going away, "I should say that for the moment the delirium was quite gone. But I did not speak much to him. Quiet is the great thing—sleep above all."

Then Maurice told him what had happened during the day, and asked him whether, supposing they found Lionel quite sane and sensible, it would be advisable to tell him that Miss Ross was in the house, or even ask her to go and see him.

"Well, I should say not—not unless he appears to be troubled again. His present tranquillity of mind is everything that could be wished; I would not try any unnecessary experiment. Probably he does not know now that he has even seen her. Sometimes they have a vague recollection of something having happened; more frequently the whole thing is forgotten. Wait till we see how the fever goes; when he is convalescent—perhaps then."

But Maurice, on his own responsibility, went into the sick-room after the doctor had left—went in on tip-toe, lest Lionel should be asleep. He was not asleep. He looked at Mangan.

"Maurice, come here," he said, in a hard-laboring voice.

"You're not to talk, Linn," his friend answered, with a fine affectation of carelessness. "I merely looked in to see how you were getting on. There's no news. The government seem to be in a mess, but even their own friends are ashamed of their vacillation. They're talking of still another lyric theatre;

you'll have to save up your voice, Linn—by Jove! you fellows will be in tremendous request. What else? Oh, nothing. There's been a plucky thing done by a servant-girl in rescuing two children from a fire—if there's a little testimonial to her, I'm in with my humble guinea. But there's nothing in the papers—I'm glad I'm not a leader-writer."

He went and got some more water for a jug of white lilies that stood on the table, and began to put things a little straight—as if he were a woman.

"Maurice!"

"You're not to talk, Linn, I tell you!"

"I must—just a word," Lionel said, and Mangan was forced to listen. "What does the doctor really say?"

"About you?—oh, you're going on first-rate! Only you've to keep still and quiet and not trouble about anything."

"What day is this?"

"Why, Tuesday."

He thought for a little.

"It—it was a Saturday I was taken ill? I have forgotten so many things. But—but there's this, Maurice; if anything happens to me—the piano in the next room—it belongs to me—you will give that to Francie for her wedding-present. I would have—given her something more, but you know. And if you ever hear of Nina Rossi, will you ask her to—to take some of the things in a box you'll find on the top of the piano—they all belonged to her—if she won't take them all back, she must take some—as a—as a keepsake. She ought to do that. Perhaps she won't think I treated her so badly—when it's all over—"

He lay back exhausted with this effort.

"Oh, stuff and nonsense, Linn!" his friend exclaimed, in apparent anger. "What's the use of talking like that! You know you were worried into this illness, and I want to explain to you that you needn't worry any longer, that you've nothing to do but get well! Now listen—and be quiet. To begin with, Lord Rockminster has got his three hundred pounds—"

"I remember about that—it was awfully good of you, Maurice—"

"Be quiet. Then there's that diabolical eleven hundred pounds. Well, things have to be faced," continued Mangan, with a matter-of-fact air. "It's no use sighing and groaning when you or your friends are in a pickle; you've just got to make the best of it. Very well. Do you see this slip of paper?—this is a check for eleven hundred pounds, drawn out and signed by me, Maurice

Mangan, barrister-at-law, and author of several important works not yet written. I took it up this afternoon to that young fellow's rooms in Bruton Street, to get a receipt for the money, for I thought that would satisfy you better; but I found he was in Paris. Never mind. There is the check, and I am going to post it directly, so that he will get it the moment he returns—"

"Maurice, you must ask Francie."

"I will not ask Francie," his friend said, promptly. "Francie must attend to her own affairs until she has acquired the legal right to control me and mine. You needn't make a fuss about a little thing like that, Linn. I can easily make it up; in fact, I may say I have already secured a means of making it up, as a telegram I received this very afternoon informs me. Here is the story: I can talk to you, if you may not talk to me, and I want you to know that everything is straight and clear and arranged. About ten days ago I had a letter from a syndicate in the North asking me if I could write for them a weekly article—not a London correspondent's news-letter—but a series of comments on the important subjects of the day, outside politics. Outside politics, of course; for I dare say they will supply this article to sixty or eighty country papers. Very well. You know what a lazy wretch I am; I declined. Then yesterday, when I was dawdling about the house here, it suddenly occurred to me that after all I couldn't do better than sit down and write to my enterprising friends in the North, and tell them that they could have that weekly column of enlightenment, if they hadn't engaged any one else, and if they were prepared to pay well enough for it. This afternoon comes their answer; here it is: 'Offer still open? will four hundred suit you?' Four hundred pounds a year will suit me very well."

"Maurice, you're taking on all that additional work on my account," Lionel managed to say, by way of feeble protest.

"I am taking it on to cure myself of atrocious habits of indolence. And look at the educational process. I shall have to read all the important new books, and attend the Private Views, and examine the working local government; bless you! I shall become a compendium of information on every possible modern subject. Then think of the power I shall wield; let Quirk and his gang beware!—I shall be able to kick those log-rollers all over the country—there will be a buffet for them here, and a buffet for them there, until they'll go to their mothers and ask, with tears in their eyes, why they ever were born. Or will it be worth while? No. They are hardly important enough; the public don't heed them. But the four hundred pounds is remarkably important—to any one looking forward to having an extravagant spendthrift of a wife on his hands, and so you see, Linn, everything promises well. And I will say good-night to you now—though I am not leaving the house yet—oh, no!—you can send the nurse for me if you want me. *Schlaf' wohl!*"

The sick man murmured something unintelligible in reply, and then lay still.

Now Maurice Mangan had spoken of his dawdling about this house; but the fact was that he had his hands full from morning till night. The mere correspondence he had to answer was considerable. Then there were the visitors and the doctors to be received, and the nurse to be looked after, and the anxious mother to be appeased and reassured. Indeed, on this evening, the old lady, hearing that her son was sensible, begged and entreated to be allowed to go in and talk to him, and it took both her husband and Maurice to dissuade her.

"You see," said Mangan, "he's used to me; he doesn't mind my going in and out; but if he finds you have all come up from Winstead, he may be suddenly alarmed. Better wait until the crisis is over—then you may take the place of the nurse whenever you like."

Shortly thereafter the old people and Francie left for their hotel; then Maurice had to see about Nina, whom they had left in the up-stairs room.

"Just as you wish," she said, with a kind of pathetic humility in her eyes. "If I can be of any service, I will stay all the night; a chair, here, will be enough for me. Indeed, I should be glad to be allowed—"

"No, no," said he, "at present you could not be of any use; you must get away home and have a sound night's rest after your travelling. I have just called the nurse; she will be down in a minute. And if you will put on your things I will send for a four-wheeled cab for you; or I will walk along with you until we get one."

All day long Nina had betrayed no outward anxiety; she had merely listened intently to every word, watched intently the expression of every face, as the doctors came and went. And now, as Mangan shut the door behind them, he did not care to discuss the chances of the fever; it was a subject all too uncertain and too serious for a few farewell words. But there was one point on which, delicate as it might be, he felt bound to question her.

"Miss Ross," said he, "I hope you won't think me impertinent. You must consider I represent Lionel. I am in his place. Very well; he would probably ask you, in coming so suddenly to London, whether you were quite sufficiently provided with funds—you see I am quite blunt about it—for your lodgings and cabs and so forth. I know he would ask you, and you wouldn't be angry; well, consider that I ask you in his place."

"I thank you," said Nina, in a low voice. "I understand. It is what Leo would do—yes—he was always like that. But I have plenty. I have brought everything with me. I do not go back to Glasgow."

"No?" said he, and then, rather hesitatingly, for it was dangerous ground, he added, "Wasn't it strange that, with you singing at those public concerts in Glasgow, Lionel should never have seen your name in the papers—should never have guessed where you were?"

"I took another name—Signorina Teresa I was," Nina said, simply.

"So you are not going back to Glasgow?" he asked again.

"No. The concert season is about over there. Besides," she added, rather sadly, "I have been—a little—a little homesick. The people there were very kind to me, but I was much alone. So now—when Lionel is over the worst of the fever—when he promises to get well—when you say to me I can be of no more use—then I return to Naples to my friends."

"Oh, to Naples? But what to do there?" he made bold to ask.

"Ah, who knows?" said Nina, in so low a voice that he could hardly hear.

He put her safely into a four-wheeled cab; then went back to Lionel's rooms to see that all arrangements were made for the night; finally he set out for his own chambers in Westminster. No, it had not been a dawdling day for him at all; on the contrary, he had not had time to glance at a single newspaper, and now, as he got some hot drink for himself and lit his pipe and hauled in an easy-chair to the fire, he thought he would look over the evening journals. And about the first paragraph he saw was headed, "Death of Sir Barrington Miles, M.P." Well, it was a bit of a coincidence, he considered; nothing more; the £1100 had been paid, and, apart from that circumstance, it must be confessed, his interest in the Miles family was of the slightest. Only he wondered what the young man was doing in Paris, with his father so near the point of death.

CHAPTER XXV.

CHANGES.

Shortly after ten on the Wednesday morning a young gentleman clad in travelling costume drove up to the door of a house in Edgeware Road, got out of the hansom, stepped across the pavement, and rang the bell. The smart little maid-servant who answered the summons appeared to know him, but was naturally none the less surprised by so early a visit.

"Miss Burgoyne isn't down yet, sir!" she said, in answer to his inquiries.

"Very well, I will wait," said the young man, who seemed rather hurried and nervous. "Will you tell her that I wish to see her on a matter of great importance. She will know what it is."

Well, it was not the business of this rosy-cheeked maid to check the vagaries of impetuous lovers; she merely said,

"Will you step up-stairs, sir; there's a fire in the morning-room."

She led the way, and when she had left him in the bright little chamber— where breakfast-things for one were laid on the table—she departed to find, perhaps to arouse, her mistress. The young man went to the window and stared into the street. He returned to the fire and stared into the red flames. He took up a newspaper that was on the table and opened it, but could not fix his attention. And no wonder; for he had just succeeded to a baronetcy and the extensive Petmansworth estates; and he was determined to win a bride as well—even as he was on his way to his father's funeral.

It was some considerable time before Miss Burgoyne came down, and when she did make her appearance she seemed none too well pleased by this unconscionable intrusion; at the same time she had paid some little attention to her face, and she wore a most charming tea-gown of pink and sage-green.

"Well?" she said, rather coldly. "What now? I thought you had gone over to Paris."

"But don't you know what has happened?" he said, rather breathlessly.

"What has happened?"

He took up the newspaper, opened it, and handed it to her in silence, showing her a particular paragraph.

"Oh!" she said, with startled eyes, and yet she read the lines slowly, to give time for consideration. And then she recollected that she ought to express sympathy. "I am so very sorry—so sudden and unexpected; it must have been such a shock to you. But," she added, after a second—"but why are you here? You ought to have gone home at once."

"I'm on my way home—I only got the telegram yesterday afternoon—I reached London this morning," the young man said, disconnectedly; all his eager and wistful attention was concentrated on her face; what answer was about to appear there to his urgent prayer? "Don't you understand why I am here, dear Kate?" said he, and he advanced a little, but very timidly.

"Well, really," said she, for she was bound to appear a trifle shocked, "when such a dreadful thing happens—your father's sudden death—really I think that should be the first thing in your mind; I think you ought not to delay a moment in going home."

"You think me heartless, but you don't understand," said he, eager to justify himself in her eyes. "Of course I'm sorry. But my father and I never got on very well; he was always trying to thwart me."

"Yes, but for the sake of mere outward form and decency," she ventured to say.

"That's just it!" he said, quickly. "I'll have to go away down there, and I don't know how long I may be kept; and—and—I thought if I could take with me some assurance that these altered circumstances would weigh with you—you see, dear Kate, I am my own master now, I can do what I like—and you know what it is I ask. Now tell me—you *will* be my wife! I can quite understand your hesitating before; I was dependent upon my father; if he had disapproved there might have been trouble; but now it is different."

Miss Burgoyne stood silent, her eyes fixed on the floor, her fingers interclasped. He looked at her. Then, finding she had no answer for him, a curious change of expression came over his face.

"And if you hesitate now," he said, vindictively, "I know the reason, and I know it is a reason you may as well put out of your mind. Oh, I am quite aware of the shilly-shallying that has been going on between you and that fellow Moore—I know you've been struck, like all the rest of the women—but you may as well give up that fancy. Mr. Moore isn't much of a catch, *now*!"

She raised her head, and there was an angry flash in her eyes that for a second frightened him.

"Magnanimous!" she said, with a curl of her lip. "To taunt a man with being ill, when perhaps he is lying on his death-bed!"

"It is not because he is ill," he retorted, and his naturally pale face was somewhat paler, "I dare say he'll get well enough again. It is because he is dead broke and ruined. And do you know who did it?" he went on, more impetuously still. "Well, I did it! I said I would break him, and I broke him. I knew he was only playing with you and making a fool of you, and I said to myself that I would have it out with him—either he or I would have to go to the right about. I said I would smash him, and I have smashed him. Do you see this check? That was waiting for me at my rooms this morning. Eleven hundred pounds—that was two days' work only, and I had plenty more before. But do you think it is his check? Not a bit! It is drawn out by a friend of his. It is lent him. He is just so much the more in debt, and I don't believe he has a farthing in the world. And that's the wonderful creature all you women are worshipping!"

Now this foolish boy ought to have taken care, but he had been carried away on a whirlwind of jealous rage. All the time that he was pouring forth his vengeful story, Miss Burgoyne's face had become more and more hard; and when he ceased, she answered him, in low and measured tones that conveyed the most bitter scorn.

"Yes," she said, "we women are worthy of being despised, when—when we think anything of such creatures as men are capable of showing themselves to be! Oh, it is a fine time to come and boast of what you have done, when the man you hate—when the man you *fear*—is lying ill, delirious, perhaps dying. That is the time to boast of your strength, your prowess! And how dare you come to me," she continued, with a sudden toss of her head, "with all this story of gambling and debt? What is it to me? It seems that is the way men fight now—with a pack of cards! That is fighting between—men, and the victor waves a check in triumph, and comes and brags about it to women! Well—I—I don't appreciate—such—such manliness. I think you had better—go and see to your father's funeral—instead of—of bringing such a story to me!" said Miss Burgoyne, with heaving bosom; and it was real indignation this time, for there were tears in her eyes as she turned proudly away from him and marched straight for the door of the room.

"For Heaven's sake!" he cried, intercepting her. "Kate, I did not mean to offend you! I take back what I said. How could any one help being jealous—seeing your off-and-on relations with him all this time, and you would never say one thing or another. Forgive me."

She turned to him, and there were still indignant tears in her eyes.

"It isn't fair!" she said. "It isn't fair!—he is ill; you might have a little humanity."

"Yes, I know," he said, quite humbly and imploringly (for this young man was in a bad way, and had lost his head as well as his heart). "And I didn't mean half what I said—indeed I didn't! And—and you shouldn't reproach me with not going at once down to Petmansworth, when you know the cause. I shall be among a lot of people who won't know my relations to you; I shall have all kinds of duties before me now, and I wanted to take with me one word of assurance. Even if it was only sympathy I wanted, why should I not come first to you, when you are the one I care for most in the world? Isn't it a proof of that, when my first thought is of you when this great change has taken place? Don't you see how you will be affected by it—at least if you say yes. I know you are fond of the theatre, and of all the flattery you get, and bouquets and newspaper notices; but you might find another way of life just as satisfying to your pride—I mean a natural pride, a self-respect such as every woman should have. Oh, I don't mind your remaining on the stage, for a time anyway; we could not be married for at least six months, I suppose, according to usual observances; but I think if you knew how you could play the part of great lady down at Petmansworth, that might have as great attraction for you as the theatre. I was considering in the train last night," continued this luckless youth—studying every feature of his mistress's face for some favorable sign of yielding, "that perhaps you might agree to a private marriage, in a week or two's time, by private license, and we could have the marriage announced later on."

"Oh, Percy, you frighten me," said the young lady, whose wrath was clearly being mollified by his persuasive words—or perhaps by other considerations. "I couldn't think of such a thing! Oh, no, no! What would my people say? And what would the public say, when it all came out?"

"I only offered the suggestion," said he, submissively. "It would be making everything sure, that was all. But I can quite understand that a young lady would rather have a grand wedding, and presents, and a list of friends in the *Morning Post*: well, I don't insist; it was only a fancy I had last night in the train, but I am sure I would rather study your wishes in every respect."

She stood silent for a little time, he intently waiting her answer.

"It is too serious a matter for me to decide by myself," she said, at last, in a low voice.

"But who else has any right to interfere?" he exclaimed. "Why should you not decide for yourself? You know I love you—you have seen it? and I have waited and waited, and borne with a good deal. But then I was hardly in a position to demand an answer; there would have been some risk on your part, and I hesitated. Now there can be none. Dear Kate, you are going to say one word!—and I shall go away down to all this sad business that lies before me with a secret comfort that none of them will suspect."

"It is too sudden, Percy," she said, lingeringly; "I must have time to consider."

"What have you to consider?" he remonstrated.

"A great many things," she said, evasively. "You don't know how a girl is situated. Here is papa coming to town this very morning; Jim and Cicely have gone up to Paddington to meet him. Well, I don't know how he might regard it. If you wanted me to leave the theatre altogether, it would make a great difference; I do a good deal for Jim and Cicely."

"But, Katie," he said, and he took her hand in spite of her, "these are only matters of business! Do you think I can't make all that straight? Say yes!"— and he strove to draw her towards him, and would have kissed her, but that she withdrew a step, with her cheeks flushing prettily through the thin make-up of the morning.

"You must give me time, Percy," she said, with downcast eyes. "I must know what papa says."

"What time?"

"Well—a week," she said.

"A week be it: I won't worry you beyond your patience, dear Kate," said this infatuated young man. "But I know what you will have to say then—to make me the happiest of human beings alive on this earth. Good-bye, dearest!"

And with that he respectfully kissed her hand and took his leave; and so soon as she was sure he was out of the house she rang for breakfast, and called down to the little maid to look sharp with it, too. She was startled and pleased in one direction, and, in another, perhaps a trifle vexed; for what business had any man coming bothering her with a proposal of marriage before breakfast? How could she help displaying a little temper, when she was hungry and he over pertinacious? Yet she hoped she had not been too outspoken in her anger, for there were visions before her mind that somehow seemed agreeable.

That was another anxious day for those people in Piccadilly, for the fever showed no signs of abating, while some slight delirium returned from time to time. Nina, of course, was in constant attendance; and when he began, in his wanderings, to speak of her and to ask Maurice what had become of her, she would simply go into the room, and take a seat by the bedside, and talk to him just as if they had met by accident in the Piazza Cavour. For he had got it into his head now that they were in Naples again.

"Oh, yes, it is all right, Leo," she would say, putting her cool hand on his burning one, "they will all be in time, the whole party; when we get down to the *Risposta*, they will all be there; and perhaps Sabetta will bring her zither in its case. Then there will be the long sail across the blue water, and Capri coming nearer and nearer; then the landing and the donkeys and the steep climb up and up. Where shall we go, Leo?—to the Hotel Pagano or the Tiberio? The Pagano?—very well, for there is the long balcony shaded from the sun, and after luncheon we shall have chairs taken out—yes, and you can smoke there—and you will laugh to see Andrea go to the front of the railings and sing, '*Al ben de tuoi qual vittima*,' with his arms stretched out like a windmill, and Carmela very angry with him that he is so ridiculous. But then no one hears—what matter?—no one except those perhaps in the small garden-house for the billiard. Will there be moonlight to-night before we get back? To-morrow Pandiani will grumble. Well, let him grumble; I am not afraid of him—no!"

So she would carelessly talk him back into quietude again; and then she would stealthily withdraw from the room, and perhaps go to the piano and begin to play some Neapolitan air—but so softly that the notes must have come to him like music in a dream.

Lord Rockminster called that afternoon and was shown up-stairs.

"I am going down to Scotland to-night," said he to Maurice, "and I have just got a telegram from Miss Cunyngham—you may have heard of her from Mr. Moore?"

"Oh, yes," Mangan said.

"She wishes me to bring her the latest news."

Well, he was told what there was to tell—which was not much, amid all this dire uncertainty. He looked perplexed.

"I should like to have taken Miss Cunyngham some more reassuring message," he said, thoughtfully. "I suppose there is nothing either she or I could do?" And then he drew Maurice aside and spoke in an undertone. "Except perhaps this. I have heard that Moore has been playing a little high of late—and has burned his fingers. I hope you won't let his mind be harassed by money matters. If a temporary loan will serve, and for a considerable amount if necessary, I will rely on your writing to me; may I?"

"It is exceedingly kind of you," Maurice said—but made no further promise.

No, Lionel had not been forgotten by all his fashionable friends. That same afternoon a package arrived, which, according to custom, Maurice opened, lest some acknowledgment should be necessary. It proved to be Lady Adela Cunyngham's new novel—the three volumes prettily bound in white parchment.

"Is the woman mad with vanity," said Francie, in hot indignation, "to send him her trash at such a time as this?"

Maurice laughed; it was not often that the gentle Francie was so vehement.

"Why, Francie, it was the best she could do," he said; "for when he is able to read it will send him to sleep."

He was still turning over the leaves of the first volume.

"Oh, look here," he cried. "Here is the dedication: 'To Octavius Quirk, Esq., M.A., in sincere gratitude for much kindly help and encouragement.' Now, that is very indiscreet. The log-rollers don't like books being dedicated to them; it draws the attention of the public and exposes the game. Ah, well, not many members of the public will see *that* dedication!"

A great change, however, was now imminent. Saying as little as possible—indeed, making all kinds of evasions and excuses, so as not to alarm the women-folk—old Dr. Moore intimated that he thought it advisable he should sit up this night with Lionel; and Maurice, though he promised Francie he would go home as soon as she and the old lady had left, was too restless to keep his word. They feared, they hoped—they knew not what. Would the exhausted system hold out any longer against the wasting ravages of this fell disease, or succumb and sink into coma and death? Or would Nature herself step in, and with her gentle fingers close the tired eyes and bring restoring sleep and calm? Maurice meant to go home, but could not. First of all, he stayed late. Then, when the nurse came down, she was bidden to go back to bed again, if she liked. Hour after hour passed. He threw himself on the sofa, but it was not to close his eyes. And yet all seemed going well in the sick-room. Both the doctor and he had convinced themselves that Lionel was now asleep—no lethargic stupor this time, but actual sleep, from which everything was to be hoped. Maurice would not speak; he wrote on slips of paper when he had anything to say. And so the long night went by, until the window-panes slowly changed from black to blue, and from blue to gray.

About eight o'clock in the morning the old doctor came out of the room, and Maurice knew in a moment the nature of his tidings.

"All is going well," he whispered. "The temperature is steadily decreasing—nearly three degrees since last night—and he is now in a profound sleep;

the crisis is over, and happily over, as I imagine. I'm going along to tell his mother and Francie—and to go to bed for a bit."

And Maurice? Well, here was the nurse; he was not wanted; he was a good-natured sort of person and he had seen how patiently and faithfully Nina had concealed her grief and done mutely everything they wanted of her. A few minutes' drive in a hansom would take him down to Sloane Street; the fresh air would be pleasant—for his head felt stupefied for want of rest; and why should not Nina have this glad intelligence at the first possible moment? So forth he went, into the white light of the fresh April morning; and presently he was rattling away westward, as well as the eastward-flowing current of the newly awakened town would allow. But very much surprised was he, when he got to Mrs. Grey's house, to find that Nina was not there. She had gone out very early in the morning, the maid-servant told him; she had done so the last two or three days back—without waiting for breakfast even.

"But where does she go?" he demanded, wondering.

"I don't know, sir," the girl said; so there was nothing for it but to walk leisurely away back to Piccadilly—after all, Nina would be sure to make her appearance at the usual hour, which was about ten.

By the time he was nearing Lionel's lodgings again, he had forgotten all about Nina; he was thinking that now, since Lionel seemed on a fair way to recovery, there might be a little more leisure for Francie and himself to talk over their own plans and prospects. He was on the southern side of Piccadilly, and sometimes he glanced into the Green Park; when suddenly his eye was caught by a figure that somehow appeared familiar. Was not that Miss Ross—walking slowly along a pathway between the trees, her head bent down, though sometimes she turned and looked up towards the houses for but a second, as if she were asking some unspoken, pathetic question. She was about opposite Lionel's rooms, but some little way inside the Park, so that it was not probable she could be seen from the windows. Well, Maurice walked back until he found a gate, entered, and went forward and overtook her. In fact, she seemed to be simply going this way and that, hovering about the one spot, while ever and anon a hopeless glance was cast on the unresponsive house-fronts up there.

"Miss Ross!" he said.

She turned, quickly, and when she saw who it was, her face paled with alarm. For a moment she could not speak. Her eyes questioned him—and yet not eagerly; there was a terrible dread there as well.

"Why are you here?" he asked, in his surprise.

"I could not rest within doors—I wished to be nearer," she answered, hurriedly; and then, fixing her eyes on him, she said, "Well? What is it? What do they say?"

"Oh, but I have good news for you," said he; "such excellent news that I went away down to Sloane Street, so that you could hear it without delay. The crisis is over and everything going on satisfactorily."

She murmured something in her native tongue and turned away her face. He waited a minute or two, until she brushed her handkerchief across her eyes and raised her head somewhat.

"Come," said he, "we will go in now. I hear you have had no breakfast. Do you want to be ill, too? Mrs. Jenkins will get you something. We can't have two invalids on our hands."

She accompanied him, with the silent obedience she had shown all the way through; she only said, in a low voice, as he opened the door for her,

"I wonder if Leo will ever know how kind you have been to every one?"

This was a happy day for that household, though their joy was subdued; for a shadow of possibilities still hung over them. And perhaps it was the knowledge that now there was every probability of the greater danger being removed that caused a certain exaggeration of minor troubles and brought them to the front. When Mangan begged his betrothed to go out for a five-minutes' stroll in the Park before lunch, he found, after all, that it was not his and her own affairs that claimed their chief attention.

"I don't know what to do, Francie," he said, ruefully. "I'm in a regular fix, and no mistake. Here is Nina—it seems more natural to call her Nina, doesn't it?—well, she talks of going away to-morrow, now that Linn is in a fair way to get better. She is quite aware that he does not know she has been in London, or that he has seen her; and now she wishes that he should never be told; and that she may get safely away again, and matters be just as they were before. I don't quite understand her, perhaps; she is very proud, for one thing, but she is very much in love with him—poor thing! she has tried to conceal it as well as ever she could; but you must have seen it, Francie—a woman's eyes must have seen it—"

"Oh, yes, Maurice!" his companion said; then she added, "And—and don't you think Linn is just as much in love with her? I am sure of it! It's just dreadful to think of her going away again—these two being separated as they were before—and Linn perhaps fretting himself into another illness, though never speaking a word—"

"But how am I to ask her to stay?" Maurice demanded, as if in appeal to her woman's wit. "There's Miss Burgoyne. Linn himself could only ask Nina to stay on one condition—and Miss Burgoyne makes it impossible."

"Then," said Francie, grown bold, "if I were you, Maurice, I would go straight to Miss Burgoyne, and I would say to her, 'My friend Lionel is in love with another woman; he never was in love with you at all; *now* will you marry him?'"

"Maurice walked back until he found a gate, entered, and went forward and overtook her."

"Yes, very pretty," he said, moodily. "The first thing she would do would be to call a policeman and get me locked up as a raging lunatic. And what would Linn say to me about such interference when he came to hear of it? No, I must leave them to manage their own affairs, however they may turn out; the only thing I should like in the meantime would be for Nina to see Linn before she goes. That's all; and that I think I could manage."

"How, Maurice?"

"Well, there is simply nothing she wouldn't do for Linn's sake," he made answer; "and if I were to tell her I thought it would greatly help his recovery if he were to know that she was well, that she was here in London and ready to be friends with him and looking forward to his getting better, then I am pretty sure she would remain for that little time at least, and do anything we asked of her. Of course it would not do for them to meet just now—Linn is too weak to stand any excitement—and he will be so for some time to come; still, I think Nina would wait that time if we told her she could be of help. Then once these two have seen each other and spoken, let them take the management of their own affairs. Why, good gracious me!" he exclaimed, in lighter tones, "haven't you and I got our own affairs to manage, too? I have just been drawing up a code of regulations for the better governing of a wife!"

"Oh, indeed!" said Francie.

"Yes, indeed," said he, firmly. "I am a believer in the good old robust virtues that have made England what she is—or rather, what she has been. I'm not a sentimentalist. If the sentimentalists and the theorists and the faddists go on as they are doing, they'll soon leave us without any England at all; England will be moralized away to nothing; there will only be her name and her literature left to remind the world that she once existed. The equal rights of women—that's one of their fads. The equal rights of women! Bosh! Women ought to be very proud and grateful that they are allowed to live at all! However, that is a general principle; the particular application of it is that a man should be master in his own house, and that his wife's first and paramount duty is to obey him—"

"You shouldn't frighten me too soon, Maurice," she said—but she did not appear to be terribly scared.

"And I mean to begin as I mean to end," said he, ominously, as they were about to cross the street on their way back. "I am not going to marry a wife who will have all her interests out of doors. I will not allow it. A woman, madam, should attend to her own house and her own husband, and not spend her time in gadding about hospitals and sick-wards and making friends and companions of nurses."

Francie laughed at him.

"Why, Maurice," said she, as they were about to enter, "you yourself are the very best nurse I ever saw!"

But it was not in this mood that Mangan received Miss Burgoyne when she called that afternoon to make inquiries. She and her brother were shown to the room up-stairs, and thither Mangan followed them. He was very polite and cold and courteous; told her that Lionel was getting on very well; that the fever was subsiding, and that he was quite sensible again, though very weak; and said he hoped his complete recovery was now only a question of time. But when the young lady—with more hesitation than she usually displayed—preferred a request that she might be allowed to see Mr. Moore, Maurice met that by a gently decisive negative.

"He is not to be disturbed in any way. Perfect rest is what the doctors ordain. He has been left a wreck, but his fine constitution will pull him through; in the meantime we have to be most careful."

She was silent and thoughtful for a minute.

"I can't see him?"

"I think not—it would be most unwise. You would not wish to do anything inconsiderate."

"Oh, certainly not. May I write to him, then?" she asked.

"It will be some time before he can attend to any letters. You have no idea how weak he is. We want him to remain in perfect rest and quiet."

"This is Thursday," she said. "Supposing everything goes well, and I called on Tuesday next, could I see him then?"

"By that time it would be easier to say," he answered, with diplomatic ingenuity. "I should think it very likely."

"It will be a long time before he can come back to the theatre?" she asked again.

"There is no doubt about that."

"But his voice will be all right when he gets well?"

"Dr. Whitsen seems to think so."

She stood undecided for a moment; then she said,

"Well, I won't write until you give me leave. I don't mind your seeing the letter, when I do. In the meantime, will you tell Lionel how awfully glad I am that he is going on well, and that we shall all be glad to have him back at the theatre?"

"I will give him the message."

"Thanks—good-bye." And therewith Miss Burgoyne and her brother Jim withdrew.

But if Maurice set his face against that young lady being allowed to see Lionel in his present exhausted condition, it was quite otherwise with his notions about Nina. He talked to the three doctors, and to Mrs. Moore, and to Francie—to Francie most of all; and he maintained that, so far from such a meeting causing any mental disturbance, the knowledge that Nina was in London, was close by, would only be a source of joy and placid congratulation and peace. They yielded at last, and the experiment was to be tried on the Saturday morning about eleven. Nina was told. She trembled a little, but was ready to do whatever was required of her.

"Well, now," said Maurice to her, when she came up that morning (he noticed that she was dressed with extreme neatness and grace, and also that she seemed pale and careworn, though her beautiful dark eyes had lost none of their soft lustre), "we mustn't startle him. We must lead up to his seeing you. I wonder whether your playing those Neapolitan airs may not have left some impression on his brain?—they might sound familiar?"

At once Nina went to the piano and silently opened it.

"I will go and talk to him," he whispered. "Just you play a little, and we'll see."

Mangan went into the next room and began to say a few casual words, in a careless kind of way, but all the time keeping watchful and furtive observation of his friend's face. And even as he spoke there came another sound—soft and low and distant—that seemed to say, "*A la fenesta affaciate—nennela de stu core—io t'aggio addo che spasemì, ma spasemo d'amore—e cchiù non trovo requia, nennella mia, ppe te!—*"

"Maurice!" said Lionel, with staring eyes. "What is that? Who is there?"

"Don't you know, Linn?" his friend said, tranquilly. "She has been here all through your illness—she has played those airs for you—"

"Nina? Nina herself?" Lionel exclaimed, but in a low voice.

"Yes. If you like I will bring her in to see you. She has been awfully good. I thought it would please you to know she was here. Now be quite quiet, and she will come in and speak to you for a minute—for just a minute, you know."

He went and asked Nina to go into the room, but he did not accompany her; he remained without. Nina went gently forward to the bedside.

"Leo, I—I am glad you are getting on so well," she said, with admirable self-possession; it was only her lips that were tremulous.

As for him, he looked at her in silence, and tears rolled down his cheek— he was so nerveless. Then he said, in his weak voice,

"Nina, have you forgiven me?"

"What have I to forgive, Leo?" she made answer; and she took his hand for a moment. "Get well—it is the prayer of many friends. And if you wish to see me again before I go, then I will come—"

"Before you go?" he managed to say. "You are going away again, Nina?"

His eyes were more piteous than his speech; she met that look—and her resolution faltered.

"At least," she said, "I will not go until you are well—no. When you wish for me, I will come to see you. We are still friends as of old, Leo, are we not? Now I must not remain. I will say good-bye for the present."

"When are you coming back, Nina?" he said, still with those pleading eyes.

"When you wish, Leo."

"This afternoon?"

"This afternoon, if you wish."

She pressed his hand and left. Her determined self-possession had carried her bravely so far; there had hardly been a trace of emotion. But when she went outside—when the strain was taken off—it may have been otherwise; at all events, when, with bowed and averted head, she crossed the sitting-room and betook herself to the empty chamber above, no one dreamed of following her—until Francie, some little time thereafter, went quietly upstairs and tapped at the door and entered. She found Nina stretched at full length on the sofa, her head buried in the cushion, sobbing as if her heart would break. Perhaps she was thinking of the approaching farewell.

CHAPTER XXVI.

TOWARDS THE DAWN.

On the Tuesday about midday, according to her promise, Miss Burgoyne called and again preferred her request. And, short of a downright lie, Mangan saw no way of refusing her.

"At the same time," he said, in the cold manner which he unconsciously adopted towards this young lady, "you must remember he is far from strong yet; and I hope you have nothing to say to him that would cause agitation, or even involve his speaking much. His voice has to be taken care of, as well as his general condition."

"Oh, you may trust me for that," said she, with decision. "Do you think *I* don't know how important that is?"

Miss Burgoyne went into the room. Lionel was still in bed, but propped up in a sitting posture; and to keep his arms and shoulders warm he had donned a gorgeous smoking-jacket, the fantastic colors of which were hardly in keeping with his character as invalid. He knew of her arrival, and had laid aside the paper he had been reading.

"I am so glad to know you are getting on so satisfactorily," said Miss Burgoyne, in her most pleasant way. "And they tell me your voice will be all right too. Of course you must exercise great caution; it will be some time before you can begin your *vocalises* again."

"How is Doyle doing?" he asked, in a fairly clear voice.

"Oh, pretty well," said she, but in rather a dissatisfied fashion. "It is difficult to say what it is that is wanting—he looks well, acts well, sings well—a very good performance altogether—and yet—it is respectable, and nothing more. He really has a good voice, as you know, and thoroughly well trained; but it seems to me as if there were in his singing everything but the one thing—everything but the thrill that makes your breath stop at times. However," added Miss Burgoyne, out of her complaisance, "the public will wait a long time before they find any one to sing 'The Starry Night' as you sang it, and as I hope you'll be singing it again before long."

She was silent for a second or two; she seemed to have something to say, and yet to hesitate about saying it.

"I hear you are going to Italy when you are strong enough to travel?" she observed, at last.

"That is what they advise."

"You will be away for some time?"

"I suppose so."

And again she sat silent for a little while, pulling at the fringe of her rose-lined sun-shade.

"Well, Lionel," she said, at length, with downcast eyes, "there is something I have been thinking about for a long time back, and if you are going away very soon, and perhaps for a considerable while, I ought to tell you. It may be a relief to you as well as to me; indeed, I think it will; if I had imagined what I have to say would vex you in any way, you may be sure I wouldn't come at such a time as this. But to be frank—that engagement—do you think we entered upon it with any kind of wisdom, or with any fair prospect of happiness? Now if I trouble you or hurt your feelings in any way, you can stop me with a single word," she interposed, and she ventured to look up a little and to address him more directly. "The truth is, I was flattered by such a proposal—naturally—and rather lost my head, perhaps, when I ought to have asked myself what was the true state of our feelings towards each other. Of course, it was I who was in the wrong; I ought to have considered. And I must say you have behaved most honorably throughout; you never showed the least sign of a wish to break the engagement, even when we had our little quarrels, and you may have received some provocation. But after all, Lionel, I think you must admit that our relations have not been quite—quite—what you might expect between two people looking forward to spending their lives together."

She paused here—perhaps to give him an opportunity of signifying his assent. But he refused to do that. He uttered not a word. It was for her to say what was in her mind—if she wished to be released.

"I am quite sure that even now, even after what I have just told you," she continued, "you would be willing to keep your word. But—but would it be wise? Just think. Esteem and regard and respect there would always be between us, I hope; but—but is that enough? Of course you may tell me that as you are willing to fulfil your part of the engagement, so I should be on my side; and I don't say that I am not; if you challenged me and could convince me that your happiness depended on it, you would see whether I would draw back. But you have heard me so far without a word of protest. I have not wounded you. Perhaps you will be as glad to be free as I shall be—I don't mean glad, Lionel," she hastily put in, "except in the sense of being free from an obligation that might prove disastrous to both of us. Now, Lionel, what do you say? You see I have been quite candid; and I hope you won't think I have spoken out of any unkindness or ill-feeling."

He answered her at last,

"I agree with every word you have said."

A quick flush swept across Miss Burgoyne's forehead; but probably he could not have told what that meant, even if he had been looking; and he was not.

"I hope you won't think me unkind," she repeated. "I am sure it will be better for both of us to have that tie broken. If I had not thought that it would be as grateful to you as to me to be released, be sure I would not have come and spoken to you while you were lying on a sick-bed. Now, I promised Mr. Mangan not to talk too much nor to agitate you," said she, as she rose, and smoothed her sun-shade, and made ready to depart. "I hope you will get strong and well very soon; and that you will come back to the New Theatre with your voice as splendid as ever." But still she lingered a little. She felt that her immediate departure might seem too abrupt; it would look as if she had secured the object of her visit, and was therefore ready to run away at once. So she chatted a little further, and looked at the photographs on the wall; and again she hoped he would be well soon and back at the theatre. At last she said, "Well, good-bye." Gave him her gloved hand for a second; then she went out and was joined by her brother. Mangan saw them both down-stairs, and returned to Lionel's room.

"Had her ladyship any important communication to make?" he asked, in his careless way.

"She proposed that our engagement should be broken off—and I consented," said Lionel, simply.

Mangan, who was going to the window, suddenly stood stock-still and stared, as if he had not heard aright.

"And it is broken off?" he exclaimed.

"Yes."

There was a dead silence. Presently Maurice said,

"Well, that is the best piece of news I have received for many a day—for you don't seem heartbroken, Linn. And now—have you any plans?—perhaps you have hardly had time?—"

He was looking at Lionel—wondering whether the same idea was in both their heads—and yet afraid to speak.

"Maurice," Lionel said, presently, with some hesitation, "tell me—could I ask Nina—look at me—such a wreck—could I ask her to become my wife?

It's about Capri I am thinking—we could go together there, when I am a bit stronger—"

There was a flash of satisfaction in the deep-set, friendly gray eyes.

"This is what I expected, Linn. Well, put the question to herself—and the sooner the better!"

"Yes, but—" Lionel said, as if afraid.

"Oh, I know," Maurice said, confidently. "Tell Nina that you are not yet quite recovered—that you have need of her care—and she will go to the world's end with you. Only you must get married first, for the sake of appearances."

"What will she say, Maurice?" he asked again, as if there were some curious doubt, or perhaps merely timidity, in his mind.

"I think I know, but I am not going to tell," his friend answered, lightly. "I am off up-stairs now. I will send Nina down; but without a word of warning. You'll have to lead up to it yourself—and good-luck to you, my boy!" And therewith Maurice departed to seek out Nina in the chamber above; and as he went up the stairs he was saying to himself, "Well, well; and so Miss Burgoyne did that of her own free will? I may have done the young woman some injustice. Perhaps she is not so selfish and hard after all. Wish I had been more civil to her."

Meanwhile Miss Burgoyne and her brother were walking in the direction of Regent Street.

"Now, Jim," she said, with almost a gay air, "I have just completed a most delicate and difficult negotiation, and I feel quite exhausted. You must take me into a restaurant and give me the very nicest and neatest bit of luncheon you can possibly devise—all pretty little trifles, for we mustn't interfere with dinner; and I am going to see how you can do it—"

"Well, but, Katie," he said, frowning, "where do you suppose—"

"Oh, don't he stupid!" she exclaimed, slipping her purse into his hand. "I am going to judge of your *savoir faire*; I will see whether you get a nice table; whether you order the proper things; whether you command sufficient attention—"

"I was never taught to bully waiters," said he.

"To bully waiters!—is that your notion of *savoir faire?*" she answered, lightly. "My dear Jim, the bullying of a waiter is the most obvious and outward sign of the ingrained, incurable cad. No, no. That is what I do not expect of you, Jim. And I am going to leave the whole affair in your hands; for while you are ordering for me a most elegant little luncheon, I have an extremely important letter to send off."

So it was that when brother and sister were seated at a small table on the ground-floor of a well-known Regent Street restaurant, Miss Burgoyne had writing materials brought her, and she wrote her letter while Jim was in shy confabulation with the waiter. It was not a lengthened epistle; it ran so:

"Tuesday.

"DEAR PERCY.—Let it be as you wish.

"Your loving

"KATE.

"P.S. When shall you be in town? Come and see me."

She folded and enclosed and addressed the letter; but she did not give it to the waiter to post. It was of too great moment for that. She put it in her pocket; she would herself see it safely despatched.

Well, for a boy, Jim had not done so badly; though, to be sure, his sister did not seem to pay much attention to these delicacies. Her brain was too busy. As she trifled with this thing or that, or sipped a little wine, she said,

"Jim, I know what the dream of your life is—it's to go to a big pheasant-shoot."

"Oh, is it?" he said, with the scorn born of superior knowledge. "Not much. I've tried my hand at pheasants. I know what they are. It's all very well for those fellows in the papers to talk about the easy shooting—the slaughter—the tame birds—and all that bosh; fellows who couldn't hit a stuffed cockatoo at twenty yards. No, thanks; I know what pheasants are—the beasts!"

"Well, what kind of shooting would you really like?" said this indulgent sister.

"I'll tell you," he said, with his face brightening. "I should like to have the run of a good rabbit-warren, and to be allowed to wander about entirely by myself, with a gun and a spaniel. No keeper looking on and worrying and criticising—that's my idea."

"All right," said she, "I think I can promise you that."

"You?" he said, looking at her, and wondering if she had gone out of her wits.

"Yes," she answered, sweetly. "Don't you think there will be plenty of rabbits about a place like Petmansworth?"

"And what then?"

"Well, I'm going to marry Sir Percival Miles," said Miss Kate, with much serene complacency.

CHAPTER XXVII

A REUNION.

"*'I have an extremely important letter to send off.'*"

Here is a long balcony, shaded by pillared arches, the windows hung with loose blinds of reeds in gray and scarlet. If you adventure out into the hot sunlight, you may look away down the steep and rugged hill, where there are groups of flat-roofed, white houses dotted here and there among the dark palms and olives and arbored vines; and then your eyes naturally turn to the vast extent of shimmering blue sea, with the faint outline of the Italian coast and the peaked Vesuvius beyond. But inside, in the spacious, rather bare rooms, it is cooler; and in one of these, at the farther end, stands a young man in front of a piano, striking a chord from time to time, and exercising a voice that does not seem to have lost much of its *timbre*; while there is an exceedingly pretty, gentle-eyed, rather foreign-looking young lady engaged in putting flowers on the central table, which is neatly and primly laid out for four.

"Come, Leo," she says, "is it not enough? You are in too great a hurry, I believe. Are you jealous of Mr. Doyle? Do you wish to go back at once? No, no; we must get Mr. Mangan and his bride to make a long stay, before we go over with them to the big towns on the mainland. Will you go out and see if the *Risposta* is visible yet."

"What splendid weather for Maurice and Francie, isn't it, Ntoniella?" said he (for there are other pet names besides the familiar Nina for any one called Antonia). "I wish we could have had our wedding-day along with theirs. Well, at least we will have our honeymoon trip along with them; and we shall have to be their guides, you know, in Venice and Rome and Florence, for neither of them knows much Italian."

"Yes, but, Leo," said Nina, who was still busy with her flowers, "when we go back with them to Naples, you really must speak properly. It is too bad—the dialect—it is not necessary; you can speak well if you wish. It was only to make fun of Sabetta that you began, now it is always."

He only laughed at her grave remonstrance.

"Oh, don't you preach at me, Ntoniella!" he said, in the very language she was deprecating. "There are lots of things I can say to you that sound nicer that way."

He turned from the piano at last and took up an English newspaper that he had previously opened.

"Ntoniè, tell me, did you read all the news this morning?"

"No—a little," Nina answered, snipping off the redundant stalks of the grapes.

"You did not see the announcement about—about Miss Cunyngham?"

At the mention of this name, Nina looked up quickly, and there was some color in the pale, clear complexion.

"No. What is it, Leo?"

"I thought you might have seen that, at all events," he said, lightly. "Well, I will read it to you. 'A marriage has been arranged and will shortly take place between Lord Rockminster, eldest son of the Earl of Fareborough, and Miss Honnor Cunyngham, daughter of the late Sir George Cunyngham, and sister of Sir Hugh Cunyngham, of the Braes, Perthshire, and Aivron Lodge, Campden Hill.' I should like to have sent them a little wedding-present," he went on, absently, "for both of them have been very kind to me; but I am grown penurious in my old age; I suppose we shall have to consider every farthing for many a day to come."

"Leo, why will you not take any of my money?" Nina exclaimed, but with shy and downcast face.

"Your money!" he said, laughing. "You talk as if you were a Russian princess, Ntoniella!"

He drew aside the reeded blind of one of the windows and went out into the soft air; both land and sea—that beautiful stretch of shining blue—seemed quivering in the heat and abundant sunlight of June.

"Nina, Nina!" he called, "you must make haste; the *Risposta* will soon be coming near, and we must be down in town to welcome Maurice and Francie when they come ashore."

In a second or two she was ready, and he also.

"There are so many things I shall have to tell Maurice," he said, just as they were about to leave the house. "But do you think I shall be able to tell him, Ntoniella? No. He must guess. What you have been to me, what you are to me, how can I tell him or any one?"

He took both her hands in his and looked long and lovingly into her upturned face.

"*Ntoniè, tu si state a sciorta mia!*" he said, meaning thereby that good-fortune had befallen him at last. It was a pretty speech, and Nina, with her beautiful dark eyes fixed on his, answered him in the same dialect, and almost in the same terms, if in a lower voice:

"*E a sciorta mia si tu!*"

Milton Keynes UK
Ingram Content Group UK Ltd.
UKHW030622061024
449204UK00004B/417